African Film and Literature

D0863700

Film and Culture Series

John Belton, General Editor

African Film
and Literature

Adapting Violence to the Screen

Lindiwe Dovey

Columbia University Press

New York

Columbia University Press wishes to express its appreciation for assistance by the Faculty of Languages and Cultures at SOAS, University of London, toward the cost of publishing this book.

Portions of the following are included here in slightly different form and are reprinted with the permission of the editors and publishers:

Lindiwe Dovey, "Politicising Adaptation: Re-historicising South African Literature through *Fools*," in Mireia Aragay, ed., *Books in Motion: Adaptation, Intertextuality, Authorship* (Amsterdam/New York: Rodopi, 2005): 163–79;

Lindiwe Dovey, "Redeeming Features: From *Tsotsi* (1980) to *Tsotsi* (2006)," *Journal of African Cultural Studies* 19.2 (December 2007): 143–64.

Columbia University Press
Publishers Since 1893
New York   Chichester, West Sussex

Library of Congress Cataloging-in-Publication Data

Dovey, Lindiwe.
    African film and literature : adapting violence to the screen / Lindiwe Dovey.
        p. cm. — (Film and culture)
    Includes bibliographical references and index.
    ISBN 978-0-231-14754-5 (cloth : alk. paper) — ISBN 978-0-231-14755-2 (pbk. : alk. paper) — ISBN 978-0-231-51938-0 (ebook)
    1. Motion pictures—Africa.   2. Africa—In motion pictures.   3. Violence in motion pictures.   I. Title.
PN1993.5.A35D68 2009
791.43096—dc22   2008042411

⊗ Columbia University Press books are printed on permanent and durable acid-free paper. This book is printed on paper with recycled content.

Printed in the United States of America

c 10 9 8 7 6 5 4 3
p 10 9 8 7 6 5 4 3

References to Internet Web sites (URLs) were accurate at the time of writing. Neither the author nor Columbia University Press is responsible for URLs that may have expired or changed since the manuscript was prepared.

For Teresa Dovey

CONTENTS

FILM STILLS

PREFACE

This book seeks to reinstate the importance of authorship as well as of spectatorship. Accordingly, it is necessary to "own up" to my authorial presence. Born in apartheid South Africa to parents involved in anti-apartheid work, I was raised in a highly politicized and violent context. The interest that I developed in the film medium in my teenage years grew out of my family's obsession with recording: my father would borrow a video camera once every few years in order to interview my sister and me about our lives, our political views, and our dreams for the future; he would also give the video camera to us and we would interview our parents on similar topics. In this way, the personal, political, historical, and anthropological potential latent in film as an audiovisual recording medium became apparent to me. As an undergraduate in the United States, I studied film production jointly with literature and found the theory and practice of film adaptation a compelling way of coalescing my interest in both art forms—cinema and literature. Adapting a South African novel, Olive Schreiner's *The Story of an African Farm* (1883), into a short film as part of my Honors thesis, I felt great pleasure in feeling as though I was returning to my "African roots." As a consequence, I decided to merge my love of Africa and my passion for film adaptation through a Ph.D. on African film adaptation.

From the time at which I embarked on the Ph.D. until the present, in my position as a Lecturer in African Film at the School of Oriental and African Studies in London, I have seen my work as twofold: on the one hand, as theoretical and critical, through my conventional academic writing; on the other hand, as practical, pedagogical, and political, in my founding of the Cambridge African Film Festival (www.cambridgeafricanfilmfestival. co.uk) and my involvement in the founding and organization of the London African Film Festival as a way of increasing exhibition and distribution of African films in the UK, through my work as a filmmaker, and through my teaching. As I began my Ph.D., I found myself reading accounts of African cinema describing it as the "last cinema" due to its notorious overlooked situation globally. As small and localized as the Cambridge African Film Festival's impact has been since its inauguration in 2002, it has nevertheless provided a forum for showing African films and the education of UK audiences on Africa through discussions with African filmmakers after the screenings. Coming to understand in a very real, hands-on sense the difficulties that face African filmmakers in getting their films distributed and exhibited has been an important part of my education as an African film critic. Furthermore, having made films myself, I am acutely aware of the institutional, communal, and practical aspects of the film medium which determine that the process of making a film is not an isolated and controlled one, but often contingent on multiple, recalcitrant factors and replete with necessary compromises. While the interpretation of one's work remains with the beholder, the particular nature of filmmaking means that frequently a brief interview with a director can clear up a great number of issues and save the critic from embarrassingly far-fetched interpretations. Personal interviews with African filmmakers, writers, and actors therefore inform this book and are a crucial part of my methodology in all my work.

In my conventional academic writing, of which this book is an example, one of my goals has been to do justice to the complexity of African screen media through providing extended, formal analyses of particular African films, while drawing simultaneously on interviews, historical sources, and sociocultural analysis in my interpretations. I had the privilege, over a steaming coffee in snow-covered Sweden, at the 2006 Stockholm African Film Festival, of asking Manthia Diawara, the first to write a book about continent-wide film production in Africa and an African filmmaker in his own right, what direction he feels African film criticism now needs to take. He said that what has been lacking within African film studies is a serious and profound consideration of the films themselves. Similarly, Keyan Tomaselli cites the great Ethiopian filmmaker, Haile Gerima, as saying: "As long as critical theory in African cinema does not make the transition to critical analysis . . . the state of African cinema, now thirty years old, remains underdeveloped" (2006:84). Françoise Pfaff makes an argument for "innovative, kaleidoscopic analysis of African films" (2004a:8), and even scholars of Nigerian video films argue that, "We need much deeper *readings* of the films, approaching them as works of art with adequate interpretative sophistication" (Haynes 1997a:10).

In African film studies, bibliographic approaches prevail, with critics recounting film narratives in an assumption that their readers will not have seen the films of which they speak. This has often been the case in the past, but as African films gain wider exposure and become more readily available for purchase, a rigorous tradition of African film scholarship needs to develop to complement this movement toward increased accessibility. Such scholarship might also broaden and enhance the work of early African film critics, who have been laboring steadily and tirelessly from the 1960s in order to secure more interest in the cinemas of Africa.[1] The work of these African film critics and theorists has been supplemented more recently by the vital work of media ethnographers who are playing an important role in drawing together cultural-materialist and textual-aesthetic points of view, thereby emphasizing the need for film academics to acknowledge the geo-historical and sociocultural locatedness of the texts they analyze in addition to their aesthetic forms (Ginsburg, Abu-Lughod, and Larkin 2002; Askew and Wilk 2002).

The ground covered by these researchers and critics is what makes this book possible. The extensive research into the contexts of film production, distribution, and exhibition in Africa—while by no means complete—has liberated me to concentrate to a greater extent in this book on the analysis of specific African films and the literary texts on which they draw, albeit consistently in relation to specific historical and political contexts and not with the assumption that texts are hermetically sealed aesthetic objects that exist outside of social life. Following media scholars such as Barber (2000), Ginsburg et al. (2002), Born (2004), and Tomaselli (2006), I have attempted to inflect my textual analysis with concern for how the texts are constituted by their social life and not in isolation from context. I attempt to analyze the films not only as texts but also as examples of material and cultural artifacts, where such artifacts emerge out of "a constellation of simultaneous social, institutional, technological, aesthetic and discursive forms" (Born 2004:96).

Nevertheless, I want to emphasize the fact that my approach is in the first instance a textual one, in that it is a response to Diawara's concerns that if African films are not treated *as* films (among other things), then we will necessarily succumb to the view that Africa has to offer the world *only* anthropological and historical objects. One of the arguments made in this book is that Africa is currently producing extraordinarily sophisticated, complex works of art—works of art that merit discussion not only in terms of their contexts but also their discourses and aesthetics. Just as all films (not merely African films) demand contextual and anthropological study, all films deserve textual analysis. While conventional film theory has not provided a means for successfully analyzing the heterogeneous genre of African screen media, nor have history and anthropology derived conclusive methodologies for doing so. It will only be through an interdisciplinary fusion of discourses—based in a profound awareness of autochthonous African practices and philosophies—that we might begin to develop adequate tools for this task.

By focusing my analyses of the African films discussed here on the ways in which violence is represented and critiqued, I do not at all intend to suggest that violence is the only, or most important, feature to be examined in African cinema. On the contrary, I argue that by dealing with violence in certain ways, African filmmakers are participating in that larger project by African critics to try to understand and work against continuing violence, thus problematizing representations of Africa as inherently violent, and contributing to the ongoing construction of Africa itself. One of the guiding principles of the Cambridge African Film Festival has been to show films that reveal the many positive dimensions of Africa—dimensions that abound, remarkably, in spite of the poverty that continues to beleaguer the continent. The resilience, spirit, and humor that many Africans reveal in the face of such dire circumstances is inspiring, just as the films discussed in this book are inspiring in that they offer a profoundly progressive and humanist philosophy to the world at large at a time of widespread violence across the globe.

ACKNOWLEDGMENTS

I want to thank Columbia University Press for its immediate interest in the original manuscript, and in particular Juree Sondker, associate editor at the Press during this time, for her stewarding of the project throughout, and Afua Adusei, editorial assistant at the Press, for handling the project in its final, crucial stages with such efficiency. I am also indebted to Roy Thomas, senior manuscript editor at the Press, for his painstaking attention to detail and enthusiasm for the project, and to the whole team at the Press for its dedication. The book has benefited a great deal from the thoughtful and engaged feedback I received from three anonymous reviewers: my gratitude to them. Many thanks to Professor Michael Hutt and the Faculty of Languages and Cultures at SOAS, University of London, for their grant to cover the cost of the images reproduced in the book; and, for permission to print these images, thanks to JBA Production, Peter Fudakowski, Cornelius Moore and California Newsreel, and Anant Singh and Videovision Entertainment. Earlier versions of parts of chapters 1 and 3 have been published as "Redeeming Features: From *Tsotsi* (1980) to *Tsotsi* (2006)," *Journal of African Cultural Studies* 19.2 (2007), and an earlier version of chapter 2 has been published as "Politicising Adaptation: Re-historicising South African Literature through *Fools*," in Mireia Aragay, ed., *Books in Motion: Adaptation, Intertextuality, Authorship* (Amsterdam/New York: Rodopi, 2005). Thank you to Taylor & Francis and Rodopi for permission to re-use this material.

While researching and writing this book, I have been inspired and helped along the way by many people. Ato Quayson's practical assistance, sharing of knowledge, encouragement, and guidance over the years is much appreciated.

I feel privileged to have the mentorship and friendship of David Trotter, and am grateful for his support, wise counsel in guiding my professional development, and feedback on various drafts of this book. At Cambridge, my work was also informed by inspiring conversations with Tony Jones, Jean Khalfa, Isabelle McNeill, Mark Morris, Adrian Poole, Emma Widdis, Emma Wilson, and Robert Young. Over the years I have benefited from interesting discussions and exchanges about African film with the following colleagues: Abdalla Uba Adamu, Michael Auret, Cameron Bailey, Lizelle Bisschoff, Paula Callus, Peter Davis, Manthia Diawara, Suzy Gillett, Faye Ginsburg, Jonathan Haynes, Matthias Krings, Kazeem Shina Lawal, Birgit Meyer, Marc Neikatar, Mahir Saul, Alexie Tcheuyap, Keyan Tomaselli, Helen Vassallo, and the participants of Salzburg Seminar 403. Sincere thanks, too, to all the African writers and filmmakers whom I interviewed for their significant contribution to this book. My new colleagues in the Department of African Languages and Cultures at SOAS have provided the friendly and nurturing academic home in which this book was completed: in particular, thank you to Kai Easton, Graham Furniss, Angela Impey, Lutz Marten, and Akin Oyètádé for their guidance, support, and friendship.

Many people and institutions have aided my research in a practical way. Thank you to the Harvard-Cambridge Committee, Trinity College (University of Cambridge), Murray Edwards College, and the Andrew W. Mellon Foundation for the generous scholarships that made this research possible. I am grateful to the following people for their generous practical assistance: Madeleine Bergh, Vivian Bickford-Smith, CinémAfrica Film Festival, Tim Dunne, the Film Resource Unit, Jens Franz, Lynne Grant (NELM), Peter McGregor (CUMIS), Jeanick Le Naour (Cinémathèque d'Afrique, French Ministry of Foreign Affairs), Matilda Wallin, Nicholas Wharton, Anny Wynchank, and Jill Young Coelho. For assistance with French translation, I want to acknowledge Alioune Sow and David Todd.

Special thanks go to Kristoffer Famm, who has supported me in so many ways, and to my family, Ken, Teresa, and Ceridwen Dovey, for their faith in me.

ABBREVIATIONS

AFL	African Film Library
AFP	African Film Production
ANC	African National Congress
AOF	Afrique Occidentale Française
CIDC	Consortium Interafricain de Distribution Cinématographique
COMACICO	Compagnie Marocaine de Cinéma Commercial (then Compagnie Africaine Cinématographique et Commerciale)
CRIFAM	Centre for Research into Film and Media
Dic	Division des investigations criminelles
ECA	Entertainment Censorship Act (1931)
ECOMOG	ECOWAS Monitoring Group
ECOWARN	ECOWAS Warning and Response Network
ECOWAS	Economic Community of West African States
EEC	European Economic Community
FEPACI	Fédération Panafricaine des Cinéastes (Pan African Federation of Filmmakers)
FESPACO	Festival Panafricain du Cinéma et de la télévision de Ouagadougou (Panafrican Festival of Cinema and Television of Ouagadougou)
FRU	Film Resource Unit
GEAR	Growth, Employment, and Redistribution program
GFIC	Ghana Film Industry Corporation

IDC	Industrial Development Corporation
NEPAD	New Partnership for African Development
NFB	National Film Board (South Africa)
NFVF	National Film and Video Foundation
SABC	South African Broadcasting Corporation
SADF	South African Defense Force
SECMA	Société d'Exploitation Cinématographique Africaine
SONAVOCI	Société Nationale Voltaïque du Cinéma
TRC	Truth and Reconciliation Commission
ZIFF	Zanzibar International Film Festival

African Film and Literature

Introduction

"African Cinema": Problems and Possibilities

There are no artificial lights to dim. Late-afternoon sun streams into the large, cinder-block theater, making visible a magical gauze of red dust as more and more bodies enter, sweating, from the Sahelian heat outside. The rows of hard-backed chairs have completely filled up, so people do what feels most natural—they begin sitting down on the cool stone slabs, the steps between the rows, until the room is so packed it would be impossible to get out without a frantic bottleneck. You can hear the police officials shouting commands at people outside of the room, people who are still desperately battling to get in, suspecting that the film to be shown will be the highlight of the next year of their lives. You are lucky to be here. You were carried in by a tide of people, past the officials, who could do nothing to check this enthusiasm, whether spectators had tickets or not. The smell of frying *brochettes* (kebabs) drifts in from outside. You crane your neck to get a glimpse of the film starting on the screen: close-ups of a water surface, long shots of a village meet your gaze.

A tingle of excitement runs down your spine as you glimpse the banner on one of the walls announcing that this is the 20th edition of FESPACO, the Festival Panafricain du Cinéma et de la télévision de Ouagadougou (Panafrican Festival of Cinema and Television of Ouagadougou), the largest and longest-running African film festival in the world. Founded in 1969 by a small group of African filmmakers, and held biannually in Ouagadougou, the capital city of Burkina Faso (the world's fourth-poorest nation), FESPACO creates the sensation that "African Cinema" is not simply an imagined body of films, not simply a slogan for a desired but impossible pan-African union, but something alive and well. After the day's screenings, people gather around the pool at the Hotel Independence to drink millet beer and enjoy late-night debates about the films. On Sundays, Burkinabé gather to pray at the Place du Cinéaste Africain, a stone memorial at two dusty crossroads dedicated to the country's filmmakers. About twenty feature films usually make up the official FESPACO competition list, spanning the entire continent from north to south. The sheer diversity of the films—examples of the multiplicity of and differences between film production in various African contexts—suggests that there are profound problems associated with the idea of *an* African Cinema. Acknowledgment of this dilemma has taken root in the recent alteration of the concept of "African Cinema" (pioneered by Vieyra 1975, Diawara 1992, and Ukadike 1994) to "African Cinemas" by certain contemporary African film critics (Barlet 2000; Turegano 2004). I prefer the term *African screen media*, which recognizes not only the plurality of styles and genres within African film production but also the increasingly diverse formats (video, television, new media) in which films are made. More metaphorically, the term *media* also reminds us, as Faye Ginsburg has argued, that films only come into being through a negotiation of sorts between maker and viewer—films are, quite literally, "mediators" (1995).

Some African filmmakers have rejected the term "African Cinema" because of the bias implied not in the word *cinema*, but rather in the word *African*. They argue that the term might be seen to imply that Africa, a vast continent of fifty-three countries and hundreds of languages, is capable of producing only a certain kind of film. As Henry Louis Gates has shown, "Africa" derives from Latin and Greek words (meaning "sunny" and "without cold," respectively), which were initially used to describe the north of the continent, but which later came to be applied to its entirety, thereby erasing its internal differences (1999:18). In opposition to totalizing accounts of Africa, which continue to assert themselves even today, contemporary postcolonial theorists have drawn attention away from the continental and toward the local—to a variety of different, specific Africas (McClintock 1992; Harrow 1999b; Haynes 1999a; Quayson 2000; Chrisman and Parry 2000; Young 2001). At the same time, certain African philosophers and writers such as Achille Mbembe (2001) and Tsitsi Dangarembga (2006) have pointed out that the desire for, or fantasy of, a continental African identity—inspired by the pan-Africanism of former leaders such as Haile Selassie, Kwame Nkrumah, and Gamal Abdel Nasser—has not foundered.

This fantasy is manifested in political organizations such as the AU (African Union), in trade-economic partnerships such as NEPAD (New Partnership for African Development), and in arts festivals such as FESPACO and ZIFF (Zanzibar International Film Festival). Although African film criticism has tended to isolate sub-Saharan Africa from North Africa in its historiographies of film production, FESPACO features the work of many North African filmmakers, who have told me in interviews that they identify as much with Africa as with the Arab world. Martin Banham too has pointed out that "historically there has been immense cultural interchange between all parts of the continent, and particularly from the Arab world into East and West Africa" (2004:xv). The fact that Egyptian cinema, thriving already in the 1920s in the form of lavish, popular melodramas, has very different origins to cinema in other African countries has not prevented filmmakers, such as Khaled el Hagar, from seeking dialogue and collaboration with other African directors. In this sense, of the three definitions of Africa suggested by Ali Mazrui—racial, continental, and power-based—the continental definition seems to be in ascendancy (1986:26–30). The desire for pan-Africanism undoubtedly has something to do with a sense of shared, past oppression at the hands of the colonizers and, in film terms, it marks Africa as a continent that "is trying to reappropriate its image" (Gaston Kaboré, quoted in Thackway 2003:2). Pan-Africanism is, however, far more than a response to colonialism.

The realities of life in Timbuktu and Maputo might be palpably different. The early militant cinema made in the ex-Portuguese (Lusophone) colonies might seem the antithesis of the burgeoning commercial video film industry in Nigeria (with a turnover of more than a thousand films a year). However, the desire of human subjects to erode boundaries and to unite into communities cannot be denied nor slighted—and neither can its potential to transform itself from imagination into reality be underestimated. The persistence of pan-African beliefs and attitudes in the African film scene cautions us against overlooking the role of desire, imagination, and subjectivity in the construction of African cinematic identities on the local, regional, and continental scales. The imbrication of imagination and reality has been theorized by scholars in a range of different fields in startlingly similar ways.

Benedict Anderson (1983) from a postcolonial perspective, Jacqueline Rose (1996) from a psychoanalytic point of view, and Brian Larkin (2002) from an anthropological stance have all explored the role that fantasy and imagination play in the construction specifically of nation-states. Anderson claims that the nation is "an imagined political community" (7) and that nationality and nationalism are "cultural artefacts of a particular kind" (4). Nations are therefore at once "imagined" and "artefacts," immaterial and material. Taking off from Anderson's concern with the nation, Rose in *States of Fantasy* concludes that "there is no way of understanding political identities and destinies without letting fantasy into the frame" (4), thereby allowing us to extemporize that cinema both frames and is framed by the nation and fantasy alike. For Rose, states exist in the concepts of "nations" as much as in the minds of nationals, and fantasizing—far from being a private, asocial activity—becomes generative of "the collective will . . . the unconscious dreams of nations" (3). Larkin, as a media ethnographer, explicitly references cinema, and the ease with which it lends itself to imagination and projection of national desire—both in the production and the reception of films. Negotiating between anthropological studies emphasizing materiality (Miller 2005) and those concerned with the role of imagination (Prins 2002; Turner 2002; Wilk 2002), Larkin argues in a study of the materiality of cinemas in Nigeria that fantasy is "the energy stored in the concreteness of objects" (319). Whether the material or the immaterial precedes the other is a question left unresolved by Anderson, Rose, and Larkin, but it would seem that they all view the fluidity between objects and concepts, the body and the mind, and nation-states and psychic states as certain. I too will explore this dialectic, and define films as cultural material artifacts as well as aesthetic texts that corral and inspire, and are corralled and inspired by, imagination, fantasy, and desire. However, I will look further than the interplay of imagination and nation to the implications of desire and fantasy for regions—both on a specific, smaller (South African and West African) scale and larger (African) scale.

The greater aim of this book is to investigate local instances of filmmaking in order to test out possible continental trends, currents, and movements. Drawing together contemporary South African and Francophone West African film adaptations of literature as the objects of analysis seemed to me a productive way of acknowledging the differences among the cinematic production and traditions of diverse parts of the African continent, while also seeking clues to possible collective African identities on different scales (national, regional, continental). My faith in this project has been inspired in part by Imruh Bakari's suggestion that the comparison of cinematic experiences in various African contexts is essential to the project of interrogating African cinema as a whole (2000:5). While the scope of the study and my unfamiliarity with languages other than English and French necessarily prevent me from covering the entirety of the African continent, a comparative study at least allows me to participate in that crucial conversation to which Kwame Anthony Appiah refers, a conversation at whose heart remains the exploration of the "possibilities and pitfalls of an African identity" (1992:xiii). In spite of the many differences identified, similar emphases in films from vastly different African contexts enables me to test out—however tentatively—the idea of Africa as a geographical and sociocultural entity with certain shared historical experiences and a certain shared vision for the future. That the contextual differences do demand serious attention and raise their own questions of integrity, however, is evident in the need for separate accounts of the histories of South African and Francophone West African film respectively (chapters 1 and 6).

While I chose to undertake a comparative study of a national (South African) and a regional (Francophone West African) cinema partly to explore African identities in a range of geographical configurations, it is also the texts themselves that have demanded this focus. Since the early 1990s in South Africa and in Francophone West African countries (Senegal, Cameroon, and Mali), film adaptation of literature has flourished, but in a significantly different way in each context. In South Africa, filmmakers in the post-apartheid era have drawn on and adapted South African literary texts written during apartheid, in what appears to be a nation-building gesture, while in Francophone West Africa, filmmakers from different nations have taken inspiration from canonical literary texts—such as the Bible or Bizet's *Carmen*—in what I will suggest is not a typical act of postcolonial appropriation, but a confident regional project of asserting Africa's place in world history. While postcolonial and political theorists are sometimes too willing to reject the power of the state, the South African film adaptations remind us that in an immediate post-apartheid context a focus on the nation is wholly understandable. On the other hand, the fact that Francophone West African filmmakers are increasingly collaborating with one another suggests that the nearly half century since decolonization in West Africa has brought about a renewed emphasis on the region as the site with the most potential to foster cultural creativity. The separate historical introductions on the development of South African and Francophone West African film production are an attempt to take into account these important differences and their influence on film practices.

African Film: Adaptation, Violence, History

The films examined here have been chosen not only because they are adaptations of literature but also because they are illustrative of a broader trend in African screen media that emphasizes the political and pedagogical responsibility of African film authors and audiences. In particular, the films highlight the filmmakers' concern with the social realities of violence, and offer ways of conceptualizing, visualizing, and critiquing violence. The representation of violence of all kinds, physical and psychical, is evident in the films considered foundational in the cinematic corpus of Africa. The first documentary film by a black African, *La Mort de Rasalama* (Raberono; Madagascar, 1947), examines religious intolerance in its celebration of the centenary of the death of the female Malagasy Christian martyr, Rafaravavy Rasalama (1810–1837), who was speared under the reign of the queen Ranavalona I. The first short film by a black African, *Mouramani* (Mamadou Touré; France, 1953), is an adaptation of a West African oral story which allegorically critiques male dominance: the film centers on a relationship between a man and his dog, but the implication is that the dog's subordinate role mirrors that of women. *Bab el Hadid* (Cairo Central Station) (Youssef Chahine, 1958), the most famous film by the "Father of Egyptian Cinema," offers a chilling depiction of the influence of modernization and Westernization in Nasserian Egypt. The first short fiction film to be made in sub-Saharan Africa by a black African, *Borom Sarret* (directed by the "Father of African Cinema," Ousmane Sembene; Senegal/France, 1963), observes the way in which the rich exploit the poor, and even the way the poor exploit one another. Sembene's *La Noire de . . .* (Senegal/France, 1965), the film that most consider the first feature-length sub-Saharan African production, explores both continuing white racism in the postcolonial era and the materialism of its protagonist, a Senegalese woman, Diouana, who decides to move to France to work as a maid.

What is evident in this brief sketch of some of the first films made by Africans is not simply their concern with exploring violent social realities, but with the kind of "introspection" by which Frank Ukadike (1994:166) and Olivier Barlet (2000:98) define many contemporary African films. As Ukadike points out, "In the 1970s and 1980s, [African] cinema became more introspective, directed toward addressing contemporary African issues—colonialism and neocolonialism, social and cultural conflicts" (1994:166). Class, religious, and gender exploitation in Africa itself are the concerns of many of the first films made by Africans. This movement in African screen media which preoccupies itself not so much with the colonial past as with the postcolonial failures of Africa, dispenses with stereotyped images of the "evil West" and "victim Africa," and is one of the criteria for African development detailed by postcolonial theorists such as Emmanuel Chukwudi Eze (1997). This kind of cinematic movement does not ignore the violence of the Atlantic slave trade, the colonial project, and apartheid, or the tremendous suffering of Africans, since this history allows us to understand more profoundly the contemporary, postcolonial forms of violence and oppression that are its legacy. However, this awareness of the past does not restrain filmmakers from searching for solutions to contemporary violence (in Africa and the rest of the world) within Africa itself. In the vein of Burkinabé filmmaker Fanta Régina Nacro's film *La Nuit de la Vérité* (2005), which offers an Afrocentric perspective on genocide both in Africa (Rwanda) and Europe (the former Yugoslavia), the filmmakers analyzed here would seem to endorse African agency in contemporary global struggles against violence, and their makers are examples of the possibility of such agency.

Rather than argue that postcolonial African film adaptation is merely a response to colonialism and colonial filmmaking, this book claims that the introspection of many contemporary filmmakers is highly progressive in the history of cinematic production in Africa. Whereas many colonial films made in Africa attempted to establish an authenticity for the colonial endeavor by celebrating the courage of white characters who defeat villainous, violent black characters, many of the first African films undermine the very attempt to authenticate identities through self-celebratory measures. The way in which African filmmakers rule out claims to authenticity is not necessarily derivative of poststructuralist ideas about the death of grand narratives. It has also emerged from Africans' quotidian experiences and understandings of the cross-cultural interactions that sabotage *any* attempt at achieving cultural authenticity. Many Africans recognize that precolonial culture cannot simply and purely be recuperated—as Sembene himself says, "I no longer support notions of purity. Purity has become a thing of the past" (1995:176). From the beginnings of African film production, then, many filmmakers show an awareness that—as David Murphy has argued—"there is no 'authentic' Africa, nor is there an 'authentic' West" (2000b:240).

If there is no authentic Africa or African Cinema, it follows that there is no authentic mode or style in which to make African films. Nevertheless, it is impossible to deny the profound interaction of the African arts with the mode of realism. Karin Barber, for example, refers to the "detailed evocations of lifelike ordinary individuals into everyday, recognizable space" in popular Yoruba art, and ultimately asks, "Is the apparent 'realism' and the portrayal of everyday life, found right across the continent in the colonial era in visual and verbal arts, a unified phenomenon or do different situations produce different 'realisms'?" (2000:15). A survey of African films suggests that different situations not only produce different "realisms" but also give rise to a range of genres grounded in the desire to interact with and impact social realities. The majority of early African films tend to work within a traditional social realist mode, inspired in part by the aesthetic mode and political concerns of Soviet social realism, and also comparable with Italian neorealism's mode of working with existing light and landscapes, nonprofessional actors, and giving preference to long, slow takes with little camera movement. From as early as 1973, however, with the screen explosion of Djibril Diop Mambety's *Touki Bouki*, the genre of social realism lost its exclusive purchase on African cinema. Manthia Diawara has made a strong case against the idea of an authentic African film language of any kind, drawing attention to the vast differences among film styles, subjects, and genres throughout Africa (2000:81). This diversity of expression does not mean that it is impossible to find trends. What *has* fortunately been banished from African film criticism, however, is the previous hitching of authorial ideology to film mode—a practice encouraged by African governments, critics, and filmmakers wishing to prescribe what modes should be used to achieve certain political ends. It is now generally accepted—and it is certainly an argument put forward in this book, which offers analysis of films that are made in a range of styles—that a film need not be made in a realist mode in order to be serious and/or political. As I will show, profound reflections on violence may come in many forms and formats, from social realism to postmodernism, from television drama to cinematic essay.

What many African films share, rather than a particular mode, is, first, an engagement with local, contemporary realities in Africa and a desire to respond to these realities. Second, many African filmmakers make creative use of the past for the sake of contemporary audiences. The latter attribute may be symbolized through the image of the Sankofa bird from Akan mythology in present-day Ghana and Ivory Coast. According to Claire Andrade-Watkins, just as the Sankofa bird "flies ahead while looking to the past," African cinema "marches backwards into the future" (1996a:145). In their recognition of the past as a source—however mediated it may be—the adaptations analyzed here form part of a subgenre of African screen media concerned with history (literary and otherwise). The Malian director Adama Drabo, for example, "describes his role as being 'to interrogate the past to reflect upon and to forge the present and the future'" (Thackway 2003:462). Another Malian director, Cheick Oumar Sissoko, argues that African filmmakers "address the past by referring to what is happening today. That is what you could call a 'political' use of this past" (Thackway 2003:40–41). Bickford-Smith and Mendelsohn (2007), in a study of African history on the screen, argue that "many history films [about Africa] use the past to raise questions about the present" (10). According to Mbye Cham, "Since the 1970s many [African films] have drawn on the African past for their film narratives, often as a means of engaging with and 'historicizing' the pressing issues of contemporary Africa" (quoted in Bickford-Smith and Mendelsohn 2007:3). The essays on South African cinema in *To Change Reels* (Balseiro and Masilela 2003) reveal this cinema's profound concern with history; Melissa Thackway designates an entire branch of Francophone West African films as "memory-history films" (2003); Tomaselli organizes his recent book on South African cinema around Ntongela Masilela's concept of the "consciousness of precedent" (2006); and Mbye Cham (2004) and Josef Gugler (2004) think through the importance of historical representation in the context of African and Western viewing of African films. I too am concerned here with the way in which African filmmakers approach literary texts *and* historical realities, adapting them so as to "embed" different forms of history in their art.

All the films discussed here are connected to one another, then, through their "updating" of literary texts as well as of historical reality itself. It is through their deliberate re-historicization of texts and realities that the film-makers critique certain forms of past violence as well as explore the provenance of contemporary violence in Africa. This book examines, for example, the way in which a feminist critique of contemporary violence comes about when the first black director to make a feature film in post-apartheid South Africa updates to 1989 a novella set in 1966, at the height of apartheid, about the rape of a black schoolgirl by her black teacher; or the way in which a Senegalese filmmaker and ethnographer reconfigures the racial and sexual anxieties of Mérimée/Bizet's *Carmen* by setting the story in the year 2000 in La Maison des Esclaves on the Île de Gorée, a site where slaves were held before their shipment across the Atlantic. I discuss the kinds of meanings that are made out of the source texts and their historical moments in the new contexts. And I closely examine the way that these adaptations are able to re-historicize violence and thereby engage viewers' capacity for rational analysis of the multifaceted sociohistorical sources of contemporary violence.

Theories of Film Adaptation

Within African film theory, most work on adaptation has focused on the transformation of African oral narratives to the screen (Shehu 1995; Diawara 1996; Thackway 2003:49–92) and not on the adaptation of literature, as Mbye Cham suggests (2005:296). This focus is unsurprising when one considers the importance of oral tales in Africa, and the way in which African film narratives often mimic structures of orality. Nevertheless, recent studies have attempted to show that literature and the written word do have tremendous value to Africans (Barber 2006), and that studies of film adaptation of literature are worthwhile (Tcheuyap 2005). Cham argues that in African cultural studies "the focus has been predominantly on the relationship between the oral and the written" and that "only scant attention" has been given to the imbrication of oral narratives, literature, and film (2005:295). Some of the first African films were adaptations of literature,[1] many of Sembene's films are literary adaptations of his own novels,[2] and many African film adaptations of oral narratives draw simultaneously on literary texts.[3] Furthermore, many African film critics see the project of African writers and filmmakers as fundamentally linked in their joint effort to portray African realities so as to affect and move readers and viewers in particular ways.

One can only imagine, then, that the dearth of specific research on African film adaptation of literature is a sign of resistance to the imposition of "Western" theory onto African artistic practices. Alexie Tcheuyap, the first African film critic to write a book-length study on adaptation (2005), follows the only path that seems viable in such a situation: he uses theory against itself. Analyzing adaptation in Africa largely from a poststructuralist perspective, he rejects film adaptation approaches focused on fidelity and medium specificity in favor of a notion of *réécriture* or a poetics of repetition. Tcheuyap aims to dismantle the deterministic authorial and media-imposed power relations constructed by conventional adaptation theory when he argues that, "The concern is . . . not the subjugation of a medium or a text, but that of the various *creative, poetic and ideological processes* implied in the *repetition that brings change to any rewriting*'" (2001:3). Tcheuyap's definition of repetition is one that incorporates difference and that clearly does not locate itself within discourses, initiated by Benjamin and pursued by Baudrillard, around modernity's modes of automatic, repetitive production. Like Tcheuyap, I want to examine African adaptation in the context of repetition-with-difference, repetition as a result of human agency rather than the simulacra of technological and industrial machinery. Like Tcheuyap, I grant equivalent status to literature and cinema, to source and secondary (and tertiary) text. However, where Tcheuyap's focus is on the adaptation of African literature to film, my focus is on the adaptation of literature to African film—the practice and reception of film adaptation *in Africa*. Tcheuyap's primary concern is with general film aesthetics, whereas my interest is in teasing out the aesthetics of African cinema. And while Tcheuyap clearly sees film adaptation of African literature as a distinct genre (thereby positioning the project in a Western framework), I attempt to ground African film adaptations of literature within the domain of African screen media, examining the ways in which these adaptations share other African films' interest in social realities and the re-historicization of the past.

Tcheuyap correctly diagnoses the problems of applying conventional film adaptation theory to African screen media. In displaying radical *in*fidelity rather than fidelity to their sources, African adaptations require a broadening of the scope of adaptation theory, which has until recently hinged on the notion of fidelity. Film adaptation theorists have tended to focus on the way in which adaptations are said to either "respect" or "disrupt" the *original* "meaning" of the literary text, as though this meaning were available in an unmediated way. Drawing attention to the prominence of fidelity as a topic of debate within adaptation studies, Erica Sheen has argued that, "The way adaptations [that are perceived to be "unfaithful"] produce not just animosity, but incoherent animosity, suggests that what is at stake is institutional definitions and identities rather than textual forms and contents" (2000:3). In a theoretical context in which "institutional definitions" are at stake, there would seem to be little place for African film adaptations that employ radical infidelity not as a sign of splendid auteurism (in the manner of the Nouvelle Vague adaptations [Horton and Magretta 1981]), but as part of a sociopolitical project. Beyond film adaptation theory, there are difficulties associated with applying theories of intertextuality derived from poststructuralism and postcolonialism. While Tcheuyap's poststructuralist perspective establishes equivalence between source text and adaptation, its denial of origins does not allow for an account of the strong sense of authorship displayed by many African filmmakers. And postcolonial theory, which often sees African rewritings of canonical texts as a form of opposition, resistance, or appropriation, cannot explain the nonadversarial way in which the West African directors studied here deal with canonical texts. Nevertheless, two theories of adaptation have proven useful on a heuristic level—performative criticism and Theodor Adorno's concept of mimesis—in that they aid the conceptualization of a specifically African form of adaptation. For while the new millenium has seen a surge in research on film adaptation,[4] little account has been taken of African practices of adaptation, or of postcolonial adaptation more generally (Dovey forthcoming).

Film Adaptation as Performative Criticism

An approach that takes into account the agency of the adapter as well as of the audience in cases of medium change has been articulated around the idea of performative criticism, which Kamilla Lee Denman argues "provides a multifaceted fictional response to a work of fiction that is not only an aes-

thetic production but a work of interpretation with layers that can be senso-
rily, emotionally, psychologically, and intellectually apprehended" (1996:iii).
In that film can be seen as a natural extension of the performance arts in
Africa, Denman's stress on the performative aspect of the interpretation
offered by, and experienced through, film adaptations is useful.

Denman's performative framework functions in the context of African
screen media since the nature of the African filmmaker's role tends to carry
with it a particular relationship to the African spectator—a relationship that
could be said to have arisen out of long-established traditions. Many African
filmmakers refer to themselves as "screen griots" (Sissoko 2003c:203), claiming a position as the inheritors of the tradition of communal West African
oral storytelling and critique.[5] Adopting this title, and translating oral stories as well as literary texts to the screen, African filmmakers are able, first of
all, to reach non-literate African audiences, and, second, to encourage audiences to react to the cinematic experience in the same way that they would
to a griot's performance of an oral tale—that is, with a critical, modifying
eye and not with the absent-minded passivity of spectators expecting to be
merely entertained. As modern-day griots, African filmmakers thus play two
roles: as the preservers and transmitters of African culture to future generations in the wake of the demise of oral storytelling; and as critical mediators
of social realities, encouraging audience response and (re)action. In relation
to the latter role, it is important to note that the oral narrative, central to
African gnosis, not only involves audience participation but also requires the
necessary modification of oral tales by audiences. Teshome Gabriel speaks
about the performance of oral narratives in Africa as a "collective effort at
mythmaking" (2002:x) that requires the active participation of the audience.
As Barber argues in relation to the production and consumption of popular
Yoruba plays in Nigeria, the proximity of the producers/actors to the audience means that "production and consumption themselves are often almost
indistinguishable" (2000:5).

In cultures where art has traditionally been seen as performative, and as
requiring audience participation in the construction of this performativity,
viewers tend to engage with films in a quite different manner from audiences
in the West. Thackway describes how during performances in West Africa
audiences play an embodied role—clapping or singing "call-and-response"
refrains—and she points out that these "participatory practices" are often

carried across into film viewing (2003:52). Screenings tend to be accompanied by vibrantly and bodily expressed identification with the characters, a great deal of loud laughter, clapping at moments when the audience supports a character's decision, and shouting when fortunes are reversed. This active participation is not restricted to West African audiences—as South African director Ramadan Suleman says, "Historically we all know that Africans or Third World people have the tendency, if they like something, to see it two or three times. . . . We have even experienced in movie houses that the audience knows movie dialogues by heart. They memorize; they even tend to talk to the screen characters!" (2002:291). This kind of identification does not necessarily end after the screening. At one point in Senegal, maids and housewives went on "strike" in order to attend repeated screenings of Sembene's *La Noire de . . .* (1965). Screenings of Cheick Oumar Sissoko's film *Finzan* (1989) caused heated debate in his home country, Mali, around the issue of female circumcision, and, as Sissoko himself says, "this kind of film was very necessary for launching the debate" (2003c:202). Sissoko's film *La Genèse* (Genesis) (1999), which he himself screened in rural areas throughout Mali with a mobile film unit, and which deals with interclan violence, also initiated important discussion between stockbreeders (*l'éleveurs*) and agriculturalists (*cultivateurs*). While I have drawn on personal interviews with filmmakers, writers, and actors to try to reconstruct the reception of the films analyzed here, there is unfortunately a dearth of information that restricts me from fully activating the performative criticism of audiences themselves.[6] One hopes that the work currently being undertaken by media ethnographers in examining the "social lives" of films as well as their textual aspects will help to bring the disciplines of anthropology and film studies into even more productive association in the future (Ginsburg et al. 2002; Askew and Wilk 2002).

Although empirical research remains scant, it is possible to analyze, from a textual perspective, the impact of performativity on the form and aesthetics of African screen media. Although the filmmaker is, of course, not present in bodily form in a film, many techniques are used so as to mimic the presence of the filmmaker/griot, including the use of voice-over, opening and closing the film with a griot, or having the filmmaker act in the film. Lack of access to funding also tends to result in a mode of production that, while determined to some extent by the inevitably collective nature of any film production, bears the strong imprint of the director, who is often compelled to take on more than one role—sometimes as writer, director, producer, editor, and actor. This means that the authorial role in African films is more marked than in Hollywood films, for example, where specialization results in hierarchies of expertise. This form of authorship in African films is not oppositional, as was auteur cinema in Europe, but can be seen as an extension of social and artistic responsibility, a role articulated by DRC filmmaker Mweze Ngangura as follows: "in Africa, for many years now almost all filmmakers have regarded themselves as authors, as people with a mission, charged with carrying a message to their people" (1996:61).

In this respect, African films share aspects of what Hamid Naficy (2001) calls exilic films—cinema made by exiles, émigrés, immigrants, and diasporic peoples who foreground their own authorial presence in their films. In an attempt to "put the locatedness and the historicity of the authors back into authorship" (34), Naficy challenges poststructuralist theory to rethink its denial of authorship and origins and to take account not only of the meanings assigned to films by spectators but also by authors, arguing that both authors and spectators are simultaneously "subjects of texts" and "subjects in history" (34). Like Ngangura, he sees film authors not as autonomous artists distinct from sociocultural contexts, as auteur theory tends to do, but as everyday men and women, both constituted by and critical of their environments. This challenge to poststructuralist theory has also been undertaken by recent postcolonial theorists such as Neil Lazarus, who argues that rather than seeing Eurocentrism as a monolithic episteme, we might see it as an ideological formation and thus as capable of critique by individual authors (2004:11–12). In drawing extensively on my interviews with African filmmakers, writers, and actors, I too intend to take human desire and intention seriously, thereby challenging the poststructuralist denial of authorship.

Holding to Stuart Hall's encoding/decoding dialectic (1973), and to Karin Barber's recognition that in many cases it is impossible to separate production and consumption in Africa, I see author and audience as two sides of the same coin. Furthermore, Barlet has warned us not to see the "African audience" as an indivisible collective, but as heterogeneous, as comprised of individuals. The project of reinstating the importance of authorship as well as spectatorship thus inevitably involves recognition of the role not only of the collective in Africa but also of the individual, something which might help us to move away from reductive oppositions of Africa's "communal-ism" to the West's "individualism." As Barber writes of the Adédjobí Theatre Company's Yoruba plays,

> A close look at the texts of these plays enables us to explore what kind "modern self" [*sic*] is in fact projected, and how individuality, autonomy, and agency are conceptualized. . . . The bipolar before-and-after narrative of modernity that traces the emergence of the universal, individualistic, autonomous, post-Enlightenment "modern self" from its particularistic, communalistic, tradition-bound antecedents is called into question by these representations. (2000:13)

Similarly, scrutiny of the South African and West African film adaptations in the chapters that follow reveals the films' profound engagement with dis-courses around the limits of both individuality *and* communalism in Africa, showing that it is impossible to simplistically hold Africa to collective prin-ciples of *ujamaa*, *unhu*, or *ubuntu* without taking into account its dynamic redefinition of modern subjectivities.

In summary, then, the recuperation of authorship as well as of specta-torship enables the possibility of performance and criticism, two concepts that are central to the claims of this book. In light of these claims, it seems important also to explore a paradigm of adaptation that devises a theory of critique while challenging the possibility of critique under certain sociocul-tural circumstances: Theodor Adorno's concept of mimesis.

Film Adaptation as Adornian Mimesis

The idea of performance suggests an *embodied* investment in film by both authors and audience, but it does not address the question of where ratio-nality fits into the picture. Theodor Adorno's concept of mimesis is use-ful to this study in that it marries the concepts of embodied and rational modes of being and sees this marriage as a prerequisite of critique. Mimesis, of course, has a long history, predating Adorno's adoption and amplification of the concept. While it is not my interest to engage with this history here, it is important to point out that mimesis has primarily been conceived of in two ways. One form of mimesis has its origins in embodiment—in bodily mimicry—and the other in Plato's idea of mimesis as imitation. The philosophy of history offered in *The Dialectic of Enlightenment* (1947), which Adorno coauthored with Max Horkheimer, traces in a fragmentary, nonlinear way how, through the Enlightenment in the West, humans attempted to distance themselves as much as possible from mimesis as an embodied mode of being (often associated with mime and dance, and with Africa) in the pursuit of "civilized culture," or rational modes of being. Adorno and Horkheimer argue that in the process of attempting to reject embodied modes of being, these modes are inevitably manifested within Western rationality itself. This sense of a dialectic is expressed in the two frequently cited assertions from *The Dialectic of Enlightenment*: "myth is already enlightenment; and enlightenment reverts to mythology" (Horkheimer and Adorno 1973:xvi). This statement seeks to acknowledge that magic and myth are already forms of cognition, of knowledge. The second thesis, that enlightenment reverts to myth, is explained by the way in which a totalizing rationality, such as that experienced in late modernity (according to Adorno), produces a complete reification of the world and assumes that it is the sole means to the truth, and thus inevitably becomes a myth (and incapable of offering critique) in that it fails to recognize its own contingency. Adorno thus seeks to locate embodiment and rationality within a continuum or constellation, with no dichotomy between them—they do not constitute a binary opposition. As soon as rationality denies the bodily, it loses its truth-value; at the same time, as soon as the bodily suppresses rationality, it forfeits its meaning-making power.

Many contemporary film and literary theorists appear to be in the process of critiquing the validation of the rational over the bodily that has dominated post-Enlightenment "Western" thought, through a new focus on the sensory and on embodied modes of being and viewing/reading.[7] Many African filmmakers, including those studied here, seem to be engaged in the opposite process: they are using the hyper-embodied medium of film to project their own versions of rationality into their films. The Cameroonian filmmaker Jean-Pierre Bekolo has said that he uses a great deal of voice-over in his films since he "was once told that no one ever hears what Africans say or what they think. And by extension such a statement would seem to suggest that Africans don't think at all" (2000:25). Similarly, El Hadj, the protagonist in Alain Gomis's film *L'Afrance* (2001), tells his white French lover who asks him if French attitudes to African immigrants have changed: "They used to say, all that Africans know how to do is play the drums; now they say, wow,

Africans all have such great rhythm!" In both cases, Africans are confined to the bodily, to the "natural" or "pre-rational." The heightened embodiment of which the film medium is capable cannot, therefore, simply be celebrated in Africa, a continent where imperialism was justified through the very polarization of European "rationality" and African "embodiment." Rather than merely succumbing to a position of resistance, through consistently asserting African rationality over embodiment, the filmmakers discussed here maintain the necessary dialectic intrinsic to Adorno's concept of mimesis. Furthermore, their films, as well as those of other African filmmakers, often move beyond the simplistic opposition of rationality and embodiment altogether to explore competing rationalities.[8] In this sense, rather than countering the "embodiment" through which European colonialists tended to classify Africans, these filmmakers would appear to be drawing positively on Afrophone philosophies which present complex, multilayered definitions of "knowledge," "belief," and "truth," and which equate "being human" with "having knowledge," with rationality (Dzobo 1992; Hallen and Sodipo 1997).[9]

Grounded in mimicry, Adorno's mimesis allows for the possibility of a different kind of relationship between subject and object—an adaptive or correlating behavior in which the subject attempts to *be like* the object, rather than control the object by identifying it. Correlating behavior, according to Adorno, allows the subject to appreciate the object's full, embodied materiality—through "sensuous knowing" or "sensuous Othering"—rather than classify the object through rational(izing) thought. It allows for identification *with* the object/Other (an embodied mode of being), rather than identification *of* the object/Other through the reifications of abstract thought. The films studied here harness embodiment by adapting to their objects— the literary texts, historical realities, and violence—in a way that "mimics" them, that approaches them closely rather than attempting to dominate or control them as do the rational discourses of academic disciplines. However, the films also access rationality through their complex re-historicization of the discourses of the literary texts and the historical moments in which they were made.

If, as I have claimed, African film adaptations operate in the manner of Adornian mimesis, it is important to examine Adorno's proposition that mimesis as critique is contingent on context. According to Adorno, under the conditions of modernity and mass culture, mimesis as "a cognitive attempt to be like the object, is . . . progressively replaced by identification, thought's attempt to subsume and classify the object" (Jarvis 1998:27). Mimesis becomes almost entirely repressed, as a result of the instrumentalization of reason, and it becomes confined to the "irrational" or "a-rational" language of art, which is increasingly viewed as separate from the rational language of science. Thus mimesis in art becomes reduced to the irrational, with the subject mimicking the object but denied the ability to offer any valid kind of knowledge of it. The classificatory mode of modern rationality, on the other hand, is faced with the dilemma of reducing the object or Other to pure concept, eliminating all embodied experience of it or affinity to it, which would seem to also invalidate the knowledge or critique thereby produced since it is not *felt*.

For Adorno, cinema produced and received under the conditions of the "mass culture industry" exploits mimesis as both adaptation and imitation for its own manipulative ends. In his view, film cannot offer a critique of society precisely because of its mimetic qualities. Thus, on the one hand, because film can produce near-perfect imitations of empirical reality, "Reality becomes its own ideology through the spell cast by its faithful duplication" and "Imagination is replaced by a mechanically relentless control mechanism which determines whether the latest imago to be distributed really represents an exact, accurate and reliable reflection of the relevant item of reality" (Adorno 1991:55). On the other hand, "the sensuous individuation of the work," which might be the means for avoiding the abstraction of identity-thinking, merely "contradicts the abstractness and self-sameness to which the world has shrunk." This is the source of Adorno's criticism of the cinema as medium, which leads him to make statements such as "Every visit to the cinema leaves me, against all my vigilance, stupider and worse" (1978:25). In the context of late modernity, according to Adorno, mimesis is able to offer critique of a totalizing instrumental reason only through the "determinate negation" of society, in the form of nonrepresentational modernist art's mimicking of rationality itself.

Adorno paints a picture of cinema as a medium not able, under late modernist Western conditions, to bring together the embodied and rational capacities necessary for mimesis as critique. As Michael Cahn has pointed out, Adorno thus associates modernity with a crisis of critique, and the question that arises is how a critique of violence is to be achieved, since critique "has to demonstrate its relevance by an involvement and similarity with what it criticizes" (1984:46). The identity-thinking of instrumental rationality, approaching the object via the abstraction of general concepts, cannot know the object in its embodied particularity, and it is mimicry which provides the means for approaching the object closely enough in order to be able to know it. Because art is the domain in which the body has not been entirely repressed, it seems to offer the means for critique, but, for Adorno, the risk is that, through its capacity to "be like" the world, art may simply work as an advertisement for the world. The most is at stake in art that deals with violence since this art risks producing an affirmation of violence by mimicking it. In Adorno's schema, cinema within a totalizing social order is able to exploit the power of mimicry, turning citizens into automatons capable of the excesses of violence witnessed in the last century. According to Adorno, the spectacular mass displays of Nazi Germany and the mass media of the American culture industry constitute technologies of the visual that have been harnessed in the service of violent manipulation and control.

While Adorno's own totalizing claims contradict his dialectical argument, and result in a reduction of the differences inherent in the "West," it is possible to argue—again, without wanting to essentialize "Africa"—that the very different relationship to screen media (and art of all kinds) in many African contexts enables rather than undermines critique through film. The active, embodied, and performative responses of many film audiences in Africa, as well as the difficulties associated with access to certain kinds of cinema in Africa (and particularly the kind of films discussed here), suggest that while film may be part of popular culture, it cannot be considered part of mass culture. Barber provides a resounding critique of generalized theories of the culture industry through her reference to popular culture in West Africa:

> Especially incongruous to popular culture in West Africa are those
> theories that assume a radical separation between production (by
> cosmopolitan technocratic elites) and consumption (by local masses),
> and which imagine these masses being unilaterally transformed by
> their exposure to the flow of internationally generated images. Local,
> small-scale West African producers are socially and physically close to
> their consumers, sharing much the same social experience and outlook.
> (2000:5)

Even the thriving video film industries of Nigeria, and increasingly of Ghana, Sierra Leone, Cameroon, Kenya, Tanzania, and Uganda, cannot be described as initiating or participating in "mass culture" given the obstacles that filmmakers working in these industries face on a daily basis, including electricity failures, delays due to religious customs (such as the muezzin's call for Muslims to pray), and piracy (meaning that it is difficult for producers to recuperate their costs) (*This Is Nollywood* [film, 2007]).

For my purposes, then, what is most significant is that it is possible to construct an idea of a *critical* branch of African screen media, since although African films can of course not be located wholly outside of a culture industry, they can be located within a public sphere that is characterized by closeness rather than the distance that has been associated with mass culture since Walter Benjamin's famous first words on the work of art in the age of mechanical reproduction (1935). This allows for a recuperation of the intentionality of both filmmaker and viewer, and it also enables a particular kind of engagement of filmmakers with their subject matter, and of viewers with the images on the screen, a relationship that makes critique possible.

· · · · ·

I have thus far made claims that African film adaptations offer performative criticism, and operate in the manner of Adornian mimesis. There are, however, three serious problems associated with the critique manifest in African film adaptations of literature that it is important to address. All three problems are related to the idea that the success of critique through film is dependent on its absorption by the audiences at whom it is aimed. The first problem is that many audiences in Africa are non-literate and will not have read the literary texts that the films adapt. In all sub-Saharan African countries, except the Seychelles, the non-literacy rate is more than 10 percent, and it is as high as 70 percent in many West African nations. While many Africans would have an oral knowledge of certain texts discussed here (such as the Book of Genesis) that can be said to substitute for having read them, in many cases it is unlikely that people will know the texts intimately. The criticism offered specifically through the literary adaptation process, then, is only accessible to those who are literate and who have access to the texts.

The second, more fundamental problem has to do with the fact that it is very difficult to see the kind of African films discussed here in Africa. At the 2007 New York African Film Festival the Cameroonian documentary maker, Jean-Marie Teno, said: "I am sick of the question, *who* are you making your films for? American filmmakers never get asked this question." If certain kinds of African films are not reaching the African public, however, the question of audience is a vital one, and it is impossible for African filmmakers and African film critics to disengage from it. The popularity and accessibility of films made in "Nollywood" (in southern Nigeria), "Kanywood" (in northern Nigeria), "Riverwood" (in Kenya), and "Bongowood" (in Tanzania), to name only a few of Africa's booming video film industries, suggest that it is not impossible for African films to reach African audiences. It is difficult to reconcile the critical achievements of the filmmakers analyzed here with the rise of low-budget video filmmaking and its attendant entertainment or "showbiz" industries. The latter has rendered obsolete the arguments around whether culture (and particularly the relatively expensive practice of filmmaking) should be sidelined while African governments attempt to deal with the urgent issues of food, housing, and job creation. People are no longer relying on inept state structures to produce and consume their culture: they are doing it themselves. If the condition for a film being considered "African" is its accessibility to an African audience, then video films are more supremely part of "African screen media" than the films analyzed here. However, the nature of critique offered by such video films has been at issue.

Nigerian filmmakers and historians such as Afolabi Adesanya and Wole Ogundele, and African film critic Kenneth Harrow, are deeply troubled by the commercial nature of the video industry and what it means for "serious" and critical African art. Alternatively, anthropologists such as Brian Larkin and Birgit Meyer express excitement at the local and global access to audiovisual media for Africans created through the video industries. What remains disturbing is the relative lack of research and discussion about the forms and functions of the video films. The general euphoria that Africans are producing and consuming their own films runs the risk of compromising important debate on the content and critique of such African films. While certain video filmmakers, such as Tunde Kelani and Ladi Ladebo in Nigeria and Bob Nyanja in Kenya, have adopted a critical voice, raising important issues around African art, ethnicity, and HIV/AIDS, other video filmmakers trade in the genres of horror, magic, and melodrama and often exhibit themes of vengeance in order to make money (Adesanya 1997:14). While such films may include social and political critique (Haynes 2006; Dovey 2007a), their chief difference from the films discussed here (and many other African films made on celluloid) is related to their representations of violence: whereas the films under analysis here offer a critique particularly of retributive violence, video films tend to affirm such violence in lieu of exploring restorative, nonviolent means of resolving social and political problems.

While we cannot deny the importance and promise that video film holds in terms of addressing the crisis of representation in African societies, we also cannot refrain from analyzing the critique offered by all African films, regardless of the format in which they are made. In particular, given the beleaguered state of the entire globe in terms of "terrorism" of all kinds, state-sanctioned violence, wars, and violence against women and children, it would appear to be vital for African filmmakers not to renounce the position they have taken up in critiquing violence. Ogunleye refers to "criticisms about the amount of blood, debauchery and violence (both physical and spiritual), witnessed on African video screens" (2003:x). While one would not want to prescribe to African filmmakers what kinds of films they and audiences should make and watch, it is vital that an intellectual community explores and debates the iconographies and impact of African films.

Specifically, the iconography of any commercial cinema (in Africa and elsewhere) must be analyzed, for, as one critic points out:

> An indigenous popular cinema will inevitably transmit and reinforce the priorities and beliefs of the society that finances it. An art cinema based in essentially nonprofit filmmaking, on the other hand, can risk interrogating that society's values and suggesting alternatives. Nigerian cinema may soon face the same problem confronted by the U.S.: how to nurture and finance a noncommercial cinema, which can act as a critique and complement to its commercial counterpart. (California Newsreel 2000)

The question, then, is not of competing alternatives, of whether to choose commercial video production *over* critical filmmaking. It is of how to allow both forms of filmmaking to flourish and to inform and develop one another. Acknowledgment of the possibility of coevalness might shift African film criticism beyond the impasse that has recently arisen over the incommensurability of the overtly commercial aims of certain filmmakers and the relatively noncommercial aims of others. On the one hand, Mweze Ngangura argues that African filmmakers can best contribute to social change through an entertainment cinema (1996). On the other hand, Clyde Taylor argues that the "desideratum of enlightenment will inevitably draw rejection from those who favour a commercial orientation. Much of the discussion among the builders of African cinema revolves around developing distribution and creating an industry: but the development of an industry could be the worst thing for the more profound social possibilities of African cinema" (2000:144). Taylor cautions critics against reifying African audiences, against assuming that "commercialised African audiences will be more resistant to trash and glitter than other societies" (ibid.).

At FESPACO 2007, there was a strong consensus that everyone involved in African film has to work, in the future, toward bridging the gap between critical African films and the African public so that their critique may be fully activated for development purposes: whether this means evolving new popular forms of film that will appeal more to local, African audiences; making more films in African languages; harnessing the democratization process that has been opened up by new technologies; creating coproduction treaties between African nations; showing African films on television; or through creating alternate distribution and exhibition strategies. In order to acknowledge the importance of African films reaching an African public for their critique to be fulfilled, I address specific issues of audience in the historical introductions to South African and Francophone West African film, respectively.

The third problem associated with the critique offered by African film adaptations of literature is as much a problem as it is proof that such films are necessary in Africa. If, according to Adorno, mimesis in a situation of late modernity in the "West" is virtually impossible given the reification of instrumental rationality at the expense of embodiment, one might similarly argue that mimesis in a situation of postcoloniality in Africa is virtually impossible given the damaging fissure of African minds (consciousness) from bodies, as described by Fanon (1967) and Steve Biko (1979). To both Fanon and Biko, writing long before Ngugi wã Th'iongo's *Decolonization of the Mind: The Politics of Language in African Literature* (1986), the true tragedy of colonialism was its effect not so much on the body as on the psyche or consciousness of the colonized. To Fanon, racism results in an emphasis on the skin color of a victim to the extent that the victim can think of nothing other than his/her skin color—his/her mind becomes preoccupied with the body/skin. Similarly, according to Biko, the minds of black South Africans were the prime weapons in the hands of the apartheid government in South Africa, and he argues that, "Material want is bad enough, but coupled with spiritual poverty it kills" (1979:28). Reconstituting an effortless dialectic between mind and body was one of the aims of Fanon's psychiatric work at Blida-Joinville in Algeria in the 1950s as well as of Biko's Black Consciousness movement of the 1970s. Both notably involved the movement from group solidarity toward a resurrection of the importance of the individual. As Biko writes: "The philosophy of Black Consciousness . . . expresses *group* pride and the determination by the blacks to rise and attain the envisaged *self*" (1979:68; my emphasis). The typical process of production and reception of fiction films—made by a collective but with a focus on individual protagonists, watched by a collective but ultimately stored within the minds of individual viewers—mirrors Fanon's and Biko's work and philosophies. The fact that contemporary African film adapters of literature are themselves engaging in mimesis—in the reconnection of rationality and embodiment—would then imply a process of healing, of overcoming the fracturing of selves, of mind from body, caused by colonialism. Biko is particularly relevant to this study in that rather than advocating a focus on the enemy's violence, and on retaliatory violence, which is another way of playing by the oppressor's rules, he called for an increased consciousness of African lives and realities.

African Screen Media, Mimicry, and Violence

The main question that this book seeks to explore, then, is how African fiction filmmakers are representing and critiquing contemporary violence (murder, war, genocide, rape) that continues to ravage the African continent. Debate persists on whether the Western media exaggerates violence in Africa (Harding 2003a, 2003b, 2003c) or portrays it accurately (Schwab 2001:3–4). Those who believe that Africa is a particularly war-torn continent tend to cite the many military coups d'état that have occurred—in 1963 (Togo), 1966 (Nigeria, Ghana, Central African Republic), 1967 (Sierra Leone), and 1968 (Mali)—as well as the civil wars that took place throughout the 1990s (in Angola, DRC Congo, Congo-Brazzaville, Liberia, Sierra Leone, Somalia, Sudan, Burundi, and Rwanda) and are currently ongoing (in Sudan, Somalia, Chad, and DRC, among other countries). They reference apartheid in South Africa, and the dictatorships of Idi Amin in Uganda and, more recently, of Robert Mugabe in Zimbabwe. While it is not my purpose to enter the academic fray about the magnitude of violence in Africa compared to other regions of the world, or how culpable the Western media is in (re)producing it, what is useful to my study is the consensus among political theorists that contemporary violence in Africa is characterized by intrastate rather than interstate conflict. Such recognition strongly suggests that much of the large-scale violence in contemporary Africa is not inherent to the continent, but is a product of the imaginary, volatile nations into which it was sliced during the 1884–85 Berlin Conference.

Similarly, in that I approach the topic of violence through African films that re-historicize earlier situations of violence, I reject claims that Africa is in the process of "*self*-destructing," as Schwab suggests in the title of his book (2001; my emphasis). Instead, I align myself with scholars who have taken the long view of history in Africa and analyzed the ways in which postcolonial violence is a metonymic displacement of colonial and other kinds of violence.[10] At the same time, I try to avoid the one-dimensional view that all of Africa's contemporary problems are a result of colonialism and apartheid, a view that patronizes Africans by assuming that they have no agency. As one international relations scholar puts it, "African wars, as with wars elsewhere, can never be attributed to a singular explanatory variable" (Bøås 2003: 43). Since I favor an approach that takes account of agency, I am concerned with how Africans themselves are responding to and representing violence of all kinds, including bodily (for example, murder or rape) and psychic/systemic violence (for example, colonial and institutional state violence). Cinematic representation of violence has been prominent in films made across the continent in the past decade, and the question of violence took center-stage at FESPACO 2007, as attested to in FESPACO 2007's special bulletin on "Violence et cinema africain" (*AfriCiné*). In the brief section that follows, I want to address the relationship of colonial Africa and violence as a way of contextualizing the discussion of contemporary African representations of violence in subsequent chapters.

Anthropologist Michael Taussig describes "the violence of the twentieth-century colonial frontier" in terms of the "mimicry by the colonizer of the savagery imputed to the savage" (1993:66). Taussig's account of the physical violence of colonial encounters is the counterpart to Homi Bhabha's notion of colonial mimicry as a form of discursive violence. Bhabha's concept of mimicry was inspired by Fanon's recognition in *Black Skin, White Masks* of the way in which colonialism bred mimicry by the colonized of the colonizers. Unlike Fanon, however, Bhabha is less interested in exploring the schizophrenic fissures with which colonialism disrupts the psyche and body of the colonized, and more interested in the schizophrenia of the colonizers as figured through colonial discourse. Fanon argues that "the European has a fixed concept of the Negro" (1967: 35)—that is, an essentially racist, dehumanizing concept. Bhabha counteracts this statement by saying that this fixed concept is actually not as fixed as it initially seems to be. To Bhabha this fixed concept emerges out of a long history and tradition of "civil" discourse, in which a stereotype of the black African is anxiously repeated. The repetition of this fixed concept or stereotype becomes a form of mimicry that represents an ambivalence, a shifting in the Western psyche between fear and desire of the black colonial subject. Bhabha thus argues that "the stereotype . . . is a form of knowledge and identification that vacillates between what is always 'in place,' already known, and something that must be anxiously repeated . . . as if the essential duplicity of the Asiatic or the bestial sexual license of the African that needs no proof, can never really, in discourse, be proved" (1994:94–95). This anxious repetition or mimicry, Bhabha claims, leads to ambivalence in the colonial text, thereby inauthenticating its supposed objectivity. It is this colonial mimicry that I want to trace in relation to the introduction of cinema into Africa. I hope to show how remarkable it is that certain African filmmakers have rejected a similar form of mimicry in their films and have instead embraced a form of (Adornian) mimesis that critiques violence.

In Africa there was no gradual exposure to new technological developments at the end of the nineteenth century, no Thomas Edison inventing electric light, no George Eastman developing celluloid, no Étienne-Jules Marey brandishing his photographic gun. Nor was there regular entertainment of the kind Georges Méliès provided to French crowds with his magic lanterns, the forerunners of our modern cinemas. There was no Théâtre Optique, no Muybridge's Horse, no Lumière brothers. Although Cinematograph screenings were given in a number of different African countries from 1895 onwards, these screenings were generally reserved for "elite" residents (usually white male civil servants), meaning that most Africans were not made aware of cinema's existence until well into the twentieth century. Cinema came hand in hand with brutal colonization, and with patronizing and racist censorship and exhibition policies. The British, Belgian, Portuguese, and French colonizing authorities largely used cinema in an attempt to perpetuate the idea that Africans (and black people in general) were an inferior and violent race that required taming and civilizing.

Films were made about Africa by European and North American filmmakers, who turned Africa into a savage, fabricated backdrop peopled by violent tribes with heathen rituals, against whom white heroes had to fight for "civilization."[11] As Robert Stam and Ella Shohat point out, these films, when shown in Africa, had "complex ramifications for spectatorship," so that "some of the major figures articulating anticolonial and postcolonial discourse symptomatically return in their writing to colonial spectatorship as a kind of primal scene." Stam and Shohat speak of "spectatorial schizophrenia," given that black Africans were made to identify with white heroes while rejecting the "barbaric" Africans depicted in the films. In this way, they argue, colonial filmmaking in Africa initiated a particular mode of "black" reception (2000:386), a mode of spectatorship that has been analyzed in depth by Manthia Diawara (1988).

Films were also made specifically *for* African audiences as early as the mid-1920s, when colonial film units were set up in various African countries—predominantly those colonized by the British and Belgians—for educational and propaganda purposes. Some films were made with a very limited form of collaboration between Africans and the colonizing powers, as in the case of the Bantu Educational Cinema Experiment, conducted from 1935 to 1937 in British East Africa, but the organizers' patronizing and essentially exploitative attitude toward Africans is evident throughout their report. Of the belief that Africans were "unable to distinguish between truth and falsehood" (Notcutt and Latham 1937:23) and that it would have been dangerous to show them "harmful films" (22), the organizers made films to "educate" Africans as to why they should pay their taxes, save their money in banks, cultivate and drink tea and coffee, and trust Western medical technology more than their own natural healers (30–73). These films, based on the assumption that the black races were by nature violent and in need of instruction and civilization, were also insidious advertisements for European products, designed to make Africans dependent on Europe and its new modern technologies. This "cinema in Africa," then, was a method of control and modernization, a further means for subjecting Africans to the legal, bureaucratic, commercial, and scientific forms of organization of the colonizing powers.

Films made about Africa and Africans, and films made for and shown to Africans, shared an assumption that Africans were inherently violent. One could argue, then, that colonial film production and exhibition were symptomatic of the colonial process as a whole. The "savagery imputed to the savage" in the earliest films made and shown in Africa is evident at every turn. It is of great interest, given the violence of colonization justified through the assumed violence of the colonized, that many of the first films made by Africans were fundamentally opposed to retaliatory violence. While, as Mbye Cham has noted, African cinema is no doubt a "child of political independence" (1996:1), its birth as a political cinema in a critical rather than revolutionary sense has not been adequately addressed.

The development of African screen media—if confined to production by sub-Saharan Africans—began only in the 1950s, concurrently with the decolonization struggle and the advent of independence in many African nations, and its genesis as a politicized art form was, in part, a reaction to colonial cinema and ethnographic filmmaking in Africa.[12] However, the overtly political origins of African screen media can be distinguished from a pre-existing political cinematic practice and discourse—that of Third Cinema, a term coined by the Argentinean filmmakers Fernando Solanas and Octavio Getino, who in 1969 published their groundbreaking manifesto, "Towards a Third Cinema." In their manifesto, Solanas and Getino reject what they call "First Cinema," constituted primarily of seamlessly constructed illusionistic Hollywood movies, which, they argue, situate the viewer as "a *consumer of ideology*, and not as the creator of ideology" (1969:51), and propose Third Cinema as an alternative to "Second Cinema," which they see as failing in its challenge to First Cinema.[13]

Solanas and Getino's work was strongly influenced by the ideas of European thinkers such as Marx and Gramsci, and by anticolonial theorists such as Fanon and Cabral, and particularly by their theorizing of revolutionary or proletariat violence (Fanon 1983; Cabral 1973). Fanon, as I have mentioned, was one of the first to address the imitative nature of colonial encounters. In *The Wretched of the Earth*, the first edition of which was prefaced by Jean-Paul Sartre, Fanon urged colonized peoples to give up their "nauseating mimicry" (quoted in Sartre 1983:8) of the European colonists, who attempted to "white-wash" (Sartre 7) their subjects. Fanon did encourage mimicry on one front, however, urging colonized peoples to mimic the colonizers' violence, and thereby transform it into revolutionary violence (Fanon 1983:28).

This is the kind of violence that so-called "Third filmmakers" attempted to promote through their films. Solanas and Getino insist, throughout their manifesto, on filmmaking as a "guerilla activity," the camera as the "inexhaustible *expropriator of image-weapons*" (58) and the projector as a *"gun that can shoot 24 frames per second"*(58). They argue that Third Cinema should incite its viewers to *action*, that the film is "important only as a detonator or pretext" (62), and that Third filmmakers should "insert the work as an original fact in the process of liberation, place it first at the service of life itself, ahead of art" (50). Film screenings in Latin America provoked demonstrations and debates, and were used for the education of militant cadres in the 1960s and, owing to the threat of government reprisal, these screenings were often guarded by armed revolutionaries (Gabriel 1982:19).

While emphasizing action rather than a change in consciousness, Solanas and Getino did argue that Third Cinema must effect the "*decolonization of culture*" (47), not only on the front of colonialism but also on that of neocolonialism. This early recognition of the centrality of culture in the development of Third World countries was taken up and endorsed by African filmmakers, and is particularly evident in those manifestos created at film festivals in Algiers in 1973 and 1975, Niamey in 1982, Harare in 1990, and Ouagadougou in 1991—manifestos that represent the first stirrings of a theory of "African Cinema" (Bakari and Cham 1996:17–36). Teshome Gabriel, however, allows us to pinpoint a key difference between Third Cinema and African Cinema in a way that other Third Cinema theorists, such as Roy Armes (1987), do not. Introducing the work of the Senegalese writer and filmmaker Ousmane Sembene, Gabriel argues that the so-called "Father of African Cinema" can be distinguished from Third filmmakers in that he views film as a political rather than a revolutionary medium (1982:22). According to Sembene,

It's not after having read Marx or Lenin that you go out and make a revolution. . . . All the works are just a point of reference in history. And that's all. Before the end of an act of creation society usually has already surpassed it. . . . The role of the artist is to denounce what he sees wrong in society [. . . but] to give solutions escapes the artist. (Quoted in Gabriel 1982:22)

Throughout his career, Sembene showed an interest in the consciousness-raising of his people, but not in inciting physical violence of any kind. His use of cinema to critique, summon reflection, or forewarn reveals his belief in the medium's critical potential. I would argue, then, that instead of seeing Sembene as a father figure simply because he was the first black sub-Saharan African to make a feature-length film, or because of what some film critics identify as his pioneering of the mode of social realism in Africa (Pfaff 1984), he deserves this title for also being the exemplar and inspiration of an African cinematic mode that concerns itself with critical awareness rather than with revolutionary action.[14] An appreciation for the critical nature of Sembene's films—although not directly addressed in this book—therefore informs my discussions of the work of other African directors.

What is most significant in this brief history of the cinema in Africa and the emergence of African film is the violence with which cinema was implemented in African contexts, and the choice that many African filmmakers have made to reject such violence and instead adopt a point of view that offers a critique of violence. Malian film critic Moussa Bolly argues that contemporary directors from Chad, Nigeria, Senegal, and Tunisia "are exploring ways of breaking the cycles of violence in which Africa is plunged. A violence which, according to them, can never be the solution to the problems of Africans" (2007:1).[15] As I have emphasized, by focusing on the ways in which violence is critiqued in African films, my view is not that violence is a staple of African cinema. Such a suggestion would fuel the erroneous image of Africa, perpetuated in much Western media, as inherently violent (Harding 2003a, 2003b, 2003c). On the contrary, I posit that by historicizing violence through the adaptation process, African filmmakers are problematizing representations of Africa as inherently violent.

At the same time, we cannot deny that many millions of people in Africa do have intimate experience of different forms of violence, which means that even more is at stake in the specific representation of violence in this context. At the current time, when violence—although not inherent—is endemic in many African countries, and cannot simply be ignored, it seems important to ask how violence is to be dealt with in literature and film. Referring to the torture of prisoners in South Africa during apartheid, J. M. Coetzee talks about the way that writers are drawn to the torture room, pointing out that "there is something tawdry about *following* the state in this way, making its vile mysteries the occasion of fantasy. For the writer the deeper problem is *not* to allow himself to be impaled on the dilemma proposed by the state, namely, either to ignore its obscenities or else to produce representations of them" (1986:364). The dilemma is similar in relation to other forms of violence, too, and the question arises as to whether film as medium is, on the one hand, able to represent violence in a way that does not appeal to the fantasies of the viewer as voyeur, and, on the other hand, whether film as medium is able to achieve a critique of violence in a way that is not available to the verbal, concept-bound, rational critique of the traditional disciplines.

Stephen Prince has provided a historical overview of screen violence, focusing on the attempt by Hollywood filmmakers to achieve verisimilitude in their representations of violence (2000b). It would seem that the professionalization of makeup artists and the invention of "squibs" have allowed for increasingly gruesome representations of violence that seem designed not to inspire critique on the part of the audience, but horrific delight. We may conclude that the realistic representation of violence in Hollywood films is largely a commercial ploy. African filmmakers, on the other hand, have attempted to represent violence realistically for educational reasons. Senegalese filmmaker Mahama Traoré, for example, has criticized Hollywood films for being "vehicles of violence, sex, and an alien culture, a culture into which we are not integrated and into which we, in fact, refuse to be integrated because we want to remain ourselves" (quoted in Adesanya 1997:13). Josef Gugler argues that "after the violence of slavery, of colonialism, and of postcolonial conflicts, gratuitous violence [in African films] seems obscene" (2003:10). He further notes that, "Violence shown in [African] films on political struggles, and . . . in particular torture scenes, can be quite unsettling to Western audiences inured to different kinds of violence'"(2003:10). Guinean film critic Fatoumata Sagnane and Benin film critic Godefroy

Macaire Chabi argue respectively that in an African film "blood does not flow" (2007:2) and that "there are not exchanges of bullets" (2007:3), but that violence is figured in more subtle, less crude ways. African governments, who have deemed Western depictions of violence and sex as a "potentially bad influence," have similarly encouraged the modest representation of violence (Meyer 2003:207). The films that I analyze provide examples of filmic conventions of representing violence that—while broadly realistic—are very different to those of commercial cinema, both in the West and in Africa. It is through these different conventions and through the re-historicization of the adaptation process that a critique, rather than an affirmation or a denial, of violence is made possible.

1 Cinema and Violence in South Africa

Cinema and Violence in Pre-1994 South Africa

In 1916 a film called *De Voortrekkers* was made by one of the first South African film production companies, African Film Production (AFP). The film tells the story of the Great Trek and ends with a historical reconstruction of the 1838 Battle of Blood River, in which about 3,000 Zulus, led by their chief Dingaan, were massacred by 464 Boers. The South African film historian Thelma Gutsche relates what happened when the imported American film producer, Harold Shaw, and the screenwriter, the Afrikaner Gustav Preller, attempted to direct the battle, having ordered all the props that they felt would ensure the most authentic, nonanachronistic production—twenty thousand assegais, five hundred period rifles, and forty trek wagons assembled into a "laager" (a circular barricade):

> At a given signal, the natives charged the laager furiously; but instead of recoiling and falling "dead," continued into the laager itself where blows with Europeans were exchanged. Mounted police . . . were forced to intervene and to prevent the natives from attacking the laager in earnest. In moving them away from the scene of the "battle," the police hustled the natives out of the laager and into the surrounding hills. Some escaped by swimming the river and one was drowned. This unfortunate occurrence badly affected the temper of the hundreds of natives now waiting sullenly in the hills and made a "re-take" impossible. (1972:314)

Gutsche notes that, prior to the production of this scene, the white filmmakers were anxious as to how they might control "thousands of natives who were expected to make a fanatic attack on a laager without losing sight of the fact that they were only acting" (ibid.). Yet when magisterial investigations were undertaken into the reasons for the black extras' seeming misunderstanding of instructions, Harold Shaw and Major Trew (the head of police) came forward with important information. The *Cape Times* on December 15, 1916, quotes them as saying that there had been "a plot to incite and irritate the natives" (ibid.). Apparently, as the black extras acting as Zulus had moved toward the laager, the white men acting as Boers had started firing at them before being so instructed. In spite of Shaw's running into the midst of the blacks and shouting to stop the whites from firing, the whites continued shooting at close range even as the blacks fled. It was only a month later that filming could be resumed, this time—Gutsche says—"with complete success" (ibid.).

This controversial first take of the Battle of Blood River was screened only once, privately, at Johannesburg's Empire Theatre. Gutsche's tone is astonishingly detached as she claims that the scene, although "extremely realistic, . . . was of course wholly inaccurate" (ibid.). The scene was perhaps "inaccurate" as a re-presentation of the events of this particular battle, but it was remarkably accurate as a symbolic reenactment of the violence of colonial mimicry. Sabotaging the script of *De Voortrekkers*, the whites joined forces to mimic a very real, contemporary script of racism and white oppression. The turmoil resulted in one man drowning, 122 people injured, and 35 people hospitalized (Peterson 2003:45). In this way the whites reproduced the overarching script of colonialism, mimicking the behavior and attitudes of their own race while being captured on film. Ironically, while the white film producers had feared that the black extras would not be able to distinguish reality from playacting, it was the white extras who engaged in a real act of provocation.

The film producers' assumption is continued in Gutsche's response to the incident. She renders near-invisible the white-on-black aggression that initiates the debacle, commenting that "when [Major] Trew saw a native pull a white man off his horse and jab at him with his improvised assegai, he realised the danger of the disturbance" (314*n*24). Although black extras had already been injured, the physical "danger" is recognized—by Trew, and by Gutsche—only when the retaliatory black-on-white aggression began. More recently, Ndugu Mike Ssali, too, fails to tell the entire story of the filming of *De Voortrekkers*, recounting events only in relation to black-on-white violence (1996:97–98), and Ntongela Masilela, in a laudatory essay about

Gutsche's film research, leaves this omission on Gutsche's part unexamined (2001:207–28). Edwin Hees, while admittedly focusing his attention on the post-Union context in which *De Voortrekkers* was filmed, also makes no mention of the startling Battle of Blood River episode (2003:49–69). What is significant is the way in which this extended oversight perpetuates the kind of mimetic projection of the initial colonial encounters, in which the whites' violence is somehow justified or made invisible and the blacks' violence is made visible. In this inaccurate schema, it is black rather than white violence that is seen to initiate a chain of violence, the metonymic displacement of violence. It is only Bhekizizwe Peterson who has drawn attention to the black casualties that resulted from the whites' behavior and from the overlapping of real and staged warfare in the process of the film production (2003:44).

In this chapter I want to highlight the way in which the genealogy of colonial and apartheid violence—directed by whites at blacks—is mirrored in much of South Africa's cinematic history. It is against such a background of violent and exclusionary cinematic nation-building that I want to situate the work of the filmmakers studied here, many of whom appear to make a deliberate decision to assert their power through a critique of, rather than affirmation of, violence. This chapter will not attempt, therefore, to offer a comprehensive history of the cinema in South Africa, ground that has already been well-covered.[1] Rather, it will interpret this history with the express purpose of exploring the relationship between contexts of violence and the cultural institution of cinema in South Africa. This historical "excavation" is specifically intended to reveal possible inspirations for the current critique of violence in post-1994 South African film adaptations of South African literature written during apartheid.

The first public screening of the final version of *De Voortrekkers* was on the seventy-eighth anniversary of the Battle of Blood River—December 16, 1916[2]—in Krugersdorp, in the presence of the then prime minister, General Botha, who wept throughout the film. Forty thousand Afrikaners traveled in the old Trek style, by ox wagon, to attend the event, which was advertised as being "South Africa's greatest historical film. . . . Historically perfect" (Gutsche 315). The film attracted huge audiences and aroused much emotion as it toured the country, and an annual screening of the film on December 16 became a national tradition (Gutsche 316), bringing it into the service of Afrikaner nation-building after the Boer War (1899–1902). The decision to film the Battle of Blood River was an attempt to authenticate Afrikaner identity, in that the reenactment of the Afrikaner victory over the Zulus almost eighty years before offered psychological compensation for the defeat and humiliation the Afrikaners had recently experienced at the hands of the British, who regarded them as a backward and boorish people. This recuperation of a heroic past also endorsed the Afrikaner "right" to continue the domination of black peoples in the present, as they moved toward the implementation of apartheid. The making of *De Voortrekkers* thus encompassed both physical and epistemic white-against-black violence on which an exclusionary racist Afrikaner nationalism was built.

While *De Voortrekkers* attempted to authenticate the Afrikaners' claim to South Africa at a time of defeat, the film *Zulu*, made in 1964 by a British production company and starring the famous British actor Michael Caine, attempted something very similar on behalf of the British—the bolstering of British pride during a time at which Afrikanerdom was on the ascendancy because of the entrenchment of apartheid. Again the narrative revolves around a battle—in this case that of Rorke's Drift in 1879, in which 100 British soldiers defeated 4,000 Zulus. While interpretation of the film has been polarized between critics who claim that it is deeply anti-imperial and those who believe that it is racist (Hamilton and Modisane 2007), I want to analyze briefly the final sequence of the film to show that in treating the Zulus "equally," the filmmakers compromise an anti-imperial message. In the final sequence of the film, the British soldiers appear to have won the battle, and the Zulu warriors to have retreated, when the Zulu warriors return to the hilltop. After initial fear, the British soldiers realize that the Zulu warriors have come back "to salute fellow braves." The cinematic construction of the scene is complex. We, as viewers, are for the most part placed among the British soldiers, and we are made to experience their terror on observing the mass of Zulus reappearing on the hilltop. However, the film also offers us closer wide-shots of the Zulus, filmed from low angles. In such a way, the filmmakers would seem to wish to establish the Zulus and the white men as "equal parties." The low-angle shots gazing up at the Zulus seem to suggest their valor as fine warriors; more than this, the narrative suggests that the Zulus are "good sports"—they have come to pay their respects to the British. We are left with the elated feeling that this has been a war played out fairly, and that the British have deserved to win. This final scene, however, is not historically accurate: the Zulus *did* return to the hill-top, not to pay tribute to the British as "fellow braves," but to get a better look at the relief column making its way into Rorke's Drift. One commentator on the film says that this "invention is perfectly in spirit with the tone of the film," which he says is to value warring armies of equal stature (film historian Sheldon Hall, in the *Zulu* DVD special feature commentary). In such a way he endorses a reading of the film that we might correlate with Robert Rosenstone's concept of "true invention" rather than "false invention" in historical films (1995:45–79). I would claim, however, that the invention is false in that it intervenes in the film's attempted production of historical authenticity, creating an ambivalence that inauthenticates it. When we take into account that the sequence is not historically accurate, we begin to see how the filmmakers have cleverly manipulated the characterization of the Zulus. The Zulus are not being "saluted" by the filmmakers so much as they are being used to authenticate the valor of the British soldiers. The war was *not* fought on equal terms, due to the superior firearms of the British, and the filmmakers therefore *require* the Zulus to pay tribute to the British since it is *only* the Zulus who can authenticate the fairness of the war.

Not only do *De Voortrekkers* and *Zulu* rely on "false invention," but they also make use of selective history, an issue not raised by Bickford-Smith and Mendelsohn in their discussion of the relationship of history to film (2007). The filmmakers did not choose to depict historic battles in which whites were defeated by blacks; they are involved in a process of representing and authenticating a specific national and nationalist identity which is an exclusively white one. *De Voortrekkers* represents the founding myth of the Afrikaner nation, whereas *Zulu* memorializes the episode in which the most Victoria's Crosses in a single battle were won by British soldiers. As such, these films can be likened to what James C. Scott has called "public transcripts"—that is, the public script in which the powerless (in this case, blacks) disguise their own "truths" in order to rehearse a script of domination. Scott points out that while both the powerful and the powerless *perform*, it is the powerful who largely determine the script. Thus, he says, "The public transcript is, to put it crudely, the *self*-portrait of dominant elites as they would have themselves seen" (1990:18). As I will argue over the following chapters, now that political power has shifted from white Afrikaners and British to black South Africans, contemporary filmmakers are notably not engaging in the manufacturing of "public transcripts" as flattering self-portraits, but rather in a critical, self-evaluatory project.

The filming of De Voortrekkers and Zulu demonstrates the complex set of conflicting interests that makes it problematic to impose theories of colonialism and postcolonialism on the history of cultural production in South Africa. Unlike the West African states, South Africa was, of course, a settler colony, and as J. M. Coetzee points out, "from being the dubious colonial children of a far-off motherland, white South Africans graduated to uneasy possession of their own, less and less transigent internal colony" (1988:11). This development is reflected in the history of cinema in the country, which has been subject to both external (Hollywood) and internal (Afrikaner and British) colonization of its production, distribution and exhibition structures.

The first film screening in South Africa (and in Africa) was given to a private, English-speaking audience at the Grand National Hotel in Johannesburg in 1895. After walnuts and wine, the guests watched a cockfight, a scene with Buffalo Bill "in one of his quick-firing exhibitions," and Carmencita, a Spanish girl, performing a skirt dance (Gutsche 1972: 8). The Standard and Diggers News of April 6, 1895, published one of many articles that raved at how "life-like" the medium was (ibid.). It is not surprising that the audience was English-speaking: when the British settlers arrived in South Africa in the 1800s, they quickly introduced a policy of Anglicization. They established English newspapers, substituted the Dutch rixdollar for their own sterling pound, and made English the only legal language for instruction in state schools. Almost all the newspaper articles covering film in the late 1890s are English publications.

In the late 1890s, along with the movement of (white) people between South Africa and Europe, came a constant influx of the most recent film-related inventions from the United States and Europe, and itinerant, foreign showmen exhibited the latest "moving pictures" primarily in the large cities such as Cape Town and Johannesburg. Many South Africans living in rural areas were thus not aware of cinema's existence until well into the twentieth century. As Gutsche describes, "Although by 1898, moving pictures were known all over South Africa, they were known only to a certain class of people. The early exhibitions of 1896 and 1897 were considered a display of the 'latest scientific wonder' and audiences were composed almost entirely of men" (32). When cinema did begin to reach the broader South African public, it was as an extension of an already-burgeoning entertainment sector—before moving pictures appeared, there were touring theaters, circuses, marionettes, waxworks, magicians, and tableaux vivant. Yet owing to the fact that cinema arrived at the same time that tension between the British and the Boers (Afrikaners) was mounting, the initial "sensationalism" of cinema was soon tempered by a recognition of the medium's political and ideological potential at times of violent conflict. When the Anglo Boer War began in 1899, foreign journalists (including Winston Churchill) flocked to South Africa to report on the war through writing, photography, and film.

Three different film companies followed the Anglo Boer War. One of them was the Warwick Trading Company, which employed Edison's assistant, William Kennedy Laurie Dickson, to make films of close-range fighting with a cumbersome Biograph camera that he carried everywhere. The soldiers regarded Dickson and his assistants as their constant companions, and the latter risked their lives in trying to film the "terrible sights," creating an early link between cinema and violence in South Africa (Gutsche 43). In the Trading Company's 1900 catalog, it proudly states that, for the first time in history, the War Office had sanctioned the use of the Cinematograph. Yet it warns potential distributors always to wait for "genuine films" and not to "fool the Public with Faked Films. . . . The 'Warwick' War and Films of Topical Events for all parts of the World are taken on the Spot and are not made on Hampstead Heath, New Jersey, France or in somebody's Back Garden" (Gutsche 46). Their notice refers to the fact that, due to the guerilla nature of the fighting between the British and the Afrikaners, foreign journalists often found that their footage could not keep the interest of British audiences back at home. An industry thus developed around fictionalized accounts of the war, with unrealistically dramatic fighting scenes (Barnes 1992). Thus, from cinema's inception in South Africa, a blurring of "real" screen violence and "faked" screen violence emerged: screen violence was manufactured, particularly for foreign audiences.

Taking pleasure in screen violence, real or fake, was not something unique to the audiences of the Boer War films. Violence has exerted a fascination over filmmakers and audiences in all contexts since cinema's beginnings. Stephen Prince points out that screen violence is "deeply embedded in the history and functioning of cinema" and has "arguably been of central importance for the popular appeal of film" (2000b:2). Similarly, Gerald Mast argues in a discussion about cinematic mimesis that "disaster, catastrophe, and other events too horrible to endure in reality have been one of the constant delights of the mimetic arts" (1983:40). What Prince and Mast do not analyze, however, is the way in which national and racial politics regulate *who* is allowed to take pleasure in watching screen violence. The history of cinema in South Africa provides ample examples of how whites attempted to curtail black viewing pleasure.

South Africa was no stranger to the colonial film units that were set up in various African countries by the British and Belgians, and by missionaries, for educational and propaganda purposes (Malkmus and Armes 1991:19–22; Ukadike 1995:49; Ssali 1996:86). A certain Rev. Ray Phillips from the American Board of Missions installed a unit in Johannesburg as early as 1919–20 for the purpose of showing a series of (heavily censored) films to black mine workers (Peterson 2003). The Chamber of Mines and the Municipal Native Affairs Department welcomed the screenings, believing that the cinema could eradicate "potential criminal tendencies" in their workers, distract them from political activities in their spare time, and educate them. The assumption was that films with violence could not be trusted on the "natives" because they were so simple-minded they would mimic the violence. When it was in the interests of whites to encourage black violence, however, they did not hesitate to use film as an aid. The Native Recruiting Corporation used films to recruit black laborers for all kinds of work, but mostly to fight for Britain in World War II (Gutsche 1972:379–80).

Just as the filmmakers of *De Voortrekkers* assumed that blacks would not be able to distinguish between reality and acting, white film exhibitors supposed that blacks would not be able to separate reality from the images on the screen. Gutsche describes the reaction of the first black film audiences as follows: "At the outset, reaction was not unnaturally very primitive and at the touring cinema shows organised by the Native Recruiting Corporation in the country, assembled audiences not infrequently rose as a body and inspected the back of the screen to discover what had happened to the people they had just seen" (1972:379). The first white film audiences, however, were equally "primitive" in their reactions: grown men leapt out of their seats when the famous film of the Black Diamond Express hurtled toward them on the screen, and the Chief of Police of Uitenhage in South Africa ran out of a film screening of *A Daring Daylight Robbery* to try to capture the thieves

(Gutsche 1972:69). In fact, as the Egyptian film critic Samir Farid has said, cinema "was the first art in the history of human existence that drew people together in their experience of it ... people of all kinds, of all races, of all cultures" (2000:191).

Although some permanent cinemas were built for "urbanized natives" in the 1920s, the low wages of black South Africans and regular white public concern with the possible criminalizing effects of the cinema on black people meant that it was difficult for black South Africans to access films (Gutsche 378–79). The question of "harmful" or violent films was one of import across the continent, but perhaps particularly acute in South Africa. In anticipation of civilians of *any* race being incited to political action by watching films, the South African government legalized a draconian Entertainment Censorship Act (ECA) in 1931, no doubt inspired by the Hollywood Production Code of 1930 which stated that, "No picture shall be produced that will lower the moral standards of those who see it. Hence the sympathy of the audience should never be thrown to the side of crime, wrongdoing, evil or sin." Similarly, every possible representation of violence was prohibited in the ECA, from "Treatment of death," to "Scenes representing antagonistic relations between capital and labour," to "Pugilistic encounters between Europeans and non-Europeans," to "Scenes of rough handling or ill treatment of women and children" (Ssali 1996:92). This may seem like an antiviolence mandate, but it could be read as that form of fascism that, as Michael Taussig argues, is "an accentuated form of modern civilisation which is itself to be read as the history of the repression of mimesis—the ban on graven images, gypsies, actors; the love-hate relationship with the body" (1993:68). The South African filmmakers studied here do not ban violence, or the body, from their films: instead, they adapt violence to the screen in a way that allows them to politicize their audiences, and to sharpen viewers' critical capacities. How, in fact, could they ban violence from their films if, to repeat the words of Michael Cahn, critique "has to demonstrate its relevance by an involvement and similarity with what it criticizes" (1984:46)?

Britain, although a trailblazer in terms of filmmaking and processing technology, and in spite of its insistence on using film during the Anglo Boer War, did not regard the cinema as an integral part of its colonization process—colonization was focused not on cultural, but on political and economic domination. This oblivion to the power of film is perhaps what created a significant gap in surveillance in the pre-apartheid era (1920–1948) that allowed one black South African, Solomon T. Plaatje, to introduce a very different tradition of cinema and cinematic viewing to black South African audiences in the 1920s—a tradition that could be seen as the forerunner of contemporary South African cinema. In his influential article "The New African Movement and the Beginnings of Film Culture in South Africa," Ntongela Masilela situates Plaatje as one of the founders of the New African Movement, a movement dedicated to the modernization and enlightenment of black South African culture in the face of the consolidation of Afrikaner power in the lead-up to the institutionalization of apartheid in 1948. The bedrock of the New African Movement was not only a belief in modern progress, but in nonracialism, as expressed by one of its leaders, Pixley ka Isaka Seme, as follows: "There is today among all races and men a general desire for progress, and for cooperation.... The greatest success shall come when man shall have learned to cooperate, not only with his own kith and kin but with all peoples and with all life" (quoted in Masilela 2003:17). Plaatje was particularly enthused by the educational and entertaining role that film—as a modern art form—might play in South Africa, and he brought documentaries about the successes of the "New Negroes" back from trips to the United States and exhibited them throughout South Africa to mixed-race audiences between 1923 and 1925 (Masilela 2003:19). Plaatje was also attuned, however, to how film might be used as a vehicle for racist ideology, and in 1931 he worked very hard to stop a screening of D. W. Griffiths' *The Birth of a Nation* (1915) at the Johannesburg Town Hall because of its violent racism (Masilela 2003:21).

Masilela sees the development of the American Mission Board's childish film program for black miners as an affront to the work of Plaatje and others, who were trying to show—in the words of another New African Movement member, H. I. E. Dhlomo—that "the African responds to the cinema as other human beings do" (quoted in Masilela 2003:23). The few films that Dhlomo was able to see, including Laurence Olivier's *Henry V*, formed the basis of his humanist, nonracial philosophy and inspired his belief in the universality of all culture. The members of the New African Movement saw film as a possible tool of modernity and enlightenment that could be harnessed for the betterment of all races. The New African Movement evolved into the Sophiatown Renaissance, heralded by writers such as Lewis Nkosi, Can

Themba, and Bloke Modisane and, I want to claim here, has subsequently resurfaced in the "enlightened" movement of filmmaking in South Africa post-1994 which, as a form of Adornian mimesis, emphasizes rationality in equal measure to embodiment. Modisane craved the enlightenment of film so much that he apparently joined in debates about particular films with white friends until he had to admit, humiliated, that he had not been able to see the film because of censorship (Masilela 2003:25).

The negative role that the American Mission Board played in South Africa, and the positive example that Plaatje and others found in the American films about the "New Negroes," reveals how complicated the cinematic relationship between South Africa and the United States has been. South Africa's strong trade relations with the United States, and the fact that English was a lingua franca, provided fertile ground for Hollywood to appropriate South Africa's nascent film industry—Meyer Levy's cinema museum in Johannesburg shows that from the early 1900s, there was a "little Hollywood in South Africa" (*In Darkest Hollywood* [film, 1993]). Hollywood played an active role as a "colonizer" of South African stories and screens, and even colluded with D. F. Malan's National Party when it came into power in 1948 by helping it to make propaganda films. It was not until the 1970s, when *The Wilby Conspiracy* (1974) was made, that Hollywood began to pay attention to the potential profit of exposing the apartheid system. This led in the late 1980s to the production of the three best-known South African anti-apartheid films, all adaptations of books and made partly in collaboration with Hollywood: *Cry Freedom* (1987), *A World Apart* (1988), and *A Dry White Season* (1989).

Today, Hollywood's monopoly over South Africa's film production and exhibition circuits, and its influence on South African filmmakers, remains an impediment to the development of a truly independent national cinema, and could be compared to France's dubious cultural patronage of the Francophone West African film industry. South Africa is not unique in Africa in occupying a fragile relationship to the development of its own images. An article by Dave Calhoun in *Sight & Sound* reveals that a new spate of *Out of Africa*–type films, made by foreigners with African backdrops, have recently flooded the international market. As Calhoun critically argues, "the obvious urgency present in such [African] films as *Bamako* and *Daratt* is a million miles away from the deflating attitude of too many international filmmakers to Africa: stunning landscapes, a fascinating past, but ultimately a continent whose people and politics are too difficult to get to grips with" (2007:35). Many of these foreign-made feature films—such as *Hotel Rwanda* (2004), *Blood Diamond* (2006), and *The Last King of Scotland* (2006)—not only reductively associate Africa with beautiful landscapes and strange animals but also with violence. Films like *The Constant Gardener* (2005) feature scenes in which inexplicable violence by one group of Africans against another occurs, consolidating in this way the pervasive media portrayal of Africa as a war-torn continent where the black races indulge in gratuitous violence.

All aspects of the South African film industry—production, distribution, and exhibition—began to come under strict state control as early as 1949. Recognizing the ideological potential of film, the newly elected Afrikaner National Party hired John Grierson, a Scottish documentary filmmaker who had initiated the successful National Film Board of Canada, to investigate state film services (Tomaselli and Hees 1999).[3] Ultimately, however, the National Party government ignored Grierson's report of 1954 and instead appropriated the radio and press to propagate their message. A decade later, they did launch the National Film Board (NFB), but its operating principles differed significantly from Grierson's original suggestions, and instead drew on the resolutions of a later report made by the De Villiers Commission (1956), which pressed for the NFB to maintain strict control over censorship and to monitor external distribution, particularly in the face of growing international opposition to apartheid. "Differential censorship" was introduced, which the Minister of Interior attempted to justify, in 1963, by arguing that "there are some films which can be exhibited much more safely to a white child of fourteen years than to an adult Bantu" (quoted in Tomaselli 1988:22). This kind of censorship mimicked that of the American Mission Board, playing out yet again white mimicry of the violence projected as inherently "black." H. I. E. Dhlomo strenuously criticized this policy, arguing that "a healthy mind in a healthy body in a healthy home in a healthy environment can see hundreds of gangster films ... without once thinking of emulating them. It is the social conditions that produce the criminal" (quoted in Masilela 2003:22). That criminals are produced through social conditions, and that post-apartheid violence is a legacy of apartheid violence, is implied in all four of the South African films analyzed in the following chapters.

The National Party was not only interested in monitoring what black South Africans were watching; it also maintained strong control over film production. Although the first films made specifically for black South Africans were made by liberal, foreign whites who genuinely believed that they were creating a "native film industry," their films are deeply conservative. The very first films with black stars—such as *Jim Comes to Jo'burg/African Jim* (1949), *Zonk!* (1950), and *Song of Africa* (1951)—are musicals that valorize the image of the smiling, singing, dancing, unthreatening black person. Although these films do harbor subversive elements—such as the black workers filmed in *Jim Comes to Jo'burg* who (unknown to the white directors) are singing a popular worker's song with the Zulu lyrics "Damn these white men who make us work so hard and pay us nothing"—they ultimately serve to confirm the racist view that black South Africans need to work hard to avoid the violent effects of urbanization on their "backward" race. *Jim Comes to Jo'burg*, for example, opens with a scrolling title that announces that this "is a simple film and its quaint mixture of the naïve and the sophisticated is a true reflection of the African native in a modern city." The scene in which the black workers sing, however, offers an ideal example of how even in the "public transcript" of inauthentic white films about blacks, blacks managed to introduce certain authentic "hidden transcripts" aimed at black spectators.[4]

In 1956 the National Party created a state subsidy scheme, which led to the development of a nationalist Afrikaner cinema, intended to sustain Afrikaner identity, just as the continued circulation and screening of *De Voortrekkers* was intended to encourage an exclusive Afrikaner patriotism in viewers. Although the subsidy was in part designed to prevent foreign film studios from buying out local companies, one of its aims was to fuel commercial propaganda films that could be used to transmit a positive image of South Africa overseas at a time of increasing international embargoes. An amendment to the subsidy scheme in 1969 further reduced funding for noncommercial film ventures, and allocated large sums of money specifically for the production of Afrikaans films. This was a covert way of reducing funding for politically subversive films, such as adaptations of Nadine Gordimer's stories "City Lovers" and "Country Lovers" (given the same names) and the two adaptations of Fugard plays made by Ross Devenish, *Boesman and Lena* (1974) and *Marigolds in August* (1978) (Tomaselli 1988:51). This amendment also severely reduced funding for film projects in African languages, which had originally been eligible for funding under the general subsidy scheme. This meant that only two feature films were made by black South Africans during apartheid: Simon Sabela's *U-Deliwe* (1975) and Gibson Kente's *How Long?* (1976). *U-Deliwe* was a 60-minute film shot on 16mm, about a young Zulu orphan who makes her way to Johannesburg, where she becomes a model. Her uncle finds her and she is forced to return to the countryside and live a solid, Christian life. This film became controversial after it was exposed that it had received funding from the apartheid government, no doubt since it supports the idea that black South Africans have no place in the city. *How Long?*, an anti-apartheid film by the "Father of Black South African Theater," Gibson Kente, was seized, and Kente was arrested and jailed for a year. The film has never been released.[5]

In the later years of apartheid, from the 1980s onwards, the South African Defense Force (SADF) increasingly gained control of the media, which it manipulated for its own military ends (Tomaselli 1988:20). Military use of the media is, of course, nothing new, and it is well known that Foucault has comprehensively theorized the ways in which visual technologies have been the means of exercising control over subject populations (1977). Allen Feldman goes further than Foucault, however, to argue that in war zones like Northern Ireland, visual technologies do more than allow for a substitution of physical violence by "ocular aggression," and that they are able to produce "the visual staging and technological penetration of the body by cameras, high-velocity bullets, or digitized bombs, which unite both seeing and killing, surveillance and violence in a unified scopic regime" (2000:49). Given the imbrication of visual technologies in the exercise of violence, film as technology clearly cannot be simply claimed as a means for working against the perpetuation of violence, which is why close attention has to be paid to the particular ways in which violence is represented in the films analyzed here.

Feldman argues that certain kinds of visual representation of violence are processed by the viewer according to a "recognition code," which allows for a kind of instantaneous classification of this violence through "idealizing nationalist, ethnic, and other cultural codes" which render the violence excusable (55). He does not draw explicitly on Adorno, but what he describes is clearly an example of mimesis as imitation harnessed in the service of identification, of labeling. Feldman also describes a schema, which he calls the "historiography of excuse," in which "prior acts of violence extenuate the commission of present and future acts." He goes on to describe this process as a form of regressive colonial mimicry, in terms that approximate Taussig's figuration of the first colonial encounters: "The rationality of excuse depends on recursive time and mimetic resemblance as narrativized by political discourse and popular memory. Through temporal mimesis and regression, each act of violence becomes typified insofar as it participates in and takes its validity from a prior aggression" (54). It is in this way that the visualization of violence is able to enact political goals in contexts such as Northern Ireland or in apartheid South Africa or in the current American "War against Terror" being waged on different fronts in the Muslim world. In apartheid South Africa, this visualization involved the constant streaming on television of images of black South African "terrorism" to convince whites that the government was justified in its (racist) laws.

Just as Burkinabé director Fanta Régina Nacro condemns violence that takes its cue from "a prior aggression" in *La Nuit de la Vérité* (2005), so too do all of the South African filmmakers studied here offer their solution to violence through a focus on the necessity of breaking violent cycles. Such a tradition has its origins in what many consider the first truly anti-apartheid film, *Come Back, Africa* (1959), directed by the American communist filmmaker Lionel Rogosin and coscripted with two of the most famous Sophiatown writers of the 1950s, Lewis Nkosi and William Bloke Modisane. The film, which was shot clandestinely in South Africa, follows the travails of Zachariah, a black man from rural pastures who comes to Johannesburg to work on the mines. Zachariah's story ends in tragedy after a gangster, Marumu, kills Zachariah's wife. One of the most striking scenes in the film features Nkosi, Modisane, and Can Themba with others in a shebeen (a township bar), discussing Marumu's violence and attempting to understand its origins. By contextualizing Marumu's violent acts in this way, the filmmakers condemn the association of violence with the urbanized black man and acknowledge its source in white apartheid violence. The shebeen scene is a remarkable example of the activation of mimesis through film: emerging from the bodies of people who were actually suffering at the time, this improvised verbal critique of apartheid violence elevates embodied knowledge to institutional knowledge, accessible to people within and outside of

South Africa. As Masilela points out, "this last intellectual generation of New Africanism still believed that rationalism, exemplified by the Enlightenment, could overcome irrational practices and obstacles" (27). Such a belief in rationalism, coupled with a profound consideration of epistemologies of the body, seems to have resurfaced in many contemporary South African films, and most powerfully in the films analyzed here.

Breaking cycles of violence was also the focus of the second anti-apartheid film, *Mapantsula* (1988), by the white South African director Oliver Schmitz in collaboration with black South African Thomas Mogotlane. In this film, the concern lies not simply with black criminal violence, however, but with the relationship between criminal and political violence, mirroring the shift to armed resistance by the anti-apartheid movement. The Defiance Campaign, initiated in 1952 by Nelson Mandela, Oliver Tambo, and others, had emphatically embraced nonviolence. However, when the Sharpeville massacre occurred in 1960, resulting in the murder of sixty-nine people during a peaceful protest march against pass laws, the ANC (African National Congress) felt compelled to adopt a policy of violent resistance. *Mapantsula* tells the tale of Panic, a "pantsula"—a gangster, in Zulu—who turns from petty crime to political consciousness. At the end of the film, when Panic finally makes the decision not to collaborate with the apartheid police, his resounding "NO!" shows that Panic has learned that his criminal behavior merely internalizes and perpetuates apartheid violence (most of his victims have been black); it is only by joining the anti-apartheid movement that Panic will begin to engage in a form of resistance that will help to eradicate white violence.

Situating *Mapantsula* in a tradition of films in which "gangsterism" becomes "enmeshed with discourses of resistance, offering a romanticised way of coping under apartheid," Tomaselli raises the thorny issue of the aesthetic representation of different forms of violence in South African films (2006:44–45). A number of contemporary South African films *do* appear to have developed out of this earlier tradition, and while important films in many ways, they also occasionally romanticize or glamorize criminal behavior (for example, *Hijack Stories* [2000] by Oliver Schmitz) or gender violence (for example, *Wa 'n Wina* [2001] by Dumisani Phakhati), through the use of sexy music or slick camera movement. On the other hand, the wildly successful SABC television series *Yizo Yizo* (2004), which realistically reveals the gritty violence of township school life in South Africa, has succeeded in conveying both the extent and pervasiveness of violence in South Africa, but without aestheticizing it. Coming close to the violence is, as I have argued, necessary, but how this violence is choreographed for fiction film is a serious issue for consideration.

Cinema, Violence, and Adaptation in Post-1994 South Africa

When South Africa became democratic in 1994, South Africans faced a decrease in political violence but an escalation in violent crime, which has led to South Africa's reputation as the crime capital of the world. The Centre for the Study of Violence and Reconciliation in South Africa published fifteen volumes between 2001 and 2005 in an attempt to scrutinize violent crime in the aftermath of apartheid and to try to find solutions to it. Representing violence is thus something of a double-edged sword for contemporary South African filmmakers. On the one hand, South African filmmakers face a history of brutal white violence against blacks, and have inherited a legacy of films they want to repudiate, in which black South Africans have been fashioned as barbarians. On the other hand, apartheid violence has been integrated into the post-apartheid era and has emerged in new forms, largely concentrated within the poorest areas of the country, such as the townships and so-called "informal settlements." It is no surprise after a system as debilitating as apartheid that violence is enacted by and against the weakest in society. As the Malian-Mauritanian director Abderrahmane Sissako says, "In his writings on the psychopathology of colonization, Frantz Fanon used to say that when the enemy is very far away and you can't reach him, then people will kill each other with machetes to assure their own death. I think it's important to reflect on this in the context of the continued violence within Africa" (2007:31). Like Sissako, African film critics (*AfriCiné* 2007) have termed violence in Africa "*violence continue*" or "continued violence" to reflect this violence's relationship to history. However, contemporary filmmakers are showing that it is not sufficient to acknowledge South Africa's history of violence; they explore questions about the nature of individual and collective responsibility for violence in post-1994 South Africa.

In the current violent climate in South Africa, it would appear to be vital to take seriously the "Father of Black South African Cinema" Lionel

Ngakane's statement that South Africans "need to recognise that at this stage of our history cinema is perhaps the most powerful instrument to foster a stable, democratic and united South Africa through feature films and documentary films about ourselves" (quoted in Blignaut and Botha 1992a:92). Ngakane here voices the desire of many citizens for a coherent and meaningful "nation"—one that has not previously existed since, despite the creation of the Union of South Africa in 1910, the newborn South African state quickly became subject to variegated socioeconomic, racial, and ethnic divisions and strife. It is only in the post-apartheid era that the state is slowly negotiating its way toward becoming a nation. In this sense, South Africa's position mirrors that of most African countries which, because of their formation through arbitrary colonial borders, have attempted to grow from geographically delineated states into imaginative nations (Laremont 2002).

Because the concept of the "nation" is largely a fantastical or imaginative one, art has a peculiarly privileged role in sustaining and questioning it. Contemporary South African filmmakers are playing an important role in narrating the new South African nation into being. *Drum* (2004), winner of FESPACO's 2005 Etalon de Yennenga, focuses on the life of Henry Nxumalo, a young journalist working in 1950s Sophiatown, a thriving township near Johannesburg, and his relations with his colleagues at the well-known magazine *Drum*. *Max and Mona* (2004) comically revitalizes the theme of rural South Africans coming to the city, with 19-year-old Max Bua—a professional funeral mourner—struggling to acclimatize to the dangerous turbulence of Johannesburg, where he intends to study to become a "white" doctor. *Hijack Stories* (2000), somewhere between a gangster flick and a comedy, realistically but humorously charts the emerging class differences among black South Africans, with an actor becoming a criminal, and a criminal becoming an actor. *Chikin Biznis—The Whole Story* (1999), which won the Grand Prix at the Vues d'Afrique film festival in Montreal, is another piquant comedy, charting the entry of its protagonist, Sipho, into the difficult world of small business in Soweto. *Tengers* (2007), South Africa's first-ever feature-length claymation film, takes a hilarious but hard-hitting look at gun violence in the province of Gauteng, while short animation films such as *And There in the Dust* (2004), *Jozi Zoo* (2006), and *Beyond Freedom* (2006), use techniques afforded by the animation process to question race, freedom, and violence in the "new" South Africa.[6] *Yesterday* (2004), nominated for the 2005 Oscar for

Best Foreign Film, quietly pictures the tale of a young mother who is living with AIDS in a village in KwaZulu-Natal. Khalo Matabane's digital docu-fiction *Conversations on a Sunday Afternoon* (2005) provides a moving look at the lives of immigrants in Johannesburg, and films such as *Jump the Gun* (1997), *God Is African* (2001), and *Cape of Good Hope* (2004) bring the multiculturalism of the "new South Africa" into focus. Issues around violence associated with gender and sexuality have found a voice in recent fiction and documentary films, such as *Proteus* (2003) and *Rape for Who I Am* (2005).

Although increasingly heterogeneous in their aims, South African films seem to share a desire to narrate the nation into being not by means of naïve optimism, but through a critique of contemporary violence. In order to move away from the violence that characterized the "old" exclusionary nationalism, they critique the cycle that perpetuates violence between white and black, and the metonymic displacement of apartheid violence that has led to increasing levels of violence between black and black. In this respect Olivier Barlet's description of the goals of many contemporary South African filmmakers is pertinent:

> Rather than meeting the expectations of right-thinking Western opinion, which would prefer to see unspeakable Whites ranged against an idealized black community, [South African filmmakers] are attempting to exorcise the scars left upon the consciousness of black people by their history. Following the path marked out by the writer Njabulo Ndebele, the cinema has taken an interest in "ordinary people," in their integration of violence into a society of violence. "We owe what we are to apartheid," said the poet Lesego Rampolokeng. Mickey Madoda Dube, exiled in the USA, took on the issue of Black-on-Black violence directly in *Imbazo, the Axe*, exploring the relationship between a son and his father, who, to survive, had been a member of the squads of hired killers paid by the regime to terrorize the black ghettos. (2000:110–11)

The themes of *Imbazo, the Axe* (1993), find articulation, too, in Dube's film *A Walk in the Night* (1998), which shows the integration of apartheid violence into a multiracial post-apartheid community. Unlike earlier expressions of nationalism in film, which relied on self-aggrandizement or blanket denigration of the Other, South African filmmakers are now rejecting "mythology-building" (Teer-Tomaselli 2001:128) and recognizing that South Africa will always be in the process of becoming a nation, and that self-critique is vital in this ongoing process.

Discourses of introspection and critique in contemporary South African cinema have no doubt been inspired by the proceedings of the Truth and Reconciliation Commission (TRC). Given that the TRC's remit was to deal with the violence committed during apartheid, any account of recent cultural production dealing with violence needs to recognize the discourses initiated in this respect. Over a five-year period, from 1995 to 2001, the TRC, presided over by Archbishop Desmond Tutu, allowed victims and perpetrators of apartheid crimes (from May 1, 1960 to May 10, 1994) to give testimony or to confess, and for perpetrators to apply for amnesty if they could prove that their crimes had been "politically motivated." While the value of the TRC has been fervently debated, one of its successes was that it was able to draw on legal, political, and religious frameworks for dealing with violence without exclusively adopting any one of these frameworks or its related discourses (Villa-Vicencio and Verwoerd 2000; James and Van de Vijver 2000). As a "liminal" institution that was able to move "betwixt and between existing state institutions" (Richard Wilson 2001:19), it was able to reformulate notions of "justice in human rights talk as restorative justice" (13).

The disciplinary struggle for control over the meaning of the TRC that followed the Commission itself has been described by Claudia Braude, who points out that many people have criticized the TRC for "excavating the past" (1996:61) and for losing its legitimacy by turning from a "waarheidskommissie" ("truth commission") into a "huilkommissie" ("crying commission") (61), with Archbishop Tutu often showing his compassion for victims by weeping with them. This was part of the TRC's appeal, however, since its nonjudiciary position allowed victims, perpetrators, commissioners, and observers to respond to the "narratives of pain" with emotion, rather than with an abstract intellectualism. Premesh Lalu and Brent Harris ask, then, what happens to narratives of pain "when they are appropriated by academics who will be expected to provide a synthesis out of what appears to be disparate episodes of personal trauma" (1996:24). The many quasi-fictional accounts that the TRC has inspired (for example, Meiring 1999; Orr 2000) seem to reflect a desire to refrain from abstracting the narratives of the TRC through the discourses of law, history, or sociology and to evoke the embodied responses of individual sufferers and perpetrators.

Films about the TRC, or film adaptations of written accounts of the TRC, are participating in the movement toward a narrative-based form of nation-building by exploring South Africa's violent past through the mode of fiction. While the first films about the TRC were documentaries, such as Antjie Krog and Ronelle Loots's *The Unfolding of Sky* (1998) and the American filmmakers Frances Reid and Deborah Hoffmann's Academy Award–winning film *Long Night's Journey into Day* (2000), a short fiction film, *Ubuntu's Wounds* (2001), was made by Sechaba Morojele while he was living in the United States. It tells the post-apartheid story of a former anti-apartheid activist residing in Los Angeles who comes face to face with his wife's murderer, a man who has been given amnesty by the TRC. Then, in 2004, four feature films about the TRC suddenly appeared. Ramadan Suleman's film *Zulu Love Letter* (2004) follows a journalist, a woman living in post-apartheid South Africa with a deaf-mute daughter, who is struggling to deal with what she sees as the "collective amnesia" of her society in the wake of the TRC. Ian Gabriel's *Forgiveness* (2004), winner of the prize for Best Film at the 2004 Locarno Film Festival, is a searing drama about an ex-police officer who comes to the small fishing village of Paternoster on the West Coast of South Africa to ask the private forgiveness of the family whose son he shot during apartheid. Tom Hooper's *Red Dust* (2004), adapted from Gillian Slovo's eponymous novel, is a courtroom drama in which an exiled white South African attorney (played by Hilary Swank) returns to her native country to represent a black political activist's TRC application for amnesty. John Boorman's *In My Country* (2004) is an adaptation of Antjie Krog's nonfictional account of her experiences reporting on the TRC, *Country of My Skull* (1998), starring Juliette Binoche and Samuel Jackson.

While David Philips has attempted to analyze the historical accuracy of TRC fiction films (2007), I am concerned with films that perform a similar *function* to the TRC, through focusing on individual narratives and harnessing an extra-statutory mode (fiction film) in order to critique violence. The work that these films accomplish extends beyond that of the TRC, however, in that the filmmakers examine not only apartheid violence but also ongoing forms of violence, racism, or hatred in post-1994 South Africa. In this way, the filmmakers suggest that South African history is not discontinuous and that the effects of apartheid cannot be bracketed between 1948 and 1994. The four films that I analyze in the following chapters are representative of this kind of work. They are the expressions of South African filmmakers who are participating in the complex dialogue initiated by the TRC around trying to understand the nuances of South Africa's violent past and present. Rather than simply vilifying the "evil" characters of the apartheid past, and thereby engaging in the kind of violent and sensational nation-building and myth-making enacted in colonial and apartheid films, such as *De Voortrekkers*, these filmmakers quietly focus their attention on the behavior of contemporary South Africans, both white and black. In order to do this, they have chosen to adapt novels written during apartheid with black protagonists culpable of criminal acts of violence—the murder of an old, defenseless white man, the rape of a black schoolgirl, the murder of a white anti-apartheid activist, and the kidnapping of a black baby. Remarkably, then, these filmmakers have shunned engagement in a discourse of "black victimhood," as one would expect in the immediate post-apartheid era, and are exploring the quandary of those black victims who become perpetrators through the metonymic displacement of violence.

Although interviews I have undertaken with the filmmakers suggest that the discourses of critique and reconciliation with which they engage are self-chosen, it is worthwhile considering alternate explanations. As filmmaker Sechaba Morojele points out, the fact that South African filmmakers have recently turned to adapting South African literature reflects not simply personal taste or political purpose, but state policy: the National Film and Video Foundation (NFVF), the major state funding body for film production, has specifically allocated funding for the adaptation of South African literature.[7] In light of this state mandate, Morojele has questioned the politics underpinning the choice of which texts to adapt to film. He asks why it continues to be literary texts by white South Africans, such as Gillian Slovo's *Red Dust* (2000) and Antjie Krog's *Country of My Skull* (1998), that are deemed most appropriate for adaptation to film. He points out, for example, that many black testimonies of the TRC have been written, but that film adapters, in order to acquire funding, still appear to require a white intermediary, as was the case with the anti-apartheid film adaptations made in the 1980s.[8] Director of *Max and Mona*, Teddy Mattera, goes further than Morojele to challenge the NFVF's allocation of funding to "reconciliation" films. He argues that many black South African filmmakers want to make films in which they explore residual anger and the limits of reconciliation, but that investors do not want to support such topics.

The complaints raised by these filmmakers are valid, and they can be contextualized within a broader debate, in South Africa, about the relationship of the TRC to South Africa's two major political discourses, liberalism and Marxism, and also within a broader global debate about justice and neoliberalism in the postcolonial era. Two dominant points of view have circulated in and about South Africa since 1994. On the one hand, there is the neoliberalism that has to a large extent been embraced by the ANC as the government of the new dispensation, and with it a belief in consumer capitalism and market economics, attracting international investment, as well as a view of the post-apartheid era as being somewhat discontinuous from the apartheid era, thus allowing for the label "the *new* South Africa" and institutions such as the TRC and the GEAR (Growth, Employment and Redistribution) program. On the other hand, there is a small but strong body of opposition to neoliberal ideas, which could be classified as neo-Marxist, where the focus is firmly placed on history, the lack of positive change that has occurred since the end of the apartheid era, the suffering not addressed by the TRC, and the need for justice, economic equality, and even revolution in the wake of growing social stratification (Parry 2005).

Interpreting the TRC from a neo-Marxist point of view, one might question to whose advantage the hearings were orchestrated. Although public discourses praise the TRC for diverting possible civil war, at the same time one might argue that it is largely the white population who has benefited from the government's policy of nonviolence and reconciliation. Many South African films have explored the Janus-faced nature of amnesty, such as Morojele's *Ubuntu's Wounds* (2001) and Gabriel's *Forgiveness* (2004), in which characters seek revenge rather than reconciliation. The films analyzed here critique violence just as they reproduce and struggle with many of the contradictions that characterized the TRC. Since two of the films adapt the work of liberal writers (Alan Paton and Athol Fugard), a major question at stake will be how liberal perspectives are translated into films made in a post-apartheid South Africa dominated itself by neoliberal politics.

I am interested in these films, then, from a historical and political as well as aesthetic perspective: as a set of adaptations made in the early years of South

African democracy, which concern themselves with questions of introspection, critique, the nation, reconciliation, the individual/collective dialectic, and redemption. No doubt new South African films will constantly broach fresh topics—and a new adaptation trend in which South African directors are turning to canonical texts has already arisen, mirroring that of the adaptation trend in West Africa. *Son of Man* (2006) translates the New Testament into a modern African setting and was nominated for the Grand Jury Prize at the 2006 Sundance Film Festival. *U-Carmen eKhayelitsha* (2005) is a South African township version of Bizet's opera, with a Xhosa libretto, which won the Golden Bear at the Berlin Film Festival. Tim Greene's *Boy Called Twist* (2004), featured at Cannes, translates *Oliver Twist* into a contemporary South African setting.

Just as West African countries have moved from a preoccupation with the nation in the immediate post-independence era toward an emphasis on the region, so too can such a shift be predicted in South Africa's future. While the current state of affairs in Zimbabwe has prevented cinematic cooperation between the two countries, Teddy Mattera has pointed to the coproduction treaty that NEPAD has already helped to forge between South Africa and Angola. South Africa has collaborated with other African nations in making films (as in the Dv8 *Africa Dreaming* [1997] series), has become a shooting venue for films from other parts of the continent (such as Jean-Pierre Bekolo's *Aristotle's Plot* [1997; see chapter 7], and Malian director Souleymane Cissé's *Waati* [1995]), and has been running training workshops for African filmmakers on the Île de Gorée (Auret 2008). South Africa's current place in continental film production is, therefore, a far cry from one hundred or even fifty years ago. It is accordingly time, as Keyan Tomaselli argues in *Encountering Modernity: Twentieth-Century South African Cinemas* (2006), for South African film scholarship to become "Africanized." Bringing South African films into contact with West African films here represents just such a move away from the isolationism of South African film criticism during the apartheid era.

The African Viewing Public

Before moving on to look at the films themselves, it is important to restate the importance of African films reaching the African public if their critique is to be fulfilled. As Eddie Mbalo, CEO of the NFVF said in an interview during FESPACO 2007, "The absolute priority is to show our films to our own people. We often heard it said that South Africans do not like their own films. The real problem is one of access; the majority of the population cannot see the films" (2007:11). The contemporary cinematic map of South Africa is a legacy of apartheid, during which black people could not attend white cinemas and there were very few cinemas in areas designated for black people. Even today there are only two cinemas in Soweto, which has a population of two million. Although most cinemas became nonracial by 1986, many black people do not have the economic means to pay to attend the screenings, and this means that the "elite who control the channels of communication are comfortable at the moment with the one million or so white cinemagoers in the country" (Suleman 2002:291). South African filmmakers thus speak of the necessity of following their West African counterparts by taking mobile film units into rural areas, and of harnessing television and digital media as a means of reaching audiences and distributing African images to the rest of Africa. There is a strange paradox here. On the one hand, South Africa has been hailed as the "future home" of African cinema due to its large annual output of films. The fact that the first Africa Film Summit was held in South Africa in April 2006, and that South African filmmaker Seipati Bulane-Hopa has recently been made Secretary General of FEPACI (Pan African Federation of Filmmakers, founded in 1969),[9] is testimony to this point. On the other hand, there is a deep divide between South African film production and access to film distribution and exhibition.

The problem alluded to by Mbalo above—that South Africans do not like their own films—is also an issue, however. South African films are not well attended even by the white population that constitutes the majority of South Africa's cinema audience. A recent article revealed that South African films—which typically range in budget from R5 million to R40 million (US$800,000 to US$6 million)—are not breaking even at the local box office. *Yesterday* brought in R1.5 million (US$250,000), *Forgiveness* R333,000 (US$55,000), and *Max and Mona* R270,000 (US$44,500), with only 40 percent of this going back to the producers after the distributors had taken their fee (Kriedemann 2005). Ironically, if a South African film does appear to be making money, it seems to no longer be thought of as South African or African by some: in January 2006, on a visit to the Labia Orange Film Theatre in Cape Town, I noticed that the Palestinian film *Paradise Now* (2005) was screening in the Labia's recently installed "Africa Screen," while *Tsotsi* (2006) was showing in one of the main screens. As Jeremy Nathan, initiator of the South African digital film project Dv8 argues, producers are not worried about returns since they feel that the value of these new South African films should not simply be judged by financial measures, but by the contribution that they are making to society in other ways—in bringing local content to screens, and in building the film industry. Nevertheless, the "contribution" of South African films in this way would seem to be irrelevant if South African audiences are not actually going to see the films. Helen Kuhn, the head of local content at Ster-Kinekor, South Africa's chief film distributor along with NuMetro, argues that, "Very few films make a profit in their own territory. It's completely unrealistic to expect them to" (Kriedemann 2005). One has only to look at the popularity of Nigerian video films, in Nigeria and across Africa, to contradict such a statement. And if one recognizes that South Africa has more than 4 million licensed television households, and that television ownership rose from 39 percent to 58 percent from 1994 to 2004 (SouthAfrica.info reporter 2005), it is clear that there are spectators who would be interested in South African films if there were alternate distribution strategies in place that would make it easier for people to see the films.[10]

Creating an alternate distribution strategy was the aim of the producers of *U-Carmen eKhayelitsha* (2005). After months of nationwide research into cinema facilities in South Africa, Spier Films discovered that only two or three cinemas exist in each of the townships, populated by the poorest South Africans, and Khayelitsha itself, the largest township in South Africa with over a million inhabitants, does not have a single cinema. Most of South Africa's cinemas are in shopping centers in the areas that were reserved for whites during apartheid, and since many people in the townships do not have access to transport, it is impossible for them to travel the twelve miles to the cinema. The producers of *U-Carmen eKhayelitsha*, however, were emphatic in their decision that the film's South African premiere would be held in Khayelitsha, and that they would first release the film in the townships of Alexandra (near Johannesburg), KwaMashu (near Durban), and Khayelitsha for a month before they would allow its general release in the more affluent parts of the country. They worked with "agents" within the townships, who helped them to settle on a ticket price of R10 (US$1.65) that would be affordable to everyone. The producers and the agents felt strongly that spectators should pay something in order to value the experience. As Mark Dornford-May, the director, comments, "It was important for us that people knew they were paying to see people work, that it wasn't just a rather nice cultural project, it was actually people's work they were watching and so therefore they needed to pay for it. But putting it into Khayelitsha itself meant that people could walk there and could afford to go" (2006).

The entire initiative has had a dramatic ripple-effect on the South African exhibition scene. On March 18, 2005, Ster-Kinekor more than halved its ticket prices to R14 (US$2.30) in 80 percent of its cinemas—the cinemas being located in shopping centers accessible to black South Africans—that will now be called "Junction" theaters. The other 20 percent of cinemas will be called "Classic" theaters, and since they are located in wealthier areas, their ticket prices will not be lowered but will remain at R34 (US$5.60). NuMetro has answered Ster-Kinekor by lowering its prices even more—to a mere R12 (US$1.98). However, a new digital cinema initiative, Shout Cinemas, which aims to launch twenty cinemas with digital projection across South Africa's townships, may render both Ster-Kinekor and NuMetro obsolete. Shout Cinemas will offer African and foreign films subtitled in African languages as well as typical township culinary fare such as *wors* (sausage) and *pap* (porridge) (Dubowski 2005).

Beyond cinema venues, the country is largely dependent on five organizations for access to African films: the Film Resource Unit (FRU), the South African Broadcasting Corporation (SABC), M-Net, the Durban International Film Festival, and the Cape Town World Cinema Festival, which runs in conjunction with the Sithengi Film Market.[11] The FRU was founded in 1986 as an underground association for distributing anti-apartheid films. Today it is an NGO that focuses on audience development and distribution of African films in Africa. It not only organizes screenings for rural communities but also engages in door-to-door distribution of African videos and DVDs, monopolizing on the fact that most South Africans have televisions, VCRs, and/or DVD players. It also has an extensive catalog of African films that are available for exhibition and purchase. The SABC, which offers three free-to-air television channels (SABC 1, 2, and 3) and one pay-TV channel (SABC Africa), is obliged to commission and program local content in South

Africa's eleven official languages. The SABC was also the main sponsor and host broadcaster of Input 2008, the thirtieth anniversary of the global television event that features the best 100 documentary films from across the world every year. Input 2008 witnessed the first time that television stations from across the African continent collectively collaborated on a major initiative. Finally, M-Net, established in 1985, has grown into Africa's most popular pay-TV company, offering a variety of channels, including M-Net East Africa, M-Net West Africa, Channel 0 Africa (focusing on youth and music programs), and Africa Magic (which broadcasts Nigerian video films across the continent). M-Net has recently become the most important distributor of African cinema in the world, having purchased the Africa-wide, broadband, and DVB-H (cellphone) rights to 364 African films, of which 70 percent are features, 18 percent documentaries, and 12 percent shorts. These films, which will make up an African Film Library (AFL), include the entirety of Sembene's oeuvre. Mike Dearham, former CEO of the FRU and current CEO of M-Net, says that the initiative is a way of keeping the rights for African films on African soil—and it was this principle that won over Sembene when Dearham met with him in Senegal just a few weeks before he passed away on June 9, 2007.[12] According to prolific African film producer Jeremy Nathan, the future of South African and African film lies in digitization. He says that South Africa's hosting of the 2010 Football World Cup has provided the "opportunity to digitize Africa" and that by this time South Africa should be broadcasting not only sport, but all kinds of programs, on every possible format—Internet, mobile phone, and satellite television. South Africa has over 5 million Internet users who would be likely to download films were they available. In fact, Nathan sees the Internet as the solution to film exhibition *throughout* Africa, where Internet use, although currently only 4.7 percent, is growing at a rate of 874.6 percent (Nathan 2007). The Durban International Film Festival, which has been running since 1979, is playing a role in situating South African cinema within African cinema more generally, as well as creating film audiences in townships around Durban, and in particular KwaMashu, that have not historically had access to film. The Cape Town World Cinema Festival and the Sithengi Film Market, which was initiated in 1997, has been a platform for South African filmmakers to reach out to the rest of the world. If initiatives such as Shout Cinemas succeed, if the FRU, SABC, M-Net, and South Africa's major film festivals continue to support African cinema and the development of its audiences, and if Jeremy Nathan's prophecies about exciting digital distribution opportunities become realities, then profound and moving South African films—such as those discussed in the following four chapters—might finally have a critical role to play in South African (and African) culture and society.

2 *Fools* and Victims

Adapting Rationalized Rape into Feminist Film

Fools invites us to explore our memory. It's important to question our pasts and to think about ourselves. The impact of apartheid won't be going away tomorrow. RAMADAN SULEMAN (1997)

Ramadan Suleman and Bhekizizwe Peterson's film *Fools* (1997), an adaptation of the novella by Njabulo Ndebele (1983), was the first feature film to be made post-1994 by a black screenwriter and director. It was made primarily with a multiracial South African audience in mind, and was supported by the South African Department of Arts, Culture, Science and Technology. It is a coproduction[1] that has achieved moderate commercial success in France,[2] has been distributed also in Belgium and Germany, and has won the Silver Leopard Award for Direction at the 50th International Locarno Film Festival in Switzerland. Occupying a unique place in history, the film will no doubt be subject to a great deal of ongoing analysis. In this respect it might be compared to a film such as *De Voortrekkers*, also produced at the dawn of a new nation, almost one hundred years previously. *De Voortrekkers* focused on a few events of the Great Trek, such as the Battle of Blood River, commemorated subsequently on "Dingaan's Day"—a commemoration to which the filmmakers of *Fools* allude in the opening scenes, and to which they return again at the end.

The purpose of *De Voortrekkers*, as I have suggested, was to glorify the Boer leaders in the battle and to promote what has been called the "central constitutive myth of Afrikaner nationalism" (Hees 2003:49). Suleman and Peterson's approach differs on every level from the approach of the creators of *De Voortrekkers*, and, in comparison, their decision to adapt a novella written in 1983 and set in 1966, about the rape of a schoolgirl by her teacher, seems remarkable. In the transitional climate of South Africa in 1997, with, on the one hand, the elation of the first democratic elections and the New Constitution still pervasive, but, on the other hand, HIV/AIDS, violent crime, and rape cases increasing,[3] one is led to ask why filmmakers might turn to the adaptation of literature rather than make films about the events occurring around them. *Fools* proves, however, that adaptation is not necessarily mutually exclusive to filmmaking on current events, and it adds a depth to these current events by historicizing them. Speaking about his decision to focus on the negative aspects of post-1994 South Africa, Suleman expresses cynicism about the idea of the rainbow nation: "[*Fools*] resurrects for me the whole question of how, today, South African politicians tell us that we live in a rainbow nation. It is fine to import a fancy African American slogan, which I learned was invented by the honorable Reverend Jesse Jackson, but when I walk into Soweto, I still see poverty; I walk around the city and it is full of misery, and I feel the contradiction inherent in the so-called rainbow nation that the politicians have failed to see" (2002:293).

Instead of choosing to celebrate black independence or the heroes of the anti-apartheid struggle, or to celebrate South Africa's fledgling democracy, the filmmakers have adapted a novella by a writer who has consistently rejected "spectacular" modes of representation in favor of a focus on the "ordinary," a novella that provides a way of reminding black people of their recent history. As Suleman says, "Black people have a history, which is to say that they need to come to grips with themselves first before coming to grips with white people" (2002:293). In his essay "The Rediscovery of the Ordinary," Njabulo Ndebele locates spectacular representation as the basis of both apartheid control and black resistance to it. He writes: "The history of black South African literature has largely been the history of the representation of spectacle. The visible symbols of the overwhelmingly oppressive South African social formation appear to have prompted over the years the development of a highly dramatic, highly demonstrative form of literary presentation" (1994b:41). In contrast to this spectacular mode of representation, Ndebele has drawn his own stories from the realm of the "ordinary," which he defines as "sobering *rationality* . . . the forcing of attention on necessary detail" (1994b:53; my emphasis). For, he argues, "Paying attention to the ordinary and its methods will result in a significant growth of *consciousness*" (ibid.; my emphasis). Not only in "Fools" but also in his short stories and in his recently published novella *The Cry of Winnie Mandela* (2003), Ndebele pays attention to the everyday life of black South Africans, eschewing easy answers to complex ethical dilemmas and frequently providing a critical look at the way that apartheid violence has been internalized in black communities.

Ndebele's writing, although produced during the time of apartheid, has been described as contributing to the creation of a post-apartheid rather than an anti-apartheid perspective on South Africa, and he has been called a "prophet of the post-apartheid condition" by Graham Pechey, who distinguishes the practice of anti- and post-apartheid discourse as follows:

> Anti-apartheid discourse demands tactical simplifications, ethico-political shortcuts and makeshifts of the kind that Ndebele's post-apartheid perspective readily understands but *always exceeds*. Post-apartheid discourse is in this sense not a new orthodoxy of "liberation" . . . it is the critical interlocutor of all projects for democratic renewal; and its theme is nothing less than the (re)composition of the whole social text of South Africa. (1994:3–4)

When asked whether he agrees with this assessment of his work as falling within the domain of post-apartheid discourse, Ndebele makes the connection between this discourse and its necessary validation of the individual:

> [Yes . . .] in the sense that the reason that I broke with . . . the protest tradition . . . was that I was trying to deliberately focus on the individual experience as opposed to the tendency of the system to massify. What the system did was to treat people—black people—as a big mass of people to whom you could *do* things. (2003a)

Similarly, many African film scholars have referred to the way in which black people have been represented as "an undifferentiated, ethnogracized mass" (Hamilton and Modisane 2007:102). In reaction, many anti-apartheid filmmakers have represented white people in the same terms: the "evil Afrikaner security police" (Bickford-Smith and Mendelsohn 2007:9) and lazy, frustrated white housewives or "madams" (as in *Come Back, Africa* [1959] and *Mapantsula* [1988]) have been fixtures in such films, themselves subject to a kind of reverse "anxious repetition." *Fools* is unusual in that it constantly negotiates between the neoliberal, post-apartheid necessity of appreciating the individual, and socialist principles of collectivity, attempting to move beyond stereotypes.

Given Pechey's analysis of Ndebele's work, the reasons for the choice of his novella by Suleman and Peterson become apparent. More broadly, the decision to adapt a literary text is explained by Suleman in terms similar to those used by West African filmmakers. Suleman says that, "Literature can inject dynamism into the cinema. I think that it can play a major role, but 75 percent of South Africans are illiterate, so the cinema can also help literature. People who have seen *Fools* may be tempted to read the novel" (n.d.; interview with Barlet). Ndebele points out that, while the film has not resulted in a noticeable increase in sales of the book, the fact that it has been shown several times on South African television, on both SABC and M-Net, has extended "the public knowledge of the book and its existence and the story itself" (2003a). The film has featured at African film festivals such as FESPACO 2003, thereby reaching a wider African audience, and has been distributed on videocassette within South Africa by the Film Resource Unit. Thanks to European financing, the film also toured through eighty South African schools, where it was screened free of charge to about 8,500 black, Indian, and Coloured students (Sé 2002).

The film has also shown at cinemas in South Africa's city centers. In May 1998, the film was released in cinemas in the Carlton Centre (a business district) and in Rosebank (a wealthy, white residential area in Johannesburg), where it played for several weeks. Although the film only had 20,000 admittances, Suleman says that he thinks the screenings were a success in terms of "constructing an audience." Contradicting the claims of others, he has expressed his doubts as to whether the building of cinemas in the townships will increase audiences. In 1994, a multiplex was built in Dobsonville, a suburb neighboring Soweto, which turned out to be a failure, constantly playing to only 6 percent of its capacity. Suleman explains that, like African youths living in the *banlieues* in Paris, young black South Africans who live in the townships want to go into the city to watch films. He says, "During apartheid we were forbidden to go to the city and be among the whites. Then, suddenly, we were free. . . . The cinemas in the city centres started to become more frequented" (quoted in Sé 2002). Suleman's observations thus complicate even further the question of audience development and film distribution in South Africa.

Viewers who have access to the film will discover that it harbors a harsh message. The film works within the domain of the ethico-political, as does the novella, but in the story of the rape of the schoolgirl by her teacher, the focus is shifted away from the consciousness of the teacher. Suleman talks in an interview about his reasons for this very significant change:

> There is the whole issue in the book where Njabulo talks about rape, but he does not deal with rape as the larger issue in the book. . . . We had a problem in adapting this part of the book because the issue of rape is very important and needed to be addressed fully. . . . And how can the rapist be the moralist? Njabulo's examination of the issue in the novel was somehow surrealistic and narrated in a dreamlike manner. The book itself is wonderful literature, but we offered a different perspective by defining rape as a terrible crime. (2002:294)

For Ndebele it is very important that the rapist should be the moralist, since the story is about the schoolteacher arriving at an understanding of the nature of the "terrible crime" that he committed three years previously, and of what made it possible for him to commit the crime. Ndebele takes the risk of drawing the reader into the consciousness of the rapist, a choice that would have been difficult in the film medium, even had the filmmakers approved of this approach. Tracing the growth of the teacher's critical awareness allows Ndebele to represent what might be described as competing epistemologies—raising questions about different ways in which black South Africans might "know" themselves. This is a question that has preoccupied Ndebele in his critical writing. He regrets, for example, that while "Africans *do* have information about themselves as the actual sufferers . . . such information has only biological validity. Only institutionalized information is subject to ideological scrutiny" (1994c:31). Ndebele's story thus turns to the "biological" site of suffering, and to embodied ways of knowing, through the mimesis made possible by fiction.

It is through the relationship between Zamani—a middle-aged schoolteacher and disillusioned former anti-apartheid activist—and Zani, the brother of the girl whom Zamani raped, that the different ways of knowing are pitted against one another. The two men meet at a train station in the novella's lengthy opening scene, in which Zani, who is returning home to the township of Charterston from his superior school in Swaziland, angrily confronts Zamani, who, owing to the expediency of the school board, is still teaching in the Charterston high school. Zani's self-assuredness, recognized by Zamani in this first scene, quickly fades after he arrives home and finds himself alienated, where people do not embrace his budding political activism and arrogance—his desire to play "God" (Ndebele 1983:230) and to "bring light where there has been darkness" (164). Stabbed on the street by a young gangster whom he accuses of having "the mind of a chicken," Zani begs Zamani to take him home. Here Zamani faces, for the first time since his crime, Mimi (the girl whom he had raped), the child born as the result of the rape, Mimi's mother Ma Buthelezi, and Mimi's sister Busi. In Ma Buthelezi's presence, Zamani feels a "strong urge to explain [himself]" (187), but he recognizes that speaking is not what is needed and manages "to resist actually saying anything" (187). It is directly after this scene that Zamani recalls and recounts his rape of Mimi.

A strange friendship develops between Zani and Zamani, with Zani visiting both Zamani and his wife Nosipho, a nurse, with whom he likes to share his freshly devised, verbose philosophies. Zamani allows Zani to address his class in protest against the imminent celebration of "Dingaan's Day," which, Zani argues—in terms too sophisticated for the young schoolchildren to grasp—represents the defeat of Dingaan's black warriors by white Afrikaners and thus should not be cause for festivity on the part of black South Africans. Zani does not succeed in sabotaging the celebration, which figures in the last scene of the novella, and from which the headmaster of Zamani's school, an admirer of the National Party, attempts to chase Zani, hurling a stone at him. The stone misses Zani, but hits the car of a passing "Boer" who, enraged, takes a whip out of his car and threatens to hit the headmaster, who runs away. The "Boer" proceeds to lash the man standing closest to him, who happens to be Zamani. After the whipping, from which the townspeople have fled, Zamani stumbles away to find Zani, who lectures at length to the elder man on the nature of victims. Before he begins his "long, painful walk" home to Nosipho (280), Zamani passes Mimi and Zani's girlfriend, Ntozakhe, but says that still he "could not look Mimi in the eyes" (279).

Although Zamani's crime is not directly decipherable in political terms, the metaphors throughout the novella work to show that it is his sense of powerlessness under apartheid that has led him—a victim—to seek someone even more powerless than himself as a scapegoat for his anger, pain, and impotence. This interpretation is latent within the novella itself, for instance when Zani lectures Zamani that "when victims spit upon victims, should they not be called fools?" (278). The filmmakers also lift this line out of its original context to use as an epigraph to the film. Although whites are completely peripheral to the plot, with only the "Boer" making an appearance in the township, the nature of white power is at the basis of all that unravels within the story. Zamani is shown to be capable of understanding his crime, although this understanding is not so much articulated as *shown* through the difference between the man, Zamani, and his alter-ego, or younger self, Zani.

The film was inevitably to lose Zamani's interior voice in the transformation or "devocalization" (Genette 1997:290) from book to film, and the filmmakers have not chosen to replicate Zamani's consciousness by means of a voice-over narrative. Irony, which is vital to Ndebele's critique of the violence made possible by certain modes of thinking or knowing, is also inevitably lost. In sacrificing this critique, the filmmakers have, in some ways, depoliticized the discourse in the novella that relates to the epistemologies of white domination. On the other hand, as I will show, they have introduced a new political discourse through their adaptation—the politics of gender. Suleman has spoken of his desire to address contemporary South African audiences, and to explore in particular the suffering of women in communities where the impotence and self-hatred of the men is unleashed on those who have least power (2002:293). This shift in the adaptation toward a more explicit politics of gender has been recognized by critics such as Kgafela oa Magogodi, who praises the filmmakers for narrativizing the "gendered body by politicizing the rape of Mimi" (2003:199) and for thereby participating in the discourse surrounding the formulation of the New Constitution, which institutionalizes women's rights and recognizes that "women in South Africa were previously treated differentially" (200).

The filmmakers have effected various changes to Ndebele's novella at the level of narrative—through the alteration of the events within, and the chronology of, the plot, the revision of certain characters' roles, and the addition of scenes. The novella's diegesis is "proximized" (Genette 1997:304) from its original 1966 post-Rivonia Trial milieu to December 1989, two months before the release of Nelson Mandela and the unbanning of the African National Congress. Rory Bester makes the point that the film thus risks omitting "a crucial context to understanding the social paralysis that is at the core of the novella" (1998), but Peterson argues that, "The '60s setting isn't really crucial . . . because we wanted the film to provoke debate and discussion now. We didn't want audiences to read this as a period piece" (quoted in Bester). However, the glossy production values and the use of a richly colored film stock could be said to aestheticize township life and to evoke a certain nostalgia for a past time, rather than to represent Charterston as "the very picture of poverty and oppression." By way of contrast, Lionel Ngakane has said that he chose to make his films in black and white since "Color makes everything beautiful. Even a slum looks beautiful in color" (2002:75).

This is indeed the case in *Fools*: the roofs of the houses at sunset create a beautiful panorama framed from above; a traditional township wedding (not included in the novella) provides further visual extravagance; exotic angles (such as unmotivated overhead shots and mirror reflections) are amply used. While the crane shots and clever cinematography evident in *Fools* are not commonly used in African films, the use of color and the imitation of the "digressive" tactics of oral tales through the "augmentation" of scenes clearly suggest that the film works in a similar aesthetic and narrative mode to many African films. It is perhaps significant that, unlike the majority of South African filmmakers, who have little to no knowledge of African cinema, Suleman has worked on the films of the highly regarded African filmmakers Med Hondo (from Mauritania) and Souleymane Cissé (from Mali), an experience which has led him to shape his own filmmaking within the aesthetic and ideological framework of West African cinema. Both Suleman and his co-screenwriter Peterson were also actively involved in the development of black South African theater during apartheid. This confirms John van Zyl's 1985 prediction that the "future of South Africa's film industry . . . will have to come from the same roots as the vigour and inspiration of its theatre" and that the "real industry of the future will be a predominantly black one" (quoted in Hees 1993).

Furthermore, Suleman's choice of certain "spectacular" cinematic techniques cannot be conflated with the kind of "spectacular representation" outlined by Ndebele at the beginning of this chapter, and it can be argued that this is the means for evoking the dignity and fullness of the characters in their setting, and for encouraging mimesis as identification with what is shown on the screen. It is in this respect that film has access to a kind of visual shorthand not available to the novel, and, as I have suggested, a greater power to invoke an embodied response in viewers. Patrick Shai, speaking of his preparation for the role of Zamani, articulates film's potential to evoke a sense of the lived experience of local viewers:

> I looked at the academic impressions [of "Fools" . . .] but I also went to the community and said, look, this is the book we're [adapting] and this is the character I'm going to be playing. . . . When [I] go to [my] community, and the shebeens [township bars] I bounce my characters off my fellow drinkers. It's the society I live in, the people I live with . . . so I try to give them space to contribute to my artistic interpretations of the characters and story. . . . It's a completely different impression from the one academics would have. Academics look at things from up here—and [in the township] what I get [is] the soul of the character, which is where I base my performance. Academics too have a soul, but often they do not project the soul—it's just about intelligence. (2003)

Shai thus suggests, from an actor's performative perspective, a new way of coming to know one's object of study—an embodied way, that supplants what Pechey has described as "the moral and the existential idioms of anti-apartheid struggle" which "shared with apartheid discourse itself a model of the subject standing outside and over against the object and atomistically separated from other subjects" (1994:8).

Aurally, too, the film has the means to evoke mimesis, and it takes full advantage of this through the use of local languages—primarily Zulu, but also Afrikaans, English, and *isicamtho* (township slang), made up from a combination of all three. Peterson says that, "On a political level . . . the use of an African language affirms the validity of such languages. Too often, making an English-language film undermines the presence of African languages" (quoted in Bester). Bringing together the embodied source of such languages and translating their rationality for viewers through subtitles creates the necessary mimetic dialectic. The film's jazz score does something similar, and also works as a historical reminder of the important role that South African musicians played in the anti-apartheid struggle. It was composed by Chikapa Ray Phiri, whose group Stimela ("Steam Train") made music during the apartheid years that undermined the regime and provided hope of freedom. Phiri describes his music as a "key to self-discovery, an outlet for personal and political frustration, and an inspiration for change" (quoted in Films for the Humanities and Sciences 2004). According to

Peterson, the film's narrative style itself "invokes the call-and-response patterns in African music and jazz. A theme is introduced, elaborated, and then repeated in different ways. It's about looking at different facets of the same thing" (cited in Bester). Again, this represents a considered harnessing of film's mimetic capabilities in conjunction with epistemologies derived from African oral and music traditions so as to avoid the reductiveness of identity-thinking.

Looking at different facets of the same thing in the film leads to a shift away from Zamani's consciousness and to the development of an array of characters. If Ndebele provides a critique of the rape through a weighing of competing epistemologies, the film provides its critique by audio-visualizing the gender politics operative in the township. In bringing the action closer in time to South Africa's political transition, the filmmakers shift more responsibility onto Zamani, whom the audience is less likely to see as a victim of structural violence that he cannot control. His culpability is extended to other sets of male characters not represented, or given peripheral significance in the novella—Zamani's drinking mates, and the council of elders responsible for allowing Zamani to continue to teach at the school after the rape. The audio-visualization of the interaction within these different groups of men shows both traditional and contemporary middle-class forms of patriarchalism in a damning way. On the other hand, the character of Zani is constructed in a more unproblematically positive way than in the novella, by being feminized—able to empathize with the women and to reveal his emotions. He is shown struggling for acceptance in the women's world rather than from Zamani, whose degeneracy and impotence are foregrounded in a scene in which he is unable to have sex with a prostitute (in the novella, Zamani's "lover" is a fellow teacher, Candu). This scene, in that it is immediately followed by a scene of Zamani running to escape a police raid, does, however, frame Zamani's sexual impotence and degeneracy in terms of the political impotence experienced under apartheid, as is the case in the novella.

While Ndebele's set of female characters could be said to be somewhat schematic—the innocent and childlike victim of rape (Mimi), her sister Busi who "exudes a whorish sensuousness" (1983:187), the intellectual girl (Ntozakhe), the idealized wife (Nosipho), and the traditional mother (Ma Buthelezi)—the film gives presence and voice to an array of strong women.

Thus the novella has been "augmented" (Genette 1997:229) with certain scenes—for example, of a *stokvel*[4] run by women in the community, including Nosipho and Busi, who, although they argue in the beginning of the film, come to each other's aid during Mimi's abortion, another vital "augmentation," which suggests in a symbolic way, as Magogodi argues, that "so long as patriarchy reigns supreme and justifies violence against women, there will be no forces of renewal in this society" (2003:195). Whereas Mimi—the victim—is an almost silent character in the novella, in the film her voice is the second that we hear. Mimi speaks in voice-over as the camera cuts from a long shot of the train to a medium close-up of Zani's anxious expression, indicating that he is recalling the words of a letter Mimi has written to him, in which she says: "I have survived two months of hell; I am now frightened of men. Whatever it is they want, must it be built on our tethered souls? I cannot wait to see you. Your loving sister, Mimi." In this way, Mimi's perspective on the rape, her suffering and her fear, preface and frame the events that follow. Her sister Busi is constructed as a strongly vocal woman and is shown early in the film berating the council of elders. Ntozakhe, who in the novella is represented only verbally, through her very intellectual letters to Zani, is shown naked in the opening scenes of the film, taking pleasure in the sexual act.

Instead of having Mimi accept her pregnancy, in the film there is an abortion[5] and Suleman said that they created this scene to "show how women can be in conflict, and when the struggle is over, how they are capable of regrouping and resolving those issues" (2002:294). He is referring here to the fact that it is Busi who asks Zamani's wife Nosipho, a midwife, to help with the abortion in spite of Busi's initial wrath toward Nosipho. Nosipho is idealized in the novella—Zamani constantly describes her in terms of her appearance, and provides an inventory of disembodied physical features: "her firm-fleshed face. Dark eyes made darker by thick eyebrows. Half-full lips, pinkish from the natural colour of blood. Smooth skin. . . . Full firm arms. Living breasts. Full hips. Large firm legs" (199). In the film Nosipho is made a more vocal character, refusing to play the role of the martyred wife when, for instance, she tells Zamani that she is not like the woman who washed Jesus' feet and then dried them with her own hair.

There is, of course, irony in Ndebele's representation of Zamani as only able to see and know his wife in these abstract, reifying terms, and he is thus made to censure himself in his own words. This is essentially the same way in which the act of rape is condemned in the novella. This scene—the crux of the narrative—is narrated in the present tense, indicating that this is how Zamani's actions were perceived at the time of the rape, and not with the advantage of hindsight. As I have already suggested, the representation of rape from the perspective of the rapist is inevitably fraught with danger, running the risk of encouraging the reader to identify imaginatively with the rapist, or at least to occupy the position of the voyeur, and thus to become an accomplice to the violence. Ndebele has Zamani describe the rape in a way that does not allow the reader to visualize the act of violence against Mimi's body. Zamani uses language strangely centered on the act of seeing and being seen, and offers a poetic description of sowing and harvesting in the mode of Romanticism, as a projection of the self onto "Nature," perceived as a unified whole in which the self can achieve an integrated identity that had been lost through the separation of being and cognition:

> "Here is the chicken," she says.
> We stand up at the same time, and I see her move towards me. I cannot see her eyes; I cannot see her cheeks; I cannot see her lips; I cannot see the bulge of her breasts beneath the dress. . . . I'm talking to her, but I do not understand my words, for words have yielded more vividly to endless years of seeing. . . . See, floating on the water, thousands of acorns, corn seeds, wheat and barley, eyeballs winking endlessly like the ever changing patterns on the surface of the water. . . . I want to come into the water, but I can't. . . . The pain of heaving! The frightening screams! And the ice cracks with the tearing sound of mutilation. And I break through with such a convulsion. And I'm in the water. It is so richly viscous. . . . Like the sweetness of honey. And the acorns, and the corn seeds, wheat and barley sprout into living things. And I swim through eyes which look at me with enchantment and revulsion. (1983:194–95)

While Zamani is made to name the parts of the girl's body that he *cannot* see, Ndebele is simultaneously asking the reader to visualize these parts—the eyes, cheeks, lips, bulge of the breasts—that draw attention to her embodiment as a young woman. Zamani cannot see Mimi in her embodied particularity because he approaches her through the alienating abstractions of Western Romanticism—and, it is implied, he is able to commit this act of violence against her precisely because he rationalizes it in this way. (There is further irony in the way that Romanticism, as the discourse which gestures toward an affinity with the irrational, is susceptible to being utilized in this way.)[6] Zamani sees and is seen by a disembodied multitude of "eyeballs," which seem to approximate the mass of people to whom the apartheid system could do things. Ndebele thus seems to desire the judgment of Zamani's act of rape as the character's attempt to differentiate himself, to "break through" into an individualized state, but simultaneously as an act of violence against the mass to which he belongs.

There is a profound irony here, too, in that the rape is not shown to be motivated, as convention might dictate, by a regression to irrational, brute, bodily instinct—by the lack of a capacity to think and act rationally. It is, on the contrary, shown to be motivated by the secondhand, rational discourses through which black people have been obliged to know themselves, and that Ndebele talks about in the passage already cited. This does not represent a desire on Ndebele's part to reject rationality per se, and he creates the sense of the necessary dialectic between rational and embodied modes of knowing through the relationship between Zamani and Zani. At the end of the novella Zamani says of Zani, "He seemed all I could have become if I were to start afresh" (278), suggesting that what is required is an amalgam of the abstract idealistic thinking of the young man and the newly learned embodied knowledge of the older man. While feeling a great love and admiration for Zani, Zamani also recognizes his naïveté, his tendency to intellectualize experience and thereby distance himself from it. It is thus with a little irony that Zamani introduces Zani to his school class as "Charterston's very own light" (215), this metaphor recalling Zani's comment to Zamani, in the opening scene, that he wishes to "bring light where there has been darkness" (164). Zani is thus characterized as the would-be representative of an enlightenment—he is unable to see, however, how his own abstractions and excessive rationality render him, as Zamani observes, "another instance of disembodiment: the obscenity of high seriousness" (217). While Zani is, to some extent, the spokesperson for Ndebele's view of apartheid—which, he claims, is a "ritual of physical cruelty" that has become "abstract," an "evil," "a philosophy" that is a "rational . . . malice" (216), it is Zamani who comes to recognize that it is this very process which he himself has internalized, arriving at a point where he could *rationally* justify his rape of Mimi.

The rape scene is given further symbolic significance through the metaphor of the chicken, which, in the shedding of its blood—as in the ritual sacrifice—could be seen to represent the girl not shown in the narrated scene. However, there is in fact a whole set of references to men as chickens: Zani is stabbed for remarking that one of the township men has "the mind of a chicken" (179), and Zamani—on arriving at the scene—describes Zani as "breathing hard and fast like a chicken that is being slaughtered with a blunt knife" (181). Similarly, Zamani asks himself, on a visit to his lover, Candu, "Why allow myself to be driven by impulses like a cock? But I have gone through this many times. The same feeling of debasement followed by rationalisation" (245). The metaphor thus seems also to refer to the men in the novella, and it is also through this metaphor that Ndebele presents men's actions as a turning in of violence against their own community, and thus ultimately against themselves. Zamani describes the chicken that Mimi has brought him as squawking "like a voice of atonement" (195), and in self-recognition, and self-destructive shame, he tears off the chicken's head, releasing it "to flutter to death freely in the dark" (ibid.). Zamani is thus shown to be both perpetrator and victim: in violating the girl who came to him in trust, bearing a gift, he has also violated himself and his people.

Without access to critique through verbal analogies and irony, the filmmakers had the challenge of depicting the rape in a way that would not allow the viewer to occupy the position of voyeur, but to see the rape—in Suleman's words—as a "terrible crime" and, more importantly, to *feel* it through Mimi's experience. Suleman criticizes Ndebele for narrating the rape in a "surrealistic" and "dreamlike manner," and in contrast to Ndebele's representation of the rape through Zamani's disembodied rationalizing consciousness, the filmmakers seem to attempt to represent the rape in an embodied way, using the visual and aural potential of the film medium to encourage the viewer to approach the scene through bodily empathy. At the same time, however, they encourage the viewer also to judge the rape by rational means, through the way that they alter the chronology of Ndebele's plot.

The sequence in which the rape scene occurs begins with a scene in which Mimi, Ma Buthelezi, and Busi prepare food together in their small, dilapidated home. Whereas in the novella this scene is one in which men are also present, in the film we see only the three women, and the filmmakers create a sense of the intimate rapport between them. The difference between their house and that of Zamani and Nosipho, with its chic, colorful décor, registers the fact that Zamani occupies a position of power not only in terms of gender, age, and his position as teacher but also in terms of economic status. The filmmakers cut to Zamani's flashback of the rape directly after a close-up of Zamani's apprehensive face, before he is to enter Mimi's house to deliver the wounded Zani. By positioning the rape scene before Zamani's encounter with Mimi and her family, the filmmakers allow viewers to judge Zamani's behavior from the perspective of the women who have struggled to make a home for themselves in this small shack.

By cutting from the close-up of Zamani's face to the scene of rape, the filmmakers indicate that the memory of the rape is unraveling within Zamani's mental space. In this way, they attribute, to some measure, the "narrativization" of the rape to Zamani, as does Ndebele. In certain ways they appear to have remained faithful, too, to Ndebele's "surreal" depiction of the rape—for instance, by shooting most of the scene with a misted filter, by using jump cuts and extra-diegetic music, and by distorting the sound, so that the voices of Mimi and Zamani echo. By cutting out of the flashback, however, to the horrified face of Zamani, who, it is thus suggested, is watching and witnessing his own crime for the first time, the filmmakers create a disjuncture between Zamani-the-rapist and the Zamani who is in the process of coming to an embodied realization of his own crime.

The visualization of the rape itself begins with a shaky, handheld shot showing Zamani and Mimi in medium close-up as Mimi hands the live chicken over to Zamani. There is no doubt in the way that Patrick Shai, playing Zamani, takes hold of Mimi that this act is not consensual, and he is made to say, "This will make a fine meal." As Magogodi points out, in township lingo, statutory rape is described as "chicken murder" (2003:193) and, in the earlier scene in which Zamani and his male drinking friends compare photographs of their lovers, one of the men comments that, "Die ding [this thing] is strictly fresh, no preservatives," thus comparing women to food to be consumed (ibid.). The filmmakers then cut to a close-up shot of the chicken, which has been dropped onto the floor. The next, handheld shot shows Mimi running to the front door to try to escape, with the sound of the chicken squawking in the background; this is followed by a close-up shot of Zamani's hand forcefully locking the door. The next shot pans quickly across the room, following Mimi as she backs away, unable to find an escape route.

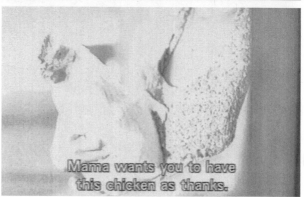

Figure 2.1
Rape sequence
from *Fools*. (Images
courtesy of JBA
Production, France)

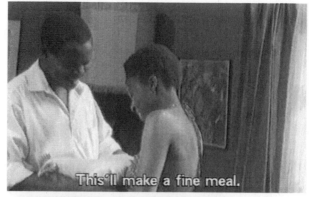

Teacher...

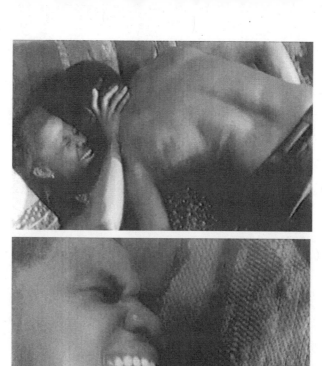

Figure 2.1 (continued)
Rape sequence
from *Fools*. (Images
courtesy of JBA
Production, France)

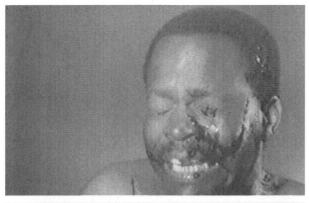

Her voice, as she says, "Teacher . . . ," works as an understated but shocking reminder of Zamani's violation of his role as the one who protects and brings enlightenment to his pupils. There is a brief shot of Zamani taking off his shirt, followed by a shot of Mimi directly from Zamani's perspective. This shot, handheld, swings back and forth, as Mimi moves from side to side trying to escape.

It might, at first, seem dangerous for the filmmakers to have allowed the camera to assume the rapist's point of view. However, it is in this shot, ironically, that the filmmakers most powerfully encourage the viewer to identify with Mimi's consciousness rather than with Zamani's. For during this shot it is not Zamani's *consciousness* (his psychological space) that the viewer is encouraged to inhabit, but his *perception* (his anatomical space). Ndebele himself has spoken of his shocked reaction to this moment in the film, recalling "the terror on the face of Mimi . . . and the realization that there was a violation of her trust" (2003a), thereby registering his extreme discomfort as spectator. Held simultaneously in the physical space of the rapist and the psychological space of victim, the viewer cannot take voyeuristic pleasure in this violation of the child by the man.

The sequence cuts next to a handheld shot in which Zamani is shown to push the screaming Mimi onto a couch; Mimi's face is shown in close-up as she continues to scream and struggles to repel Zamani. At the moment of penetration Suleman cuts to a shot of Zamani's window—the window the community will soon break with rocks (in retribution for the "breaking" of Mimi)—and to the sound of a baby crying, highlighting Mimi's youth and foreshadowing the baby she will abort as a result of the rape. The window is shattered and Zamani echoes the community's sentiment by breaking the chicken's neck. He is left with blood dripping from his face, and it is in this shot that the extra-diegetic music suddenly stops, and Zamani is left repeating "I am a respectable man" over a silent background. The sudden use of English in a scene that is otherwise wholly in Zulu is striking, and the effect is similar to that created by Zamani's use of the discourse of Romanticism to rationalize the rape in the novella. The chicken, however, instead of being compared through simile to a "voice of atonement" as in the novella, now becomes a witnessed object that we also *hear* squawking as Mimi tries to escape. The chicken's cry is transformed into an aural motif by the filmmakers, who augment Ndebele's story by showing Zani listening to Mimi's cries as the baby is aborted. In the film the chicken does not work as a metaphor for the men, but, as in the novella, it does symbolize the metonymic transfer of violence onto women as scapegoats in an oppressed society.

Ndebele, through the metaphor of men as chickens, and also through the character of "Forgive Me," generalizes the abuse of women by their own men whereas, in the film, the chicken allows for the generalization and embodiment of the pain experienced by the women. In the novella, "Forgive Me" is mentioned only once, in a letter written by Ntozakhe to Zani:

[Zamani] reminds me of the man who lives alone about five houses away from us. . . . Some say he killed his mother, others say it was his wife he killed; some vow he raped his niece. . . . But for as long as I can remember, he has been getting up very early in the morning, and going up and down our street three times, all the while shouting: "Forgive me! Forgive me! Forgive me! . . ." [. . .] Nobody knows his real name; but we all call him, "Forgive Me." Now isn't that an example of someone for whom atonement has become the very condition of life? (253–54)

In the novella "Forgive Me" is a foil, a very minor character, who nevertheless carries the burden of justifying Ndebele's strategy of having the rapist as narrator and moralist. "Forgive Me" is a protected figure in the community because he is the embodiment of atonement. It is implied that Zamani will achieve the same kind of status through his act of atonement, taking a whipping from the Afrikaner on behalf of Zani. In the first scene of the novella, Zani reminds Zamani of how he used to whip a schoolchild "until his skin peeled off" (161). Later Zamani describes being whipped by the Afrikaner in precisely the same words: "It was as if my skin was peeling off" (275). Ndebele thus makes it clear that it is only the experience of physical pain that can bring Zamani to a realization of the nature of his violation of his pupil.

But Zani—who has not witnessed the whipping since he runs away—remains caught up in the rational discourse of political analysis. As the wounded Zamani approaches Zani, the older man notes, "I had expected to see pain in his eyes, but I found instead, a pensive look" (277). Zani, oblivious to Zamani's suffering, remarks: "I suppose they are still dancing, drinking, singing, and fornicating. . . . And that's the point of it all. . . . We're just drifting. All without the liberating formality of ritual" (ibid.). What Zamani has just done, however, represents precisely the "formality of ritual"—the ritual of voluntarily taking on the role of scapegoat. In this way, Ndebele-as-author implies that Zani has not yet crossed the threshold of pain, the threshold beyond which there is nothing left to *say*. All that Zamani can do is "[stand] silently next to [Zani]" (ibid.). The novella thus traces the "enlightenment" of a male character who, apparently paradoxically, moves to a position of enlightenment, not through an emerging rationality, but through a progressively embodied response to his situation. Zani appears to "educate" Zamani in the conventional way, bringing the book knowledge of his superior education in Swaziland, but what Zamani learns in this encounter is the relative impotence of rationality, abstraction, and analysis—or worse, its ability to corrupt—so that the rape is constructed not as a return to bestial, embodied instinct, but as a Romantic abstraction.

The figure of "Forgive Me" becomes an important symbolic character in the film. This is done, it seems, not to further emphasize the politics of gender, but to broaden the filmmakers' critique, reminding audiences of hegemonic abuse of power in apartheid South Africa and beyond. The film opens with an establishing wide-shot of "Forgive Me," in half-silhouette against the sunset, climbing down from the hillside to the township; and "Forgive Me" reemerges at various points throughout the film, wandering the streets or stoking his smoking rubbish heap; in the denouement, "Forgive Me" comes to Zani's aid by trying to distract the angry Afrikaner. However, he represents not personal atonement, as he does in the novella, but rather, political atonement on behalf of the entire black *and* white community. For the film version of "Forgive Me" is not the perpetrator of a crime against his own family but—as one of Zamani's friends explains—a victim of the "German war," who has returned home insane. Thus, he does not chant for his own absolution, but prays on behalf of an unknown people, eerily transfigured in paintings of distorted faces on the wall behind his lair—possibly the white people who co-opted him into the war, possibly the Germans, possibly the black people of Charterston. He calls out: "Forgive *them*, God, for they know not what they do" (my emphasis). His role thus changes from that of the traitor, receiving protection from his community in return for attempting to atone for his sins against them, to a victim of white violence in a far-removed society, and a scapegoat disburdening all humanity of its sins, personal and political. Rather than remaining a local character with a local meaning, "Forgive Me" appears to have been fashioned into an international character, partially inside the story and partially without, maintaining a critical distance, but from beneath rather than above his society. His role, particularly at the end of the film, seems to be to deflect attention away from Zamani's individual crime to humanity's crimes, and to situate the black-on-black violence in South Africa in the larger context of white-on-black apartheid violence, and the vast scale of the white-on-white violence of the Second World War.

The difficulties of representing interracial relations, and in particular ongoing white racism, are articulated by Suleman as he recalls the choices he and Peterson faced when adapting the final scene of the novella:

> We had dilemmas within ourselves about the end . . . Do we let the teacher laugh off the pain, or does he defend himself and kill the white man? The logical way to kill him would have been with a hail of stones. We remembered South Africa as a violent place; our struggle was violent, and we were all fond of throwing stones. Njabulo wrote about this so

beautifully, which made it a challenge for us to show someone laughing off pain and using that pain and laughter to destroy his enemy. . . . This image, rather than killing off the white man, we thought, presents a more powerful argument. . . . It is basically saying to South Africans that throwing stones or using a gun is not the only way left for us to deal with our current problems. We wanted to state that there could always be alternatives. (2002:294–95)

The specter of the violence of Afrikaner nationalism is present both at the beginning of the film, in an announcement on television of the forthcoming "Day of the Covenant" celebrations (with the striking image of Afrikaner Weerstandsbeweging members with their swastika-like flags), and at the end, in the aborted commemoration of this day, which, in post-apartheid South Africa, celebrates reconciliation. Through a close-up of Ntozakhe's hand picking up and then dropping a stone in this final scene, however, the film makes a powerful comment about the need, in post-apartheid South Africa, for black South Africans to reject retributive violence against whites, something which they are now in a position of power to enact.

At the same time, it must be acknowledged that the way in which the Afrikaner is represented does constitute a form of stereotyping. By framing him with low angles, making him look disproportionately huge and threatening, the filmmakers visualize him as a monstrous symbol of oppression. Perhaps rather than unnecessary stereotyping, however, this is a necessary strategy to encourage audiences not to forget the horrors of apartheid. Ndebele has commented on black people's responses to the white violence in the final scene of the film in a way that suggests that the adaptation has already been important in reminding viewers of their shared history of suffering and oppression under apartheid:

[O]ne of the things that [black] African viewers found disconcerting . . . is how one white man with [a whip] gets all those people running away. . . . And there were many people who felt, surely it wasn't this bad. But in fact it was, because what you had were three million white South Africans with a very well-trained army. . . . And I think it came through very well in the movie that if you have the monopoly of instruments of violence and destruction, you can control large numbers of people who don't have those things. (2003)

The novella concludes with Zamani seeking out his wife Nosipho, who is childless, is a nurse (a symbol of *personal* healing), and is also the daughter of a priest (signifying the importance of private rather than public redemption). One is led to imagine that he will seek forgiveness from his wife as representative of the suffering women of the community. In the novella, Zamani does not escape his outcast status in the community—Mimi and Ntozakhe shun him after the whipping, and it is *Zamani* who stumbles away to search for *Zani*. In the film, it is Zani who searches for Zamani, in what appears to be the filmmaker's desire to stage reconciliation between the generations. Zamani, however, stumbles away from Zani, and scrambles up the hillside to where the film begins, either to assume the mantle of, or ask pardon from "Forgive Me," as the community's most recent victim of white brutality and the scapegoat of the Afrikaner's misdirected wrath. According to Suleman, however, the image of Zamani taking over the place of "Forgive Me" does not suggest that Zamani has been redeemed of his own horrible crime, nor that the film's tragedy is a redemptive one offering catharsis to the viewer. Rather, Suleman says that, "[Zamani] joins ["Forgive Me"] at the end of the film, as I do not believe in the Redemption: Zamani's suffering must continue until he is judged" (n.d.; interview with Barlet).

Made in 1997, in the post-apartheid era that Ndebele had to conjure through his imagination, the film reverses the orientation of the novella's closing gesture. Under apartheid, Ndebele's protagonist has to learn how to escape the process of "massification" imposed on him by the system; he has to realize his individuality, his full personhood, by refusing to allow the system to destroy even his soul, and he has to take responsibility and atone for the rape that he has enacted against a young girl. In 1997 and beyond, the film of *Fools* seems to work in the opposite direction, reminding young people—the generation that was not exposed to, or is already forgetting, the worst atrocities of apartheid—of their collective history and responsibilities, as well as of the need to critique the escalating violence (particularly of a sexual nature) against the weakest in society. As Suleman says, "In *Fools*, I wanted to say that we can exteriorize this hatred, that we can restore tolerance by working on ourselves. That seems to me to be the duty of the filmmaker, and of artists in general" (n.d.; interview with Barlet). His view is shared by Zola Maseko, director of *Drum* (2004), who argues that in the latter film he was trying to encourage black South Africans not to betray their race by preying on one another through violence, but by working together (2008). *Fools* plays the very important role, then, of provoking viewers into critically considering their own role and responsibility in current South African society, where a woman is said to be raped every twenty-six seconds (Phillips 2001). While the film could be accused of a lack of cohesion in contrast to the novella—one critic even calls it a "failed adaptation" (Renders 2007)—it is remarkable as one of the few post-1994 South African films that breaks the silence on the horrific reality of rape in South Africa. As I will argue in the following chapter, this silence unfortunately pervades Gavin Hood's *Tsotsi*, in spite of the film's critique of other forms of contemporary violence.

3 Redeeming Features

Screening HIV/AIDS, Screening Out Rape in Gavin Hood's *Tsotsi*

On an April afternoon in 2006, in the city of Pretoria, a woman called Olga Botha left her car with its engine still running as she opened the gate to her driveway. A moment later, she turned around to see that her car had been hijacked. Inside it was her baby. Botha's mobile phone was also in the car. When police called her number, a man answered and said that he had been expecting the call. He said that he did not want the baby, and agreed to drop it off at a school for the police to collect. He followed through on his word, and soon mother and child were reunited. The baby was unharmed. For those who have seen the film *Tsotsi* (2006), this scenario will sound uncannily familiar. As one of the policemen notes, the incident—which occurred a month after the film became the first from South Africa to win a Best Foreign Language Film Oscar—was a "total simulation of the *Tsotsi* movie." He goes on to say, "I think this movie is playing an important role among criminals out there—maybe it encouraged him to have a soft heart" (BBC 2006b).

Whether this extravagant example suggests that the film *Tsotsi* is reforming perpetrators of violent crime in South Africa can only be a matter of speculation; more interesting to consider is how the policeman's response to the incident might reveal the opening of a public discourse in South Africa around the effects of the film medium in general, and particularly in relation to violence. The policeman and the BBC journalist who wrote the article about the incident take for granted that we are confronted here with a "copycat" incident—with life mimicking film. They suggest, in this way, that the film has offered a critique of violent crime which has been understood by at least one criminal. This example represents one possible effect of the film *Tsotsi*—an effect that corroborates the theory that contemporary African film adaptations are making positive, critical interventions in society. It would be all too easy, however, to write off the film's relationship to, and effect on, violence through one sensational post-film incident.

One might just as easily cite the fact that within weeks of the film's Oscar win, real *tsotsis* (a particular kind of South African gangster, whose history I will discuss later) began to sell pirated DVD copies of the film, clearly not heeding the film's anti-theft message. The director Gavin Hood's response, that these "criminals" have "greedy souls," indicates the gap that exists between Hood's expectation that South Africans will obey the law since this means that they are "investors" in local films, and the reality of what South Africans can afford (BBC 2006a). With commercial DVDs priced at 200 rand (US$30) each, one can understand why many South Africans wanting to see the film would opt for an illegal copy at less than 50 rand (US$7). The pirated afterlife of the film is a complex example of the film's effects, signaling a desire by South Africans to see the film, but also a disinterest in following the film's advice in terms of crime. Notably, the pirated version of the film, which was stolen from the cutting room, was given a different ending from the film finally released, the implications of which I will address later.

In spite of the pirating of *Tsotsi*, the film is the first post-1994 South African production that has succeeded in making a major breakthrough in reaching both international and local audiences. The film outperformed Hollywood blockbusters in South Africa, where it brought in US$70,000 in its opening weekend. As Helen Kuhn, local content manager for Ster-Kinekor Distribution said, "It's a quality film and we always believed it would play well, but it's extremely encouraging to see that it is crossing over to all audiences and that cinemagoers are embracing it. . . . It's clear that South African audiences were very enthusiastic and supportive of South African talent on the big screen" (reported in IDC 2006). Notably, *Tsotsi*'s best playing site was in Pretoria, the hometown of two of the film's stars. *Tsotsi*'s success at reaching local and international audiences has persuaded one of its major funders, the Industrial Development Corporation (which provided 50 percent of the film's funding) to invest an extra US$17 million in South African feature films, documentaries, and television series (South Africa 2006/2007:120). It is clear, from *Tsotsi*'s box office results, and from the enthusiastic public response to the film in South Africa, that any critique that *Tsotsi* might offer has reached a broad, diverse audience.

I argued in the previous chapter that the primary way in which *Fools* offers a critique of contemporary violence against women and children in South Africa is through its updating and re-historicization of the diegesis of the novella on which it is based. In *Tsotsi*, it appears that the novel's diegesis is updated so as to offer a critique of a variety of forms of contemporary violence: domestic abuse, the systemic violence of epidemics such as HIV/AIDS, and particularly violent crime (such as hijackings and burglary). However, considering interviews in which Hood and producer Peter Fudakowski speak about their reasons for updating the novel, it becomes clear that this was both a commercial and an ideological decision. Hood felt that the novel's humanist, redemptive themes would hold more valence for audiences if couched within familiar settings (thereby suggesting that the novel's themes have been preserved rather than altered), and Fudakowski stressed that only modernization of the novel would make the film financially viable (the film's budget, at US$5million, was larger than that of *Fools* [1997] and *A Walk in the Night* [1998], but not of *Cry, the Beloved Country* [1995]). This would seem to suggest that any critique that results from the re-historicization of the novel might have been purely expedient rather than expressive. I will argue, furthermore, that the film focuses on certain forms of contemporary violence at the expense of another, very pressing kind of violence in South Africa: violence against women and children, and particularly baby rape. Although the film had the potential to offer a very powerful critique of gender and sexual violence, in the vein of *Fools*, it succeeds only in conjuring a complex and contradictory message.

All of director Gavin Hood's films have concentrated on contemporary violence in South Africa. In Hood's first short film, *The Storekeeper* (1998), which won him an Academy Award nomination, an old man who runs a general store is repeatedly burgled. When his nightwatchman is murdered by the burglar, the old man decides to take the law into his own hands. He devises an intricate pulley-system by means of which a gun will fire if someone attempts to steal something. When he leaves to attend his daughter's wedding, he locks the store and puts up a notice warning people not to enter. While he is away, a little girl climbs through one of his windows to try to steal a lollipop, leaving the film with a tragic ending and a strong message condemning retributive violence. The film has no dialogue, and with an all–South African cast and subtle cinematography, it shows Hood's potential for summoning South Africa's violent realities. In his first feature-length film, *A Reasonable Man* (1999), Hood offers a fascinating exploration of the violence made possible through the scientific rationality of a "Westernized" legal system. In this film, a young man is charged with murder after he accidentally kills a baby, believing that it is a Tokoloshe, an evil spirit in which many black South Africans believe. In this way, the film—which is based on an actual legal case from the 1930s—stages a confrontation between competing epistemologies in a similar way to *Fools, Cry, the Beloved Country* (1995), and *Karmen Geï* (2001).

One of Hood's tools in elaborating a critique of violence in his films has been his realistic representation of South African society, and his films would therefore seem to partake in a postcolonial movement that values historical and geographical locatedness. Although he trained at the UCLA film school and has embraced a Hollywood mode of production on his sets, Hood has also worked for South Africa's Department of Health, making short educational dramas. As a result, he fuses slick, high production values with a focus on gritty social realities. As I have emphasized, what distinguishes many African films is not necessarily their realism, but rather the dialogic manner in which they attempt to engage realities, and *Tsotsi* is no exception to this rule. The emphasis is not on portraying violence in all its gruesome reality as conventional Hollywood directors tend to do, but in contextualizing scenes of violence within an authentically audio-visualized social environment.

In *Tsotsi*, Hood insisted on an all–South African cast and, in the case of the leads, the acting has that rare, magical quality of nonprofessionals that one sees in De Sica's *Bicycle Thieves* (1948). The revelatory weight of Tsotsi's moral transformation falls onto the young actor Presley Chweneyagae, whose moving performance lends the film a raw and heart-wrenching power that the novel cannot hope to achieve. It is difficult even to use the term "performance" to describe Chweneyagae's presence—his spontaneity both rescues the film from slipping into sentimentality and threatens to spill over the film's neat boundaries, particularly in the final sequence. Notably, actual *tsotsis* in South Africa, who were interviewed by a journalist to see whether the film was "true to *tsotsis*," were alone in their criticism of Chweneyagae, whom they said was a great actor but not authentic in the role; they said that he looked too "sloppy" and "soft" to be a *tsotsi*, and that his "*taal* [dialect]" was "off" (Sosibo 2006). Hood was infuriated by this article, and gave his explanation of Tsotsi's characterization as follows:

> The "sharp" gangsters those guys missed are in the movie, they just aren't the lead, and that's what made them uncomfortable. One of them said, "Money is neither clean nor dirty, it's just money." How is that any different from the gangster Fela who can only define "decency" as "making a decent fucking living"? I spent three years making educational dramas in the townships. I met these guys and most of the ones working for the rich gangsters are just kids, wearing a mask of some sort. Some are real aggressive; some, like Tsotsi, are just silent. This movie is about peeling back the mask, to find the "decent" kid underneath. (Quoted in De Bruyn 2006)

What is interesting in the debate between the director and the real *tsotsis* is that it revolves less around Chweneyagae's performance and more around the definition of a *tsotsi*. This raises the question of whether the film, in the first instance, portrays Tsotsi realistically or not.

Most reviewers of the novel and film of *Tsotsi* ignore the history and specificity of the term *tsotsi* by paraphrasing it for non–South African audiences as "hooligan" or "gangster." "Tsotsi" is difficult to translate: it refers to a type of streetwise criminal who operated in the larger South African townships, and particularly in Sophiatown, from the 1930s onwards. The *tsotsis* spoke what is called "tsotsi-taal," a mixture of Xhosa, Zulu, Afrikaans, Sotho, Tswana, and even Spanish, and which is the ancestor of *isicamtho*. The term's origins supposedly lie in the phrase "zoot suit"—which *tsotsis* of the 1930s and 1940s used to wear—and which was later adapted into the Sesotho word *tsotsa*, which meant to "dress flashily." The brilliant black journalist Henry Nxumalo (1918–1957), who worked for *Drum* in 1950s Sophiatown, showed a good deal of interest in (and compassion for) *tsotsi* violence—somewhat ironically, since he was himself tragically murdered by a *tsotsi* in 1957. In an article in the 1950s he wrote:

> They are made every day on the Reef [the "gold reef" area around Johannesburg]. . . . It is true that when a young boy takes the wrong turn

it is partly his own fault; but the amount of crime in a city varies with the well-being or poverty of the mass of its citizens. With the grinding poverty and the sea of squalor that surrounds the "Golden City," it is not difficult to understand the rest. There is a struggle for existence, and the individual intends to survive. (Quoted on Rotten Tomatoes 2006)

Nxumalo's historicization of the *tsotsi* is important. It is impossible, as certain critics have done, to claim that the questions about *tsotsi* violence first raised by Fugard in the novel are "so fundamental, so awesome, that their specific cause—in Sophiatown—has relatively minor importance" (Daymond 1981:86). Tsotsi's existence as a *tsotsi*, in a specific place and time, is vital to the story's implicit questioning of the individual's relationship to his/ her environment. It is not my purpose here to delve into a deeper history of the *tsotsi*, which has been charted by others (Glaser 2000; Rebelo 1981:17–18), and whose representation in films such as *Come Back, Africa* (1959), *Mapantsula* (1988), *Max and Mona* (2004), and *Drum* (2004) deserves a separate study. What is important to the debate between Hood and the *tsotsis* cited above is the fact that two different brands of *tsotsi* developed from the 1950s onwards—on the one hand, the slick, smartly dressed gangsters who tend to operate on big money from whites or Asians (represented in *Tsotsi* by Fela); on the other hand, the young, marginalized boys who operate out of the desperation of poverty and who tend to serve the former kind of *tsotsi*. Hood's protagonist clearly belongs to the latter group and, as such, provides a counterargument to those who assert that the film's central character is a soft, unrealistic portrayal of a *tsotsi*. Chweneyagae's small size, and the vulnerability in his eyes, make him appropriate for a role in which Hood wants viewers to see that this character is a boy, a 19-year-old, rather than a man already hardened in his ways.

Hood's realistic portrayal of Tsotsi might be credited to his fidelity to Fugard's Tsotsi. However, there are a number of ways in which Fugard's attempt at representing Tsotsi realistically is compromised. Fugard began to write *Tsotsi* in 1961, on a boat conveying him and his wife, Sheila, back to South Africa from England. They had been shocked into returning after the 1960 Sharpeville massacre, which saw sixty-nine peaceful protestors shot by apartheid police while participating in a protest against pass laws. This incident no doubt impacted the writing of *Tsotsi*, as did the ongoing demolition of Sophiatown by the apartheid government (begun in 1953 and completed in 1963). Fugard, however, abandoned *Tsotsi* as soon as his play *Blood Knot* (1961) catapulted him to international recognition. Fugard's 1962 journal entries impart his own feeling about the novel's worth, and his reasons for abandoning it:

> The novel has aborted. Read what I had written to Sheila last night. Her silence and my own feelings as I progressed from one muddled paragraph to another were enough. I don't consider the work wasted. The characters are with me now. They'll come out one day. In any case this business of writing "prose" because a publisher wants "prose," is wrong. I'm a playwright. (Walder 1984:51)

The critic Stephen Gray has recounted the story of the discovery of Fugard's abandoned manuscript in 1978 in a box that Fugard had donated to the National English Literary Museum, and his experiences of editing it into shape for publication in 1980 (Gray 1981). He explains that a "flurry of excitement unprecedented in the local publication of South African fiction" (Gray 1981:59) accompanied Quagga Press's announcement of the book's arrival on shop shelves. This excitement was followed by mixed reviews, both in South Africa and internationally. Much of the controversy around the novel boils down to a disagreement over whether Fugard's "heavy-handed parable" written in "sentimental" prose compromises his "determination to look as closely and unflinchingly as possible at the violence and ugliness in the black township" (Jacoby 1983:174). While certain critics nominate it as one of the best South African novels of its time (Niven 1980:500), most agree that it has many faults, foremost among these being its explicit allegorical/parable-like form (Daymond 1981:86). Fugard's novel is ultimately a "morality drama," argues Derek Cohen (1984:282). Cohen situates Fugard's mode of writing in *Tsotsi*—a form of white liberal humanist writing imbued with white pathos and sympathy for black pain and suffering—within a category that he calls "missionary art" (1984:273). Missionary art is art with a message, art that "becomes lost behind the larger structure of the artist's mission and *his*, rather than *its*, impulses determine the course of events" (1984:274). Such art forgoes critique in lieu of bolstering its own ideology.

The novel takes place over six days, and primarily registers—through the genre of the psychological thriller (Gray 1981:59)—the change in consciousness of its eponymous protagonist, a hard-core criminal living in Sophiatown, after he is surprisingly left saddled with a baby. The baby has a profound impact on Tsotsi, a robber and murderer and would-be rapist, whom we learn has blocked all memories of his violent past in which his mother was arrested by the apartheid police during a pass raid, leaving Tsotsi homeless. The baby not only awakens a desire in Tsotsi to remember and reclaim his past, his identity, and his true name (David Madondo), but leads him first to a renunciation of violence, then to God, and, finally, to heroism (or anti-heroism), as Tsotsi attempts to save the baby's life as bulldozers arrive to demolish Sophiatown. Tsotsi loses his life in the attempt, but dies with a redemptive smile that is "beautiful, and strange for a tsotsi" (Fugard 1980:226).

Whereas the film of *Tsotsi* retains the novel's problematic status as morality drama by preserving Fugard's sentimental, redemptive themes, the audio-visualization of the story rescues it from certain liberal humanist pitfalls. The novel is narrated in the third person, but is focalized through the characters living in Sophiatown, thus attempting to present their thoughts to us directly. Not only is Fugard faced, in this attempt, with a protagonist whose "nonexistent consciousness must be treated from within" (Daymond 1981:87), but he is also confronted with the contradiction that it is due to the "unavoidable advantages of being a white writer in South Africa" (Cohen 1984:273) that he is able to carry out this project. Cohen expresses concern at the chasm of experience—an effect of apartheid—that separates Fugard as master of the "sophisticated language of the existential philosophers" (1984:283) from his protagonist. While at times the narrator's voice does ring unlikely, at other times it is all too explicit, making the allegorical links on behalf of the reader, as when the narrator remarks: "[The baby] had become the repository of Tsotsi's past. The baby and David, himself that is, at first confused, had now merged into one and the same person" (1980:175).

One could make the argument—as many, including Fugard, have done—that Fugard's writing style is much better suited to theater and film than to prose fiction. One critic points to Fugard's excessive use of "dramatic techniques, such as scene-setting and exposition" (Spaanderman 1982:21), and David Hogg, the first to write about the novel, argues that "Fugard's prose-narrative is dramatic, in that it offers, or strains towards offering, the tale without the teller" (1978:76). Fugard's role as an actor, as a theater director who enjoys working through improvisation, and as a screenwriter and film actor, perhaps do confirm that the dramatic media of theater and film provide a more sympathetic outlet for his artistry. Although Fugard was not involved in the adaptation of *Tsotsi* to film, he has had a very productive relationship with the film director Ross Devenish, with whom he has adapted two of his plays to film, *Boesman and Lena* (1974) and *Marigolds in August* (1980). Indeed, in the adaptation of *Tsotsi* to film, the problem surrounding Tsotsi's unlikely "articulation" of his own story is dropped and, in this sense, the film's depersonalized third person perspective offers a much more realistic representation of Tsotsi. Hood has acknowledged that the novel was a particularly difficult one to adapt to film since it is ultimately about Tsotsi's deeply interior, psychological journey. As he comments:

> The book is brilliant, but it's a book and it's an interior journey and a lot of those interior psychological journeys are difficult to translate into the film medium because, what are [you] going to do, have voice-over saying what
> · he's thinking? You have to find visual ways of generating a sense of what he's thinking. (Quoted in Axmaker 2006)

In finding visual as well as aural ways of conveying Tsotsi's consciousness, Hood has succeeded in solving part of the liberal dilemma that undergirds the novel. Although Hood occupies a similar position to Fugard as a white South African focusing his art on the black experience, the collaborative nature of film allows Hood to share authorship with black South Africans who understand the violent realities of township life better than he does, and whose input imbues the film with a great deal of authenticity.

If a novelist or filmmaker is to offer critique, however, it is not sufficient to portray a situation realistically or authentically. Critics of Fugard's novel have explored the implications of his desire simply to "bear witness to what happens in [his] time" and to "talk to other South Africans about what is happening here and now" (quoted in Frassinetti 1990–91:9). Fugard has famously made an analogy between his white skin and thorn trees: "Thorn trees don't protest the endless drought of the Karroo. . . . Thorn trees don't pray; they just try to live" (ibid.). What is problematic in this statement is the equation of "whiteness"—a constructed category—with a particular type of tree, and the suggestion thereby that whites should simply accept their own existence within apartheid—which, through its analogy to an "endless" drought, would also appear to be beyond critique. Similarly, in *Tsotsi*, Fugard's message to black South Africans seems to be "just try to live." In preparatory notes before he wrote *Tsotsi*, Fugard reveals his novel's primary interest: "criminal: completely shrouded in darkness. At a moment—a stab of light and pain. This followed, developed, in the span of a short time leads to the full Christian experience" (quoted in Foley 1996:148). In the final part of the novel, on the urging of one of his gang members, Tsotsi sets out to find "God"; his search leads him, unsurprisingly, to a church where the gardener, Isaiah, tells him that God wants people to "be good," to "stop stealing, and killing and robbing" (1980:218). Tsotsi walks away from the church feeling "unnaturally light"; Fugard suggests that the transformation within his consciousness has led to an alteration within his body:

> Walking was no longer the weight of his legs coming down on the hard, resistant earth; but a sensation of drifting as if the shimmering noonday heat was running in the streets and carrying him along with it. . . . He had passed beyond even feeling the sting as the grains of sand whipped into his flesh. (219)

The Christian "solution" presented by the novel is problematic in that it constructs a silence around the particular foundation of Tsotsi's violent criminality—apartheid violence, which has robbed Tsotsi of a mother. Fugard seems to imbue Isaiah's words with none of the irony they might carry when one considers that they should really be directed toward the apartheid government as the chronic criminal within this context. As one critic points out, "Fugard does not condemn the Government actions nor does he attempt to give any solutions" (Rebelo 1981:22). His message seems to be fundamentally liberal-existentialist: "carry on" and "be."

Hood in the post-apartheid era, unlike Fugard in the apartheid era, does appear to level critique at institutionalized violence, at the cycles of violence and poverty that have produced the likes of Tsotsi. In this way, Hood offers criticism of the novel itself which, set as it is between the Sharpeville massacre and the demolition of Sophiatown, one would expect to be far more engaged in a critique of institutionalized, state violence. In fact, Hood goes so far as to find a visual symbolism for revealing the fact that the violent South African past has been integrated into, and is largely responsible for,

Figure 3.1
Widescreen shots
from *Tsotsi*. (Images
courtesy of Peter
Fudakowski)

South Africa's violent present. He does this by finding a way of simultaneously focusing on individual characters and the environment in which they
exist: through using widescreen Super35mm film stock (aspect ratio 2.35:1).
Hood had first been exposed to the widescreen format during his direction
of a Polish film, *In Desert and Wilderness* (2001), and fell in love with it since
it gives one "the opportunity to express emotion in a shot" due to being able
to capture an individual's face *and* a landscape in the same frame (quoted
in Axmaker 2006). In the film's first sequence, the zoom-in on Tsotsi's face
when his gang asks him for instructions reveals Tsotsi's cold-eyed expression in the foreground while the rust colors of the township are simultaneously evident in the background. In the next sequence, in which Tsotsi and
his gang strut through the township streets, the same effect again renders a
tension between individual and collective destiny—for all his arrogance and
attempts to set himself apart, Tsotsi cannot escape his literal or figurative
background. Hood also uses a second, more conventional cinematic tech-

Figure 3.2
Flashback shots
from *Tsotsi*. (Images
courtesy of Peter
Fudakowski)

nique for relating Tsotsi to his background and environment: the flashback. However, he revitalizes this technique by eliminating the typical dreamy dissolve from "present time" into "past time" and simply cuts into it directly. In this way, Hood establishes an immediate connection between Tsotsi the teenager and Tsotsi the child, suggesting that they are one and the same person: Tsotsi the teenager is the result of Tsotsi the frightened, brutalized boy.

One might argue, too, that the film extends its local critique of the cyclical nature of violence by means of its aural reference to the way in which South Africans are attempting to exorcise violence—through music. The film's soundtrack, featuring Zola's hard-hitting *kwaito*—a specifically South African–derived form of hip-hop dance music, with strong bass and recited vocals—immediately and unrelentingly locates the film in present-day South Africa, where *kwaito* is heard in homes, shopping centers, on radio and television, and in shebeens and clubs. The use of *kwaito* is particularly appropriate in the film since this form of music was developed by a group

Figure 3.3
HIV/AIDS
billboards from
Tsotsi. (Images
courtesy of Peter
Fudakowski)

of gangsters in Sophiatown in the 1950s, who called themselves the "Amak-waito." Their name, in turn, comes from the Afrikaans word *kwaai*, which means "vicious" or "angry." The incorporation of *kwaito* music into everyday life in South Africa either represents a strange form of acceptance of violence or makes peace with the notion that the channeling of violence into art can absorb the shock of actual violence, or even pacify it. Whereas Fugard's tale strains toward telling a universal story about a criminal individual, Hood's audio-visualization of the novel prevents Tsotsi from being divorced in the viewer's mind from a historical and geographical location.

As I mentioned earlier, in *Tsotsi* Hood offers a critique of different forms of contemporary violence, including domestic violence, criminal violence, and systemic violence. He introduces a critique of the pervasive, systemic violence of HIV/AIDS in the first moments of the film, with prominent bill-board posters announcing, "We are all affected by HIV/AIDS." By showing Tsotsi's mother dying of AIDS, rather than being taken away during a pass raid, as in the novel, Hood suggests that HIV/AIDS has replaced apartheid as the greatest threat to South Africa's future stability and peace. Indeed, it is believed that about 10 percent of the South African population is infected, with approximately 300,000 people dying every year. However, by raising the issue of HIV/AIDS in *Tsotsi* without making the slightest reference to the patriarchal violence which often leads to the transmission of HIV/AIDS, Hood can be accused of silencing a very important and urgent form of contemporary violence in South Africa. As I will proceed to show, the seed for such a critique is latent in the novel, but Hood failed to take it up.

In the novel, the major event that changes the course of Tsotsi's life involves sexual violence against a woman. Tsotsi has beaten one of his gang members, Boston, into unconsciousness, and is ruminating in a grove of trees when a young black woman, scruffily dressed and visibly frightened, hurries into the grove carrying a shoebox. Tsotsi attacks the woman in the following way:

> He caught her by one arm and swung her into the darkness, his hand
> cutting short the scream of terror that had fallen from her lips like
> splintering glass. A second move forced her against a tree and there, with
> his body pressed against hers, a knee already between her legs and his
> hand still on her mouth, there he looked into her eyes. She struggled once
> but he held her firmly. . . . He studied her calmly, her eyes, her neck with
> the pulse of an artery under the warm skin, deliberating his next move
> while the warmth of her body crept into his and her breasts, full and firm,
> panicked under the weight of her chest. (1980:41)

A cry from the woman's shoebox distracts Tsotsi and—noticing his fascination—the woman hands the shoebox to Tsotsi in what can be interpreted as a sacrificial offering of her baby in lieu of herself. Fugard's narrator confirms that the cry of the baby in the shoebox has "saved" the woman (41)—from what, he does not say.

In the film, this scene is transfigured when, after beating up Boston, Tsotsi blindly flees, not into a grove of trees, but away from the township—across its desolate no-man's-land—into an affluent suburb of Johannesburg during a sudden thunderstorm. Seeking shelter beneath a tree, Tsotsi witnesses an expensive car turning into a driveway. Unable to activate the automated driveway gate, a smartly dressed black woman gets out of the car and tries to contact her husband through the intercom. Tsotsi instinctively sees his opportunity: he points his gun in the woman's direction as he gets into her car and shuts the door; when she opens the door, he shoots her in the legs, and then drives away. It is only when he reaches the highway that a baby cries from the back seat and Tsotsi turns around and sees what he has accidentally stolen. The film does not mimic the novel's "doubling" of events through different characters' viewpoints. However, it introduces an entirely new narrative thread—that of the baby's parents. The story, although centered on Tsotsi, vacillates between the experiences of Tsotsi, and the baby's parents (in hospital, since the mother has become paralyzed from the waist down due to Tsotsi's gunshot). In this way, the film not only introduces a discourse around class difference in post-apartheid South Africa, but it also raises the stakes of the plot: in the novel, there is no one to whom Tsotsi can return the baby; in the film, the viewer is constantly made to wonder if Tsotsi will redeem himself. The narrative impetus and ethical emphasis is thus centered on the concept of redemption.

Although one could argue that the alteration of this scene from the novel stems from the filmmakers' desire to offer a critique of violent crime (hijacking being a common occurrence in Johannesburg), it is a change that is troubling since it silences the novel's crucial description of how Tsotsi acquires the baby. When Tsotsi waits in the grove for the woman, we are told that he "didn't know what he was going to do but his fingers flexed at his side" (40). Although there is no explicit naming of rape in the novel, it is quite clear that rape is one of the actions that Tsotsi is considering in this episode. The abuse of women reveals its ugly face throughout the novel, leaving Fugard open to criticism that he himself downplays this abuse through euphemism and through his particular characterization of "willing women." Fugard employs euphemism at the moment when Tsotsi, leaving the shebeen after beating up Boston, passes "the woman [two of his gang members] had taken out earlier, returning now with wet thighs for the drink she had earned" (28). Boston, a "positive" foil to Tsotsi, was expelled from school for raping a girl (we find out later in the novel), which, he explains to Tsotsi, was an accident. In particular, Fugard characterizes Miriam (a new mother in the township whom Tsotsi forces to breastfeed the baby) in highly problematical terms which suggest that "natural" womanhood involves acceptance of rape. The first time Tsotsi forces Miriam to breastfeed the baby, we are told that

With the first pull of his [the baby's] greedy mouth on the nipple a sudden wave of erotic feeling passed through her body. With an imperceptible movement her thighs relaxed. If Tsotsi had meant what she had first thought to be his intentions and had taken her at that moment, she wouldn't have fought him for long. The baby had that effect on her, and before long his alien, rapacious sucking opened the deepest reservoirs of her milk. (138)

The unfortunate similarity between the terms "rape" and "rapacious" in this passage suggest not only the link between Tsotsi and the baby but between Woman's "natural" need to nurture babies and her "repressed" erotic willingness to be raped. The passage is focalized through Miriam, but would appear to have been imagined from the point of view of Fugard's fantasy of femaleness, perhaps nurtured itself by male-authored Western literary and artistic images of "willing submission" to rape—for example, Leda's "terrified vague fingers" and "loosening thighs" (Yeats), as reproduced in hundreds of paintings. On Tsotsi's second meeting with Miriam, Fugard focalizes the encounter through Tsotsi's perspective, a perspective dominated by the young man's appraisal of Miriam's appearance: "One baby had not marked her, or if anything only turned a girl into a woman; the moment of ripening, they said in the township. You only speak of a tree after picking the first fruit" (176–77). While we might read this description as stemming from Fugard's critique of the gender violence at the heart of the township, the metaphor created here between women and fruit to be plucked is subtly threaded throughout the novel, and is disturbingly pervasive in township lingo and thought in contemporary South Africa.[1] Not a single review comments on the gender/sex violence at the heart of the novel, and the film—through its alteration of the means by which Tsotsi comes into possession of the baby—effectively silences this discourse as well. Furthermore, the film (unlike the novel) offers a sentimental, highly unrealistic suggestion that a love affair will develop between Tsotsi and Miriam, the woman he has forced at gunpoint to breastfeed the stolen baby. While the film does show violent crime, then, it nonetheless refrains from revealing the gender violence that has been rampant in South African townships from the 1950s to the present day and which is difficult to ignore in the novella, however much Fugard eroticizes or euphemizes it.

African film critics such as Moussa Bolly harshly castigate filmmakers who show "fascination with the representation of violence" (2007:1). Most

African filmmakers seem intent on distancing themselves from fascination and glamorization of violence in lieu of preserving their own modest manner of representing violence. While the cinematic rendering of violence in *Tsotsi* is generally authentic and critical rather than gratuitous and glamorous, the privileging of certain forms of violence raises the question of fault through omission: whether *Tsotsi* distorts South African realities not through the violence it shows, but through the violence it does *not* show. Most disturbing to a viewer who is well acquainted with the realities of the post-apartheid landscape is the way in which the film's silencing of the rape at the novel's core paves the way for a much more pervasive silence around the sickening reality of rape in general. Given the prevalence of baby rape in South Africa—and particularly by HIV-infected men—one could argue that a film that brings together the issue of AIDS and a stolen baby within the same frame is complicit if it remains silent on the link between HIV/AIDS and baby rape. Researcher Charlene Smith points out that although there was a 400 percent increase in child rape from 1988 to 2003, the myth of raping a virgin as a cure for HIV/AIDS only came into the media spotlight after the horrific phenomenon of baby rape was revealed through a documentary film, *The Dark Heart* (2004), directed by Cliff Bestall and Pearlie Joubert. Smith presents the frightening statistics: in 2002, children below the age of twelve made up 40 percent of South Africa's annual one million rape victims (2003). Part of the criticism of child rape, researchers suggest, should be directed toward the government, which has not made antiretroviral drugs available to people with HIV/AIDS, who are resorting to myths in their desperation for a cure from the disease. There are other explanations for child rape, however, as the documentary film, *No Past to Speak Of: A Story of Infant Rape in South Africa* (2006), commendably discusses in detail. Hood of course was not setting out to make a film about baby rape, but had his chief goal been to critique contemporary violence through re-historicizing Fugard's novel, he might have chosen to focus his attention on the most unspeakable violence of all—a form of violence that has also notably been underrepresented in fiction film.[2] As it is, for those who are aware of the worst side of South African society, the issue of baby rape festers silently beneath the surface of the film as a violent truth waiting to break through.

Lucy Graham explores the history of the silencing of rape in literary narratives, and, specifically, the way in which silence around rape is used as a structural, self-reflexive device in J. M. Coetzee's *Disgrace*—as a doubling back on the "differences between male and female scriptings of rape" (2005:256). Graham cites Higgins and Silver (1991) who "concede that elision of the scene of violence in texts about rape both emphasizes the violence and suggests the possibility of making it visible" and who suggest that "the omission of the rape scene in male-authored texts could expose 'the ambivalence of the male author caught in representations of masculinity and subjectivity he may question but that he ultimately leaves in place'" (ibid.). Fugard's description of rape in the novel is at best ambivalent, and one might generously conclude that Hood has elided adaptation of the rape(s) in the novel to sidestep the difficulty of dealing with this very ambivalence. One might, again generously, suggest that Hood has censored the "making visible" of rape in his film because of the more sensational, realistic dimensions of the film medium compared to literature, or to vet the spreading of the myth of curing HIV/AIDS through raping a virgin, which—it has recently been suggested—originated through people's consumption of media programs about the myth (*No Past to Speak Of* [2006]). In a less generous gesture, one might compare Hood's removal of rape in his adaptation to the excessive visualization of rape in Belgian director Marion Hänsel's film adaptation *Dust* (1985) of J. M. Coetzee's *In the Heart of the Country* (1978). Male "modesty" at representing rape might be reinterpreted as male collusion in perpetuating the silence. As Graham points out, there are complex historical reasons for contemporary violence against women and children in South Africa, and a feminist re-historicization of the issue of rape in *Tsotsi* would have been welcome in this respect.

If one accepts that the film of *Tsotsi* has an agenda other than feminism, how may this agenda be understood? Hood has said that, "The issues in the film are very much about the gap between the haves and have-nots, if you want to politicise it in some way." He goes on to admit, however, that, "Really we wanted to make a film about a young guy who's angry and struggling with his own identity who becomes a young man. In a sense it's a coming of age story, a universal story, but it just happens to be set in quite an extreme place" (quoted in Zomorodi 2006). The latter view would appear to absolve the broader South African community of reflecting on issues of wealth disparity. The film seems less to offer a Marxist critique of class division than a liberal resolution of it in which private property and individual rights are respected. For the confrontation between the rich and the poor ultimately resolves itself, in the final redemptive sequence, when Tsotsi—in a highly unbelievable plot turn—returns the baby to its wealthy parents. After Tsotsi has left the baby, in a cardboard bag, outside the parents' home, he cannot resist taking one final look at the child with whom he has come to identify his innocent past self. One of the policemen guarding the parents' house spots Tsotsi and immediately summons his fellow policemen to the scene. The camera angles and montage position our sympathy, as viewers, clearly with Tsotsi: while the high, point-of-view shot from the policeman's perspective cannot prove to viewers that Tsotsi's intentions are good, the low-angle shot of Tsotsi looking lovingly into the baby's eyes confirms for viewers that he has fully redeemed himself from violence. No further critique of violence is possible on the director's part, since the character has critiqued and redeemed himself, as it were.

This gesture is a neoliberal one: the viewer feels catharsis because Tsotsi has made the right decision; the film does not attempt, in the final analysis, to offer solutions to the poverty and disease that have fuelled Tsotsi's violence. The film could be criticized, then, for subtly endorsing the status quo. A kind of Christian critique of materialism is made manifest through the characters of Miriam and Morris, who are representatives of the philosophy that financial security does not necessarily bring happiness. Morris, in spite of being a destitute, crippled beggar, still finds reasons to keep living; like the character in the novel, he tells Tsotsi that he likes to feel the sun on his skin. Similarly, when Tsotsi tries to pay Miriam for her help, she says she does not want the money. These characters' perspectives are contrasted with that of the weathered, money-hungry gangster Fela. It was this critique in the film that apparently struck President Thabo Mbeki, and Hood describes Mbeki's comments on the film as follows:

President Mbeki said something quite . . . quite . . . hmm, I don't know what the word is. Quite unusual for a politician. . . . Most politicians don't admit to any kind of mistake, but Mbeki said perhaps we have made a mistake in focusing so much on what we're doing in terms of housing and schools, and the integration of schools. Perhaps we haven't focused enough on the soul of the country. (Quoted in Kennedy 2006)

Within a Marxist framework, a focus on the "soul" without a simultaneous focus on material conditions is not sufficient. Both Hood's and Fugard's *Tsotsi* seem to suggest, in neoliberal fashion, that the poorest South Africans should "just try to live."

The group that is *truly* redeemed, through *Tsotsi*'s message and within South African society at large, is the white sector of the population. In this respect, the double meaning of the word *redemption* is apt: redemption means not only a freeing from sin (apartheid) but also has the commercial connotations of "paying off" or "exchanging." Accordingly, we might venture to ask to what extent white South Africa has literally bought its own purgation. In an article written in 1991, titled "Fugard and the Liberal Dilemma," Derek Cohen makes the link between Fugard's liberalism and the neoliberalism adopted by the ANC. Cohen argues:

> The ANC and Fugard appear to be closer than before. . . . The ANC is looking remarkably like the defunct South African Liberal Party [to which Fugard has said that he would have belonged had he joined a political party] in both economic and political ambition. Nelson Mandela himself has stated that the ANC is not wedded to socialism. This will come as no surprise to those who have watched during the last few years as the ANC has entered into negotiations about a nonracial South Africa with the moguls of big business in South Africa, whose object is of course to ensure that they and their business interests survive. It seems, in short, that the liberal capacity for accommodation has been borrowed by the revolutionaries and the businessmen and has tempered their fervor. Liberalism has become the site where agreement has been thought possible. (1991:18)

The (global) tension between Marxist and neoliberal ideologies will no doubt have a determining influence on South Africa's future, and it is by no means an easily reducible one.[3] At present, however, neoliberal proponents are winning out, with politicians privileging questions of the country's economic position in the world over the question, recently raised by Desmond

Tutu, of the discrepancies in wealth within South Africa. Rather than challenge the neoliberal status quo, the film of *Tsotsi* would seem to accept it-accepting, in the process, Fugard's own existentialist notion (which he says is the theme "that has gone through all [his] work") that "man can only really experience his existence through pain" (Hough 1980:125). We witness the immense pain of Tsotsi, the character, in both novel and film; we confirm our own existence (and guilt) through sharing this pain; but, after this pain and empathy, no further solution to South Africa's collective problems are suggested, in either novel or film. The film thus sacrifices the rational at the expense of empathy—the bodily—rather than achieving the necessary balance. In this way it is different from *Fools*, in which the directors take a long view of the future, suggesting that atonement over time will bring about change, as well as the translation of embodied modes of knowing into new forms of African rationality.

If we turn, in conclusion, to the final sequence in *Tsotsi*, perhaps it is possible, however, to uncover something of a proposed solution to South Africa's problems. As Tsotsi is taking his final look at the baby, policemen arrive in their cars with whirring lights and squealing sirens. Panicking, Tsotsi picks up the baby and runs into the road, where he is prevented from moving further by the presence of policemen on all sides, holding him at gunpoint. The policemen begin to yell at Tsotsi that he must put the child down. It is the baby's father, when he arrives on the scene, who quietens the policemen and tells them to lower their guns. What follows is the most powerful sequence in the film: an almost silent series of cuts between the two men—father and Tsotsi—as the father approaches Tsotsi and waits until Tsotsi hands the baby over to him. Rather than assume the conventional aspects of a shot/reverse-shot sequence, this series is less interested in forwarding the narrative, it seems, and more invested in establishing a poignant visual counterpoint of the similarities and differences between the two men: they are both young and black; the baby's father is privileged but has nevertheless been scarred by the violent society in which he lives (since his wife is now paralyzed), while Tsotsi has suffered from a background of poverty, the death of his mother due to AIDS, and a father whose violence forced him to run away and live as a street child. This sequence is not so much concerned with reconciliation as

(continued on page 117)

Figure 3.4
Closing sequence
from *Tsotsi*. (Images
courtesy of Peter
Fudakowski)

Figure 3.4 (continued) Closing sequence from *Tsotsi*. (Images courtesy of Peter Fudakowski)

Figure 3.4 (continued)
Closing sequence
from *Tsotsi*. (Images
courtesy of Peter
Fudakowski)

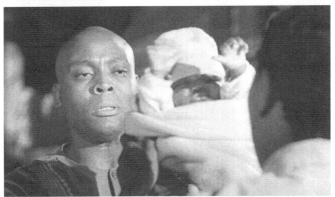

115

Figure 3.4 (continued)
Closing sequence
from *Tsotsi*. (Images
courtesy of Peter
Fudakowski)

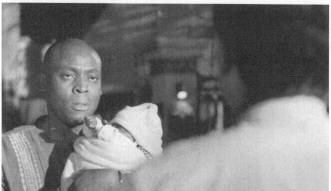

it is about hard-hitting, factual juxtaposition: the one man could just as easily have been the other. The sequence establishes equivalence between the two men, suggesting that it is only class that divides them.

The sequence is notably not accompanied by the pounding beats of *kwaito* that feature throughout much of the rest of the film. Nor is it accompanied by the saccharine sounds of Vusi Mahlasela's vocals, which tend to signal, in other parts of the film, when the viewer is to feel empathy for the characters. The reconciliation figured is all the more powerful for this meaningful silence, and the actors—Chweneyagae and Rapulana Seiphemo—need no music to heighten the power of their performances. The sense of chance—the spontaneity of Chweneyagae's performance—heightens the sense of the film's indexical ability to capture the faces, voices, bodies of real South Africans, something which the novel—although now a rare historical recollection of the lost world of Sophiatown—could not do.

Although Hood shot two alternative endings—one in which the policemen shoot Tsotsi (notably, this was the ending used in the pirated versions, probably intended to make a martyr out of Tsotsi), and one in which Tsotsi manages to escape—he decided against these endings for the following reasons:

> In the end, after much debate, it seemed to me that killing Tsotsi . . .
> was not as dramatically powerful as having him surrender with dignity.
> I felt that, despite the many socioeconomic problems facing the new
> South Africa, there is far greater cause for hope today than there was
> during the sixties under apartheid. The post-apartheid government
> has emphasized and practiced an extraordinary policy of forgiveness
> and reconciliation. So, it seemed to me that a less tragic, more open-
> ended and even slightly hopeful ending might be more appropriate,
> less sensational, less predictable and potentially more moving. It might
> also keep people talking after a screening: debating what might be an
> appropriate punishment for Tsotsi. Killing him made him a saint. And
> he isn't a saint. He's a young thug who ultimately, bravely, is willing to
> take responsibility for his actions. In this sense he is redeemed. And
> with this acceptance comes hope for forgiveness and the possibility,
> however small, of a second chance. Just as there is hope in the new
> South Africa despite the many challenges we still face. (Quoted in
> Rotten Tomatoes 2006)

In this way, Hood acknowledges that Tsotsi does achieve redemption for his violence and, as such, the film looks back to Fugard's redemptive Christian liberalism, and forward to the redemption of South Africa itself from violence. At the same time, however, Hood very powerfully leaves the final critique of Tsotsi's violence to contemporary viewers. Although the focus on what should happen to Tsotsi might detract from consideration of more systemic, institutionalized forms of violence—such as violence against women and children, and class disparity—at least Hood opens a space in which viewers can debate the consequences and solutions of Tsotsi's actions. The film—a feature about redemption—might, then, be said to have its own redeeming feature, in that it avoids the ideological pressure asserted through Fugard's "missionary art" in lieu of a more dialogic approach.

4 From Black and White to "Coloured"

Racial Identity in 1950s and 1990s South Africa
in Two Versions of *A Walk in the Night*

Whereas *Fools* and *Tsotsi* raise questions about gender violence (or the lack of representation of it) in contemporary South Africa, *A Walk in the Night* and *Cry, the Beloved Country* examine the continuation of racially motivated violence in the "new" nation. At the core of the literary texts of *Fools* and *Tsotsi* we find a scene of black-on-black sexual violence while at the heart of *A Walk in the Night* and *Cry, the Beloved Country*—both the novels and film adaptations—is the murder of a white man by a Coloured or black man. How the respective directors of *A Walk in the Night* and *Cry, the Beloved Country* represent and frame this act of cross-racial murder in their film adaptations of the novels is notably very different: the Coloured director of *A Walk in the Night*, Mickey Madoda Dube, condemns the violence of his Coloured protagonist as anachronistic; whereas the white director of *Cry, the Beloved Country*, Darrell James Roodt, chooses to make visible the white violence that has initiated this act of black violence. Both directors then, in confirmation of Ukadike's (1994:166) and Barlet's (2008:98) descriptions of African cinema's "introspective" qualities, turn inward to level critique at their own racial communities in South Africa rather than critiquing the Other and thereby, perhaps, provoking retaliatory violence. On a further positive note, the similarly free social context in which Dube and Roodt are making their films today is glaringly apparent when one notes the contrasting situation of Alex La Guma and Alan Paton as Coloured and white writers respectively within late 1940s and 1950s South Africa.

La Guma, author of the novella "A Walk in the Night" (1962), wrote the book under house arrest and, due to censorship in apartheid South Africa, had to publish it in Nigeria and market it outside South Africa. His second and third novels, *And a Threefold Cord* (1964) and *The Stone Country* (1967), were published in East Berlin. As J. M. Coetzee pointed out in 1974, with reference to Lewis Nkosi's stringent critique of black South African writing during apartheid:

> So much of the intelligentsia is in prison or in exile, so much serious work has been banned by the censors, that the work of black South African writers has become a kind of émigré literature written by outcasts for foreigners. There can thus be no argument, as in independent Africa, that a vital if crude national school of writing will eventually both educate and be educated by its audience, for the work of the South African exile is deprived of its social function and indeed of the locus of its existence in a community of writers and readers. At his desk he must generalize the idea of an audience from a "you" to an indefinite "they." (344–45)

The unpredictability of audience is manifested in "A Walk in the Night" precisely through what Coetzee calls the generalizing appeal to a "they" rather than a "you." La Guma deprives his diegetic characters of vision; in particular, his protagonist, Mikey, cannot "see" what is going to happen to himself. Instead La Guma "locates change and development in his reader's synthesizing intelligence" (Coetzee 1974:352). A chasm is introduced, then, between characters and reader: the characters relegate their dire situation to fate; the reader, on the other hand, is let into the secret that La Guma's naturalist mode is inflected by the South African context. For the devolution here is not—as in conventional naturalist fiction—the result of a human flaw (Trotter 2000), but is hastened by the systemic flaw that is apartheid.

By having his film adaptation of the novella, *A Walk in the Night* (1998),[1] shown on television, the director Mickey Madoda Dube has been able to reinstate a connection between character and audience where it was lost during apartheid. Dube's own personal story reveals the very different conditions under which he has worked compared to Alex La Guma. Born in Soweto in 1960, he studied drama at the University of Witwatersrand before winning a Fulbright scholarship to undertake an MFA at the University of Southern California School of Cinema and TV. His first film, the short *Imbazo, the Axe* (1993), which examines black-on-black violence in South Africa, won multiple awards, and since then Dube has written, directed, and/or produced documentaries, television shows (including the South African version of *Sesame Street*), and commercials in South Africa and abroad. In addition to a five-part series on the Truth and Reconciliation Commission for the SABC, he has made documentaries about black South African art, Robben Island prison songs, and global warming. He has also recently completed a short film adaptation of Njabulo Ndebele's short story "Mozart: The Music of the Violin" (1984), which questions the importance of European epistemologies in Africa. Dube has also taught film at the Newtown Film and Television School.

While Dube has access to a local audience that La Guma did not, he has also commented on how slowly institutional change is occurring in the South African film and television industries. *A Walk in the Night* was the pilot for the SABC television series called *Places and Dreams*, which was to feature eight film adaptations of South African literary texts. No film was made beyond *A Walk in the Night* because, Dube says, "It takes the television a century to make a decision" (quoted in Sé 2002). Like Morojele and Mattera, he has also questioned the politics surrounding who is allowed to make films in South Africa, and who has access to resources. The fact that *A Walk in the Night* was made on a pitiful budget of approximately R8,000 (roughly $1,200) per minute is reflected in the film's low production values and its gritty aesthetic. Accordingly, Dube has challenged the kind of film criticism that is being undertaken in South Africa, and took exception to filmmaker Andrew Worsdale's "trashing" of the SABC's *Dramatic Encounters* short film series, of which Dube was the supervising producer. Dube argues that, "Anyone who watches these films will agree that, as flawed as they are, they are to varying degrees very commendable for first-timers. There is a lot in them that clearly surpasses most of the dramas we see on our screens. There is no doubt talent here and it should be encouraged rather than stubbed out like cheap, stale cigarettes" (Dube 1999). He recognizes the importance of critique but says that in South Africa's fragile, fledgling film industry, constructive criticism is what is needed. While I want to recognize, similarly, that *A Walk in the Night* and *Fools*, unlike *Cry, the Beloved Country* and *Tsotsi*, are the debut films of the first Coloured and black filmmakers in post-apartheid South Africa, it would be patronizing to evaluate them on different terms due to this fact. Although these films, as first-time productions, inevitably have flaws, they also offer insights and innovations (sometimes as a result of their flaws) not evident in the films by more established directors. They have also been made, commendably, more with a South African than international audience in view.

Dube cowrote *A Walk in the Night* with Molefi Moleli and well-known former anti-apartheid activist and novelist Mandla Langa, and they clearly intended the film to reach a wide South African audience. Largely in Afrikaans, the film has English subtitles, but they are not complete, suggesting that *A Walk in the Night*'s ideal audience will be one familiar with Afrikaans, some Xhosa or Zulu, and with South African slang. The film has not received much critical attention—perhaps because of its formal "flaws"—although Josef Gugler refers to it in his comprehensive book on African cinema as a "visually stunning film" that "surprises" in its characterization of whites as "even more brutal and murderous than they are in [La Guma's] novella—at a time when the African National Congress is established in power" (2003:104). The adaptation surprises in many other ways, however, and leads one to ask why the filmmakers have chosen, in the post-apartheid era, to adapt a novella set in the 1950s, grounded in Marxist politics, and at whose climax is the murder of a white man by a Coloured man.[2] My comparison of the novella and the film—of the way in which each works in a particular way in its specific historical context—does not, of course, claim to be representative of the average television viewer's appreciation of the film. Very few viewers might be expected to have read La Guma's novella, but, as in the case with the other adaptations analyzed in this study, the film—through its re-historicization of the narrative—demands of its viewers a critical awareness of the historical sources of their contemporary experiences of violent reality. This would appear to be one of Dube's aims given that he has lamented the fact that South African audiences are "desensitised" (1999).

When considered in its context of production, La Guma's "A Walk in the Night" is as surprising as Dube's film, given that it turns inward, at a time when white apartheid violence was at its height, to critique the integration of violence into a predominantly Coloured community. Unlike the black protest writing of the 1960s and 1970s that is characterized by the overt expression of political goals, "A Walk in the Night" is remarkable for its representation of the effects of apartheid as system, rather than its use of explicitly political rhetoric. The book is perhaps particularly striking in this respect when one takes into account that La Guma was one of South Africa's most politically involved literary writers during apartheid. His father was at one time the president of the South African Coloured People's Congress, and La Guma joined the Young Communist League in 1946, at the age of twenty-one, and was tried alongside Nelson Mandela in the Treason Trial of 1956. After being acquitted in 1961, La Guma was placed under house arrest for five years, after which he went into exile.

Ursula Barnett attributes La Guma's "powerful and realistic portrayal of the violence and suffering of the black man in South Africa" in "stark and naturalistic terms" to his political involvement, thereby finding the allegory of the man in his literary work (1983:24). In support, Barnett cites Wole Soyinka, who argues that "A Walk in the Night" is "a near obsessive delineation of the physical, particularised reality of a South African ghetto existence . . . a total statement both about the reality of that situation and on the innate regressive capacity of man in a dehumanised social condition." Both Barnett and Soyinka place La Guma's writing in the category of naturalism, but they also point to another element in "A Walk in the Night"—the fact that its subject matter is concerned with the "violence . . . of the black man in South Africa" and the "innate regressive capacity of man in a dehumanised social condition" (Soyinka quoted in Barnett, 24). The development in La Guma's writing, from "A Walk in the Night," his first published novella, to *In the Fog of the Season's End* (1972), is charted by Gerald Moore as a move from a philosophy of "endurance" to one of "resistance" (1980:112). Similarly, J. M. Coetzee argues that La Guma's novels do "become progressively more political" (1974:345). Moore and Coetzee refer primarily to the change in the way in which La Guma's protagonists are characterized: the protagonist of "A Walk in the Night" is an ordinary Coloured man who becomes a criminal, whereas the protagonist of *In the Fog of the Season's End* is a Coloured political activist who is "saved" by a black political activist who refuses to speak under torture at the hands of the white apartheid police. As Moore observes, the publication of the latter text "marked the convergence of [La Guma's] fiction with his own long-held position as an uncompromising revolutionary" (1980:107).

La Guma's early work, such as "A Walk in the Night," is written less under the influence of politics and protest literature than under the auspices of an international naturalism and interest in modernity. This is perhaps due to the fact that its setting is the early 1950s, a time in which apartheid was still being institutionalized through the introduction of a series of repressive laws, such as the Population Registration Act (1950), the Separate Representation of Voters Act (1951)—which removed Coloured people from the common voters' roll—and the Natives Act (1952), which forced black people to carry identification with them in the form of "passes" at all times. These laws intensified throughout the decade, and violent black resistance began only after the slaughter of peaceful protestors in Sharpeville in 1960. As Peter Davis notes,

> [The 1950s] was a period of mass removals of Africans from their homes, clearing "black spots" for whites to occupy. It was a time of increasing repression of opponents of the ruling National Party, of censorship, of the introduction of laws forbidding interracial sex, of draconian restrictions on movement and job opportunities for nonwhites, of severe limitations on education, of the growing power of the Special Branch. At the same time, paradoxically, it seems to have been a period of great optimism for Africans. The recent war had opened up new vistas, there was an increasing awareness of the world, a growing militancy for rights for Africans, and, emanating from the world forum of the United Nations, the sense that colonialism and the colonial ethos were in retreat, racism everywhere in decline. (2004:8)

The anxiety of and desire for a modern, internationalist perspective (sizzling off pages of *Drum* magazine at the time) is readily apparent in La Guma's writing, and Coetzee has pointed out that the predecessor texts for "A Walk in the Night" are largely by North American naturalist and/or modernist writers, such as James Farrell, Richard Wright, and Upton Sinclair. If, according to David Trotter, the genre of "[naturalism] added a new pattern to the small stock of curves describing the shape lives take (or adapted an old one from classical tragedy): the plot of decline, of physical and moral exhaustion" (2000:199), La Guma takes up both of naturalism's signature features in "A Walk in the Night." He describes the everyday lives of a cast of poverty-stricken characters, and he adapts *Hamlet*'s metaphors of moral and physical decay to the South African context. Trotter associates naturalism's plot of decline with what he calls bad or disillusioning messes (2000:5–6). These disillusioning messes in apartheid are not embodied messes, but absurdly rational messes—there is a contradictory logic to them which results in the metonymic displacement of violence from white to black, as La Guma shows in "A Walk in the Night." What "A Walk in the Night" does share with the larger body of naturalist fiction is the impulse to declass or declassify, "by discovering its protagonists among the lowest of the low" (Trotter 2000:22). The novella also declasses, however, in a quite literal sense, due to its unique, specific setting.

The novella is set in District Six, a suburb of Cape Town where about 60,000 people—of many races, but mainly Coloured—lived together until 1966, when the area was razed and declared a "whites only" area under the 1955 Group Areas Development Act (Rive 1987; Breytenbach 1997). That this demolition occurred only four years after the publication of "A Walk in the Night" means that the novella is itself part of a historical archive of a lost place in South African history—a place that gave some hope that South Africans of different races could live peacefully side by side. La Guma can refrain from classifying Mikey as "Coloured" at this time because people in District Six would have overlooked this difference; as we will see in Dube's version, "Coloured" identity becomes politicized through the experience of segregation under apartheid and is still manifest in the post-apartheid era. The story, in the novella, begins with the protagonist Michael Adonis (Mikey) walking home from work having just been fired by his white boss. Mikey's anger—described by the third-person narrator as a "knot," "pustule," and "growth" with typical naturalist glee (La Guma 1967:1)—is fueled when he is targeted and beaten by a white policeman for no apparent reason. Mikey remains ignorant of the origin of his anger, and he is unable to make the link between the harsh treatment by the white boss and the white policeman as indicative of an oppressive white racist political system. The climax of the story shows Mikey venting his unspoken rage on Uncle Doughty, an old Irish actor who has long lived in the same tenement as Mikey and shown a paternal concern for him. Doughty dies, and Mikey flees in fear. A young Coloured boy, Willieboy, is seen by the tenement's inhabitants leaving Doughty's room, and they accuse him of murdering the old man. The two white policemen arrive at the scene of the crime and pursue the innocent Willieboy. The more senior policeman, Constable Raalt, kills Willieboy (a crime explained by the narrator as arising out of Raalt's suspicion of his wife's infidelity), in spite of his colleague's protestations. Mikey, unaware of the murder of Willieboy, lounges in a bar, about to be initiated into a street gang. The novella closes with a series of four images, confirming Trotter's view that naturalist stories "could only ever end in an image" (2000:23). These images are: a cockroach gorging itself on a mess of "liquor and vomit," a man smelling the "staleness of the ruin that was his body" (1967:95), another man gathering "writhing" seaweed which moves "like beckoning hands" (96), and a pregnant woman "feeling the knot of life within her" (96). Although these do not nearly approach the disgust of Trotter's example (from Émile Zola's 1883 novel *Pot-Bouille*) of "a foetus sliding onto a bed in a pool of shit and bloody mucus," they are not devoid of nausea, of a sense—if not of hopelessness—at least of confusion. Even the hope engendered through the promise of life is complicated and twisted through the implication that the foetus is knotted, puzzled.

Coetzee describes La Guma's District Six as a stereotype of the ghetto, a bounded pit of poverty and fragile stability that "seethes with internal violence" (1974:349). He points out that the ghetto is only stable, however, in comparison with the rest of the city and system in which it is encapsulated—it plays a stabilizing role by "absorbing the consequences of unequal black-white contact" (350). Closed off, seemingly working according to its own inner logic, the ghetto integrates the structures of the "rational" external system to the point where the inhabitants successfully accomplish what the system desires—as Raalt's colleague puts it, "to kill each other off" (1967:39) in an apparently "irrational" way. This introverted "irrational" violence then becomes the means by which the administrators and legislators of the system justify their own "rational" and "civilized" intervention, whereby they establish, in the words of one of the Coloured characters in La Guma's novella, "law and order" (59). The fact that the Coloured characters refer to the individual white policemen by the abstract noun "the law" emphasizes their perception of these agents of apartheid as the embodiment of an inscrutable and intransigent power. As Asmal, Asmal, and Roberts argue, "It is one of those rare strokes of brilliant propaganda that the apartheid regime so pervasively used the legal system to give a semblance of order to cruelty and oppression" (1997:54). Coetzee, too, speaks of "the bitter ironies of crime and punishment in a state in which Law and Crime overlap" (1974:352). The irrational system of apartheid with its violence against the black body politic was thus disguised beneath a mantle of rationalism, and it is no coincidence that La Guma sets his novella in the decade in which this rationalization through the law largely occurred.

According to Coetzee, La Guma reenacts the system of apartheid through the very structure of his novella, highlighting the metonymic displacement or scapegoating set in motion by apartheid. Coetzee describes the racial dynamics of scapegoating in the novella as follows: a white man fires a black man (Mikey), who in his rage accidentally kills a white man (Doughty); the black people in Doughty's tenement blame the murder on an innocent black man (Willieboy), who runs away; a white policeman (Constable Raalt), inwardly angry with his white wife, grows even angrier when he discovers that it was a white man who was murdered; the policeman's white compatriot urges him not to do anything, but rather to "Let these hottentots kill each other off" (39); the white policeman pursues the innocent black man and kills him; the guilty black man is co-opted by a black gang. Coetzee suggests that, through these dynamics, the novella offers a critique of apartheid as a system which requires above all that the transference of violence flows in the direction of white to black or black to black, not from black to white or (worst of all) white to white (1974:346). He argues that the metonymic displacement of violence under apartheid "may begin in the white city or the black ghetto, but it must end in the ghetto and its last victim must be black" (351).

The climax of the novella, however, clearly marks a transgression of Coetzee's pattern: the murder of a white man by a Coloured man. While this white victim is not the last victim in the chain of violence, his murder adds a dimension not recognized by Coetzee. Although Coetzee does acknowledge that most of La Guma's characters are "from a single milieu, the Colored working class" (1974:346), he ultimately simplifies the racial identities of La Guma's characters—as black and white—in order to justify his reading of the novella.[3] Doughty is not a white South African, but a poverty-stricken, alcoholic Irishman, and his utterly marginal status reinforces the arbitrariness of his scapegoating and murder by Mikey. Mikey's act does not represent any kind of protest against disguised, institutional white violence, but only perpetuates more gratuitous violence. However, the characterization of Doughty allows for a more complex analysis of Mikey's violence than Coetzee allows. La Guma makes much of the fact that Doughty was married to a Coloured woman and treats Mikey as a son. The father-son relationship between Mikey and Doughty is further highlighted by the analogy between Doughty and Hamlet's father's ghost. Overlooking this, Coetzee argues that La Guma uses Shakespeare's play merely to increase the literariness of his text—to "fingerprint" it with Literature (1974:351). This is not only to ignore the exploration of Coloured identity in the novella at a time when the government had recently invented this racial category but also to neglect the tendency of naturalist writers to adapt classical or Shakespearean tragedy for their own specific ends.

The title of the novella and film comes from a line in *Hamlet*, and the novella also features an epigraph from Hamlet's father's ghost's speech, which is repeated by Doughty later in the novella. The speech comes from act 1, scene V:

> I am thy father's spirit;
> Doom'd for a certain term to walk the night,
> And for the day confined to fast in fires,
> Till the foul crimes done in my days of nature
> Are burnt and purged away.

By making Doughty utter this speech, La Guma suggests that Mikey's murder of him is a form of patricide. Earlier in the scene, Mikey reacts negatively to Doughty's patronage and retorts that he does not have any "white uncles" (1967:25). In this way, Mikey's problematic position as a Coloured person is not elided (as Coetzee's reading implies), but is integral to the displacement of violence onto the ghostlike father figure of Doughty from whom Mikey wants to distinguish himself. The violence becomes, in this way, less random and more meaningful in a domestic sense.

Although La Guma wrote the novella in the early 1960s, the story is set, as I have mentioned, in the early 1950s. The 1950s backdrop is conveyed not only through generalized description but also by Mikey's specific reference, at one point, to having seen the film *The Gunfighter*, a B-grade Hollywood western released in 1950. Apartheid legislators were, in this year, evolving new forms of excessively personalized surveillance and ratifying them with specific laws: for instance, in 1949, mixed marriages were banned, while in 1950 the Immorality Act, which outlawed any kind of sexual act between people of different races, was passed. The state thus set in motion a new form of terrorism, attempting to monitor people's most intimate actions. They invaded homes, breaking down doors if necessary, to try to catch mixed couples in the act of making love, and undergarments were used in court as forensic evidence of sexual behavior. The novella thus takes place at a time when new barriers between races were being constructed, and when the possibility of Coloured people merging or even maintaining an affiliation with whites (or blacks) was rapidly disappearing.

Mikey's murder of Doughty in this context is more than an accidental transgression of the system of displaced violence that Coetzee describes, and implies an unconscious desire to establish a cultural identity (and on La Guma's part, a political identity), free from the taint of white blood. In political terms, this draws attention to the uneasy alliance between La Guma's Marxist politics of class and the racial politics mobilized in the resistance movement against apartheid. Beyond this, the novella constructs a complex set of multiracial relationships and confused cultural identities: in spite of apartheid, the characters are immersed in a multiracial and multinational milieu with Coloureds, Indians, white South Africans, white Portuguese, white American sailors, and even a Puerto Rican (55), living together and demonstrating sometimes contradictory attitudes and allegiances. While Mikey rejects the idea of white patronage, he says that American whites "are better than ours, I bet you" (16), but that American "negroes isn't like us" (ibid.).

All of this, then, leads one to ask why the filmmakers chose to adapt this novella in 1998, and how they attempt to make it speak to audiences in post-1994 South Africa. The setting is shifted from District Six in the 1950s to what appears to be the multicultural and crime-ridden inner-city suburb of Hillbrow in Johannesburg in the 1990s. The number of characters is reduced through the conflation of some of those from the novella so that the figure of Mikey is made to carry a great deal more significance. The first scene of the film shows Mikey at work in a steel factory, in conflict with a white foreman who will not allow him to take time to go to the toilet, and who calls him a "kaffir." Mikey quickly rejects this racist insult, used in relation to black rather than Coloured South Africans, and tells the foreman never again to call him that. The scene is intercut with shots of Doughty, wearing a pink paper hat, reciting the speeches of Hamlet's father's ghost at length, as though in performance. The next scene takes place outdoors, with vérité-like documentary shots of Johannesburg's busy Central Business District as South Africans go about their daily work. Mikey finds Joey working as a prostitute in the street and takes him to a restaurant, where he vents his anger to Joey over the fact that he was fired from the factory for simply "needing to take a piss." He viciously condemns his white boss for being a racist, but at the same time lashes out at the black immigrant African waiter, Ngugi, and tells Joey he thinks of himself not as a "so-called Coloured, but a real Coloured," thereby augmenting the novella's interest in Coloured identity at a time when people who have been labeled "Coloured" for fifty years are struggling to think of themselves as anything else. Walking home that evening Mikey is humiliated by a white policeman, Brown (the equivalent of Raalt, renamed with irony of course), who beats him up for no reason while his fellow white policeman looks on apprehensively.

Mikey's anger is shown to grow over the course of the film, which, like the novella, spans solely one night. Mikey vents this anger not only on white characters—such as the old white man Greene, whom Mikey despises for implying that he is "half-white"—but directs his rage toward everyone, leading the Coloured barman to tell him, "We all got our problems, Mikey." Although Mikey at first appears to cheer up when Doughty joins him and Greene in the bar, he soon becomes irritated with Doughty for calling him "my boy." Staggering home with Doughty, Mikey lets the old man fall on the pavement and then, laughing, urinates on him. Back at the block of flats, Doughty asks Mikey to help him to bed but, instead, Mikey shouts at Doughty once again for calling him "my boy," before pouring wine all over him, then striking him on the head with the bottle, killing him. Unlike La Guma's Mikey, the film version of Mikey pursues the white policemen who pursue Joey. In the film's denouement, the policeman, Brown, shoots Joey, then—after turning to shoot Mikey—is shot dead by his fellow *white* policeman. The irony in the film's narrative, which is not present in the novella, is that while Mikey has been trying to protect Joey from violence throughout the film, it is ultimately Joey's association with Mikey that leads to his death. What accentuates the domesticity of both murders (of Doughty and Joey) is that Doughty is fashioned as a father figure to Mikey, and Mikey as a father figure to Joey. Mikey's attempt to rid himself of any white identity leads to the death not simply of two innocent people, but two people who are closer to him than anyone—his surrogate "father" and surrogate "son."

Whereas La Guma's Mikey is apolitical in his ignorance (leading to the chasm between character and reader), Mikey in the film is a politicized character whose politics are shown to be dangerously anachronistic, revealing Dube's desire to speak to contemporary South African audiences about racially motivated violence. There are several ways in which it is made apparent that the filmic Mikey's resentment is not grounded in ignorance, but in some understanding of apartheid's systematic injustices and of their perpetuation in the present. Whereas the novella begins with Mikey walking home *after* he has been fired, the film begins by visualizing Mikey at work. The viewer's empathy is engaged through the foreman's harsh and sadistic treatment of Mikey, and through the effects created by cinematography and montage. The film's opening shot (in lieu of the usual wide-angle, establishing shot) features a close-up of fire sparks from Mikey's torch at the steel factory. The scene of Mikey's firing flashes up again and again during the film, thereby keeping white racism alive in the spectator's consciousness. The film magnifies Mikey's violence and his desire for a political explanation to injustice: in the bar scene, when the old white man, Greene, tells everyone to "cut out politics," Mikey threatens Greene with a knife.

Mikey has no easy outlet for his rage, and the spectator is encouraged to feel his claustrophobia from the framing used throughout the film: barring the film's second sequence in which the streets of Johannesburg are filmed in long shot, no establishing shots are provided, with most of the film comprised of medium or close-up shots. The soundtrack also works throughout the film to foreground Mikey's growing frustration: a smooth-sounding jazz plays over the shots when Mikey is relatively at peace, whereas an ominous grating noise, incorporating the sounds of the steel factory, rises to a heightened pitch when Mikey's anger grows. A visual analogy impresses on the viewer the displacement of racism that Mikey comes to enact against Doughty: the low angle of the shot of Mikey urinating in the first scene of the film (before he is fired) is replicated in the shot in which Mikey urinates over the drunken Doughty. Similarly, Mikey reenacts the debasement that he experienced on being fired from work for "needing to piss" by debasing Doughty through liquid: he pours the wine over Doughty's head, as a kind of bizarre funereal balm, before killing him.

In the novella, we experience events from an all-seeing, bird's-eye-view perspective. But in the film we experience events from Mikey's point of view—which is largely a haptic point of view, since we are made to feel more than witness Mikey's anger. By engaging his viewers in this way, and

Figure 4.1
Fire shots from *A Walk in the Night*. (Images courtesy of California Newsreel)

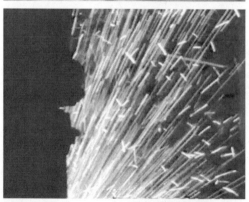

by suggesting that they know and feel as much as Mikey does, Dube challenges the audience to rethink its attitude to violence. The film suggests that in post-1994 South Africa, in spite of the fact that the legacy and effects of apartheid are still felt by many, violence can no longer be directed against an unjust political system. With perhaps the most progressive constitution in the world, there is no longer any monolithic center of power against which a character like Mikey can protest. As a result, he acts out his anger on a powerless figure like Doughty. Whereas I have suggested that Mikey's murder of Doughty in the novella can be read as representing an unconscious desire to disavow any genetic links or affiliation with whites, thereby conveying a sense of dis-ease with the Coloured identity, Mikey in the film professes to take pride in his Coloured identity and, unlike La Guma's Mikey, he is shown to be explicitly racist in his attitudes. Instead of distancing himself from whites to integrate with blacks, as La Guma's Mikey does, Dube's Mikey is particularly racist toward blacks. For instance, in the restaurant scene Mikey verbally abuses the waiter Ngugi, an immigrant from another part of Africa.

Figure 4.2
"Urination" shots
from *A Walk
in the Night*.
(Images courtesy
of California
Newsreel)

When Ngugi asks for Mikey's order, Mikey hisses that he wants "tamatie sous" ("tomato sauce") on his chips—deliberately using Afrikaans in order to alienate Ngugi.[4] When Ngugi leaves, Mikey swears in Afrikaans: "Bloody foreigner . . . hierdie goed is nou everywhere" ("Bloody foreigner—this rubbish is now everywhere"). After the encounter between Mikey and the waiter, the camera tracks in toward Mikey, showing the new South African flag pinned on the wall behind his head. The film's visual irony is clear: Mikey's xenophobia represents an underside of the "new" South Africa, an ugly, grating aspect that does not conform to the notion of the Rainbow Nation, where all the different races live together peacefully.

Mikey in the film demonstrates a viciousness that suggests that his crime is perhaps not accidental, as it is in the novel. Leading up to the film's climax, he is shown to construct his relationship with Doughty in increasingly symbolic and abstract terms, by means of which—it is suggested—he is able to rationalize his violence against Doughty. This symbolism is achieved largely through the way in which La Guma's use of *Hamlet* is amplified in the film. If Coetzee saw La Guma's summoning of *Hamlet* as a superfluous display of literariness, one wonders what he would have to say about the far more extensive and theatrical (even melodramatic) use of Shakespeare's play in a film made for television. It should be noted, however, that South Africans of all colors, who have been fortunate enough to receive a secondary education, would be familiar with certain of Shakespeare's plays, and in particular the tragedies (Bowen 1993). One of the members of the New African Movement, H. I. E. Dhlomo, extolled Shakespeare's plays (and, in particular, *Hamlet*) and encouraged black South Africans to take inspiration from Shakespeare for the development of their culture. Contrary to reductive views that equate the Western world with literacy and the African world with orality, Dhlomo argued that "great plays are in themselves great literature and should be read as such, rather than experienced only in stage performance" (quoted in Masilela 2003:23).

Images of Doughty reciting the ghost's speech are intercut into *A Walk in the Night*'s first sequence in which Mikey is fired. Flashbacks are used throughout the film not only of Mikey's firing but also of Doughty's baleful recapitulation of the ghost's words, as though these scenes are being replayed in Mikey's consciousness. Doughty tells Mikey how much he loved Mikey's mother, and reminds Mikey of how, when Mikey was a boy, he would try to teach him lines from *Hamlet*—clearly an intimate, domestic memory for Doughty. Mikey responds by reciting lines from Hamlet's "To be, or not to be" speech (act 3, scene I):

> To be, or not to be; that is the question:
> Whether 'tis nobler in the mind to suffer
> The slings and arrows of outrageous fortune,
> Or to take arms against a sea of troubles,
> And, by opposing, end them. To die, to sleep—
> No more, . . .
> . . . .
> For who would bear the whips and scorns of time,
> Th' oppressor's wrong . . .

These lines might be seen to represent Mikey's desire for revenge, but they also imply a state of impotence and inertia—an existential dilemma. Doughty, in the role of Hamlet's/Mikey's father's ghost, therefore seems to fulfill two related functions in the film. On the one hand, he could be seen to represent the absent or "ghostlike" white oppressor, while, on the other, he could be read as Mikey's real father. Mikey chooses to reject the second interpretation, and to see Doughty symbolically as a white oppressor against whom he must enact revenge.

The abstract nature of authority figures, and the resultant turning inward of violence, is described by Naomi Segal, who says that "abstracts cannot bleed and the symbolic (the fathers) are what they are by being abstract. . . . That is why the body-blow is always against an other who can be hit . . . the child, the animal, the woman. No one can hit the fathers: they are the abstraction and institution of power" (1994:142). Under apartheid, however, for those who were politically aware, anger could be harnessed in the service of protest against oppressors who—as well as exerting an abstract form of power through surveillance and terrorism—had a concrete and embodied presence (in whites). However, in the post-apartheid context, the oppressors have no more (or less) status than ghosts. Mikey's brutal treatment by the white foreman and the policeman can no longer be regarded as political in an explicit way, and—rendered impotent by the "ghostly" or intangible nature of power in this context—Mikey turns his anger inward against the powerless old man who treats him affectionately as a son. The way in which

Figure 4.3
Ngugi sequence from
A Walk in the Night.
(Images courtesy of
California Newsreel)

the domestic ties between Doughty and Mikey are augmented in the film makes Mikey's crime all the more reprehensible and emphasizes the way in which political violence has been converted into domestic violence in post-apartheid South Africa. As I have emphasized, Mikey's paternal links to Joey similarly work in this way to suggest that Mikey's impotent anger leads to the death of his "son." It is also significant that, whereas—in the novella—the pregnancy of the wife of a minor character, Franky Lorenzo, is a sign of hope, Mikey rejects his unborn baby, carried by his girlfriend Zelda, further signaling the self-destructive nature of this violence.[5]

At the same time, however, the film works to historicize this integrated violence, refusing the simplistic unhistoricized labeling of such violence as "criminal." This historicization is, I would argue, achieved largely by means of the anachronisms displayed through characterization. Mikey's anger, politics, and color consciousness are shown to be anachronistic, and there is also anachronism in the characterization of the white foreman and policeman who abuse Mikey. As Gugler points out, it is surprising that Dube chooses to represent all the white characters who are in positions of authority as omnipotent at a time when whites no longer have the monopoly on political power in South Africa. The choice to retain La Guma's white policemen overshadows the fact that a large proportion of the police force in post-apartheid South Africa is black. Furthermore, under the 1995 Labour Relations Act, "Unfair Dismissal" is prohibited, and Mikey's need to relieve himself during a shift could not lead to his being fired. The white characters also continue to use racist terms such as "kaffir" and "hottentot" that are recognized and would be punishable today as hate speech. Certain effects of the change from the medium of literature to film have magnified this stereotyping: by removing access to Brown's consciousness, Dube represents Brown not as a person caught up in a web of both personal and political problems, as does the novella, but unproblematically as a white racist.

The anachronisms could be read as simply a degree of confusion and incoherence occasioned by the adaptation of a novella from an earlier period. Less kindly, one might ask whether the filmmakers are themselves guilty of reductive characterization. However, sporadic incidents of white brutality against black people do continue to occur in post-apartheid South Africa, as is evident in the January 2008 massacre of four Skielik inhabitants by 18-year-old Johan Nel and the 2008 revelation of abuse by white Free State University students of black residence hall workers, which was filmed in September 2007.[6] One could argue that the anachronisms work in two ways in the film: first, as a reminder of the real brutalities as well as the abstract omnipotence of apartheid—something that cannot simply be excused and forgotten on the grounds of its being "political"; and second, as a warning to South Africans to remain alert to ongoing racist behavior in the present. These anachronisms could therefore be read as a reaction against that manufactured "discontinuity" between past and present that some writers, such as Richard Wilson, have argued characterizes South Africa's TRC. Wilson posits that, "Unlike some nationalist visions of the past in, say, Britain or France, the new South African nation is not naturalized by reference to its ancientness, but in its affirming of the uniqueness of the present. The new South African identity is constructed upon a discontinuous historicity, where the past is not a past of pride, but of abuse" (2001:16).

In order to deal with its "past of abuse," there is a tendency to disconnect from it, and to see the arrival of the "new South Africa" or the "Rainbow Nation," with its New Constitution and the enshrining of human rights, as having ushered in a golden era of racial harmony. The film appears to resist this wholly optimistic vision, and would seem in this way to participate in a critical discourse that refuses, in the words of Bronwyn Harris, to valorize the "popular representation of South Africa as a 'miracle' nation" while in reality post-1994 South African society is dominated by a "culture of violence" in which "violence is upheld as the primary 'solution' to daily problems and challenges" (2003). While recognizing the harsh reality of this "culture of violence," it is important that it be historicized and not seen as inherent to particular groups or individuals. This is an urgent task in a context in which, as Harris points out, children of all races "instead of relating their present-day circumstances (including high levels of violence and inequality) to the nation's history [. . . locate] them within personal attributes and individual characteristics, such as 'courage' or 'failure.'" At the same time, Harris recognizes that a "social silence about racism" pervades South African culture, and that ongoing vocal critique of racism is needed—critique that recognizes that "racism in South Africa is a complex phenomenon [and] cannot be reduced to 'black and white' issues alone" (2003). Certainly, by highlighting the particular experience of a Coloured man in post-1994 South Africa, Dube is contributing to the movement to recognize the complexities of apartheid's racial legacies.

Through the process of re-historicization through adaptation, Dube seems to offer one answer to Michael Green's pertinent question as to how a work of fiction can "make of history something both resistant to being simply appropriated by the present and yet relevant enough to relate meaningfully to the present" (1999:130). By keeping the past alive while also making a statement about contemporary South African society, *A Walk in the Night* participates in that critical process which, as Green argues, is the only way to reconstruct the South African nation. The film makes of its historical material "a moment of resistance that leads to an intervention within its own moment of production or consumption" (Green 1999:130). The potential of the adaptation derives partly from the opportunity it affords for drawing the past into the present, while also—through its fictional status—acknowledging its own contingency. Thus, while on the one hand the context of La Guma's novella and the particular forms of violence it critiques are evoked (sometimes anachronistically, as I have shown), on the other hand the film also addresses some of the new forms of violence, most significantly xenophobia, and other forms of racism, that Harris argues have arisen during South Africa's transitional period (2001a; 2001b). The May 2008 xenophobic riots and murders in South Africa, exactly a decade after the making of *A Walk in the Night*, show that films may also speak to future, unanticipated violence. Dube's film is arguably more relevant in 2008 than it was in 1998, and, in light of the horrendous killing of more than fifty African immigrants, would no doubt serve a very useful purpose if screened for contemporary South African communities.

It would seem, then, that part of Dube's goal is to recognize that there is no discontinuity between the apartheid and the post-apartheid eras: as Maingard has said, "While there are moments and events that delineate points in history signifying change or the potential for change, there are ways beyond time in which, in the experience of life in South Africa, the syntagmas of history overlap" (2003:116). Rather than suggesting that his film's setting is separated from La Guma's 1950s milieu by half a century, Dube builds into the fabric of the film the weight and consequences of those fifty years. The consequences Dube paints, however, are not necessarily what one would expect. Dube's critique of Mikey's character is largely aimed at the supremacy with which Mikey cherishes his Coloured identity, which is at odds with the frustrating experience of liminality experienced by many Coloured people in post-1994 South Africa.[7] Whereas La Guma's perspective is naturalist and modernist, Dube's is social realist and postmodernist: his relentless focus on Coloured identity—and an unusual Coloured identity at that—and on different forms of racism erodes the "black" and "white" terms in which South Africa's history is often reductively characterized.

Working in a more positive and optimistic way, Dube's ending revises La Guma's conclusion by allowing for a transgression of the scapegoat system—what could be called, using Gerard Genette's term from *Palimpsests*, "racial transpragmatization" (1997:312). Thus Brown, after shooting Joey, is shot dead by his fellow *white* policeman. The way in which this scene is edited engages the viewer's own preconceptions concerning racially motivated behavior. There are no fewer than nine cuts between close-ups of Brown and Mikey looking directly at each other. We then hear the gunshot before we see who has fired the shot, or who has been shot. It comes as a shock that Brown has not shot Mikey, as the history of white-on-black violence would lead us to expect. The killing of Mikey by Brown (not figured in the novella) would have constituted yet another white-on-black murder, affirming that the apartheid laws of violence continue to hold. Rather, the killing of Brown by his fellow white policeman, while an incident highly unlikely to come about in reality, seems to symbolize a new, albeit ambiguous, hope for interracial reconciliation, as opposed to white racist collusion in South Africa. The significance of this alteration of the novella's plot is reinforced by the framing of the shot in which the killing occurs: Brown, in close-up, falls out of the frame to reveal the younger white policeman still holding the gun that killed him.

In its "infidelities" to the novella, *A Walk in the Night* suggests that in post-apartheid South Africa individuals have a measure of agency and are no longer simply "overwhelmed by social forces." The filmmakers rupture the indomitable abstract system of violence that Segal sees as responsible for scapegoating, or the metonymic displacement of violence. While the film portrays violent white authority figures continuing to exercise their power over nonwhite characters, through their final gesture the filmmakers also suggest that the totalizing system of apartheid—which has extended beyond April 27, 1994—is beginning to crumble. Both Brown and Mikey are in the wrong, but Mikey's behavior is explained by being historicized. Portrayed as cognizant of this very explanation, it is implied that Mikey has to take responsibility for his actions, however accidental. While the novella, through its structure, offers a Marxist analysis of apartheid as system, the film, through changes in both characterization and structure, works in

Figure 4.4
Gunshot sequence
from *A Walk in
the Night*. (Images
courtesy of
California Newsreel)

Figure 4.5
Closing shot from
A Walk in the Night.
(Image courtesy of
California Newsreel)

some ways as an existential tragedy, emphasized by Mikey's utterance of the "To be, or not to be" lines from *Hamlet*. This is a tragedy, however, without catharsis or redemption. In this respect, the closing shot of the film might be read as an attempt to shift *out* of the genre of the individual tragedy, to a more positive and collective view of the future. A long wide shot framed from the center of a road reveals young black men and women marching solemnly toward the spectator.

In its complication of interracial and intra-racial relationships, and its exploration of trans-ethnicity, Dube's *A Walk in the Night* participates in the same wave of new South African filmmaking as Les Blair's *Jump the Gun* (1996), Akin Omotoso's *God Is African* (2001), Mark Bamford's *Cape of Good Hope* (2004), Teddy Mattera's *Max and Mona* (2004), and Khalo Matabane's *Conversations on a Sunday Afternoon* (2005), all of which provide a plea for a vibrant multiculturalism in South Africa and, in some cases, a critique of South African xenophobia against African immigrants. These films also provide hope for a future in which a more experimental cinema might emerge, for they eschew traditional techniques and media. *God Is African*, made by a Nigerian-born South African, signals a shift to a new kind of cinema made *by* African immigrants in South Africa. It reverses the assumption that "diasporic" cinema owes its provenance only to the migration of colonized peoples to the metropolitan sites of Paris, New York, and London. The film has thus been praised for the fact that it "offers something revitalising in an industry where innovation means simply reversing traditional black and white roles" (Ian Harris 2004). Both *God Is African* and *A Walk in the Night* attempt to move beyond reversal, beyond reaction, beyond even reconciliation and redemption, to engage in that introspective criticism that Barlet recognizes as a strategy of African filmmakers, a strategy that is necessitated by the fact that the "new conditions make it impossible to think in binary terms: it is time for introspection. . . . One must go beyond resentment and scour one's own imagination in one's need to reconstruct one's self-image" (2000:110). This is precisely what Dube does, courageously challenging the behavior of all South Africans, while also providing hope that in spite of the fact that South Africa's worst violence is still concentrated in the most impoverished areas of the country, the laws of violence are in the process of changing.

5 Audio-visualizing "invisible" Violence

Remaking and Reinventing *Cry, the Beloved Country*

In 1995 a new film adaptation of Alan Paton's novel *Cry, the Beloved Country* (1948) appeared, with advertisements hailing it as "the first major film to be made in the newly democratic South Africa" (Beittel 2003:70). Anant Singh had bought the film rights when Nelson Mandela was released from prison in 1990 (Beittel, 71), no doubt anticipating the collapse of apartheid, but he waited for apartheid to officially end in 1994 before making the film, with Darrell James Roodt as the director. The film is the second adaptation of the novel, and so can also be considered a remake of the 1951 film, scripted by Paton himself, and directed by Zoltan Korda. My interest lies with the 1995 film, but I will draw attention to certain similarities and differences between the two films as a way of illuminating the choices made by Roodt and Singh, and of linking those choices to the historical—and historic—moment at which the later film was made.

Although the 1995 adaptation of *Cry, the Beloved Country* (to which I will refer as *Cry*) predates *Fools* and *A Walk in the Night*, I have chosen to discuss the latter first because they represent the beginnings of an alternative and independent filmmaking practice in South Africa. Roodt and Singh are well known as a commercially successful South African director-producer team,[1] and it can be—and has been—argued that their choice of Paton's novel for adaptation at this time was opportunistic (Beittel, 81). The novel, described as "the great raiser of popular awareness of South Africa . . . the most influential South African novel ever written" (Nadine Gordimer, *Observer*, quoted on the back cover of Paton 2002), in some ways does seem like the obvious choice for a commercial film in post-apartheid South Africa. Beittel claims that "Singh and Roodt clearly hoped that *Cry* would be their break-through 'serious' film, and they went to great lengths to promote their remake as more than just a commercial venture, to capitalize on the current international interest in South Africa and on the continuing popularity of Paton's novel" (2003:81).

The novel and the 1995 film can be seen as "bookends" situated at either end of the apartheid era. The novel appeared just a few months before the electoral victory of D. F. Malan and the National Party on May 26, 1948. The premiere of the 1951 film adaptation (directed by Zoltan Korda and starring Sidney Poitier and Canada Lee) was sponsored by the Institute of Race Relations and had as its guest of honor none other than Malan himself, with whom Paton is shown shaking hands in newsreel footage (*In Darkest Hollywood* [film, 1993]). The black actors were not allowed to attend the screening, and they were also forbidden to live in white areas of Johannesburg during the production of the film. The 1995 film, on the other hand, was launched just as the country began to make the transition to democracy, and Nelson Mandela was the guest of honor at the premiere. Whereas Paton's novel turned out to be prophetic in many ways, Roodt talks about the "massive hindsight" with which he was able to approach the making of the film (Pretorius 1994:33). Notwithstanding the motives suggested by Beittel, the careful timing of the film creates the expectation that this adaptation might profit from the space opened up—immediately post-apartheid—for a new and different reading of this novel, the meaning and value of which were so strongly contested during the apartheid years. And with the hindsight available to viewers and critics almost a decade after the film's appearance, it also becomes possible to consider whether the film anticipates in any way the forms of discourse set in motion by the proceedings of the TRC, which began in the same year that the film was released.

Roodt has given some sense of his motives for making the film in an interview, saying, "It is the pain of remembrance with which I have imbued the picture. . . . We are trying to understand the past, and for me, the new direction of films in South Africa will be about retelling history" (Pretorius, 33). The retelling of history is never neutral, I have argued, in that it always involves harnessing and interpreting the past in the service of the present or the future. Beittel, however, criticizes what he sees as Roodt and Singh's focus on the past, arguing that while the 1951 film "seeks to influence the *present* and the *future*," the 1995 film "is determined [only] by the tragedy of the apartheid *past*" (2003:73; my emphasis). He also complains that, although the remake "promised a 'post-apartheid' perspective on Paton's novel, presumably offering [also] a different ideological stance than the original film adaptation" (71), the "intention to 'retell history' is guided by the project to tell only its bright side" (86), which results, he argues, in "a conception of history that is monumental" (84). Beittel argues that this "monumentalizing" of history "freezes the process of the present continuous reinterpretation of the past into a series of neatly connected 'facts' and magnified, isolated 'events'" through which "memory is reduced to memorial" (84).

Cry is set at the time of the novel's writing, and does seem to be more focused on the past than the present, unlike Suleman's, Hood's, and Dube's adaptations, which update the literary texts. Roodt and Singh's focus on the past suggests that they are clearly targeting an international as well as a local audience. It is nevertheless possible to argue that the 1995 film attempts a critique of the metonymic displacement of apartheid violence into the present. I will argue that the 1995 film of *Cry* draws on and enhances the mimetic power of the novel to offer this critique, and that by focusing on a form of violence largely silenced or obscured by the novel, it shows the novel's critique to be flawed and contradictory.

In this respect, I would suggest that, despite its commercial orientation, which leads to a tendency to oversimplify, and despite its conventional commercial aesthetics, the film deserves a more generous reading than the one given by Beittel. Rather than view the adaptation as opportunistic, we might recognize that Singh and Roodt's decision to both adapt the novel and remake the 1951 film at this time does raise interesting questions about "the continuing historical relevance" of Paton's novel, exposing it to renewed critical debate and interpretation. Given the status of this novel in South African literary and intellectual history during the apartheid era, the fresh debate that the filmmakers have generated is in itself valuable, whether or not one endorses their interpretation. Indeed, Braudy has argued that "even the most debased version" of a cinematic remake offers "a meditation on the continuing historical relevance (economic, cultural, psychological) of a particular narrative." He goes on to say that, "A remake is thus always concerned with what its makers and (they hope) its audiences consider to be unfinished cultural business, unrefinable and perhaps finally unassimilable material that remains part of the cultural dialogue" (1998:331).

I will go beyond Beittel's reading, then, to argue that the film does not "monumentalize" or "memorialize" history by telling only its bright side, and that it does offer a different ideological stance than both the novel and the 1951 adaptation, evident in its critique of the novel and the earlier film's faith in the judiciary. The 1995 film shows how the judicial branch of the Law participates in systemic racist violence, and in this sense it can be compared to *A Walk in the Night*, in which the policing branch of the Law is shown to perpetuate the metonymic displacement of violence down a chain of descending power within the community. Like *A Walk in the Night* and also *Fools*, *Cry* also works to forestall this ongoing metonymic displacement of violence onto powerless scapegoats, although in this case not primarily within the communities of the dispossessed, but within post-apartheid South Africa more broadly.

In order to understand the nature of the "unfinished cultural business" that the 1995 film deals with, however, it is necessary to begin by looking at the kind of intervention in South African cultural and intellectual life that the novel represents. Paton wrote the novel in a mere three months, from September to December 1946, while on a tour of prisons and reformatories in England, Canada, and the United States, in his capacity as the director of Diepkloof, the largest reformatory in South Africa. Nine publishing houses expressed their interest in the manuscript within weeks of receiving it, and the novel was published, without a single change, in February 1948. It immediately met with the highest praise from reviewers; the first printing sold out on its first day, and during Paton's lifetime the book sold 15 million copies, and was translated into more than twenty languages, including Afrikaans and Zulu (Gerstung 2001:23–29).

The story is set in 1946 and tells the tale of two fathers, each of whom loses a son. The white father, James Jarvis, is a wealthy farmer in Natal; the black father, Stephen Kumalo, is a minister of religion in the same area. Their sons are both in Johannesburg: the white son, Arthur, is an outspoken critic against racial injustice; the black son, Absalom, turns to crime, and shoots and kills the white son (whom he does not know) in a foiled burglary attempt. The black son is found guilty of murder and hanged. These are the two acts of violence around which the narrative is organized, and they are framed by the systemic violence, described by Arthur Jarvis, before his death, as responsible for black criminal behavior in South Africa. A chain of causality is thereby implied, with whites' treatment of blacks resulting in black violence, and this black violence acted out in the random killing of a white man, and then retribution exacted (by the "white" Law) through the hanging of a black man. The novel ends with a scene of reconciliation between the two fathers, with James Jarvis forgiving Absalom for killing his son, and Stephen Kumalo having to reconcile himself to his son's death by hanging. This ending works to cancel out the violence, or at least to obliterate the essentially political cause that first sets the chain in motion, by focusing on the individual grief and reconciliation of the two fathers. Arthur Jarvis's writings, the only explicit "revelation" in the novel of the systemic violence of apartheid, and the novel's own gesture toward a political reading of Absalom's seemingly arbitrary crime, are, through this ending, to a great degree silenced and forgotten.

In one of the few readings which approaches the novel from the perspective of literary discourse rather than political discourse, J. M. Coetzee has described this ending as cathartic, arguing that as the great exemplar of the religious tragedy in South African literature, the novel is "apolitical or quietistic" (1974:17). No text can be thoroughly apolitical, however, and the novel is, of course, an expression of Paton's own liberal politics. Like La Guma, Paton was also heavily involved in the arena of politics, but unlike La Guma's Marxist politics, Paton's South African Liberal Party was situated right of center in relation to other South African political parties. Maintaining its commitment to nonviolence and gradual change even in the face of apartheid's increasing brutality, it remained a party dominated by whites (Nixon 1991:501). Paton himself founded the party in 1953, initiating a political movement whose evolution and role in South Africa has been subject to a great deal of scrutiny (Robertson 1971; Rich 1984; Simkins 1986; and Nixon 1991). At an address given at Yale in 1973, Paton described his particular version of liberalism as embracing the sanctity and autonomy of individuals, free choice, nonviolence, Christian principles, and the Rule of Law (Gerstung, 28). The novel—along with the rest of Paton's literary oeuvre—has without fail been read as operating within the discourse of Paton's liberalism, with Paton regarded as the preeminent representative of "liberal humanist" writing in South Africa, which spanned a period from the 1920s to the 1960s (other representatives being William Plomer, Laurens van der Post, and the early Nadine Gordimer). Although Fugard's perspective changes across his works—from his collaborative workshop plays to his more abstruse "theater of the absurd"—his point of view in *Tsotsi*, as I have argued, is decidedly liberal humanist.

Ironically, Paton's novel, whose intention was to promote reconciliation, has strongly polarized critics. Its critics may be divided into those who are supportive of liberalism and therefore applaud the novel's thematization of liberal values, and those who—often from a Marxist perspective—have strongly criticized what they see as the contradictions within the novel, stemming from the paradoxes within liberalism itself. Many black intellectuals fall into the second group, and have found the novel insipid and paternalistic (*In Darkest Hollywood* [film, 1993]). In the shebeen scene in *Come Back, Africa* (1959), Lewis Nkosi, Can Themba, and Bloke Modisane engage in a lengthy discussion, and condemnation, of Paton's novel on account of its liberalism—its assumption, as Nkosi puts it, that all of South Africa's racial problems can be solved "over a cup of tea." Wole Soyinka, in his well-known essay "From a Common Backcloth," remarks that "Alan Paton's *Cry, the Beloved Country* simply debases the gift of sympathy" (1988:13). In these words Soyinka refers to many black African readers' dismissal of the way in which Paton fashioned Stephen Kumalo as an idealized black supplicant to whites, and therefore as not fully human. Ezekiel Mphahlele, in *The African Image* (1974), criticizes the novel for a similar reason, arguing that in it "human nature is falsified because there are bad characters as against good ones—in two distinct groups" (quoted in Beittel 2003:77). The literary critic Stephen Gray has critiqued the novel on similar, but slightly different, grounds. Situating *Cry* within a literary and film movement he calls the "Jim Comes to Jo'burg" trend (referring to the 1949 film), Gray argues that *Cry* draws on the popular theme of "the rural black man's encounter with the white-controlled industrialised city" (1985:61). Gray argues that, in spite of the belief that *Cry* was the first to initiate this theme, the novel in fact reiterates concerns that had been in motion since the publication of Douglas Blackburn's *Leaven: A Black and White Story* (1908). He argues, however, that *Cry* altered the theme by focalizing its narrative not through the typical "Jim" character (which would be Absalom in this case), but through a character who is opposed to the urbanization of the black man from beginning to end: the Reverend Stephen Kumalo, whose brother John, sister Gertrude, and son Absalom, have all disappeared from the hills of Natal to the city of Johannesburg, and whom he attempts to "reform" by enticing back to the countryside. Gray crucially suggests that one of the reasons that the novel has had such sustained international appeal is that readers have been able to identify more easily with the Christian liberalism of the Reverend Kumalo than with the modern, urbanized black characters. Notably, the "Jim Comes to Jo'burg" theme has survived into the post-1994 period, with films such as Teddy Mattera's *Max and Mona* (2004) revitalizing and parodying it from a comic black perspective that erodes Paton's division between the "white city" and the "black countryside."

Those critics who have been supportive of Paton's novel tend either to celebrate the principles of liberalism to defend Paton's work (Iannone 1997), or to reveal the complexity and nuanced nature of Paton's particular version of liberalism (Morphet 1983; Foley 1998). More recent interpretations, such as that provided by Foley (1998), fall back on biographical readings of the novel, pointing to the parallels between Arthur Jarvis and Paton himself, and particularly to their shared interest in historicizing black crime. Through his reformatory work Paton developed a deep intellectual interest in crime and violence, and it was his belief that whites—through their treatment of blacks—were responsible for black criminality in South Africa. One of Arthur Jarvis's writings is an almost exact replica of one of the many articles that Paton published in the journal *The Forum* from 1943 to 1945, titled "Who is Really to Blame for the Crime Wave in South Africa?" (Foley 1998:67).

A spokesman for liberalism over many years, Foley uses Paton's political and reformatory "fieldwork" to refocus discussion on the novel's attention to community rather than to individuals, thereby challenging those who criticize liberalism on the grounds of its concern with personal destiny alone. Foley points out that in 1946, the year in which the novel is set, South Africa in fact "seemed to be on the verge of a political liberalisation," with Jan Smuts having written the Preamble to the United Nations Charter after the Second World War (1998:88). He thus argues that Paton's novel, far from focusing only on individuals, engages with the politics and social issues of a particular moment, and that it offers practical solutions to some of the societal problems it reveals (63). He further supports this argument by drawing attention to book 1, chapter 9 of *Cry*, in which the reader is provided with a collage of black voices speaking of the difficulties of finding adequate housing in the slums of Johannesburg, and he draws on other critics, such as Callan (1982) and Pajalich (1992), who praise the novel for creating "a multitude of voices" and for being fundamentally "dialogic" (quoted in Foley 1998:86).

Foley thus redefines Paton's liberal perspective as one that attempts to avoid a monologic approach, arguing that "one of the distinctively liberal features of the novel is its willingness to confront complex problems and to present a variety of competing viewpoints on the subject rather than a rigid, monolithic ideological perspective" (1998:85–86). In contrast to what he sees as the novel's complex engagement with its sociohistorical moment, Foley argues that "almost fifty years later, Darrell Roodt's film version (1995) of the book concentrated almost entirely on the basic story line, and quite ignored the question of social restoration which the novel explores" (63–64). Beittel's criticism is similar, and his point that the film works as a "morality play," with certain "evil" characters pitted against "good white liberals and black clergy" (2003:85) is reminiscent of Soyinka and Mphalele's criticisms of the novel.

While these criticisms are largely valid in their identification of a tendency to oversimplify characters and social issues in the film, and therefore of a certain reductiveness, I suggest that the film could be read—generously—as reclaiming the right to focus on the individual, a claim made possible by the historical moment at which the film was produced. Recalling the words of Njabulo Ndebele, it can be argued that this shift to the individual is also necessary to the creation of a truly post-apartheid perspective. In the years preceding 1994, the country had been engulfed in a bloodbath of political violence set in motion by apartheid policies and state violence, but committed by several factions in the service of different political agendas. And in this climate, as the overview of critical responses to the novel has shown, the only valid perspective from which to comment on art of any kind was a collective political perspective. It could be argued that, waiting for 1994, the filmmakers seized the opportunity to focus on the storyline and on individual characters, to move away from the depersonalized rationality of mass politics, and the rationality of a critical discourse responsive to this political context. Again generously, this could be seen as a reclaiming of the right to celebrate the mimetic qualities of art (literature and film), and in this way to celebrate the sensuous and particular, the unique qualities of the individual that had been occluded for so long by the imperative to sustain the collective struggle against apartheid on every front, including the arts.

This may seem like an extravagant claim, and the focus on individuals may be seen as premature in the immediate post-apartheid period. The film does, however, differ significantly from the novel in terms of which individuals it chooses to focus on, and it is necessary to begin by examining the novel's focus, in order to argue for the significance of the filmmakers' choices. In the novel, it is the fathers who occupy center stage, with the first and third sections focalized through Stephen Kumalo, and the second section focalized through James Jarvis. At the same time, however, the heterodiegetic narrator maintains the power of intervention throughout and, as stand-in for the author, constitutes a further level of paternal (although invisible) authority in the novel. Those critics like Foley, who support the novel on the grounds of its "creating a multitude of voices" overlook the way in which this narrator achieves an almost "autonomous" status "as one who may be trusted to guide the reader through the moral quandaries of the novel" (Medalie 1998:104).

There are two further levels of paternal authority in the novel, occupied by the Judge as representative of the Rule of Law, and by a Christian God. The Judge is given an entire chapter (book 2, chapter 11) in which to expound his rational(ized) argument for finding Absalom guilty and sentencing him to the maximum penalty—death by hanging—and for acquitting Absalom's accomplices, who have also been shown to be guilty. It is an ingenious argument, relying on "rational" logic to endorse the "*sacred* duty of a Judge to administer [the Law]" (Paton 2002:171; my emphasis), and Paton's narrator argues that, "Even the black men have faith in [Judges], though they do not always have faith in the Law" and that "Even if there were one there [in court] greater than the Judge he would stand, for behind the Judge are things greater than any man" (137). Much is made of the fact that the lawyer Carmichael takes on Absalom's case "*pro deo*" (111), creating a spurious link between the Law and God. In this way, it is implied that the Judge is an extra-historical figure, whereas what this figure represents is a judicial system in which the insistence on impartiality arises out of and perpetuates a form of instrumental rationality. While the writings of Arthur Jarvis are the means for historicizing black crime, laying the blame on whites, and for criticizing white South Africans' racist version of Christianity, the novel as a whole endorses colonialism while lamenting its imperfect performance.

The 1995 film casts a different light on James Jarvis and shifts the focus from the fathers to the sons, but before going on to look at how it does this, I wish to situate this discussion about the sacred status of the Law in relation to mimesis. The workings of the Law within the TRC have been described by Sara Osborne (2000), who draws on René Girard's understanding of mimesis. Like that of Adorno, much of Girard's work is grounded in a bio-anthropological notion of mimesis, although his writing on mimesis ends up taking a very different turn. I do not have the space here to elaborate on this difference, but Osborne's use of Girard is relevant to my interpretation of *Cry* because she focuses on Girard's detailed analysis of the way in which the Law has evolved out of sacrificial cultures in order to distinguish retributive and restorative forms of justice.

For Girard, "culture itself is nothing more than a system of violence control" (Osborne 2000:101), with modern culture evolving out of a progressive repression of the atavistic tendency in nonindividuated human communities toward violence. This repression, a form of rationality in itself, is first evident in premodern ritual sacrificial systems, which enact a form of rational abstraction in their nomination of a "scapegoat" (or substitute) to expend excess societal violence and friction. This structure is then "mimicked," in the evolution to modernity, by certain institutions, such as the Law, which abstracts and depersonalizes individuals so that they, too, are given a status which approximates the sacred (Girard 1986). Like Adorno, Girard argues that humans are fundamentally mimetic beings, and like Adorno, he also argues that there is good and bad mimesis. However, unlike Adorno, Girard sees mimesis as "an *automatic* human response to our social environment" (Osborne, 89; my emphasis), and thus not necessarily as an alternate form of cognition. Mimesis, for Girard, is "morally neutral"—it is capable of drawing us "down paths to violence or away from violence" (Osborne, 100). The crucial question in Girard's theory of mimesis thus becomes, "Which Ultimate Authority triggers our desires and compels mimesis?" (ibid.) since it is the morality of this Ultimate Authority that will determine whether we engage in good or bad mimesis.

Osborne, in her article relating Girard's ideas to the TRC, provides a useful overview of Girard's definition of the Ultimate Authority in retributive justice systems, such as the Law. She writes:

> Good Violence deters Bad Violence. The Bad Violence for *all* social groups is revenge, because its reciprocal nature is potentially never-ending. . . . Girard proposes that Good Violence is universally embodied in practices that replicate a cathartic scapegoat sacrifice which interrupts escalating revenge with a powerfully diverting transcendent experience. . . . The act of expulsion which follows destroys both the conflict and the surrogate (however, the source of the conflict, not directly addressed, will appear again and require another sacrificial resolution). . . . Girard describes this formula for cultural stability as "unanimity minus one" because the social bond generated in this process is always at the expense of a scapegoat "victim." . . . Because of, and in spite of this notable exception, in order to remain effective the means and ends of Good Violence must remain absolutely sacred and never questioned. . . . Girard says, "Only the transcendental quality of the system, acknowledged by all, can assure the prevention or cure of violence." (Osborne 2000:86)

Reading Paton's novel through Girard, it is possible to argue that the Judge (endorsed by the similarly "autonomously" positioned narrator) represents this kind of sacred and transcendental system, with Absalom as the scapegoat that allows the fathers to become reintegrated into their community, ensuring cultural stability as attention is deflected from the real "source of the conflict" (apartheid).

The irony is that Paton goes to great lengths to justify the Judge's decision on the grounds of its basis in logic, in modern Western rationality. This irony is highlighted by Medalie's argument that Paton shows a loathing, throughout the novel, for any mass activity, and particularly for black revolutionary mass action to which the politician John Kumalo appeals, and which "suggests devolution, a regression to a lower, non-individuated life form. Collectivist behaviour and violence are thus presented as part of the same atavistic impulse" (1998:97). According to Medalie, Paton expresses deep ambiguity toward the notion of "Africa" itself, and it could be argued that, while the Judge represents the positive Ultimate Authority, John Kumalo, with his "bull voice" (Paton 2002:157), represents the negative Ultimate Authority who could trigger a "regression" to what would be regarded as bad violence, enacted through the bad mimesis of collective insurrection against authority.

The Judge makes a modern sacrificial victim out of Absalom, as Medalie suggests when he argues that "Absalom's crime is clearly not equal to his punishment, and there is sympathy for him as a result; yet, at the same time, we are asked to accept the punishment as *judicially* correct. . . . The judge's role is almost hieratic, suggested by his comment that his duty is a 'sacred' one" (1998:103). This sacrifice is made to ensure catharsis within the novel's diegetic community, thereby deflecting "a systemic semi-consciousness about the questionable morality of arbitrary surrogate victimizing mechanisms" (Osborne 2000:86–87), particularly in a society as *un*just as apartheid South Africa. Similarly, but on a larger, extra-diegetic scale, Paton-as-author turns Absalom and Arthur into the sacrificial victims of his own "Ultimate Authority" so that the fathers (and through them, readers) may learn about the horrors of South Africa and further violence be prevented (until, of course, a new sacrificial victim becomes necessary).

While the authority figures in the novel, then, are granted transcendental status, the two sons become victims, sacrificed for the sake of reconciliation between the fathers, to save the community and to maintain cultural stability. The sacrificial status of the sons is evident, too, in the biblical metaphors of the novel: Absalom of the Old Testament was the much loved but aberrant and ultimately lost son of King David, and John Kumalo refers to Absalom as Stephen Kumalo's "prodigal son." Arthur Jarvis, on the other hand, is characterized as a Christ-like figure (there are pictures of Christ crucified on Arthur's study walls [Paton, 125])—who, in a sense, gives himself up to become a sacrificial victim, since, unlike the other characters, he refuses to be constrained by fear. In this way, the stories of Arthur and Absalom, rather than being individualized by Paton, become generic, and—through the author's use of metonymic displacement—these characters become the sacrificial victims, not only of the logic of the Law but the logic of the novel itself, which works to ensure catharsis and redemption for readers.

The Judge and the narrator/author's "Ultimate Authority" can both be said to operate along the lines of retributive justice, which as Osborne points out, "appears abstract, procedural, and narrow in pursuit of impartiality or neutrality, the ideal of Blind Justice" and which embraces "a norm of proportional punishment as good and just" (2000:81). Osborne contrasts retributive justice with restorative justice, such as that offered through the TRC. Restorative justice, she argues, "insists that all crime is personal, evidence of a broken relationship between victim, offender, and community . . . 'justice' to be just must go well beyond addressing the specifics of the act which effected the break" (80). Within the discursive framework of the TRC, as Osborne points out, it is the African notion of *ubuntu* (the idea of humans existing only through other human beings) that constitutes the "Ultimate Authority" (98–99), with violence dealt with in a way that is personalized, but grounded in a local sociohistorical context, and with the potential to heal the community rather than simply forestall the next round of conflict.

Turning now to the 1995 film of *Cry*, I will look at how the film can be located in relation to these two different discourses of justice, and to the forms of authority upon which they are dependent. There is no heterodiegetic narrator in the film, as one would expect given the nature of the medium, which rarely allows for narrators. However, given commercial cinema's general dislike of narrators, it is significant that the filmmakers have chosen to make Stephen Kumalo an autodiegetic narrator.[2] In this way the chain of white authority figures is dispensed with, and viewers are required to judge events, and the behavior of the white father, from the perspective of the black father. This is particularly evident in the scene of Arthur's funeral, in which the voice of Stephen Kumalo (James Earl Jones), delivers—over evocative music—an altered version of some of the novel's most frequently cited passages, rewritten by scriptwriter Ronald Harwood so that Kumalo would appear to address the fears of whites living in contemporary South Africa. The passage is recited over images of James Jarvis at his son's funeral, intercut with images of white policemen beating black men and women:

> There is fear in the land, and fear in the hearts of all who live there, and fear puts an end to understanding, and the need to understand. So how shall we fashion such a land when there is fear in the heart? The white man will put more locks on his door and get a fine, fierce dog. But the beauty of the trees, and of the stars, these things we shall forego. Cry, the beloved country, for the unborn child that is going to inherit our fear. Let him not love the earth too deeply [here the image cross-fades from white policemen beating black men and women to James Jarvis's face as he stares directly at the viewer]. Let him not be too moved when the birds of his land are singing [here the image cross-fades into a medium shot,

showing a line of white people waiting to shake Jarvis's hand after the funeral]. Nor give too much of his heart to a mountain or a valley. For fear will rob him of all if he gives too much. Yes, cry, cry the beloved country.

The conflating of Kumalo's words "fear will rob him of all" with a sequence of images in which Jarvis refuses to shake a black man's hand suggests that the greatest loss to South Africans in post-apartheid South Africa will be their inability to forgive one another.

Whereas the 1951 film remains faithful to the novel by showing Jarvis shaking hands with black people at Arthur's funeral, a good deal of emphasis is placed on Jarvis's rejection of the black man's hand in the 1995 film. The sequence moves from a close-up of the face of the black man who has approached Jarvis, to a close-up of Jarvis's face; the camera then cuts to a close-up of the black man's hand, outstretched, and to Jarvis's white hands slowly being lowered. Beittel devotes much attention to this difference in his comparison of the 1951 and 1995 films. He argues that

> Unlike the 1951 film, the later version does not initially dramatize Jarvis's metamorphosis at the funeral through the symbolic language of the handshake; it occurs only later, when it is literally announced by Jarvis himself. . . . [In] the name of realism, the second adaptation suffers from a lack of the psychological complexity of character rendered through symbolic language in the first. (2003:83)

It is possible to argue, however, that the 1995 film magnifies James Jarvis's racist and vengeful views not in order to satisfy the criteria of a historical realism, but in order to critique contemporary white notions of retribution and to historicize contemporary black violence. Whereas in the 1951 film James Jarvis immediately rejects the possibility of retribution, saying "What difference would it make?," in the later film, while identifying the body of his dead son, he is made to say: "Bloody kaffirs! Whoever did this, find them, hang them."

The conventional, linear representation of the funeral in both the novel and the 1951 film is replaced with a striking montage in the 1995 film, with cuts between close-ups of James Jarvis's (Richard Harris's) stern face, staring

(continued on page 164)

Figure 5.1
Funeral sequence
from *Cry, the
Beloved Country.*
(Images courtesy
of Videovision
Entertainment)

Figure 5.1 (continued)
Funeral sequence
from *Cry, the
Beloved Country.*
(Images courtesy
of Videovision
Entertainment)

Figure 5.1 (continued)
Funeral sequence
from *Cry, the
Beloved Country.*
(Images courtesy
of Videovision
Entertainment)

at the viewer, and slow-motion scenes of white police brutally beating black people in the townships. Taken as a whole, the funeral scene's effect is to render visible the institutional white violence enacted on blacks during apartheid *simultaneously* to rendering visible the grief of Jarvis at his son's funeral. The film thus suggests that it is not singularly Absalom's act of violence that has made a victim of Arthur. Instead, it shows that Absalom himself, by his association with the black people subjected to police brutality, is a victim of the violence legitimated by the apartheid state. The alteration of the line from Paton's novel that asks, "Who knows how we shall fashion a land of peace where black outnumbers white so greatly?" (clearly the words of a white person), to the question, "So how shall we fashion such a land when there is fear in the heart?" (which could be the words of either white or black), implies that the responsibility of rebuilding the South African nation will be a shared task.

Perhaps the most important way in which the 1995 film could be said to contribute to a discourse of restorative rather than retributive justice is in its focus on the sons—the victims of violence—rather than the fathers. This focus is achieved primarily through the way in which the 1995 film deals with the two scenes of violence around which the novel is constructed—Arthur's murder by Absalom, and Absalom's hanging. The choices made by Roodt in relation to these scenes are thrown into relief when compared with the choices made by Korda in the 1951 film. The earlier adaptation is part of the same historical moment as the novel, and Beittel argues that it "vividly and faithfully follows the novel by portraying black South Africans as innocent but corruptible peasants and white South Africans as misguided but redeemable tyrants" (2003:80), and that it reproduces the paternalistic ideology of the novel. Where the 1951 film does deviate significantly from the novel, however, is in Paton and Korda's decision to visualize the first of the two scenes of violence—that is, of Absalom and his accomplices breaking into Arthur Jarvis's house and Absalom shooting Arthur. By adding this scene, the filmmakers would seem to corroborate the Judge's decision that Absalom is guilty, particularly as the way that this scene is composed and performed suggests that Absalom does not shoot Jarvis purely out of fear, as he later claims in court.

The sequence begins with a medium close-up of Absalom and his two accomplices tying scarves around their mouths. We hear Absalom ask, "Are you sure it's okay?" One of the other men says, "The woman and the children are away—it's only the servant that is there." These comments would appear to remove any intent to murder on the part of the men—they are interested, it seems, only in breaking into the house to steal. However, one of the men does ask Absalom whether he has the revolver, and Absalom nods. A cut to a medium close-up of Arthur writing in his study establishes that there is in fact someone, in addition to the servant, present. Piercing music, similar to that used in classical Hollywood crime films of the 1940s, rises in pitch as the sequence cuts between the master shot in which the men enter the house and quick, insert shots in which Arthur becomes aware of the disturbance downstairs. We see Arthur get up from his desk and the camera tracks with him as he heads downstairs, with the intensity of the music rising; a low, medium shot reveals the house servant shouting "Master!" as one of the men (not Absalom) pulls him by the neck. As Absalom's accomplices run away in the background of the next shot, we see Absalom turn back and crouch down, facing inside the house. While a wide shot of the garden shows Absalom's accomplices running away, a medium close-up shows Absalom, in the house, taking aim and firing the gun. What is clearly established in this sequence is the free choice that Absalom has at every moment: he could refuse to carry the revolver; he could leave the house at the same time as his accomplices; he could choose not to fire.

As in the novel, the scene of Absalom's hanging is not shown, but what is shown is the impact of the death sentence on Absalom and Stephen Kumalo through close-ups of their distraught faces and the sounds of their sobbing. On account of this the authorities might have deemed the film "instructive" to would-be black "criminals." In the 1951 film, then, there is on the whole a visualization and critique of black crime, but a screening out of white violence. It is significant, in this respect, that the scenes that were censored from the 1951 film were those in which Arthur's writings about the white basis to black violence were shown. And even these scenes reveal self-censorship on the part of the filmmakers: James Jarvis is shown *silently* reading his son's manuscripts, or there are stills of certain (carefully edited) pages of the manuscripts. These stills do not focus on Arthur's most provocative ideas, that whites are responsible for "native crime," but on his ideas which attribute "native crime" to the breakdown of traditional black society, and the black exodus from rural areas to the city. It is perhaps for these reasons that the then-prime minister, D. F. Malan, was willing to endorse the film, through his presence, with his wife (who was seated beside Paton), as guests of honor at the Johannesburg premiere. The 1951 film was clearly not perceived to be subversive in any way, and may have been seen as supporting the apartheid policy of creating rural "homelands" for black communities defined on ethnic grounds.

Whereas the critique of white violence is *textualized* in the novel and, to a lesser extent, in the 1951 film, in the 1995 film the white-on-black violence is *audio-visualized* in the slow-motion scenes of police brutality edited into the funeral scene, thus granting this violence its full embodied force. The 1995 film also takes Arthur's words, "native crime is a result of white crime," and repeats them in voice-over until they almost become a refrain, thereby relentlessly historicizing Absalom's act of violence against Arthur. Like the novel, but unlike the 1951 film, Roodt and Singh choose *not* to show the scene of black-on-white violence—Absalom's murder of Arthur. Whereas this scene marks the climax of the 1951 film, the central event of the 1995 film is the scene of Arthur's funeral. Perhaps the most significant choice they make, however, is to show—in vivid and emotional detail—Absalom's death by hanging, which, it is important to remember, is neither described in the novel nor shown in the 1951 film.

In many ways, the techniques used in this final scene mirror the techniques used in the funeral sequence: the filmmakers create what seems to be an audiovisual version of "polyphony," of simultaneous experience. After a scene in which Stephen Kumalo encounters James Jarvis, who expresses his solidarity with Kumalo, we are shown a wide shot of Kumalo walking toward the rising sun in the Ixopo mountains. The music shifts from its uplifting melody, during the encounter with Jarvis, to a poignant melody, slowly growing in volume. At the same time, we hear Kumalo in voice-over, speaking lines from various parts of the novel that amount to a critique of any human institution that takes on the role of God by implementing the death penalty. As the shot of Kumalo cuts into a slow-motion shot of Absalom being handcuffed by two, white, uniformed officials, we hear Kumalo say, "Wise men write many books in words too hard to understand. This, the purpose of our lives, the end of all our struggle is beyond all human wisdom." A blue-silhouetted, slow-motion shot shows Absalom being led toward the room where he will be hanged, and this is followed by shots, also in slow motion, and either in medium close-up, or close-up, of Absalom's face, full of fear. Still in slow motion, the camera lingers on his limbs and his bare feet, and the viewer is asked to pay the closest of attention to the unique details of this beautiful young body about to be rendered lifeless by the hangman. A close-up shot shows a pair of white hands as they pull the lever to open the floorboards beneath Absalom's feet.

It seems remarkable that Beittel would argue that the 1995 film "silences Absalom's death in order to celebrate the triumph of Arthur's life" (2003:86) when the sequence of Absalom's hanging is the most powerful scene, in a haptic, embodied sense, in the entire film. The combination of the close-up of the white hands, and their anonymity (we do not see to whom they belong), conjures a sense both of the individual human agency involved in institutional violence, and the attempt of humans within such institutions to conceal this human agency. In being forced to dwell on the details of Absalom's embodied suffering at the moment of his death, the viewer is confronted with the intensely personalized effect of the sacrificial scapegoat mechanism embedded in a legal system grounded in a notion of retributive justice. Through its embodied power, the scene as a whole works to expose the contradictions of liberalism's simultaneous belief in the Rule of Law and in a policy of nonviolence. And it speaks for a humanism that can embrace equally a white man like Arthur Jarvis, and a young black man who has committed a crime. Absalom is not absolved of all responsibility for his crime, however, even though it is framed by a particular political and sociohistorical context. As in the novel, the Judge asks Absalom why, if he carried a gun only to scare away others, he carried it loaded, and Absalom cannot answer. In this respect the film can be compared with *Fools*, *Tsotsi*, and *A Walk in the Night*, which balance individual responsibility against the determinism of a historicized perspective.

Like Suleman, Hood, and Dube, Singh and Roodt are able to engage in critical commentary relevant to contemporary audiences, even though they have not chosen to proximize the novel's story. The novel itself offers much potential for a critical analysis of contemporary South African society, because as Foley points out:

(continued on page 174)

Figure 5.2
Hanging sequence
from *Cry, the
Beloved Country.*
(Images courtesy
of Videovision
Entertainment)

Figure 5.2 (continued)
Hanging sequence
from *Cry, the
Beloved Country*.
(Images courtesy
of Videovision
Entertainment)

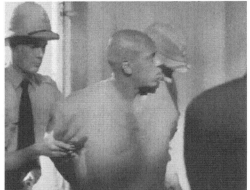

Figure 5.2 (continued) Hanging sequence from *Cry, the Beloved Country*. (Images courtesy of Videovision Entertainment)

Figure 5.2 (continued)
Hanging sequence
from *Cry, the
Beloved Country.*
(Images courtesy
of Videovision
Entertainment)

Many of the problems and debates raised in the novel persist in the South Africa of today as the country struggles to throw off the injustices of the past and to normalise itself. Problems such as unemployment, poverty, insufficient housing, inadequate educational opportunities, as well as, most evidently, the unacceptably high crime rate, remain crucially pertinent. In fact, reading the novel today inspires the uncanny feeling that, in terms of its portrayal of social ills, it might have been written in 1998 rather than 1948. (1996: 89)

The high rate of crime, which often involves extreme and apparently gratuitous violence, has resulted in calls to reinstate the death sentence, which was abolished when the ANC came into power. Roodt and Singh offer a critique of contemporary crime, but at the same time historicize it, and make a powerful case against a retributive system of justice which relies on the further sacrifice of life. In this sense, the film does not, as Berardinelli claims, simply show "the path of tolerance and compassion that the leaders of South Africa have finally found" and thereby "quiet one of Paton's great concerns: that 'when the white man turns to loving, the black man will have turned to hating'" (1995), but is admonitory, warning South Africans against a continuing lack of mutual tolerance. The choice to readapt and remake *Cry* in 1995 thus seems far from arbitrary, and not merely opportunistic.

At the U.S. premiere of the 1995 film, Nelson Mandela praised it for being a "monument to the future," and for bringing to the screen "such strong emotions about the terrible past" (Beittel 2003:70). By calling it a "monument to the future," Mandela suggests that the film concentrates not only on the "terrible past" but also addresses that "unfinished cultural business, unrefinable and perhaps finally unassimilable material that remains part of the cultural dialogue" to which Braudy refers. And by pointing to the "strong emotions" that the film evokes, Mandela recognizes its embodied as well as rational power. It is this power which accounts for the popular appeal of the novel, evident in the response of an early critic, who praises it for doing "what no discursive work in political science, sociology, economics, or anthropology could ever do; it makes us understand 'how it feels' to be a South African [in the 1940s]" (Collins 1953:46).

It is a power also evident in the 1951 film, which, although it makes use of some foreign actors and exhibits a mélange of influences (including that of the classical Hollywood style), contains some remarkable neorealist scenes. Cinematographer Robert Krasker captured the everyday life of people in the rural village of Nokweja (the equivalent of Ndotsheni in the novel) and in the slums of Johannesburg, in Pimville and Sophiatown. Handheld vérité shots show people in the Ixopo hills or in the city, traveling on trains, or trudging to work. We see people huddled at the window of a thatched hut to watch the rain; a woman with braided hair holding a child to her breast. These shots invest the film with deep historical significance, allowing the viewer to see beyond the film's fictional framework, and providing a documentary record of those anonymous people who were living and suffering under a racist white system. It seems that it was because of this real rather than staged indexicality that black viewers tended to be more forgiving of the 1951 film than of the novel. The well-known black South African actor and playwright John Kani says, "I know it is by a white. But we saw ourselves in it." Lionel Ngakane, who plays Absalom, says, "It was about us. It was shot in our locales. We were boys exactly like [the ones depicted in the film], who came from the country [to the city] and couldn't find work" (*In Darkest Hollywood* [film, 1993]). The 1951 film is remembered for catapulting Ngakane into a career as an actor, filmmaker, and founding member of FEPACI, winning for him the title of "Father of Black South African Cinema."

I like to imagine what the impact of the 1995 film might have been if the filmmakers had been more courageous, by casting South African actors in the main roles, and by not resorting to a conventional Hollywood style. As it turns out, their commercial approach did not pay off. The film was not a box office success, although it did achieve good reviews in the United States, Europe, and South Africa, and won the award for best film at the Southern African Film Festival in Harare in 1996 (Beittel 2003:82). From the perspective offered by this book, the film's main achievement lies in its activation of mimesis, bringing together a focus on the sensuous, particular details of Absalom's body at the moment of hanging, and a rational critique of the contradictions of the Law under apartheid. In both instances, the film emphasizes the importance of the individual and draws attention to the question of how the South African community as a whole is to be restored after a system as damaging as apartheid. Furthermore, by concentrating on the sons rather than the fathers, *Cry*, like *Fools*, *Tsotsi*, and *A Walk in the Night*, devotes specific attention to the next generation, to the "inheritors" of apartheid abuse and a tentative post-apartheid hope.

6 Cinema and Violence in Francophone West Africa

We have been the object of the gaze. We don't want to return the gaze, we want to look elsewhere. TEDDY MATTERA, New York African Film Festival (2007)

Colonial Francophone West Africa and the Cinema

After a hurried croissant and a café crème, I make my way down the industrial rue Ferrus and take the escalator up to the French Ministry of Foreign Affairs. It is midsummer but Paris is cold. I take a lift up to the floor on which the Cinémathèque Afrique is housed. Waiting for me in the chilly viewing room beside the Steenbeck flatbed viewing suite are a number of film reels—solitary copies of some of the earliest films made by Africans. As I string up the celluloid into the gates of the Steenbeck to settle in for a day of viewing African films in Paris, my mind cannot help wandering to French filmmakers Alain Resnais and Chris Marker's film *Les Statues Meurent Aussi* (1953). Through confrontational images and a philosophical voice-over, the iconic French directors challenge the way that France has appropriated African art and divorced it from its context. More than fifty years later, one might just as easily ask what most of Africa's early cinematic treasures are doing locked up in a Parisian archive. As the evening begins to set in, I leave the archive, my mind brimming with images from scratched versions of Sembene's *La Noire de . . .* (1965), Ababacar Samb-Makharam's *Et la neige n'était plus* (1966), and Med Hondo's *Soleil O* (1969). After a glass of wine and falafel with friends, I head to the Rue de la Clef, to the Cinéma Images d'Ailleurs, to watch Moussa Sene Absa's *Madame Brouette* (2002), a Technicolor tale of a feisty Senegalese woman defining her own life in the bustling urbanity of Dakar. During one day in Paris, I've been able to see more African films than most Africans have access to in a year. No wonder

Burkinabé director Dani Kouyaté calls Paris the "capital of African Cinema" (cited in Cookson 2003). More accurately, one might call Paris the capital of Francophone African cinema.

Given that the next three chapters analyze films that hail from Francophone West Africa, it is necessary for me to contextualize them within the history of French imperialism and the introduction of cinema to its colonies. Since this chapter mirrors the history of South African cinema, I do not intend to provide a comprehensive history of cinema in Francophone West Africa (which is provided in Diawara [1992] and Ukadike [1994]), but rather to interpret this history through the practice and concept of violence. Since the film medium's invention, France has held the reigns on film production, distribution, and exhibition in its (ex-)colonies. No African living under French imperial control was able to make a film in Africa until the end of colonial rule in the 1950s and 1960s, and the films that were circulated in Africa were European, usually French, films. Rather than restricting what Africans could watch through establishing colonial film units designed to regulate censorship and production (as the British did throughout Africa), the French screened a variety of films with the hope of inculcating French values and a taste for French "civilization."

On the surface, then, the French colonizing authorities were not concerned with preempting "inherent" African violence through repressive censorship, as were the British and Belgian colonizers; they asserted their economic control under the guise of and through the establishment of cultural programs. The republican French ideals of liberty, fraternity, and equality reemerged in the public mindset in 1870, the year in which the Third Republic was instated. Hand in hand with these ideals came France's *mission civilisatrice* (civilizing mission) and the policy of assimilation, the idea that colonial peoples should be made into "black Frenchmen" through the establishment of cultural institutions identical to those in France. As Claire Andrade-Watkins notes, "France's colonial policy of direct rule and assimilation perpetuated the idea that France and the colonies were a *family*, bound by the French language and culture" (1996:113; my emphasis). The complex and contradictory ways in which the French attempted to create a regional Francophone family based on culture, and particularly cinema, will be the focus of the analysis that follows. However, I will also examine the ways in which a regional identity preexisted the arrival of the colonial powers in West Africa, showing that there are multiple sources for contemporary West Africa's emphasis on regional identity and regional filmmaking trends (including the adaptation of canonical literature).

As cinema began its march toward incorporating and integrating diverse cultures into a modern, global visual economy, metropolitan France was attempting to consolidate its overseas "possessions" into one grand French family. One glance at a colonial map shows just how vast the French West African territory was: except for the large, British-dominated countries of Gold Coast (now Ghana) and Nigeria, the French controlled most of West Africa. While the French colonial procedure was more subtle than the undisguised brutality of the Portuguese, British, and Belgian imperial regimes, Conklin assures us that there can "be little doubt that colonization under the Third Republic [1870–1940] was in large part an act of state-sanctioned violence. On the crudest level, the French forcibly 'pacified' those West African groups who resisted colonization. On a more subtle level, French rule rested upon a set of coercive practices that violated their own democratic value" (1997:9–10). What becomes apparent from the fissures in the rationality of the *mission civilisatrice* (ironically built on the principle of rational development) is that the French did not regard the Africans as "brothers," as equal human beings, but as violent barbarians. Conklin cites the words of Gabriel Charmes, a well-known Third Republican journalist: "If France were able to establish itself permanently in North Africa, to penetrate to central Africa, to make its influence felt in the entire Sahara and to win the [Western] Sudan; if in these immense regions where only fanaticism and brigandage reign today, it were to bring—even at the price of spilled blood—peace, commerce, tolerance, who could say this was a poor use of force?" (1997:13).

While Charmes could see "only fanaticism and brigandage" in Africa, Robert Smith has shown in his book *Warfare and Diplomacy in Precolonial West Africa* (1976) how similar West African cultures of violence have been to all historical conflicts. Smith argues that a "fundamental cause of most West African wars—and, indeed, the most prevalent cause of wars in any part of the world—was the desire of the more vigorous societies for territorial expansion and to exercise a measure of physical control over their neighbours" (29–30). What made precolonial West African cultures of war different from certain Western and Islamic cultures of war is that the victors did not attempt to acquire and dominate the losers' land—rather they established a "loose tributary" relationship with the defeated group (30). While it is not my purpose in this book to schematize different forms of national and regional violence, I am interested in Smith's attempt to historicize all cultures of violence—whether they be precolonial West African, colonial European, or imperial Islamic. His work helps us to move beyond the Manichean figuring of violent European colonizers pitted against peaceful African victims; it also clearly banishes the idea of violence being inherent to African cultures and societies. Rather, Smith draws our attention to the universality and multidimensionality of violence, and suggests that precolonial West African wars had the positive outcome of integrating the West African region through continued conflict and coalitions. Similarly, the fact that most postcolonial African conflicts have been intra- rather than interstate has led to a strengthening of regional identity through people's perception that in the dearth of national cohesion, only regional integration will help to solve the violence (Laremont 2002). Given that many intra-state wars are effects of arbitrary colonial borders, one could argue that colonization paradoxically led to the strengthening of a West African regional identity as much as to its destruction.

The French colonization process in West Africa had its own coherence, partly stemming from its universalizing republican ideology, and partly from the pragmatic French concept of *mise en valeur* (rational economic development)—the need to pool human and material resources in West Africa to raise the standards of living. Conklin points out that, "Most of the West African territories were poor and many were landlocked. Administered as autonomous colonies rather than a single unit, Paris argued, they would never prosper" (1997:23). In 1895, the year in which public film shows captured the imagination of audiences in Paris, London, and Berlin, France established the Government General of French West Africa in Dakar, a centralized civilian base for the rule of the federated states of West Africa—the AOF (Afrique Occidentale Française)—they were still attempting to annex. The AOF endured for sixty-one years, until 1956, the year before Ghana became the first West African country to achieve independence. Although Conklin argues that French civil-military tensions and the size and diversity of West Africa conspired to prevent the federation from working, and although Frederick Cooper criticizes the French policy of development for controlling "the extent and the means by which this would come about"

(2005:206), the desire to improve standards of living in West Africa was (arguably) one of the few positive policies it devised. One might therefore posit that although West African regional identity took a violent blow when the European colonizers began to slice up the land into nations after the Berlin Conference of 1884–85, the peculiar form that French imperialism took fortified the regional identity of Francophone West Africa.

It is important to acknowledge, however, how tenacious the bonds were that existed among very different precolonial West African cultures—so tenacious, in fact, that many have survived colonization. People share languages—especially those of the Mandingue family—across the region; most of the areas colonized by the French had been previously colonized by the Almoravid Islamic invaders in the eleventh century and were thus predominantly Muslim; certain institutions, such as the family and the griot, were and are ubiquitously valued; particular violent practices—such as slavery—were widespread in West Africa even before the arrival of the Europeans; and many West African countries share myths of origin and legends, such as that of Soundjata Keïta, adapted to film in Dani Kouyaté's *Keïta! Le heritage du griot* (1995). One might therefore argue that a regional West African identity developed in the precolonial era through exchange and conflict, although this identity was of course by no means monolithic or homogeneous. Whether this wider, regional West African identity or a specific Francophone West African identity is more marked in Francophone West African films can be resolved only by deeper analysis of the history of cinema in West Africa, and of the films themselves.

In his historical survey of black African cinema, Frank Ukadike offers a detailed account of French cinematic involvement in its colonies (1994:30–70). In non–French West Africa, the cinema was initiated through the British Film Units in the Gold Coast and Nigeria, and by British missionaries in Sierra Leone, who used the "Magic Lantern" to try to convince local populations of the "historical reality" of Christ (Ukadike 1994:30). In French West Africa, on the other hand, cinema came hand in hand with entertainment. In 1905 the Lumière brothers' films *L'arrivée d'un train en gare de Ciotat* and *L'arroseur arosé* were screened in mobile cinemas by a French circus troupe in Dakar, alongside animated cartoons. Very little is known, however, about fiction film production in Francophone West Africa in the early colonial period. We know from Ukadike that George Méliès directed

his short films *La marche de Dakar* and *Le cake-walk des nègres du nouveau Cirque* in Dakar and that racist stereotyping of blacks and Arabs was
in evidence already in these films (1994:31). From the "Father of African film
criticism," Paulin Soumanou Vieyra (1969), we know that the Frenchman
Georges Régnier made the black-and-white romance, *Paysans Noirs/Famoro
le Tyran* (1947), in Upper Volta (present-day Burkina Faso). Although this
fiction film was the first to represent Francophone West Africa in a realistic
light, it harbored a colonial message: the story centers on the "rescue" of the
Voltaïque people by the French colonial army from a black despot. In Soudan (present-day Mali), a short morality tale, *Un enfant d'Ireli* (1958) told a
story of Dogon honor.

Much more extensive research has been undertaken, mostly by David
Slavin (2001), in relation to French colonial cinematic production in North
Africa. Although Slavin does not cite Conklin as one of his sources, many
similarities emerge from a comparative reading of the former's work on
North African–French (cinematic) relations and the latter's work on West
African–French relations in the colonial period that might be used to imagine the state of colonial Francophone West African cinema. Specifically,
Conklin's central argument—that France's colonizing system was inspired
as much by cultural and ideological motives as by economic and military
principles—is illustrated beautifully by Slavin's close analysis of a range of
films made in or about North Africa between 1919 and 1939 by French directors. Slavin sees France's *mission civilisatrice* subtly inscribed into the very
weave of these films which, "by disseminating colonial mythology . . . helped
Frenchmen transcend narrow identities and redefine themselves as bear-
ers of civilization to the colonized" (2001:4). Although French colonial policy ostensibly rejected the creation of racial barriers (seeking assimilation
and association rather than apartheid), Slavin makes a strong case for the
way in which racial and gender identities were emphasized and essentialized in French colonial cinema and in French colonial law. Using Algeria
as an example, Slavin shows how in this context white French settlers created apartheid-like laws restricting the movement and liberties of Algeri-
ans. Such racist laws have reappeared in contemporary French society—for
example, in the 1993 amendment of the French naturalization laws (Code de
la Nationalité), which has made it even more arduous for children of foreigners born in France to attain French citizenship. While Slavin distinguishes

between 1920s colonial films which "supported policy goals in Morocco" and 1930s films which "praised the Foreign Legion," ultimately he argues that all French colonial films worked to create a sense of solidarity among whites and to engage the fantasies of whites—and particularly of white men.

In terms of French colonial film distribution and exhibition, more is known about Francophone West Africa. Melissa Thackway points out that the French authorities "preferred to import French films that reinforced perceptions of French moral and technological 'superiority' than to teach or encourage Africans to make their own films" (2003:7). Following World War I an association of cinemas was created in France's African colonies for the distribution and exhibition of imported films only. This association, called COMACICO (Compagnie Marocaine de Cinéma Commercial), changed its name in 1926 to Compagnie Africaine Cinématographique et Commerciale. It was followed in 1939 by SECMA (Société d'Exploitation Cinématographique Africaine). These two companies operated throughout West Africa, and particularly in Francophone West Africa, and even as far afield as the island of Madagascar (Vieyra 1983:18). The former owned eighty-five cinemas, and the latter sixty-five (Barlet 2000:233). Even after independence, COMACICO and SECMA controlled the West African distribution circuits and refused to show African films, although this duopoly was challenged in 1970 by Burkina Faso's nationalization of its exhibition through SONAVOCI (Société Nationale Voltaïque du Cinéma). In 1979, COMACICO and SECMA were replaced by CIDC (Consortium Interafricain de Distribution Cinématographique), an African-managed regional syndicate based in Ouagadougou, Burkina Faso, and which collapsed in 1984 due to incompetence and lack of funding (Barlet 2000:234). Since then, Swiss and French companies or Lebanese cinema owners have tended to control the market, showing Hollywood, Bollywood, and kung fu films.

Although many of the films shown by COMACICO and SECMA had offensive racial and gender subtexts, Ukadike reveals the strange contradictions in which the French sometimes engaged in relation to stereotyping of Africans and blacks on film. He recounts that when D. W. Griffiths' *The Birth of a Nation* was shown in France in 1915, the government immediately banned it "for fear its volatile contents might incite French racists or offend Africans" (1994:32). While the covert reason for this decision was related to French interests in World War I—in which the French employed African soldiers—Ukadike concludes that "this measure is the epitome of 'respect and dignity' toward the colonized, whom they could have easily dehumanized if they had so desired—as in the American example, when, during World War II, German prisoners were treated better than African-American soldiers" (1994:32–33). Ukadike goes on to lament that this action did not mean, however, that the French depicted Africans in a "positive light" in their own films (33). If Africans were not portrayed as violent, they were depicted as embodying obsequious servitude—as carbon copies of the smiling black African face used in Banania advertisements in the colonial period.

Although one can argue, then, that a Bhabhaian type of colonial mimicry is manifest in French colonial films just as much as it is in films like *De Voortrekkers* and *Zulu*, James Genova has drawn attention to the difficulty of applying the concept of mimicry to the colonial French West African context in a Fanonian sense. In *Colonial Ambivalence, Cultural Authenticity, and the Limitations of Mimicry in French-Ruled West Africa* (2004), Genova examines the idea of mimicry from the perspective of the colonized rather than the colonizers. His main concern is the *évolué* class, the French-educated West African elite, particularly as it existed in Senegal, the seat of the French presence in West Africa. Due to its special status within Francophone West Africa, Senegal brought the contradictions inherent in France's assimilation policy into focus.[1] The French found most West African peoples unsuitable to be citizens, meaning that only Senegalese people living in the four "communes"—Dakar, Gorée, Saint-Louis, and Rufisque—were granted French citizenship, while the rest of the West African inhabitants were considered *sujets*. Genova examines the relationship between the *sujets* and the *évolués*, and the way in which the latter participated in the debates around African and French authenticity that took place in the 1910s in Paris and Dakar and which were to determine whether Africans had a right to attain French citizenship. As Genova points out, the debates became more charged in the wake of World War I, in which the West Africans had fought for the French. Both mimicking the French, but also highlighting the paradox between French desires for both familiarity with and difference from their colonies, the *évolués* played a central role in this arbitration. Having to situate themselves "astride the divide between French and African cultures" (Genova 2004:274), the *évolués* contributed to a critique of the assumed authenticity or integrity of both France and Africa. However, in a diplomatic context, the *évolués*, Genova argues, mimicked discourses of authenticity that essentialized Africans as fundamentally rural-based, embodied, and collectivist people. Genova accords responsibility for the initiation of such discourses not only to the colonial authorities but also to ethnographers, and particularly Maurice Delafosse, who wrote numerous books and manuals on West African languages and cultures. Somewhat contentiously, then, it could be argued that it was Frenchmen who helped to author now-outdated African concepts and movements such as *négritude*, coined by Senegalese president Léopold Sédar Senghor, the Martinican Aimé Césaire, and Guianan Léon Damas in the 1930s.

The African film directors who are the focus of this study are diametrically opposed to those Africans who embraced and participated in the *négritude* movement. As Genova elucidates, the very concept of *négritude*— based on a celebration of the "inherent" embodied nature of black people as opposed to the "inherent" rationality of whites—was derived from racist white colonial views that attempted to consolidate what was respectively authentic about Africa and France. Contemporary African directors are concerned with revealing both the embodied and rational nature of African peoples, thereby contributing to the new African "enlightenment" of which many scholars have spoken (Taylor 2000; Wynter 2000). However, African directors have arrived at this position of being able to turn their gaze "elsewhere" only by first working through the implications of colonial and ethnographic filmmaking. While, as I have argued, colonial filmmaking tends to reject the African body, ethnographic filmmaking has always privileged closeness to the African body, leading both to celebrations and critiques of its project. Ukadike argues that, although both the British and French initiated travelogues that were the founding films of anthropological cinema, it was Frenchmen such as Felix-Louis Regnault (the first ethnographic filmmaker) who "opened up new aspects of inquiry that led to a better understanding of diverse cultures" and made of their films "a genuine and well-intentioned endeavor" (1994:45–46). Ukadike would seem to recuperate a moral superiority here for French ethnographic filmmaking, suggesting that while all cultures have been subject to the gaze of other cultures, the *nature* of the gaze is what matters. He praises Regnault's earliest films about Africa—the first showing a Wolof woman making pots, filmed in 1895—for accurately and sensitively portraying African culture for educational purposes (1994:46).

Many other French ethnographic filmmakers followed Regnault to West Africa. In Upper Volta (present-day Burkina Faso), Jean Capron and Serge Ricci examined fishermen's lives and their ritual sacrifices to the gods of the water in *Noces d'eau* (1953). Guy le Moal, director of the Institute of Research of Upper Volta, made many ethnographic films about the religious function of masks among the Bobo-Fing. In Soudan (present-day Mali), Marcel Griaule made films about the Dogon peoples, such as *Au Pays Dogon* (1938) and *Sous les masques noirs* (1938).

Although certain ethnographic filmmakers attempted to exalt the "benevolence" of the French colonizers in West Africa—such as Eric Duvivier and A. Luzuy in *Paysans du Niger* (1959)—others contributed to the origins of an anticolonial French cinema. While it is not my aim here to give a comprehensive analysis of ethnographic film, I want to challenge readings of the most famous ethnographic filmmaker in Africa, Jean Rouch, that situate him as colonial filmmaker. A focus on the work of Rouch also proves that certain ethnographic filmmakers, far from consolidating colonial control, undermined colonial violence through their contribution to a vital, creative, regional culture in West Africa that moved across Francophone and Anglophone borders. In 1941, at the age of twenty-four, Jean Rouch went to work for the Free French Army's public works in the colony of Niger. He befriended many West Africans, marking the beginning of a lifetime devoted to ethnographic research and filmmaking throughout West Africa. Far from confining himself to one area of West Africa, Rouch worked in many different countries and also explored the links between Francophone and Anglophone countries, as in his films on migrancy, such as *Jaguar* (1954).[2] Rouch's role in the development of African cinema has inspired fervent debate: some value his substantial contribution to film production structures in West Africa, while others, including Sembene and Med Hondo, argue that his films regard Africans as "insects." The European critic Gaston Heustrate goes as far as to call Rouch a "paternalistic 'scientist'" (quoted in Barlet 2000:8). Rouch, however, was by no means a conventional ethnographic filmmaker; not only did he encourage collaborative filmmaking, but he also launched certain Francophone West Africans into filmmaking careers, such as Oumarou Ganda, the Nigerien director who starred in Rouch's film *Moi, un noir* (1958), and the first African woman director, the Senegalese filmmaker Safi Faye, who starred in *Petit à Petit* (1968). It would be too simple to condemn Rouch's films on account of Rouch's identity as a white Frenchman and anthropologist who came to learn about and film black Africans. It is possible to analyze his films in a way that does not align them with the general patronizing attitude toward Africans evident in French colonial films, but as deeply complex and collaborative works, owing some of their authorship to Africans themselves. Rouch referred to his own work as "shared anthropology" due to the fact that he developed his subjects and scenarios in collaboration with the Africans with whom he worked (Feld 2003:87).

Les Maîtres Fous (1954), a film that Frank Ukadike severely critiques for presenting Africans as savages (1994:50–51), offers a perfect example of the complexity of Rouch's film work and its contribution in particular to the debate on violence, colonialism, and mimicry in African history. The film is about the Hauka, a cult that was active across West Africa from the 1920s to the 1950s. The Hauka was made up of men and women who became possessed, went into a trance, and took on the roles of typical white colonial figures, such as the governor general, the engineer, the doctor's wife, and the corporal of the guard. It is believed that the Hauka was founded by a Nigerien man who fought in World War I and who, on returning to his home village, entered a trance during a ceremony and took on the role of a white soldier. Although *Les Maîtres Fous* was filmed in Ghana (then the British colony of the Gold Coast), many of the participants in the cult were migrants from Niger. The French authorities were ruthless in their attempts to suppress the cult in Niger, as were the British authorities in the Gold Coast. Rouch was invited to film one of the meetings of the cult on a farm, which he juxtaposes with footage of the cult members in their "normal" lives, working for the *travaux publics* or as fishermen. While the images of the cult members entering trance are quite graphic and disturbing (we witness them eating a sacrificed dog), Rouch alerts viewers to the reasons for showing these images in his preface to the film. He writes:

> The producer, on presenting to spectators these documents without
> concession or dissimulation, warns them of the violence and cruelty
> of certain scenes. However, he wants to allow spectators to participate
> completely in a ritual which is a particular solution to the problem of
> readaptation, and that indirectly shows how certain Africans represent
> our Western civilization.

The final words of this preface ("how certain Africans represent our Western civilization") offer the key to analyzing the film—this film is not so much about Rouch's gaze, but about Rouch attempting to replicate faithfully the Haukas' gaze. In other words, this film offers a reversed gaze of Africans at Europeans and could, as such, be called a "reverse ethnographic" film.

In the first place, Rouch was invited by the Hauka to film the event, so the Hauka were fully complicit in the existence and organization of the film. Second, the film offers a view of an excess mimicry that becomes an act of resistance to colonial rule in that it goes much further than Fanon's concept of polite, civil mimicry, and Bhabha's concept of mimicry in civil colonial discourse. Here we have men who mimic not the supposed rationality of the colonial masters, but—as Rouch's title indicates—the madness, the irrationality of the colonizers. This act of mimicry reveals, in a very powerful way, that the colonial enterprise—of both the British and the French—was in fact uncivil and irrational to the core. Through Rouch's film, then, we have access to a resistant, anticolonial form of mimicry on the part of the colonized themselves—not through discourse, but through a performance with their bodies. Such an interpretation of the film contradicts Ukadike's statement that Rouch's films could be safely exhibited because they were not subversive.

The first screening of Les Maîtres Fous proves that the film was entirely subversive. Rouch presented the film at the Musée de l'Homme in 1955 and audiences were utterly shocked by it. The film was promptly banned in Britain and the Gold Coast, but it won the Grand Prix at the Venice Biennale. Criticism of the film came from Africans and colonial powers alike: Africans (reading the film at face value) claimed that the film reinforced racist images of Africans as savage beasts, while colonial powers (predictably) objected to the disrespect colonial figures were shown by the Hauka participants. As Rouch has subsequently pointed out, the Hauka was a purely colonial phenomenon—as soon as colonial power subsided, the possession rituals stopped. In voice-over in the film he reminds us that, "There was never a Hauka called Kwame Nkrumah." In other words, the Hauka was a violent ritual spun from the web of colonial violence itself: the Hauka members were not inherently violent or savage; their behavior held up a mirror to the violence of the British and the French in West Africa. Rouch's voice-over throughout the film suggests that the ritual was a release from the humiliation of colonial oppression.

What is so striking about Rouch's film in the body of anticolonial cinema is that it critiques both French and British forms of colonial rule. Other anticolonial French films tended to focus solely on French rule. In the first French anticolonial film, *Voyage au Congo* (1927), director Marc Allégret follows his uncle André Gide's travels in the Congo. Notably, the film grew out of Gide's book of the same name in which the author harshly critiques the French colonial system. After Allégret's film, the French government in 1934 introduced the Laval Decree, which required that any film to be made in France's colonies first be approved. Nevertheless, a few more anticolonial films did come to fruition, all by Frenchmen rather than Africans. IDHEC (Institut des hautes études cinématographiques) student René Vautier's *Afrique 50* (1950), which documented anticolonial uprisings in the Ivory Coast and Upper Volta (present-day Burkina Faso), was banned in Africa and in France (Ukadike 1994:49). In 1952, Présence Africaine commissioned Chris Marker and Alain Resnais to make *Les Statues Meurent Aussi* (1953), which Sembene called "the best film ever made on Africa, colonization, and traditional art objects." It was banned for ten years (Ukadike 1994:49). Although filmmakers such as Vautier and Rouch were keen to develop Africans' filmmaking skills, the Laval Decree meant that the first West African filmmakers had to make their first films in France rather than on African soil. Mamadou Touré's short film *Mouramani* (1953) and the Africa Film Group's *Afrique Sur Seine* (1955) were both made in France. The latter film, no doubt inspired by Rouch's work, reversed the ethnographic gaze of Europeans at Africans and observed Africans and Europeans living in Paris. In the postcolonial period, however, West African filmmakers quickly rejected an approach that merely "reversed" the gaze in lieu of one that turned the gaze resolutely onto Africa itself.

Cinema, Violence, and Adaptation in Contemporary West Africa

Francophone West African cinema has endured a continuing neocolonial relationship with France since independence was gained in the late 1950s and early 1960s. In a study of France's cinematic relationship with its ex-colonies in Africa from 1961 to 1977, Andrade-Watkins examines whether it was "neocolonialism, paternalism, or a genuine effort to assist in the development of an autonomous and self-sufficient African cinema" that led France to set up the Ministry of Cooperation (in 1961) for its ex-colonies, and through it, the Bureau of Cinema (in 1963), which resulted in the production of 125 of the 185 African shorts and feature films made by 1975 (1996:112). Andrade-Watkins reveals how the Bureau's "investment" in African filmmakers, through providing financial and technical assistance, has been a dubious resource for filmmakers who have agonized over whether they have a truly independent cinema, free of compromise to French values, or not.[3] Although the situation improved a great deal between 1969 and 1977, Andrade-Watkins concludes that unfortunately the ultimate goal of the Bureau seems to have been the "continuation of Franco-African cultural hegemony, no more, no less" (1996:126). She labels the political independence of the 1960s a "*de jure* independence" and laments that the French colonial policy of assimilation has not disappeared, but has instead been "rearticulated, reappearing under the guise of *cultural expression*" (ibid.).

Since 1977 the situation does not seem to have improved. As Burkinabé director Dani Kouyaté explains, "It's rare [for us] to make films alone these days. . . . The [postproduction] labs are over there in the West and it's not possible for us to work without Westerners" (quoted in Cookson 2003). Postindependence Francophone African governments have also posed a problem, however. They have failed to provide state funding, and they have also continuously censored African films, supposedly on sexual and religious grounds, but generally with political ends in mind (Boughedir 1995). Diawara argues that the possibility of national production has been obstructed by African governments' "repression of counterhegemonic views or alternative hegemonies" (1992:80). Souleymane Cissé was imprisoned on account of making *Den muso* (1975), which was critical of Moussa Traoré's regime in Mali, and Sembene's films that are critical of neocolonial practices in Senegal, such as *Xala*, or of Islamic practices, such as *Ceddo* (1976), have been censored or banned. It was in fact in part owing to pressure by censorious and fearful African governments that France's Bureau of Cinema halted its assistance to filmmakers from their ex-colonies (Andrade-Watkins 1996:125). In 1984, the Ministry of Foreign Affairs began a new program of funding and support called Le Fonds Sud Cinéma. While it has led to the production of many African films, it has been controversial in that it finances films from non-African countries as well, reducing the amount of funding available.

Perhaps as a response to criticism, in 2004 the Ministry created a fund specifically for African film, the Plan Images Afrique program.

According to Diawara, French neocolonialism continues under the guise of the European Economic Community (EEC). On the one hand, Diawara points to the fact that the EEC has "begun to erode France's power to sustain bilateral economic, political, and cultural relations with francophone Africa, which guaranteed the steady production of a certain kind of African film" (2000:81). On the other hand, he argues that the French have actually succeeded in reproducing "Francophonie" at the level of the EEC by referring African film projects submitted in Paris to Brussels. He argues that, along with "social problem films" that have been funded by European organizations that "thrive on portrayals of Africa's tragic situation" (2000:84), the films funded by the EEC are interested in African images only at the level of anthropology—as images of the "reality" of Africa. This is a movement that prevents African films from being seen *as* films—as works of art that have an equal role to play on the world stage of culture, and that have critiques to offer that are aimed at the entire globe. It is against knowledge of such neocolonial structures that we must approach the history of film production in independent Francophone West Africa, just as it is important to bear in mind that South African filmmakers' "national" focus may be a result of state objectives rather than subjective desires. Nevertheless, it is heartening to note that, in spite of the effects of neocolonial domination by the French funding bodies and by African governments, a strong Francophone West African cinema has existed, whereas Anglophone West African cinema has, until recently, been scant. One could argue, then, that France did bequeath something of cinematic value to its ex-colonies, whereas in Ghana and Nigeria the burden fell on individuals (such as Sean Graham and Segun Olusola) to maintain and try to exploit the resources of the old Colonial Film Units (Diawara 1992:5–9). Furthermore, although Francophone West African directors have complained that French funding bodies have favored certain filmmakers (such as Sembene and Abderrahmane Sissako), at least the French have placed importance on the need for African directors. In the early days of independence in Ghana and Nigeria, on the other hand, Ghanaians and Nigerians relied on foreign production companies and directors, not believing in the potential of their own people.

While a number of films, such as *Mouramani* and *Afrique sur Seine*, were directed by Africans during the colonial period, the first film to be directed by an African on African soil was Ousmane Sembene's *Borom Sarret* (1963), made only three years after Senegal gained its independence from France. One might expect that this film would concern itself with critiquing Africa's colonial oppressors, or perhaps the way that colonizers used cinema itself as a tool of domination. It is, however, a quiet film, simply about a day in the life of a poor donkey-cart driver in Dakar. Not a single white character appears in the film. What the film critiques is the class divisions in recently independent Senegal itself, and it juxtaposes various scenes of exploitation. As Manthia Diawara comments, "Sembene evinces a critique of postindependence regimes such as Senegal which, in his view, had failed to include men like the *borom sarret . . .* in the modern state in Africa" (2000:83). Diawara points to other West African films—such as Souleymane Cissé's *Finye* (1982) and Sembene's *Guelwaar* (1992)—that "enfold in their narratives the discourse of dignity, self-reliance, and the failure of African governments to uphold these values" (2000:83). It is this approach—of turning away from the West as "evil Other" to critique instead Africa's *own* failures (however much they are inherited from the colonial era)—that sets West African filmmakers apart from other early so-called "Third filmmakers." Instead of founding a cinema based on Fanon's concept of revolutionary violence, as did many Latin American filmmakers, certain West African filmmakers founded a cinema based on critique—and, more than that, on self-critique, on what Barlet calls "introspective criticism." As Sembene says, "The filmmaker must live within his society and say what goes wrong within his society" (quoted in Pfaff 1984:15). Embodied cinema is not sufficient, according to Sembene; critique is only made possible through rationality, and vice versa. In an interview, Sembene has said, "through nothing more than just supplying these people with ideas, I am participating in their awareness" (Perry and McGilligan 1973:40). As I hope to show, this "introspective criticism" is particularly marked in West African film adaptations of canonical literary texts where the very provenance of the term *canonical* is interrogated, and the gaze is not directed so much at Europe as at Africa.

It is natural that the first African films focused determinedly on Africa. If the initial step by Francophone West African filmmakers toward the creation of an "African Cinema" was the rejection of early colonial images, the second step was claiming the right to make ethnographic images of their own people. Souleymane Cissé has said that his film *Yeelen* (1987), the first African film to win a prize at the Cannes Film Festival, was "in part made in opposition to European ethnographic films" and that he "wanted to make a response to an external perception, a perception by white technicians and academics, an alien perception" (quoted in Barlet 2000:8). In this way, Cissé suggests that his film responds to a crisis of representation—to the idea that, as Stam and Shohat have expressed it, stereotypes stem from the "powerlessness of historically marginalized groups to control their own representation" (1994:184). At the same time, Cissé implies, through the term "in opposition," that his film is an act of postcolonial appropriation through which he is reclaiming the right to gaze at his own people. The third step that West African filmmakers have taken, however, is to turn away altogether from responding to alien perceptions.

When Clyde Taylor speaks of the shift in African cinema to a new "enlightened" language that shows "relative indifference to the European gaze as something to be feared or avoided" (2000:140), all of the three films he analyzes hail from Francophone West Africa. One of the films is Senegalese director Djibril Diop Mambety's *Hyenas/Hyènes* (1992), which might be situated at the origin of the trend of Francophone West African adaptation of canonical texts. In part based on the Swiss writer Friedrich Dürrenmatt's modernist play, *The Visit* (1956), and in part on the story of a character Mambety had previously conceived in his film *Touki Bouki* (The journey of the hyena) (1973), *Hyenas* tells of the return of an elderly millionairess, Linguère Ramatou, to her home village of Colobane. During the course of the film, we learn that Linguère Ramatou initially left Colobane when her lover, Draman Drameh, rejected her after she became pregnant. She has therefore returned to Colobane with a mission: in exchange for her riches, she wants Drameh to be killed. The villagers at first reject this inhumane proposition, but slowly their greed overwhelms them: they begin to accept "loans" and gifts from Linguère Ramatou, they try to encourage Drameh to take his own life, they increasingly use the rhetoric of morality to rationalize their greed for Ramatou's promised fortune, and—in the final scene of the film—in an act of collective ritual violence, they devour Drameh, the scapegoat, like a pack of hyenas, leaving nothing behind but his clothes. This scene is remarkable in its visualization of the sacrifice: the villagers, all dressed identically in old rice bags, encircle Drameh, humming as they slowly move toward him, obstructing from view the act of killing. It is only as the villagers disperse that the viewer sees Drameh's heap of clothes, the absence of his body.

Taylor and Kobena Mercer read *Hyenas* as symbolic of a mode of African filmmaking that addresses a universal humanity. Furthermore, Diawara's acknowledgment of the film's magical realist genre—as opposed to Sembenian social realism—would seem to confirm this intended global audience. Taylor argues that "[the] film is singular in leaving no ideological or sociological space for any viewer to hide, African or foreign, black or white, female or male, in witnessing the moral crisis of contemporary humanity from an African viewpoint" (2000:142–43). Mercer agrees with Taylor's reading, but goes further in making the following comment about the film's particular relationship, as an *adaptation*, to its source text: "The universality of the narrative resides not in the translation into an African context of a European story originally set in a Swiss village, but in the way Mambety observes the human capacity for violence when shared responsibility is instead polarised onto the scapegoat within the logic of retributive justice" (2000:146). Mambety's film draws self-confidently on Dürrenmatt's play, not so much appropriating it as using its insights to critique violence both in Africa and throughout the world, wherever individuals or communities have been scapegoated in the metonymic displacement of violence and retributive justice. Mambety himself says that *Hyenas* "tells a human story to the whole world" (2002:125). In this sense, *Hyenas* is representative of a mode of filmmaking that is evident in the work of many contemporary West African filmmakers, and particularly in the work of the West African film adapters analyzed here. It has by no means been an easy road, however, to the validation of a film such as *Hyenas*, with its use of a foreign source, as profoundly "African."

There has been a long history of film scholarship that has debated the definition of African cinema, and its styles and sources.[4] Diawara identifies several important and related issues that have preoccupied African filmmakers and film critics since 1955, and which, it is implied, might be the means of establishing the identity of African cinema. The first issue concerns the content and aesthetic style considered most appropriate to the broad political goals of African filmmakers. Diawara draws attention to the mandate for films made in a social realist mode, and which would challenge neocolonialism, that the Second FEPACI (Fédération Panafricaine des Cinéastes/Pan African Federation of Filmmakers) Congress of Algiers in 1975 attempted to impose on African filmmakers in pursuing its interest in film as a tool of political and cultural development:

> [The FEPACI decided that] filmmakers should question the images of Africa and the narrative structures received from the dominant cinema. The question for the FEPACI was how to insert film as an original fact in the process of liberation, how to put it at the service of life, ahead of "art for art's sake." . . . It was in this light that several filmmakers condemned *Le bracelet de bronze* (1974) by Tidiane Aw and *Pousse Pousse* (1975) by Daniel Kamwa for being overwhelmingly spectacular and less committed to demystifying neocolonialism. On the other hand, the films of Sembene, Med Hondo, and Mahama Traoré were praised for deemphasizing the sensational and commercial aspects and emphasizing the instructional values. (1992:42)

Diawara is critical of the narrowness of the Second FEPACI mandate, clearly modeled on Solanas and Getino's 1969 manifesto. While he has recently charted what he sees as the development of West African cinema from the social realist or Sembenian mode identified and praised at the Second FEPACI Congress, to the postmodernism exemplified by Mambety's films of the 1970s, to the "griotic narrative" mode of films featured at FESPACO in 1995, he by no means adopts a prescriptive stance. He argues that "there are variations, and even contradictions, among [African] film languages and ideologies, which are attributable to the prevailing political cultures in each region, the differences in the modes of production and distribution, and the particularities of regional cultures" (2000:81). He suggests, therefore, that to associate the notion of a political or critical cinema with films made in a particular aesthetic mode no longer resonates with African film criticism.

Rather than debate the political value of certain aesthetic categories, Diawara has called for practical measures in which West African states might "adopt a regional imaginary and promote the circulation of goods and cultures which are not sequestered or fragmented by the limits imposed by the nation-states." He argues that, "What is urgent in West Africa today is less a contrived unity based on an innate cultural identity and heritage, but a regional identity in motion which is based on linguistic affinities, economic reality, and geographic proximity" (2000:82). In this way, Diawara calls for the development of a West Africa focused on contemporary issues rather than on the past. In that he imagines "a new map of West Africa" with all seventeen countries included and "with Dioula (also known as Bambara, Mandinka, and Wangara), English, French, Hausa, and Yoruba as the principal languages of films," Diawara emphasizes the need for a West Africa that will begin to supersede its colonial heritage (2000:82).

Given that more than forty years have passed since political independence was gained in the various West African countries, and given the new currents in cultural production in the region, the term *postindependence* does not seem to be relevant today in the way that *post-apartheid* is still relevant, and useful, in South Africa. It is difficult, for example, to speak of a coherent postindependence culture in the West African countries in the way that one can conceptualize, theorize, and debate what constitutes post-apartheid South African culture and cultural practice. There is, of course, an equivalent problem in defining the postcolonial on a purely temporal level, where changes inevitably brought about over time proceed at different rates and in diverse ways in distinct geographical spaces. It follows that, if the colonial configurations running across West Africa are waning in importance—not historically, since the colonizers' mark is tragically indelible, but in relation to African writers' and filmmakers' contemporary concerns—then the terms *Francophone*, *Anglophone*, and *Lusophone* are perhaps also beginning to lose their valence. Thackway has summarized the critique that has been leveled at these terms owing to the way they give rise to the problematic assumption that Africa is identifiable and knowable according only to its colonial histories (2003:1–2). Thackway nevertheless continues to use the term "Francophone" as a way of grouping the films in her study, not to uphold the "primacy of France/French as a cultural reference," but as a way of reflecting the "real convergences in the region that arise from common linguistic ties, a shared legacy of French colonization, and the inheritance of convergent political and economic structures and continuing (neocolonial) ties with France" (2003:2).

Both Diawara's and Thackway's points are valid and require acknowledgment. Since the three adaptations that will be the focus of my analysis here were all made by directors who hail from countries that were colonized, in different measure, by France (Senegal, Mali, and Cameroon), I have deemed it necessary to take into account West Africa's history of French colonialism and neocolonialism. Similarly, I have attempted to show that the particular form French imperialism took may be one of the reasons why a strong regional culture of filmmaking has developed in Francophone West Africa, leading to trends such as the adaptation of canonical texts. Francophone West African identities are crosscut, however, by national allegiances, with Diawara arguing that Africans still "fight, kill and die" for the nation-state, and that people's passion for soccer, music, and film is appropriated for nationalist causes and creates negative competition among West African states (2000:82). At the same time, it is possible to discern a concerted local effort to rehabilitate a dynamic West African culture that transcends national and colonial boundaries. Kolawole Owolabi points out that this effort has already manifested itself in the founding of ECOWAS (Economic Community of West African States) in 1975, which has "the objective of integrating the nation-states of West Africa and thereby serving as the 'vanguard integration scheme for other subregional groups in Africa'" (1996:82). Owolabi argues that this kind of integration is an attempt to foster the kind of regional interactivity—through agriculture, trade, and shared language and culture—that was "seriously disturbed by the colonial experience" (85), with the balkanization of West Africa into nation-states. Notably, contemporary violence in West Africa is also being addressed through regional rather than national frameworks. The suppression of violent conflict has been delegated to two bodies within ECOWAS: ECOWARN (ECOWAS Warning and Response Network) and ECOMOG (ECOWAS Monitoring Group). The former organization monitors peace and conflict, with a focus on preemption and prevention, while the latter operates as an association of West African armies that can intervene in national and regional conflicts. There is also a need to address forms of violence other than civil war, however, such as the recruitment of child soldiers, gender violence (in particular female circumcision and the abuse of so-called "witches"), religious conflict, continued hegemonic violence through Western institutions and companies such as Shell, and a certain degree of violent crime. Corroborating Owolabi's point that political and economic integration must be preceded by cultural rehabilitation (92), contemporary West African films are playing the role of critiquing such violence, as in *Moolaadé* (Senegal/Burkina Faso, 2004), *La Nuit de la Vérité* (Burkina Faso, 2005), *Bamako* (Mali, 2006), *Ezra* (Nigeria, 2007), and *Teranga Blues* (Senegal, 2007). They are showing that film is an important site through which people might begin to rehabilitate and reimagine Africa in general, but also rebuild West Africa's regional imaginary. With the failure of national cinemas in West Africa,[5] the argument has followed that there "cannot be a viable African cinema on the national level alone. There can only be on the regional and inter-African level" (CIDC cited in Diawara 1992:82).

While the term *Francophone* is useful in certain ways, it can only dubiously be attached to the film adaptations studied here, given the diversity of languages featured (Wolof, Bambara, French, and English), the range of settings (Île de Gorée, northeastern Mali, and Zimbabwe), the varied nationalities and ethnicities of the actors (Wolof, Bambara, and South African), and the diversity of their concerns. These film adaptations critique not only the violence of colonialism and neocolonialism but also U.S. global imperialism, the Atlantic slave trade and its effects, the Almoravid invasions that in the early eleventh century brought most of West Africa under Islamic control, forms of violence that have their roots in "traditional" West African culture (such as particular forms of gender violence), ethnic and religious conflicts, and forms of violence that have developed syncretically, as a result of these multiple forces. They are therefore concerned with collective identities on a much broader basis than simply the "national." Although West African film adapters have, like South African adapters, drawn on their own national literature[6] as well as their own texts[7] and "familial" texts,[8] they have also transformed intra-national performance texts,[9] texts from other nations in their region,[10] texts from outside their region,[11] Western texts which may be used not in their entirety but adapted only in part,[12] and—of course—canonical texts. West African filmmakers can thus be seen to be participating in the definition and redefinition of individual, familial, communal, national, subregional, regional, and continental identities—in other words, human identities, through the practice of adaptation. Where the adapters of canonical texts differ from many of their fellow West African adapters is that they turn to books written before the colonial era that have been upheld as the foundational texts of Western art, religion, and philosophy.

The trend of adapting canonical texts in sub-Saharan Africa appears to have arisen largely in West Africa in the 1990s, some thirty-odd years after sub-Saharan Africans began to make their own films. Whereas the first celebrated African authors, such as Chinua Achebe and Ngugi wã Th'iongo, quickly turned to the adaptation and deconstruction of canonical texts such as Joseph Conrad's *Heart of Darkness* (1902), African filmmakers spent their first thirty years seeking out *African* inspiration for African images—thus African oral tales and African literary texts were popular sources for the first African films. There was a vivid excitement in these years about the possibility of creating unmediated African images of Africa on the screen, whereas it was accepted that literature in non-African languages was already mediated. It is somewhat surprising, then, that in the 1990s certain filmmakers did begin to turn to canonical texts. As I have already mentioned, this interest in canonical sources in West African cinema seems to have been taken up more recently in South Africa, with some similar and even identical sources.

The radical infidelity with which the filmmakers are treating such sources allows for the rethinking of assumptions around the fidelity criterion in film adaptation theory, and also of postcolonial theory's assumptions about the use of foreign sources in African artistic production. As I have stressed, in film adaptation theory, until recently there has been resistance to—or at least suspicion of—infidelity. Part of this resistance is due to the preoccupation in film adaptation studies with adaptations specifically of canonical texts and the attendant investment in the preservation of "high" culture. On the other hand, postcolonial theorists have theorized the use of canonical texts by African artists in terms such as "repudiation," "appropriation," and "going mainstream" (Marx 2004). *Repudiation* can be defined as an oppositional stance in which writers attempt to rid themselves of reliance on any non-African source; *appropriation* as the anticolonial and postcolonial strategy of rewriting the oppressive configurations of racial and gender identities in certain canonical texts (particularly *Heart of Darkness* and *The Tempest*); and *going mainstream* as the alteration of old canons by new canons which incorporate postcolonial literature (Nixon 1987; Bowen 1993; Marx 2004). It would appear that contemporary African artists have been subjected to a tremendous amount of pressure to (re)turn to the repudiation stance, rejecting all use of foreign sources and/or languages in African writing and filmmaking. *U-Carmen eKhayelitsha* (2005), for example, came under attack from the South African Minister of Arts and Culture, Pallo Jordan, who has argued that African filmmakers should be drawing on African rather than European sources (Donaldson 2000:21).

In the first instance, the radical infidelity of the West African films analyzed here poses a problem for film adaptation concerned with the preservation of "high" culture. In Africanizing the narratives of the texts, these films challenge the Western barrier between high and low/popular culture, a distinction that does not generally exist in Africa. These films are radically unfaithful to such a degree that in many instances they are only loosely related to the source text, meaning that the chapters that follow will be shorter on the whole than the South African ones, in which it was possible to do closer, comparative analysis. In the second instance, the particular choices made by the West African filmmakers as to which canonical texts to adapt and how to approach them renders questionable whether these texts are conventional canonical texts at all, and whether they in fact belong to the "West." In reviving many of the anxieties expressed in the original, Joseph Gaï Ramaka's *Karmen Geï* interprets *Carmen* as a text profoundly concerned with class, racial, and gender differences at a time in French history remarkably similar to the West African present. Cheick Oumar Sissoko's adaptation of the Old Testament challenges Western assumptions that his film is a rewriting of solely the Christian narrative and correctly relocates the Book of Genesis as the shared property of Islam, Christianity, and Judaism. And Jean-Pierre Bekolo takes Aristotle's concept of "mimesis as difference" at face value and engages with the *Poetics* in such a tenuous way that the film can only provisionally be called an adaptation. These films cannot, then, be easily classified as conventional adaptations of canonical texts, as repudiations, appropriations, or as "going mainstream." They are much more comfortably grouped with popular West African cultural forms that, Barber argues, are "open and incorporative in mode, and . . . hospitable to foreign elements" (2000:6).

The trend under analysis reveals that West African filmmakers do not fear the Western gaze, but self-confidently assume their right to critique human culture and practice at large, with whatever sources or tools they feel are useful. As Dani Kouyaté says,

> The question is whether or not you alienate yourself by using a given tool. I try to make use of a tool intelligently, to achieve what I want to achieve. That's what matters—using it without selling one's soul, by making unavoidable concessions, by adapting. Our ancestors used to say, "When the rhythm of the music changes, the dance must change too." It just so happens that the music has changed today. (Quoted in Barlet 2002b)

In a similar way, the film adapters studied here adapt to and reclaim canonical literary texts, questioning their allocation to the sole ownership of a mythical "West." Instead of meekly adhering to the meticulously defined canonical categories and lineages established since the Enlightenment, these filmmakers are turning to canonical texts to resituate them as part of human heritage. They thus align themselves with postcolonial theorists who critique Eurocentrism while refusing to banish Western frameworks altogether, thus showing an interest in "developing contestatory dialogues between Western and non-Western cultures" and between competing rationalities (Young 2001:65–66). It is true that, by radically revisioning the texts, these filmmakers to some extent "shoot back" at Europe, through critiquing colonialism and the cultural hegemony it imposed on much of Africa, as well as continued forms of neocolonialism and global imperialism. For non-African viewers to see canonical texts refashioned from this uncompromising African point of view could be said to correlate with what Taussig describes as "the unsettling confrontation of the West with itself as portrayed in the eyes and handiwork of its Others" (1993:xv). At the same time, however, West African filmmakers adapt these texts self-confidently and self-critically, through a profound focus on African localities and an assertion of Africa's place within human history.

The African Viewing Public

Like South African filmmakers, West African filmmakers are vocal about the fact that they find adaptation particularly attractive due to its potential for making written literature accessible to non-literate African audiences. Sembene informed me in an interview that he wishes to make films for his own people, and sees film as a pedagogical, political, and social tool. He stated that reaching a wider audience among his own people in Senegal was his primary reason for adapting his literature to film. With a non-literacy rate of 55 percent for men and 74 percent for women, Senegal does not have a large reading public (Gugler 2003:vii). In 1965, the time around which Sembene made his third film, and second film adaptation, *La Noire de . . .*, not even 1 percent of Senegalese women had been taught to write or even to speak French (Pfaff 1984:114). This is one of the reasons that West Africans have become infatuated with film, television, radio, music, and football.

However, many of the film adaptations analyzed here have not had much chance to reach the African publics at whom they are aimed, making it necessary to explore briefly the state of film distribution and exhibition in contemporary West Africa.

It is impossible even to mention West African cinema today without invoking "Nollywood," southern Nigeria's thriving video film industry, and its spin-offs across the continent. Participants at African film conferences across the continent in 2007—from FESPACO to the Zanzibar International Film Festival—have heatedly debated "Nollywood"'s example. In spite of Nigerian video films' notoriously poor quality, "Nollywood" represents the first industry in sub-Saharan Africa to succeed in creating a large domestic audience for African film and thus sustainable funding. "Nollywood" has not only been popular in Nigeria; the films have rapidly spread across the continent, and to the diaspora, and are being enjoyed and appreciated by Africans everywhere. The films can be bought at shops, stalls, hairdressers, and through illegal vendors all over the continent, as well as in other parts of the world. This popularity has led M-Net, South Africa's first pay-TV company, to program Nigerian films on their Africa-wide channel, Africa Magic.

It is important to acknowledge, in the first instance, that the video film explosion has its origins in earlier forms of popular art in Africa, and particularly in Yoruba traveling theater (Jeyifo 1984; Barber 2000) and Igbo Onitsha Market Literature (Adesanya 1997:18). Barber, as I have already mentioned, defines popular art as equally constituted by producers and consumers, and says that it "can be taken to mean the large class of new unofficial art forms which are syncretic, concerned with social change, and associated with the masses" (1987:23). As opposed to "people's art," which Barber argues is "the spontaneous expression of the ordinary people who have not yet been conscientized," popular art "furthers the cause of the people by opening their eyes to their objective situation in society" (1987:7). In terms of contemporary film production, we reach something of an impasse here: for while the Anglophone West African industry is revitalizing the connection between producers and consumers, it has largely been concerned with entertainment and profit-making, and has sanctioned retributive violence (Haynes 1997; Meyer 2003; Ogunleye 2003). On the other hand, the Francophone West African and South African filmmakers discussed here are concerned with social change and the critique of violence, but most of them

have not adequately anticipated the chasm between their type of film production and African audiences.

The Nigerians who founded "Nollywood" very astutely analyzed the
social, political, and historical climate in their country. Having been colonized by the British, Nigeria and Ghana had very little in the way of film
structures bequeathed to them and, except for a handful of celluloid productions, a film industry still did not exist in the 1980s. Furthermore, finding that the government film bodies and the Nigerian television stations
were not going to provide financial support, Nigerians had to devise a way
of producing their own films: hence their budgets of only US$6,000–9,000
and their shooting schedules of only a week or two. These filmmakers also
cleverly realized that the demise in cinemagoing would increase their own
audiences: due to political unrest and conflict in Nigeria, night curfews, and
violence against women, people stopped attending cinemas in the 1980s and
preferred to watch videos in the safety and comfort of their own homes. This
trajectory has a gendered dimension to it: although Yoruba men see movie-
going as a family affair, Igbo and Hausa men prefer to socialize outside the
home on their own, meaning that the possibility of leaving their wives and
children with video entertainment at home has had great appeal (Adesanya
1997:19).

It is of course much cheaper for people to own televisions, VCRs, and
DVD players than to attend the cinema, the factor largely responsible for the
immense popularity of Nigerian films across the continent. In some contexts, people would like to attend the cinema for the "big-screen" experience
(Larkin 2002), but cinemas are fast disappearing, not only due to unprof-
itability but also neocolonial structures. As Abderrahmane Sissako has
pointed out, his film *Bamako* may not be widely seen in Mali, where it was
filmed, since "in 1990 the big financial institutions forbade the government
to subsidize culture and forced the state to sell the [cinema] theaters," meaning that there are only three cinemas in Mali today whereas there were forty
previously (2007). In his critique of the gap between African films and African audiences, Barlet alerts us to the decline in numbers of cinemas across
the continent: Ivory Coast, which used to have seventy-five cinemas, now
only has thirty; Guinea-Bissau has only ten; Namibia only seven (2000:237).
More than this, however, Barlet stresses the atrocious state in which many of
these cinemas exist. Privatization is not helping the situation, but is abetting

the conversion of cinemas into shops and supermarkets (Barlet 2000:238). The devaluation of the West African currency, the West African CFA franc, in 1994, meant that the film exhibition industry became even more untenable since ticket prices had to be raised. The rise of religion throughout West Africa has also resulted in many cinemas being bought off and converted into churches and mosques.

The alternative to the "big-screen" experience is the video hall, which is growing in stature and popularity throughout Africa in spite of its frequent involvement with piracy. The most fascinating example of the video hall is perhaps in East Africa, in Uganda, where 650 halls now exist. A star system is developing around people known as "VJs" (video jockeys), who do live translation into Ugandan languages of the dialogue in the films (often entirely reinventing the films' plot lines). One of the only ways to keep the "big-screen" experience alive, according to Barlet, is for African filmmakers to accompany their films to cinemas, which has been shown to greatly improve the box office takings and which also ensures that the filmmaker receives his/her money after the screening (2000:241). This practice has its antecedent in the ciné-bus, which used to take films into the rural areas (ibid.). Certain filmmakers, such as Sembene, even used to take their films into the villages by means of bicycle. Village screenings on mobile airscreens continue today and are wildly popular: at the Zanzibar International Film Festival (ZIFF) in 2007, the laughter and cheers from the audience of a free screening outside of the Old Fort (a Portuguese colonial relic) practically drowned out the film being projected inside the fort for which the wealthier audience had paid.

In spite of the difficulties of distributing and exhibiting African films in Africa, the "Nollywood" example shows that there are alternatives. The enjoyment that audiences are continuing to derive from screen media— whether it be in traditional cinemas, in video halls, or at home—also suggests that optimism about the future of African film in Africa is not misplaced. Film festivals such as FESPACO, ZIFF, and Journées Cinématographiques de Carthage (in Tunisia) have thrived against great odds, and new festivals have sprouted up in Rwanda ("Hillywood") and Uganda. Nevertheless, the vital questions about the distinction between "popular" and "people's" art which Barber raised in 1987 have not been resolved, and merit ongoing debate.

7 Losing the Plot, Restoring the Lost Chapter

Aristotle in Cameroon

I was sure that if our world inspires pity and fear, it's not by
accident. Like an alchemist, Aristotle resigned [*sic*] that mixing
pity and fear would produce catharsis that would save us all from
violence. I looked to the Bible for a way out. There I was condemned
for the Original Sin. Not only that, God had put a curse on the
black man. JEAN-PIERRE BEKOLO, *Aristotle's Plot*

Cameroonian director Jean-Pierre Bekolo's second feature film, *Aristotle's
Plot* (1997), opens with Bekolo relating in voice-over that he has been commissioned by the British Film Institute (BFI) to make a film for its "Century of Cinema" series. Asked by his grandfather who else will contribute
to the series, Bekolo mentions names such as Bernardo Bertolucci and Jean-
Luc Godard, highlighting the irony surrounding this request for an African filmmaker to make a film celebrating cinema's centenary, when Africans
began making their films sixty years after Europeans and Americans. Bekolo
chooses to begin his parodic account of the history of film twenty-three centuries ago, "at the root of European storytelling—Aristotle's *Poetics*," thereby
producing an "adaptation" of Aristotelian philosophy into a contemporary
African context. Bekolo thus situates African cinema—with its complex and
troubled relation to European and American film, and to colonial and neocolonial history—within the ongoing debate on art and mimesis.

Within film theory in general there has been a continuing debate about
the aesthetic relationship of cinema to the other arts, and particularly to
theater, sculpture, painting, and literature, a debate essentially orchestrated
around concepts of intertextuality and mimesis. Film adaptation theory
could be seen to have developed out of this debate, and it has focused in particular on film adaptations of canonical literary texts. Recent works on film
adaptation classify adaptations according to canonical authors (for example
Shakespeare or Jane Austen), canonical auteurs (Stanley Kubrick or Akira
Kurosawa), or oeuvres (adaptations of classics) (Naremore 2000; Sheen 2000;

Cardwell 2002). In the piece of voice-over quoted above, Bekolo reflects on the limitations of adapting canonical texts in Africa. He looks to the "Great Books" in history for an explanation of the "pity and fear" inspired by "our world" and for a means of salvation from its violence. Rejecting the fatalistic alchemy of Aristotelian tragedy, he turns to the Bible, only to find that the "black man" is to blame for it all. The violence of "our world," of Africa in this case, is, in this view, inherent in Africans, meaning that there is "no way out." As Sylvia Wynter has argued, secular discourses of evolution have not helped to remove the stain, the dead-end for Africans, since "the source of evil now came to be sited in humankind's postulated enslavement, not now to *Original Sin*, but rather to the random and arbitrary processes of bio-evolutionary Natural 'selection' and 'dysselection' [*sic*]—with all peoples of African descent wholly or partly thereby being, in consequence, lawlikely [*sic*] inscripted as the ultimate boundary marker of nonevolved, dysselected, and therefore barely human, being" (2000:36).

Considered in such a bleak light, what might canonical texts have to offer the African film adapter? After all, to what extent will Africans be able to activate their own imaginaries through such texts when Africans have been subordinated and ridiculed in the fantasies and imagination of the West for centuries? Is imagination yet another Western invention that can only be *re*claimed by Africans, or is this very idea itself a Western conspiracy of sorts? Bekolo struggles with such thoughts, but he also seeks out the possibilities involved in an African adaptation of Aristotle's *Poetics*. He praises Aristotle as a writer of "how-to books which are extremely poetic" (2002:220), suggesting that what *Aristotle's Plot* imitates or adapts in its mixing of discursive and mimetic modes is not the content of the *Poetics*, but its ways of knowing. Bekolo engages discursively, in voice-over and dialogue, and audio-visually, through allusion and parody, with the Bible, Hollywood cinema, and African film history. The film performs, in this way, a kind of wide-ranging visual literary and cultural critique, and the point has been made that *Aristotle's Plot* therefore belongs not only to the corpus of African cinema but also to the body of theoretical work *about* African screen media (Shea 1988), which is why I include it first in this second section of the book. The explicit philosophical commentary of Bekolo's film places it at the extreme end of a spectrum of strategies of adaptation in African film, and of the three West African adaptations analyzed here, it is the one that is most self-reflexive about adapting canonical or foreign sources, thereby contributing to this section in both a mimetic and discursive sense.

Choosing to engage with what is recognized as the foundational text in the canon of Western literary criticism, Bekolo enters a millennia-long debate about the function of the arts, and about the nature and the role of mimesis. The debate is ongoing and complex, but if one asks what the *Poetics* might mean to Bekolo, and also to members of local audiences exposed to the canon of literature and philosophy through a Westernized education system, the significant features would have to be the structure of drama, the emotions of pity and fear elicited by the experience of watching tragedies, and Aristotle's apparent rebuttal of Plato's view that poetry is dangerous because of its capacity to arouse the base, irrational emotions. More broadly, it seems possible to say that the *Poetics* has come to be regarded as the initiator of a tradition in which there is a focus on audiences and their responses to art, and a focus on the epistemological worth of the emotions aroused by art, thereby producing a link between the aesthetic and the ethical.[1] Furthermore, given how loose his adaptation is, Bekolo appears to take for granted that mimesis, apparently involving the study of similarity and resemblance, paradoxically demands also the study of alterity and dissimilarity. Aristotle is, after all, the founding figure in a lineage of philosophers and theorists (Erich Auerbach being the one exception) that have devoted their attention to the gaps and elisions implied by the very definition of mimesis. There emerges a tacit acceptance of the impossibility of exact replication in both nature and art, and a preoccupation with the notion of the imperfect copy.[2] This is, of course, a tradition to which Adorno's concept of mimesis has contributed in important ways.

Modeling his approach on that of the *Poetics*, then, Bekolo produces a playful and provocative performative criticism of the role of cinema in African contexts, and thereby achieves what a book on the same topic cannot achieve. Bekolo's criticism, like my own, focuses on mimesis and violence in film, but, situating African film in relation to the culture industry, it goes beyond the boundaries I have set for my analysis and requires that I go back to Adorno's commentary on mimesis and the cinematic medium. In arguing that film adaptation has the potential to offer a critique of violence, and that this potential is enhanced in certain African contexts by the active roles of both producers and spectators, I have been conscious of using Adorno's concept of mimesis against the grain of his views on film as medium. I have had to bracket Adorno's views on adaptation: his argument that "all mass culture is fundamentally adaptation" (1991:58) in that it offers the consumer "predigested" products in a process of *two*fold reification; his claim that a sense of conflict is absent in the experience of watching "a filmed version of a novel" where everything is predetermined, and events are denied "the power of the oppositions involved" and "the possibility of freedom within them" (1991:62).

I have claimed exemption from Adorno's criticisms of film and of adaptation by drawing attention to the radical infidelities of these adaptations, and to their location within African popular culture that operates in certain kinds of public spheres. My analyses have been framed by my argument that these films have a marginal status, situated outside, or on the periphery of, the global culture industry, as defined in philosophical terms by Adorno (1991) and Wynter (2000), and in anthropological terms by Powdermaker (1950). The "dream factory" of Hollywood takes center stage in Bekolo's film, which highlights Africa's location within the contexts of global capitalism and postmodernity. This fact brings me face to face with Adorno's most forcefully expressed criticism of film as the preeminent medium of the culture industry, and of adaptation and Baudrillardian repetition as the prototype of mass cultural products. Whereas the other films analyzed here offer a critique of violence in specific historical and geopolitical contexts, Bekolo's film makes no mention of a particular African country (we learn from the credits that it was filmed in Zimbabwe and that most of its actors are South African). The fact that the film is in English seems to be less a commercial move than a deliberate reference to globalization and film's relationship to it. While Bekolo might seem to be nodding, in this way, to modernity's modes of (decontextualized) repetition, we might also read his film—the only one analyzed here that disengages completely from the idea of the "national"—as the first African film to address the whole continent about the impact of imported screen violence on African viewers.

The dynamics of African film production, distribution, exhibition, and reception are portrayed with sharp wit in *Aristotle's Plot*. Bekolo's humor is trained on the fictional character Essomba Tourneur (known as "E. T." in the film), an African *cinéaste* (filmmaker), typically returned from Europe, wheeling film cans around in a trolley, and referencing the difficulties of trying to make films in Africa, with its paucity of production facilities. Bekolo also extends his humor, however, to African spectators, enthusiastic about playing an active role in the creation of their own cinema, yet nevertheless enthralled by imported Hollywood films. In such a way, Bekolo references U.S. trade policies that ensure that Africa receives a huge proportion of U.S. film exports. Although the United States allows less than 13 percent of its domestic film market to consist of "foreign films" (most of these being European films made under the auspices of U.S. studios), half the profits made by multinational film companies (most of these, once again, North American) derive from screenings in the Third World (Hondo 1996:40). Burkinabé filmmaker Dani Kouyaté laments that African films cannot compete with North American films for screen space in Africa, since North American films have already made large profits in the United States and Europe before they reach Africa, and can thus be sold to cinemas at insignificant rates (cited in Cookson 2003).

E. T.—named, of course, to reference both the Hollywood character and the alienation of the *cinéaste*—has the naïve ideal of bringing "quality African cinema" to the African public. His main opposition is a group of gangsters who are obsessed with imported action films. These gangsters, nicknamed after real-life stars such as Van Damme, (Bruce) Lee, and Schwarzenegger, are led by "Cinema," who has earned this name from watching ten thousand films—none of them African, he says, since African films are "shit." The episodic plot follows the confrontations between these two warring parties (E. T. and the gangsters) as they endeavor to take control of the single cinema in town. Shootouts and chase scenes abound, in a parody of kung fu and Hollywood action films. The viewer is guided through these scenes, and alerted to their irony, by the commentary of E. T., who represents Bekolo himself.

The absurdly repetitive cycles of violence enacted by the gangsters (and which the Law, represented by a lone policeman, can do nothing to curtail) are presented as the effect of the gangsters' adaptation to what they see on the screen, and in this sense Bekolo's film can be read as endorsing Adorno's, Powdermaker's, and Wynter's views on the culture industry. In "The Schema of Mass Culture," Adorno argues that, in the context of the culture industry, mimesis no longer becomes the means for critique and takes the form of gestures emptied of meaning as viewers "fasten on the culture-masks proffered to them and practice themselves the magic which is already worked upon them. They become a collective through the adaptation to an over-mastering arbitrary power" (1991:82). Although in "Transparencies on Film" Adorno is more forgiving of the film medium, and suggests that a "liberated" form of filmmaking which could "enlist . . . collectivity in the service of emancipatory intentions" may exist (1981–82:204), he continues to make statements such as: "The movements which the film presents are mimetic impulses which, prior to all content and meaning, incite the viewers and listeners to fall into step as if in a parade" (ibid., 203). Bekolo's film shows how the violence of a non-African context is metonymically displaced onto an African context via a globalized culture industry, but his critique extends also to African viewers, who are shown to be particularly susceptible to the mimetic effects of film. In an interview Bekolo describes how gangs of young people gather outside the cinemas in Douala after viewing kung fu and Hollywood action films, and says that "it is here that violence seen in the movies is acted out" (2000:27). Toward the end of the film, a radio news program announces that "no one in Hollywood is dying," implying that local viewers are unable to distinguish between life and these cinematic images of violence. Similarly, Bekolo includes numerous scenes in which he frames the spectators who are watching films, thereby asking the viewer of *his* film to reflect on his/her position.

If the on-screen spectators are shown to be acting out an imported script, Bekolo himself expresses a sense of being circumscribed by an agenda not of his own making, thereby raising the question of whether repudiation, appropriation, or acceptance of foreign sources is necessary:

> The question of influence is an important one and, God knows, I'm not immune to it as evidenced by my use of Aristotle's formula or my inclination for Hollywood. Sometimes I don't seem to be myself; I seem to lose control because my whole project is structured by someone else's formulation. Such ambivalence generates the type of engaging debate that I'm advocating here for the African cinema. (2002:26–27)

It must be acknowledged that *Aristotle's Plot* is a jumbled parody of the gangster, western, and action film genres, enjoying its mimicry as much as its critique of these forms. However, it is not the first African film to engage such genres in this way, meaning that, paradoxically, it is as much an adaptation of

African gangster films as of American genres. Already in 1966, the Nigerien director Moustapha Alassane made *Un Retour d'un Aventurier*, a 30-minute African parody of a western. And in Malian-Mauritanian director Abderrahmane Sissako's *Bamako* (2006), when the villagers turn on the television at night, they are presented with a mock western called "Death in Timbuktu" starring a range of filmmakers and actors (such as Zeka Laplaine, Elia Suleiman, and Danny Glover). The random shooting of women and children is shown by Sissako to inspire laughter and clapping from the viewers.

The way in which Bekolo uses the *Poetics* demonstrates that the integration described by Adorno is neither universal nor complete. *Aristotle's Plot* suggests that the very distinction between high and low art necessary to Adorno's claims holds little relevance in many African contexts. Nevertheless, more so than *Karmen Geï* and *La Genèse*, which refute fidelity to and appropriation of their sources, *Aristotle's Plot* juggles with the concepts of repudiation, appropriation, the mainstream, fidelity, and universality. Bekolo both positions his film in a tradition of Aristotelian-inspired storytelling and, at the same time, expresses his anxiety about its being subsumed by an imported culture, in the same way that the responses of local audiences are controlled by an imported culture industry. Thus E. T. comments that

> A plot has a beginning, middle, and an end. But I still wasn't sure which chapter I occupied. I suspect the decision to invite me to celebrate the centenary of cinema could only be a subplot, 23 centuries old. Aristotle's plot. I was already trapped in the narrative my grandfather warned me to avoid.

At FESPACO 1995 the only way in which the centenary of cinema could be "celebrated" was through a retrospective of colonial films that were almost a century old. Although the retrospective was important in that it reminded people of their historical oppression, it would also seem precisely to "trap" people within a plot—the plot of Western cinema's history—that is alien to them. Rather than merely succumb to this entrapment, Bekolo decides to work out into which chapter of the *Poetics* he has been forced, and how to reinsert Africans into their own chapter. E. T., at first following Aristotle's principles to the letter, comes to wonder then, "why Chapter Two of the *Poetics* is missing"—Chapter Two being, of course, the "lost" chapter on comedy.

Bekolo restores what is missing, as it were, by means of his parodic approach, endorsing his African perspective that "humor and satire are basic elements of culture" (2002: 229). Indeed, Bekolo's chief criticism of the *Poetics* is that, while it addresses tragedy—a genre of importance in African storytelling—it does not deal with comedy (Bekolo 2000:26).

E. T. eventually comes to reject Aristotle's notion that his story should necessarily "inspire pity and fear" or induce a cathartic response in audiences. E. T. compares Aristotle's tenets with those of his grandfather,[3] who, he says, would liken the effects of catharsis to those of chewing on a kola nut (a slightly narcotic foodstuff), and catharsis itself to "the sweetness and bitterness of life." The film as a whole constitutes a refusal of the assumption that, as the only African participant in the BFI's project, Bekolo should make a film that deals with tragedy and violence, or give preference to evoking an audience's emotions of pity rather than its sense of humor or its intellect. By refusing to make a tragedy, Bekolo holds to his argument, expressed in an interview, that there is a subtle and perhaps unconscious conspiracy among funding bodies that provide money particularly for documentaries about "tragic" African situations (what Diawara calls "social problem" films). These kinds of documentaries, Bekolo argues, find easy exhibition on television in the West, and in this way "tragedy is pushed on Africa" and Africa is "manufactured" as a tragic and violent place (2002:220). Bekolo believes that this is in part what is "keeping [Africa] down" and he offers the counterargument that "Africa is everything but tragic" (ibid.).

The fact that this short film (70 minutes) of very uneven quality, with poor lighting and sound, and with many of its actors pulled in off the streets, has elicited a fair amount of critical commentary is testimony to the fact that popular culture in Africa is not identical with a culture industry. Perhaps predictably, *Aristotle's Plot* has generated some debate as to the "adequate critical-theoretical apparatus" for approaching a film such as this (Haynes 1999a:26). Again predictably, Bekolo's film has been categorized as postmodern—no doubt the easiest way to account for its stylistic features, its parodic approach, and its reliance on paradox. Evidence of the unsettling effects of its comic aspects are evident in Haynes's comment that "Bekolo's verbal riffs on the soundtrack often follow a trajectory towards nonsense; so does the film as a whole, with its concluding dumb jokes about life and death in cinema, as if seeking to shed responsibilities by plunging into the ludic" (1999a:38).

Operating from a particular "postmodern postcolonial" paradigm, Haynes categorizes the film in terms of a postmodernism defined as endorsing the ludic/nonsensical at the expense of the responsible/rational, and negatively contrasts Bekolo's "popular" project with the "original revolutionary project of African film" (1999a:40). While he recognizes that "Africans have reason to be distrustful of postmodern postcolonialism as another foreign regime that tends to compromise crucial projects" (1999a:21), he is skeptical of African film criticism that continues to "be dominated by Third Worldist terms of cultural nationalism, sometimes inflected by Marxism" (1999a:23). He argues that the hybridity of Bekolo's films demands a theoretical paradigm which acknowledges that Bekolo is "a cagy and attitudinous guerrilla roaming the postmodern globalized mediascape" (1999a:27).

Certainly, some of Bekolo's cinematic tactics do seem postmodern in a Euro-American way, and Bekolo has openly acknowledged his use of American and European cultural forms and film styles. Bekolo opens his first feature film, *Quartier Mozart* (1992), with a hybrid performance of language that mimics Spike Lee's *She's Gotta Have It* (1986). *Quartier Mozart*, like *Aristotle's Plot*, is hybrid both in its characterization and its use of language. It presents culturally hybrid characters, such as Atango, who is a graduate of the Sorbonne, and sexually hybrid characters, such as Queen of the Hood and Myguy. It is linguistically hybrid in the way that it embraces and transforms French for its own imaginative ends. In addition to the oral performance of French, the actual French in the film is inflected with local words that lend it a new flavor—words such as "gombo," which means a good plan. The characters also use French words whose meaning has been transformed in the African context. For example, "drapeaux"—or curtains, in French—is the word used to describe people whom you just pass on the street without noticing. A "bordelle," which refers to a brothel in French, in Cameroonian French becomes a "woman of little virtue." It becomes impossible, in the final analysis, to decide what is authentically French or Cameroonian. Just as *Aristotle's Plot* confidently uses, struggles with, and transforms *The Poetics*, *Quartier Mozart* confidently uses, struggles with, and transforms French and European influences in general (the reference to Mozart being a clear example, and one shared by Ndebele in his story "Mozart: The Music of the Violin," adapted by Dube). These films thus seem to work within the postcolonial realm that stresses the intercultural or the transcultural—the "mutuality of cultures in the colonial and postcolonial process" (Ashcroft et al. 2000:119).

Whereas Haynes refers to Bekolo's style as a "postmodern visual assault" (1999a:29), the critic Clyde Taylor wants to interrogate the efficacy of the terms "postmodern" and "postcolonial" for African films—even for films as daring as Bekolo's (2000). In this way, he echoes the common concern with how to construct an appropriate theoretical and critical apparatus for analyzing African cinema. Taylor argues that postcolonialism and postmodernism as fields of study developed outside of Africa, and are thus not applicable to African screen media. He argues that the "shoe-horning of African reality within the frames of Europe-centered history satisfies a need of the colonizing mentality" and that the notion of an African postmodernism is absurd (2000:136). Even more pointedly, Taylor critiques postmodernist theory for "racism by default"—in other words, racism by exclusion or "dysselection," referring to the work of Barthes, Derrida, Foucault, and Kristeva. In his own criticism, Taylor attempts to answer difficult questions about African film without relying on the application of what he calls "alien terms." He sees Bekolo's style of filmmaking not as postmodern but as popular—an attempt to move beyond African films about the rural condition and to make films that will speak to an urban African public. He thus locates *Aristotle's Plot* within that "newer film language" of African cinema that shows "relative indifference to the European gaze as something to be feared or avoided." He proceeds to point out the ways in which the playful sexuality of *Quartier Mozart* has its origins not in Western cinemas but in prior African films, such as *Visages des Femmes* (Désiré Ecaré, 1985) and *Bal poussière* (Henri Duparc, 1988). Nevertheless, Taylor has to admit that Bekolo does unabashedly reference "Western, modern languages, themes, and values" (2000:140). He also finally concedes that "there is no denying the mutual involvement of Africa and Europe over the last four centuries and the overwhelming significance of this involvement for African social development, otherwise one takes the position that slavery, colonialism, and neocolonialism had a negligible impact on African people" (136). Haynes, on the other hand, argues that Bekolo's references are decidedly and liberatingly postmodern, taking into account that Bekolo has worked as a music video director, studied screenwriting with Christian Metz, worked in both France and the United States, and has talked about the profound influence of Spike Lee on his films (1999a:27). Haynes thus argues that in *Quartier Mozart* and *Aristotle's Plot*, the "First World is always present as a source of technology, commodities, and styles, and as a place to go, but it is not a controlling force . . . the dynamic of colonization is really over. Agency is all with the Africans, mostly involving structures they make themselves" (1999a:29).

In his films, Bekolo would appear to assume his prerogative to draw on, adapt, and critique a range of sources and models. All of Bekolo's films have involved a dose of both mimicry and mimesis, although his models change. Olivier Barlet points out that Bekolo's most recent film, *Les Saignantes* (The Bloodletters, 2006), is "a rewriting of [poetry], not only in its aesthetics but in the way it renews and reconstructs Africa's image and more precisely that of the African city" (2007). Barlet exempts the film from a Baudrillardian repetition, arguing that "*Les Saignantes* isn't the result of an imagery that can be reproduced endlessly, whose mercantile intentions the video clip and advertising reveal. On the contrary, this astonishing, provocative, impertinent, fun, and perfectly paranoiac film develops a real poetry" (2007). *Les Saignantes*, like *Aristotle's Plot* before it, cannot be associated with the mass reproductions of the culture industry. This is not to say that Bekolo thinks he will always succeed in his attempts at mimesis. In *Les Saignantes*, Bekolo reflects in voice-over on his own attempt to appropriate the science fiction and detective genres: "How to make a science fiction film in a country that has no future? How to make a detective film in a country where you can't hold an inquiry?" Ultimately it is the African public sphere—the economic and sociopolitical realities that Africa faces, and the modes of production and reception that have been preserved—that isolates African forms of adaptation from the mass culture industry.

Bekolo's adaptation of the *Poetics* engages with one of the foundational texts involved in the exercise of European cultural domination and offers a strong critique of contemporary American cultural domination. In this way, the film can be aligned with a postcolonial project that has as its goal the making visible and critiquing of new forms of imperialism. The acknowledgment that forms of power, identity, and knowledge are always emergent has led to a view of postcolonialism which frees it from the deterministic sense of the past inscribed in the "post" and focuses on the present and the future in what has been called "an anticipatory discourse" (Childs and Williams

1997:7). This is a discourse which could be said to have an affinity with modernism's project of ongoing enlightenment as this was conceived by Adorno: as Bernstein points out, "Adorno's primary concern was not with the future of art but with salvaging those elements most under threat from enlightened reason: sensuous particularity, rational ends, a substantial notion of individuality, and authentic happiness" (1991:19). It is possible to argue, then, as Taylor does, that African films be measured "not simply by their contributions to the ideological advancement of African political consciousness, as in the past," but by their contribution to "an African enlightenment that has been under way for a century," an enlightenment that "has much to offer the world . . . in correction of the exclusionary humanism of Euro enlightenment" (2000:140–41).

Bekolo's film is a cautionary reminder of the extreme vulnerability of the kind of cultural practice that I describe in this book, but it also makes explicit the tenacity that is implicit in the kind of creative endeavor of all the filmmakers considered here. Toward the end of *Aristotle's Plot*, the gangsters join forces to build a new movie-house called the New Africa. As they put together bits and pieces of old and new materials, the leader of the gangsters, Cinema, says: "We'll take what we can get. If it's old and it's good, fine. If it's new and it fits, excellent." Standing back to admire the new movie-house, a bricolage of multicolored fibers and fabrics, Cinema says: "*This* is the real Africa." In one of the final pieces of voice-over, E.T. celebrates a hybridity representative of the dynamic, site-specific modernities of contemporary Africa, in a way that suggests that, more fundamental than Bekolo's concern with the cinema, is his concern with Africa's survival. Bekolo's film, along with all the films analyzed here, is a testimony to the positive effects of mimesis in keeping African identities alive. In the final analysis, E.T. situates Africa within the world at large, within a humanist universe: "Is there anything in this cinema which is not African? Fantasy, myth, we got. Walt Disney, we got. Lion King, we got. Massacres, we got. Comedians, music, we got. Paul Simon, we got. Aristotle, catharsis, and kola nut, we got. What don't we got?" By Africanizing the origins of cinema in this way, Bekolo critiques the protectionist attitude of certain African leaders who believe that African filmmakers should draw only on "African" sources. Cinema, opera, and the monotheistic religions may not be indigenous to Africa, but Bekolo, Ramaka, and Sissoko—among others—have Africanized them to the extent that they now belong also to Africa and its cultures. Beyond this, Bekolo's, Ramaka's, and Sissoko's films have a vision to offer not simply to Africans, but to the world at large. As Abderrahmane Sissako says, "Without wanting to be pejorative, I would say that white people have had the privilege of seeing others without being seen for three thousand years. Today, Africans are making films, they can project their gaze elsewhere, outside their continent. I consider that a priority" (quoted in Thackway 2003:200).

8 African Incar(me)nation

Joseph Gaï Ramaka's *Karmen Geï* (2001)

Carmen has achieved mythical as well as canonical status through the countless literary, musical, theatrical, and cinematic adaptations of Prosper Mérimée's novella (1845–1847) and Georges Bizet's opera (1875). Each of the adaptations inevitably offers an interpretation of *Carmen*, and, in addition to these performative interpretations, there is a large body of critical work that offers responses to the novella and/or the opera through various disciplinary discourses. It is therefore almost impossible to approach the original without preconceptions, and *Carmen* has been, in this sense, subject to the process that André Lefevere calls refraction, that is to say, a canonical text that may be largely known through versions other than the original (1984:217). With regard to cinema alone, the University of Newcastle upon Tyne's Centre for Research into Film and Media (CRIFAM), which undertook a three-year research project to identify all the films inspired by *Carmen*, has located seventy.[1] Among these is *Karmen Geï* (2001), by Senegalese filmmaker Joseph Gaï Ramaka, purportedly the fifty-third film adapter of *Carmen*, but the first African to envision Carmen in any form. His film was followed shortly afterward by Mark Dornford-May and Pauline Malefane's South African version of the opera, *U-Carmen eKhayelitsha* (2005), showing that the West African trend of adapting canonical texts to film has inspired a similar trend in South Africa.[2]

When asked why he chose to adapt *Carmen*, Ramaka reveals his familiarity with both Mérimée's text itself, and with various refracted versions of the story:

Carmen is a subject that has been treated in every language, and I asked why not in my culture and language. But the real reason [for choosing *Carmen*] was that I grew up in St. Louis [a city in Senegal] surrounded by women: my grandmothers, my aunts, my cousins, who had a bearing that I found again in Mérimée's text. This Spanish woman [Carmen], so strong and free, with a sense of freedom pushed to the extreme, I often found again in those women who surrounded me, and who continue to surround me. Thus, I had no desire to search elsewhere. When I saw the different versions of *Carmen*, such as Godard's film [*Prénom Carmen*] or *Carmen Jones*, I found incarnations of Carmen that I already knew. (Quoted in Barlet 2001)

Two points of interest emerge from Ramaka's response. The first is his "Why not?" attitude to the idea of an African *Carmen*. He implies that if *Carmen* can be adapted in Germany, England, or the United States, there is no reason why it should not be adapted in Senegal. He does not suggest that his version is an attempt to subvert or appropriate the story in the service of a discourse of racial politics or postcolonialism, and if this *had* been his agenda, he would have been more likely to have a black Carmen confront the white historians, ethnographers, and critics who have attempted to explain and circumscribe her (particularly as her dark complexion is a mark of her Otherness in the original). His version of *Carmen*, as will become apparent, is strongly anchored in Senegalese culture.

The second point of interest is the way in which Ramaka, in describing his experience of strong and free women as the source of his personal affinity with the story, appears to locate his adaptation within the discourse of feminism. It would, however, be reductive to approach the film solely through the discourse of feminism, although this, along with the discourse of cultural politics, is one of the interpretive frameworks most commonly applied in readings of the novella and the opera. I will argue that Ramaka's *Karmen Geï*, like Ndebele's "Fools," stages an encounter between different modes of cognition. I will also argue that it works against the imposition of critical discourse, and, in doing this, *re*performs many of the thematic and aesthetic "anxieties" of the first version of the story and the opera, thereby challenging interpretations of the original *Carmen* as a racist or patriarchal work.

Peter Robinson (1992) and Susan McClary (1992) both situate the novella and the opera as fundamentally in dialogue with nineteenth-century French culture. Mérimée's *Carmen* was first published in 1845 in *La Revue des Deux Mondes* (Review of the Two Worlds), set up initially as a travel journal devoted to providing the "civilized 'world' of France" with accounts of "exotic landscapes and adventures in what today we call the Third World" (Robinson 1992:1). Robinson describes this context as follows:

> For several decades, French culture had manifested a fascination with
> history: the desire to rediscover the truths of the past, to place France at
> the head of a continuum of scientific progress, to assert its supremacy over
> lesser cultures. . . . This agenda was coupled with a fascination with the
> exotic, the bizarre and the supernatural, often resulting in stories very
> much like *Carmen*: stories in which a sober, high-minded French narrator,
> representative of French superiority and civilization, visits an area alien to
> him and reports upon what he finds. The events reported will always in
> one way or another surpass those he could live himself as a rational,
> dispassionate Frenchman. (1992:1)

McClary describes Bizet's context in similar terms, drawing attention to his attraction to "exotic subject matter" (1992:17) and to the "Orientalism" that was in high fashion in France at the time (33). She also highlights the fact that many of Bizet's works have narratives that include a *femme fatale*—also a preoccupation in late-nineteenth-century French cultural production (18).

Mérimée's *Carmen* received little attention on its publication, and it was Bizet's opera that elevated *Carmen* to fame (Robinson 1992:1). Bizet had to struggle to convince one of the directors of Paris's Opéra-Comique, Adolphe de Leuven, that his adaptation of Mérimée's text was not too scandalous for the stage (McClary 1992:19). De Leuven's fears were confirmed when the first audiences of the opera voiced their racism and sexism in their written criticisms of Bizet's work. As McClary notes:

> At the heart of each of the original reviews—whether pro or con,
> moralistic or stylistic—lies some crucial notion of difference. Comettant,
> Lauzières, and Banville focus on differences of gender, race and class—the
> intrusion of female sexuality, an unwashed "Orient," the music of low-life
> dives—and the violated integrity of both *opéra-comique* as genre and the
> Opéra-Comique as institution. (1992:115)

The initial reactions to the opera in Paris diverged remarkably, however, from those at *Carmen*'s premiere in Vienna. Whereas those in Paris had noted "difference" *within* the opera's diegesis—the aesthetic tension between its "Wagnerian" and "non-Wagnerian" elements, and the narrative tension between its "lascivious" heroine and "victimized" hero—those in Vienna delighted in the opera due to its being *entirely* foreign, as either "French" (Brahms), "pretty" (Tchaikovsky), or "African" (Nietzsche) (McClary 1992:116–18). These laudatory readings, which helped to promote the opera and secure its place in the operatic canon within ten years of its opening (McClary 1992:120), were, of course, equally as engaged in the Othering and exoticization of difference as were the explicitly racist and sexist criticisms of audiences in Paris. Both audiences were involved in the *re*staging of the Othering and exoticization apparently internal to the opera and novella.

Audiences today might respond to *Karmen Geï* in a way that is similar to the responses to the opera in Vienna, given the film's all-Senegalese cast, its striking lead actress Djeïnaba Diop Gaï, its theatrical use of brightly colored Senegalese boubous and costumes, the mixture of Wolof as well as French dialogue, and its extensive use of Wolof proverbs and indigenous Senegalese music and choreography. Some critics, no doubt at a loss as to how to "discipline" the film's difference, have called it a "quasi-musical" (London Lesbian and Gay Film Festival 2003), a "musical drama" (Amarger 2001), or even a "dance revue" (Gugler 2003:186). Music does seem to motivate much of the narrative—with saxophonist David Murray's jazz score threaded throughout, and with certain scenes literally orchestrated by the music and rhythms provided by Doudou N'Diaye Rose's *sabar* drummers, Julien Jouga's choir, and El Hadj Ndiaye's songs. Ramaka, however, rejects the classification of the film in any way, and when asked whether he was attempting to make a "musical comedy," says:

> I do not ask myself this question. . . . I do not make a great difference
> between that which is said, that which is movement, and that which is
> sung: this is a gamut among which we wander—the only thing that needs
> to be maintained is the tempo. . . . Everything is a question of tempo:
> the emotion that we express determines the need either to sing or speak
> it. Thus, I do not ask myself the question of knowing if I am making a
> musical comedy, or a baroque opera. . . . I have tried to let go and, often

with the help of others, to become a "baby" again and to ask myself what this baby is telling me. (Quoted in Barlet 2001)

In this proverb about the baby, Ramaka expresses an approach that involves attentiveness to and respect for his sources, an attempt to adapt *to* them, rather than impose certain generic conventions upon them. The hybrid nature of *Karmen Geï*, which is only eighty-two minutes long, is nevertheless one of its most remarkable features, and I will return to this later. First, however, it is necessary to further explore the contexts of production and reception of the novella and the opera.

McClary points to the way that critics of *Carmen* have sometimes read it as a story about tragic lovers. She argues, however, that to read the narrative "in this fashion is to ignore the faultlines of social power that organize it, for while the story's subject matter may appear idiosyncratic to us, *Carmen* is actually only one of a large number of fantasies involving race, class, and gender that circulated in nineteenth-century French culture" (1992:29). McClary argues that while Bizet's *Carmen*, through its recourse to exotic melodies and its fetishization of Carmen, participates in the wave of Orientalism that swept through France in the nineteenth century, it primarily articulates a conflict between France and its Others by focusing on "the racial Other who has *infiltrated home turf*" (34; my emphasis). She refers to Napoleon's expedition to Egypt in 1798 and subsequent invasions of the Orient (29–31), as well as to France's defeat in the 1870 Franco-Prussian War (32), as examples of France's confrontations with Others outside its national borders. But she also points to the working-class Commune revolutions in France in 1830, 1848, and 1871 (35) and the stirrings of a women's liberation movement (37) as events which highlight French fear not only of its pure status and identity abroad but also at home. Thus both the novella and the opera are seen to have participated in the representation of a profound identity crisis of the French nation—threatened both from within and without—that evolved during the nineteenth century.

Evlyn Gould (1996) situates the two works not only in relation to the crisis with regard to the Other in nineteenth-century France, but in relation to the anxieties of nineteenth-century European culture in general. On the basis of this argument, she explains the plethora of film adaptations of *Carmen* in the 1980s in relation to the "still-hard-to-define notion of a greater European identity" (9) in the wake of the creation of the European Union. Gould challenges those critics, including Robinson, who have read the reincarnation of *Carmen* through these 1980s film adaptations (all made by men)[3] as a form of "assault against emancipated women" at a time of "renewed feminist activity" (11). She argues instead that the tensions between nationalism, bourgeois imperialism, and pan-European sentiment of the 1800s have been highlighted by contemporary adapters of the myth who are attempting to "envision a new Europe or to further pan-European thinking in direct response to destructive nationalisms and attendant concerns regarding immigrants and their free movement (that bohemian 'roving') across national borders" (11) in the twentieth century.[4]

Feminist critics, Gould argues, ignore some of the profound issues around national and European identity with which Mérimée and Bizet were concerned, and which film adapters of the story in the 1980s resumed and reworked. She charts the various feminist readings of *Carmen*,[5] arriving at the conclusion that she herself is "less interested in being for or against the potentially misogynistic aspect of Mérimée's *Carmen* than in the formal tensions that allow for mutually exclusive readings: Is Carmen a dangerous femme fatale, or is she one of Elaine Showalter's liberated 'New Women'?" (1996:15). What is being played out here is the familiar disciplinary contest over meanings where the dominant interpretations in this case, as I have suggested, are related to the discourses of feminism and cultural politics.

Within these discourses, *Carmen* may be read, on the one hand, as contributing to an exclusionary cultural politics, or as representing women through stereotypes that exclude them from the realm of masculine rationality; on the other hand, *Carmen* may be read as subverting dominant discourses—racial and ethnic or sexist. The reading would appear to depend upon whether Mérimée and Bizet are seen to be working in a self-reflexive mode or not. Gould argues that Mérimée, Bizet, and later the filmmaker Carlos Saura (in his 1984 flamenco adaptation) *stage* rather than participate directly in the exoticization of the Other, thereby problematizing the notion of a coherent European identity. She argues that, in order to do this, Mérimée engages "the aesthetic politics of historical narrative" while Bizet engages the aesthetic politics of "operatic narrative" (1996:8). Mérimée, she says, pits "a historian against a writer who unmasks him," Bizet creates a "jarring contrast between music and spoken dialogue," and Saura repeats this procedure by contrasting the aesthetic politics of choreographic and cinematic narrative (8). Thus she implies that, through these contradictions, the works deconstruct themselves. In my reading of *Karmen Geï*, I hope to show that Ramaka's adaptation demonstrates a high degree of fidelity to the tensions and self-reflexiveness of the novella as it has been interpreted by Gould, and engages with the shifting and conflicting epistemologies and anxieties "performed" in Mérimée's novella.

Gould argues—drawing on Hayden White's *Metahistory: The Historical Imagination in Nineteenth-Century Europe* (1973)—that Mérimée's *Carmen* stages the tensions around the competing definitions of history at the time of its production. She points to the mercurial climate surrounding the creation of "history," which had been instated as a discipline at the Sorbonne in 1812, and to its "pose of objectivity" that was no doubt a reaction to historians' own insecurity about their subject (1996:61). An article that appeared in *La Revue des Deux Mondes* in the same year that *Carmen* was published in this journal, for example, claimed that history was a science that involved the recounting of facts (ibid.). Gould notes that the structure of Mérimée's novella conforms to the conventional structure of nineteenth-century historiographical writing, identified by White, which included four phases: the research phase, the representation of events as a chronicle, the "emplotment" of these events, and a concluding overview and interpretation of the events (White 1973:5–42; Gould 1996:65). Gould argues, however, that Mérimée makes use of this structure precisely in order to transgress it, to erode the boundaries that separate historical and literary writing, and to suggest that there may be limits to the truth that historical narrative is able to provide.

While I would wish to agree with Gould's analysis that Mérimée establishes a critical distance between himself and his narrator in order to question the veracity of historical narrative, I would go further to suggest that the novella stages the broader contest between rational and embodied modes of knowing. It also, in some senses, anticipates the (inevitably) rationalist disciplinary discourses that will attempt to circumscribe its meanings. I will argue that Ramaka's film does the same thing by different means, and that it questions the dominance of rational modes of thinking—while not denying the value of the rational faculty—from the position of a culture that was constructed as the irrational Other within those modes of thought.[6]

As Gould argues, the contest between the scientific or rational mode of history and the literary or fictional mode is achieved in the novella through the ironic distance between the author and the unnamed narrator (who, nonetheless, shares many of Mérimée's traits, such as a profound interest in both historical knowledge and mysticism). The irony emerges in the opening passages of the novella, with the narrator outlining the serious purpose for his writing as the desire to resolve the question of the exact location of Caesar's final battle against the champions of the republic—a question "which keeps all of learned Europe in suspense" (Mérimée 2001:11). The narrator then states his desire to tell a little story, which, he claims, will not detract from the real question at hand. At the end of the novella, however, the narrator does not return to his original premise for historical research (to the *discipline* of History), but has become sidetracked by his "*petite his-toire*" or "*little* story" (ibid.; my emphasis) of Carmen, leaving it to the reader to judge whether he has furthered knowledge and, if so, what kind of knowledge this is.

The first chapter demonstrates the classificatory thinking of the French narrator as he initially encounters the character of Don José and struggles to read and interpret a man who does not, it would appear, conform to his supposedly rational and civilized way of being. Thus, for example, the narrator prides himself on identifying Don José as a bandit, but wrongly identifies him as another bandit by the name of José Maria. He also attempts to display his ethnographic knowledge, noting that the bandit does not pronounce the letter *s* as Andalusians would, and concludes that he must be "a traveler like me, only less of an archaeologist" (2001:13). The narrator tries out a string of identificatory names and similes with which he attempts to "know" Don José: at first sight he is "a young fellow" (12), who, after displaying an air of hostility, becomes "the unknown" (12, 13, 14). After some time, the narrator notes that "he began to humanize himself" (13), as though the man is a wild beast requiring taming. After Don José has gorged himself on the narrator's food, the narrator pities him as "a starved wolf" and a "poor devil" (14), as *sub*human. The narrator cannot seem to decide what exactly Don José *is*, evidenced by his return to the term "the unknown" (15) and, finally, "the stranger" (ibid.), before he finally names him, correctly, Don José (16).

The narrator constantly struggles to assimilate what he is *seeing* with what he already *knows*—mostly gleaned from canonical texts. There is one moment, however, at the end of Chapter One, when the narrator experiences a moment of ambivalence after he has saved Don José from the guide who informs on him. In a frequently cited passage, the narrator wonders

> [if] it was reasonable to save a robber, and perhaps a murderer, from the gallows, simply because I had eaten ham and rice with him, in the Valencian manner. Had I not betrayed my guide who was maintaining the cause of law and order; had I not exposed him to a villain's (possible) vengeance? But the obligations of hospitality! . . . A savage prejudice, I said to myself; I will have to speak for all the crimes that this bandit is going to commit. . . . However, is this *instinct of conscience that resists all reasoning* really a prejudice? (2001:20–21; my emphasis)

By wavering on that "instinct of conscience" that "resists all reasoning," the narrator seems to acknowledge that there may be alternative ways of knowing the world and making judgments. However, he rejects the liberal path of reason and follows his moral instinct. In this way, the narrator colludes with Don José in Carmen's death—there is profound dramatic irony in his statement that he will have to "speak for all the crimes that this bandit is going to commit." His writing of Carmen-the-story can therefore be seen as an allegory of his implication in Don José's murder of Carmen-the-character.

The meeting with Carmen is framed by this encounter with the man who will turn out to be her lover and her murderer. Chapter Two opens with a staging of a different form of knowledge that the narrator must struggle to assimilate: he has come to Cordoba to do archival historical research in the library of a Dominican convent, but is faced on his first evening with a local tradition, when at dusk, the town's women bathe in the Guadalquivir River, while the men try to make out their forms in the dark. Once again, the narrator attempts to understand this scene through the lens of his classical education—he argues that "with a little imagination, it is not difficult to conjure Diana and her nymphs bathing below, without having to fear the fate of Actaeon" (22). As Robinson points out, "The evocation of Diana is particularly telling. By remaining outside the woman's world, the tremulous male is left to be satisfied by fantasy alone, thus protecting him from the dangers of real, physical contact with the women who—like Diana—seem quite capable of destroying him" (1992:6–7).

Ironically, while attempting to distance himself, through abstraction, from the dangerous form of unassimilable, embodied knowledge that these women represent, the narrator is approached by Carmen, who, as McClary points out, "represents virtually all available categories of alterity: inscrutable 'Oriental,' menacing worker, lawless criminal, *femme fatale*" (1992:43). The narrator, strongly attracted to Carmen in spite of the fact that her person does not conform to Brantôme's (Pierre de Bourdeille, seigneur de Brantôme) inventory of female features constituting beauty, agrees to go home with her to have his fortune told. He admits that, although he has long been "cured" of his predilection for "the occult sciences" (Mérimée 2001:24), he still harbors "a certain attraction of curiosity to all superstitions," although he quickly attempts to reign in this attraction by taming it into a question of origins— saying that he is eager to learn "from where the bohemian magic arose" (ibid.). The reader understands that the "bohemian magic" in which the narrator is most interested is Carmen herself, and that he wants to understand this magic in a carnal rather than intellectual manner. Before the narrator can consummate his attraction for Carmen, Don José interrupts in a rage, thereby "saving" the narrator from Carmen's magic. Notably, Ramaka picks up on this interpretation of Carmen and, as will later become apparent, his celebration of Karmen's embodied mode of being is mirrored in his celebration of the continuation of various kinds of so-called "magic" and occult practices in Senegal.

In the third chapter the narrator/historian bequeaths the role of narrator to Don José, whom, he discovers on his return to Cordoba, has been arrested and imprisoned for the murder of Carmen. Don José relates the story of his encounters with Carmen, whom, he claims, corrupted him, converting him from an ambitious soldier and law-abiding citizen to a murderous bandit. Don José's narrative gives a sense of an intimate knowledge of Carmen not available to the historian—he knows her because, under the influence of her powerful attraction, he has been drawn into her world and has become like her. In the end, however, he wants her to forsake her bohemian lifestyle and her other lovers, to travel with him to the New World, and he kills her because he cannot control her. Applying Adorno's logic of the sacrifice to this act, it could be argued that it is fear of complete regression to the "uncivilized," undifferentiated realm that Carmen represents, of the symbolic death that this suggests—death being the reminder of nature in culture—that makes Don José project his own suppressed situatedness in nature onto Carmen. He sacrifices her in a gesture of self-preservation, but ironically sacrifices himself as well.

The narrator and the reader come to know Carmen through the mimetic features of the narrative—through Don José's storytelling—rather than through the scientific discourse of ethnography, which follows in the fourth chapter. This fourth chapter was added in 1846, a year after the publication of the novella, and it might be speculated that Mérimée attempted in this way to justify his story about the gypsy girl and recuperate it for respectable society. This chapter reads as a strange ethnographic study of gypsy culture and language, and, like Chapter One, can be interpreted as ironic, as an inadequate academic "exposé" of what Don José has illustrated through his tale: that bohemians (and particularly bohemian women) are dangerous and ungodly. Robinson argues that the point of the fourth chapter—sealed with the gypsy proverb *En retendi panda nasti abelga macha*, which Robinson translates as "Into a closed mouth enters no fly" (1992:2)—seems to be to foreground the French narrator's appropriation and silencing of Carmen's language through his narrative, just as Don José appropriates and silences her body in the diegesis by killing her (Robinson 1992:14). The men can thus be read, Robinson argues, as "brothers-in-arms, fighting the same battles and enduring the same vicissitudes" (1992:6).

This is an oversimplification of the relationships, however, since Don José has been subject to the classificatory thinking of the narrator, who projects his fear of the irrational onto the bandit, with Don José, in turn, projecting *his* fear onto Carmen. Carmen accepts her fate passively, as if she cannot escape this role of sacrificial victim. Don José will die too, sentenced to death by the Law, and the narrator "dies" out of the life of the mimetic narrative, and into the mortification produced by the scientific language of the fourth chapter. Since Carmen is already dead, by dissecting her race and her language the narrator engages in what Adorno would call identity-thinking as "mimesis of what is dead" (Jarvis 1998:31). Jarvis explains that,

> Mimesis, for Adorno . . . is not the attempt to make a copy of nature but
> the attempt to become like nature in order to ward off what is feared;
> but what remains to be feared when instrumental reason has apparently
> brought a feared nature under control? Death is an inextinguishable
> reminder of nature in culture. The whole nexus of self-preservatory

thought and action, Adorno and Horkheimer suggest, mimics death, strives to become inorganic, object-like in its attempt to ward off death. (1998:31)

After Don José has murdered Carmen, the French narrator—the spokesman for "instrumental reason" and the new "scientific" history—mimics this very death in what can be seen as another fruitless attempt at self-preservation, an attempt to turn his "petite histoire" into an "inorganic, object-like" anthropological statement.

This logic of the sacrifice, entailing the metonymic displacement of violence, is also at the core of Ramaka's film. It is of no small significance, given this reading of Mérimée's *Carmen*, that the first African to adapt *Carmen* to film is himself a visual ethnographer, who, before making *Karmen Geï*, directed a number of ethnographic documentaries about the rainmaking rituals of Lebou fishermen in his native Senegal. He has also made a short film *So Be It/Ainsi soit-il* (1997), adapted from Wole Soyinka's play *The Strong Breed* (1964), which he transforms in such a way as to make a statement about the incommensurability of French and African modes of being. In his controversial last film, *Et si Latif avait raison* (2006), a semi-adaptation of the nonfiction work, *Un Opposant au pouvoir/L'Aternance Piégée* by Senegalese writer Abdou Latif Coulibaly, Ramaka harshly considers the government of Senegalese president Abdoulaye Wade. The latter film has resulted in Ramaka's constant interrogation by the Division des investigations criminelles (Dic) in Dakar, and in a public uproar, mostly carried out through a Senegalese news Web site called Rewmi.

Although several African filmmakers—such as Souleymane Cissé and Manthia Diawara—have attempted through their films to reappropriate the practice of ethnographic filmmaking in Africa, Ramaka takes a somewhat different stance in relation to ethnography. He argues that

The question of the ethnographic gaze . . . is not who is doing the looking, but the content of ethnography itself. You have to know what you want to see before you know how to look at it: is it to be the Other as what he is and whom I am going to *dissect* or, alternatively, the Other in so far as I feel an *affinity* with him and he with me. (Quoted in Barlet 2000:9; my emphasis)

It is significant that Ramaka insists that it is not important *who* is doing the looking, seeming thereby to imply that the ethnographer need not have the same gender, racial, or cultural identity as the Other at whom he or she looks. His words here echo those of Ukadike in his praise for the films of French ethnographer Regnault, and also reverberate with the progressive views of contemporary media ethnographers (Askew and Wilk 2002; Ginsburg et al. 2002). In addition to this, it is significant that Ramaka places the Other, as the "content of the ethnography," at the center of the attempt to know, but conflates the nature of the Other with the ethnographic method, so that the Other both constitutes and is constituted by the mode of cognition. And the modes of cognition available are "dissection"—the mode of scientific rationality, which, in the identification *of* the Other through classificatory thinking, kills in order to know; and "affinity"—the mode of mimesis as identification *with* or adaptation to the Other.

Rather than engage in a "dissection" of *Karmen Geï* at the expense of an "affinity" with the film, I want—in the vein of Laleen Jayamanne's (2001) and Francesca Castaldi's (2006) mimetic criticism, in which they "sense" as well as analyze texts—to try to conjure, through words, the striking opening atmosphere of *Karmen Geï* before moving into analysis. I want you to imagine, first of all, the opening sequence of *Karmen Geï*, and what your reaction to it would be. Loud drumbeats, handclapping, and singing erupt already during the opening credits, white text on black. When the screen bursts open into the first wide, frontal shot, it shows a magnificent black woman—clearly Karmen—sitting on a chair with her thighs open, her body covered only with a loose black cloth. Black women in colorful, traditional Senegalese dress (boubous) are dancing behind Karmen to the loud drumbeats that accompany the scene. The image cuts to a close-up of Karmen's face, which is very dark in skin tone, then the camera quickly tilts down to a close-up of her thighs opening and closing in time to the drumbeats. A cut to a close-up of another woman's face reveals that it is not a man who is the main recipient of Karmen's seductive dance. A close-up reverse shot of Karmen's face confirms that she is gazing directly at this other woman. Another close-up reverse shot of the other woman's face establishes that the film's space is being created by the gaze between these two women. Now the scene cuts to a wide shot in which the woman at whom Karmen is gazing is shown to be wearing a stiff, khaki-colored uniform. A sequence of traveling shots follows, in which Karmen rises from her chair and dances for the pleasure of the women around her, but specifically for the woman in uniform. Karmen eventually dances up to the woman in uniform, provocatively dancing between her thighs. Karmen succeeds through her dance in getting the khaki-clad woman to rise and imitate her movements, which thrills the women around them, who run to dance beside them. The scene cuts at this point to a wide, high shot looking down on the space in which the women are dancing. High walls enclose the courtyard, and officials in uniform stand guard on the wall. A whistle is blown, after which all of the dancing women flee inside. The camera now tilts up and pans past the officials in uniform, past cannons, to rest on an image of the sea, with a city in the background. The film's title, *Karmen Geï*, appears in red lettering over this image.

The first set of images in this opening sequence—focusing on Karmen's thighs opening and closing—would seem to tempt feminist criticism. After all, when Senegalese director Joseph Gaï Ramaka chose to adapt *Carmen*, he decided to turn his lens onto a canonical European literary text and opera that, as I have argued, have consistently been interpreted by feminist critics. These critics have generally held to one of three points of view: *Carmen* offers a model of bold female independence; *Carmen* engages in a fetishization of the female; or *Carmen* deconstructs the male desire to fetishize the female. Unsurprisingly, critics of *Karmen Geï* have echoed each of these viewpoints in their analysis of the film. One critic praises the film for its beauty, calling it "a black incantation . . . free and full of grace" (Philippe Azoury, quoted in Powrie 2004:284), thereby seeming to define Karmen herself as "free." Another critic condemns the film for its fetishization of Karmen as "Woman," arguing that "Karmen becomes pure spectacle," that she "never frees herself from the male gaze of the camera," and that she thus "functions as little more than an erotic object, the point of contact between voyeuristic apparatus and spectator" (Garritano 2003:159). A third critic argues that while certain films use attractive female actresses "as a simple source of visual pleasure," Ramaka fashions Karmen as a particular kind of "sexual icon" who "uses her sexual power to obtain not only personal pleasure, but to stimulate cultural subversion and incite political dissent" (Woolfalk 2003). In each case, critics seem unsettled by the difference with which this black

(continued on page 239)

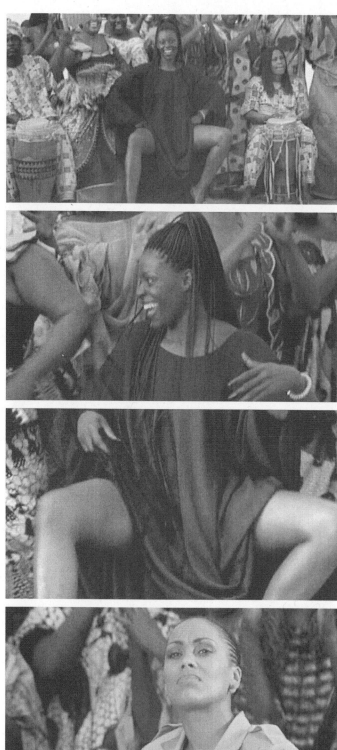

Figure 8.1
Opening sequence from *Karmen Geï*. (Images courtesy of California Newsreel)

233

Figure 8.1 (continued)
Opening sequence
from *Karmen Geï*.
(Images courtesy
of California
Newsreel)

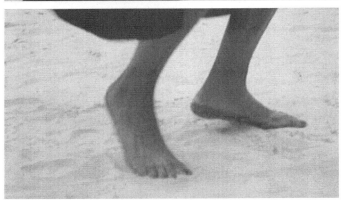

Figure 8.I (continued)
Opening sequence
from *Karmen Geï*.
(Images courtesy
of California
Newsreel)

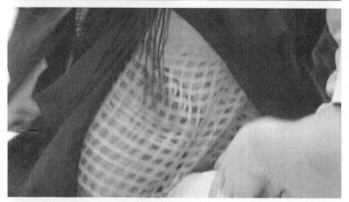

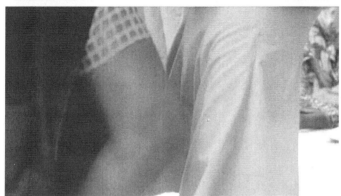

237

Figure 8.1 (continued)
Opening sequence
from *Karmen Geï*.
(Images courtesy
of California
Newsreel)

woman presents them. As a whole, the split in the responses to Karmen's representation into positive and negative readings of sexual and racial difference can be likened to Bhabha's concept of both fetishism and the stereotype in colonial discourse, in which the "unfamiliar" is fixed within a repetitious discourse that vacillates between delight and fear, desire and anxiety.

Ramaka himself seems to anticipate that his black, Senegalese version of *Carmen* will inspire such critical ambivalence. The opening sequence of his film thus appears to be edited in such a way that each successive set of images deconstructs and undermines the previous set of images, thereby offering a logic that anticipates and wards off external criticism. Whether one believes that Karmen is subject of, or subjected by, the images of her body in the first set of images becomes irrelevant when the second set of images reveals that Karmen is gazing at—and inspiring the gaze of—not a man, but a woman. Through this gesture, *Karmen Geï*'s opening sequence not only breaks pleasurable conventions but also prevents the type of criticism that depends on Mulvey's idea of the "gaze" in which an active male look is positioned opposite a passive, to-be-looked-at female (1988a). The viewer's gaze is, as it were, rendered irrelevant through the spatial dynamics of the film, which—through the tight series of shots and reverse shots of Karmen and another woman actively sharing and enjoying the gaze—cut the viewer out of the equation. This appears to be one of the ways in which Ramaka seeks to weaken the viewer's inevitable power as the owner of an active look in relation to the film's passive "to-be-looked-at-ness."

Certain critics' ambivalence over the representation of Karmen's identity as a black woman returns in other critics' alternatively positive and negative analyses of the representation of Karmen's sexuality—her lovemaking with men and women alike. The film has been interpreted as a celebration of homosexuality and/or bisexuality, having been screened and applauded at almost every major Lesbian and Gay Film Festival around the world since its release. Nonetheless, certain Senegalese viewers have been enraged by *Karmen Geï*'s engagement with homosexuality. The film was originally released in July 2001 without problems, in spite of the fact that homosexuality of any kind is considered an illegal practice in Senegal, where 95 percent of the population is Muslim. In September 2001, however, a group of men from the Senegalese Islamic brotherhood called the Mourides violently broke into a cinema in Dakar where Ramaka had been invited to speak, and threatened to burn down the cinema and to kill Ramaka. They were protesting a scene in *Karmen Geï* in which Angelique (the woman with whom Karmen dances in the first scene and who commits suicide in the film due to her unrequited love for Karmen) is given a Catholic burial, over which Ramaka has overlaid a *khassaïde*, or religious poem called a "Kalamoune." This *khassaïde* was composed by the founder of the Muslim Mouride Brotherhood, Cheikh Ahmadou Bamba Mbaké (Powrie 2004:288). The Mourides—to which the Senegalese president Abdoulaye Wade belongs—did not object to the use of the chants for a Catholic funeral, but to their use in the burial of a lesbian. The film was locked up, with government officials claiming that it insulted ten million Senegalese, but was eventually released. Both the celebration of *Karmen Geï* by international lesbian and gay film festivals, and the protest against *Karmen Geï* by the Senegalese Mourides, are motivated, ironically, by a similar interpretation of the film as a "representation"—a making visible—of homosexuality, which is constructed in either a positive or a negative way. These responses do not take into account the possibility that Ramaka is not simply making visible "blackness," "femaleness," and "homosexuality," but is offering a discourse that engages with competing epistemologies. This discourse is made manifest in the third set of images in the opening sequence of the film.

The viewer is now alerted to the fact that the woman whom Karmen entices to dance—Angelique—is dressed in uniform, and that the sequence is playing out in an all-female prison where Angelique is in fact the warden. Ramaka creates a great deal of suspense around what is to happen between Karmen and Angelique through the lengthy montage of jump cuts of Karmen dancing closer and closer to Angelique. Whereas parts of Karmen's body are filmed in isolation through close-ups, Angelique's body is represented as a whole—until Karmen's gyrations above her lap make it necessary for the filmmaker to isolate those parts of her body around which Karmen dances. Far from "fetishizing" the character of Karmen through these close-ups, Ramaka appears to have a different logic at work. He shows how, very gradually, Karmen succeeds in getting Angelique to *mimic* her bodily movements—to forget her institutional role as preserver of the Law (rational knowledge), and to give in to a bodily mode of being. The charge that Ramaka falls into the trap of equating the "black woman" with "bodily unreason" is contradicted by the fact that while Karmen does seem to represent an embodied mode of being, Angelique—also a black woman—is a representative of rationality. Not only does Angelique's status as prison warden confirm this, but her Christian name and faith locate her as a symbol of neocolonial institutions within this context. Rather than creating a binary opposition between these two women, however, Ramaka uses their love affair as a way of exploring the complex relationship between embodiment and rationality. Karmen, who exists from one bodily impulse to the next, cannot give herself to Angelique, in spite of acknowledging to her friend Samba that Angelique is the only person she really loves. Angelique's attraction to Karmen is fatal, and—unable to deal with her overwhelming *bodily* desire to be with Karmen—she commits suicide, or "sacrifices" herself in the manner of Christ. The tension between embodied and rational modes of knowing is thus figured in the relationship between two black women, rather than—as a more conventional postcolonial adaptation of *Carmen* would have it—between a black woman and a white man.

As the embodiment of an archaic form of mimesis based on the body, Karmen could be said to represent both the positive adaptive force through which the subject engages in assimilative behavior toward the Other, and also an acquisitive and aggressive behavior toward the Other (Spariosu 1984b:xvi). Both of these behaviors are intensely threatening to those intent on self-preservation through the sacrifice of the self as body, the suppression of the inner nature of human beings (Jarvis 1998:31). The threat is of a regression out of culture "back into the horror of the diffuse" (Adorno quoted in Brunkhorst 1999:59) and ultimately of death, since it is death that is the reminder of nature in culture. The positive and negative aspects of mimesis are conjured, in the first two sequences of the film, by the juxtaposition of two dances that have a different intent. In the first sequence, as I have shown, Karmen encourages Angelique to join her in a dance of cohesive mimesis. In the second scene, on the other hand, Karmen engages in a form of aggressive, competitive mimesis as she dances *against* another woman—the fiancée, Majiguene, of Lamine (the film's Don José equivalent). Karmen first attempts to "charm" Lamine, then insults him for "swallowing up the country"—a reference, perhaps, to corrupt Senegalese politicians, but also to the rational modes of thinking he stands for, as a representative of the Law. Majiguene (the film's Micaëla equivalent) rises to confront Karmen, hitching up her white wedding dress and challenging Karmen to a dance, suggesting that Karmen has succeeded in making the fiancée forget the institutional etiquette of the wedding. No word is uttered: the entire challenge occurs through music, song, dance, chant, and gesture. After the ritual of the dance competition has been going on for some time, Karmen can no longer contain her aggression and she pushes Majiguene to the ground and violently pulls back her head.

While the focus in Mérimée's novella is, in my reading, on the limitations of rational modes of knowing, Ramaka's *Karmen Geï* shifts the focus to the power (both positive and negative) of embodied modes of knowing. Not having access to the irony or self-reflexive devices of the novelist, Ramaka creates a sense of the "constructedness" of his film through the fragmented and discontinuous relationship between scenes, in which song and dance play a dual role of suggesting political resistance, and guiding the narrative. Karmen is not constrained by a narrator as Carmen is, and is presented in a way that enhances and celebrates her freedom, as for example in the scene of

Figure 8.2
Aggressive dance
sequence from
Karmen Geï.
(Images courtesy
of California
Newsreel)

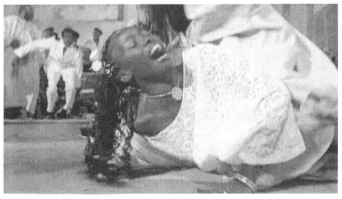

243

her seduction of Angelique. But she is nurtured and protected by two male lovers—Massigi, a singer, and Samba, a smuggler—who seem to suggest the necessary engagement with rational modes of knowledge. While her relationship with Angelique and Lamine—both of them representatives of the punitive aspects of the Law—enacts a strong challenge to rationality, while trying to win it over, her relationship with Samba and Massigi is, rather, one of affinity.

In a scene near the close of the film, Karmen, knowing she is soon to die, goes to see Samba, the lighthouse keeper, whom we learn was her first lover and who brought her to an understanding of herself, at the age of fifteen. Karmen tells her mother, Ma Penda, that Samba understands her "so well." But Ma Penda reminds Karmen that when "[Karmen's] loins shudder, [Samba] gets seasick." Massigi, the artist, represents for Karmen another grounding place when she struggles to cope with the external world: it is to Massigi that Karmen goes when she and the other smugglers are caught by the police. Karmen's relationships with Samba and Massigi are not without some form of dependence, a quality absent from Mérimée and Bizet's Carmens. It is therefore difficult to apply a straightforward feminist reading, celebrating pure female independence and freedom, to Karmen Geï.

Still, if one considers the way in which Ramaka locates his characters within a particular sociocultural context, a certain feminist argument can be found. If one takes into account that the dance performed in the opening sequence, in which the women move their pelvises in a provocative way, is not fabricated but is a specific and typical Senegalese dance, the sequence takes on a new significance. The bodies, in this reading, become nationalized, since the dances are specific to the rituals and pastimes of Senegalese women. Ramaka cannot be accused of fetishizing his female actresses; rather, he locates them within a particular context—Senegal—in which women have both cultural and specific identities. African dance scholar Francesca Castaldi has explained that the phrase the "feminization of poverty" is particularly relevant in Senegal, where, in spite of numerous households headed by women, far more women than men are unemployed and women make up two-thirds of Senegal's informal sector, currently under threat due to the government's "beautification" of the built environment for the purposes of tourism (2006:73). In resistance to their economic sidelining, women have, over the years, initiated mutual-aid associations, one of which is known as *mbootaay* and to which the opening sequence in *Karmen Geï* would appear to be metaphorically related. As Castaldi points out,

> A *mbootaay* gathers women of the same age within a neighborhood for purposes of mutual assistance. . . . To raise money, a *mbootaay* may organize a *soirée* in one of the city's nightclubs, hiring a popular *mbalax* group to entertain the crowd, or paying *géwëls* (Wolof griots) to play for a *sabar* in the streets of the neighborhood. . . . The *sabar* events organized by the *mbootaay* also serve to involve individuals in community affairs by the common practice of naming the *sabar* after a person. . . . To be chosen as the name bearer of a *sabar* is an honor and an onerous responsibility. (2006:75).

The opening sequence of *Karmen Geï* is fashioned as a *sabar*, in which it is conventional to have six male *sabar* drummers (known also as *géwëls*) pounding out rhythms that initiate the *sabar* dancing, the most popular and pervasive kind of dancing in Dakar. The dancing is characterized by its circular formation, with women moving in a provocative, energetic way very close to one another. As Castaldi points out, it is typical for women at *sabars* to dance duets with one another (explaining Karmen's dance with Angelique), and the "skills of the dancers seem to correlate with the permission and appreciation of risqué bodily exposure: the more skilled a dancer, the more she will undress and expose in the dancing circle" (2006:82)—hence Karmen's "authorized" exposure of her body. The idea that Karmen has earned the social right to behave as she does in public would suggest that in Senegal her explicit sensuality is not resistant so much as it is normal. Where it *would* be considered resistant, however, is in religious circles.

Although *sabar* dancing originated in the Wolof and Séréér ethnic groups in Senegal, it has now become a universal form of dance, due to what Castaldi explains as the "Wolofization of dance: regardless of the ethnic identity of the social subjects, *sabars* are part of the expressive repertoire of Dakarois" (2006:76). While the *sabar* has thus been responsible for eroding ethnic divisions in Senegal, it has notably heightened religious differences, since the "erotic femininity" displayed in *sabar* dances is countered by "good" women's chaste participation in religious events (ibid.). As Castaldi argues, "The *sabar* kinaesthetic competes with an Islamic kinaesthetic, which defines a different ethic of aesthetic presentation and display, linking feminine propriety to a kinetic regiment of modesty and restraint" (2006:80). Castaldi notes that on Senegalese television music videos of *sabar* dancing tend to replace female with male dancers for purposes of Islamic propriety, in spite of this not being a "realistic" representation of *sabar* events. In reality, men who are not *géwëls* are excluded from *sabars*, partaking "of the dancing as distant spectators, strategically located on the roofs of buildings that surround the *sabar* circle; but as such distant observers, they are dispensable"(2006:81).

This point leads me to the final shot in the opening sequence of the film, in which the camera's perspective moves to a position on the roof of the prison, looking down on the circle in which the women are dancing. Knowledge of the specific nature of *sabar* events allows one to interpret this scene as realistic rather than metaphorical—the metaphorical interpretation being that the male prison guards who look on possess Foucauldian panoptical control over the women. Through its realism this scene does make available, however, a specifically Senegalese feminist message, since the audio-visualizing of an actual social practice—*sabar* dancing—underlines the censorship of such "unofficial" images from the national media.[7]

In the final shot of the first sequence of *Karmen Geï*, the camera pans away from the prison to the image of the city across the water. There can be no doubt for those who know Senegalese geography that this city is Dakar and that the place where the dancing has taken place is thus the Maison des Esclaves—the House of Slaves—on the Île de Gorée, the point from which slaves were embarked for destinations in the New World during the transatlantic slave trade (1500s through the 1800s). The film's setting is one of the few ways that Ramaka can be said to make a statement that is political in the conventional sense. By turning the House of Slaves into a contemporary, all-female prison, the explicit suggestion is that women are the modern-day slaves of neocolonial Senegal. In one sense the setting evokes a meeting point between cultures—a point of arrival as well as a point of departure. It acts as a reminder, not only of the horrific earlier trade in human beings but also of the current issue of African immigration to France. Ramaka has referred to an identity crisis in contemporary France similar to that of Mérimée's period—an identity crisis that now has to do with African immigrants. The only way that the French are able to psychologically manage this African "infiltration" is through violence or, as Ramaka claims, through believing that the Other is "in a transit zone, here for a certain time before returning to Africa" (quoted in Barlet 2000:118). While, on the one hand, the "French person is incapable of taking on board the many identities settled on his territory," at the same time Ramaka argues that the African immigrant to France also refuses to admit to himself/herself that he/she is there: "The 'Other' does not pay us any heed because he doesn't know we're here. But we ourselves don't know we're here" (quoted in Barlet 2000:118).

However, the setting is also significant in the sense that, in the meeting of sea (on which the European traders and colonizers first arrived) and land (Africa as geographical place), is evoked the initial encounter between different modes of cognition, between cultures exhibiting a different relationship between being and cognition. The historicization of the story in this way prevents it from suggesting that the characters conform to some archetypal version of femininity; rather, they are anchored in a time, a place, and a particular culture. The women are neither reified nor demonized—while Karmen seems to represent both the positive and negative aspects of embodied modes of being, Angelique—as a representative of the Law—is shown to be a sad but sympathetic character. Ultimately, these women are bodies—just as the male characters are bodies—confronting the viewer in all their materiality. In confirmation of an "embodied" reading of the film, Phil Powrie points out that Gaï Ramaka's intention, before even shooting the film, was to use the body as a strategy: "I will show many bodies, naked bodies, dancing bodies, young bodies, old bodies, but the camera will seize in them the desire which they inspire rather than the libido they might unleash" (Powrie 2004:285).

Beyond his choice of setting much of the film within the House of Slaves, there is also Ramaka's description of the meaning of his adaptation in terms of its setting in Dakar, which the director has described as a "magical" and "chaotic" site of urbanity. In this way, Ramaka suggests that magic and modernity continue to coexist in certain parts of Africa, just as Adorno suggests they coexist in any culture in the world. The director talks about what it means for him to live in Africa and to make films in this context:

In Africa, the relation to the universe is very harmonious and spiritual, whereas the ecological approach in Europe is more secular. . . . That spirituality confers on me a certain serenity in my positioning in the world. *I don't need to know* if it is scientifically possible to cause thunder by making a sound, but I find it splendid that the sound is sometimes answered with thunder. The approach to life this produces is extraordinary. (Quoted in Barlet 2000:83; my emphasis)

Ramaka's film can thus, in part, be seen as weighing the different modes of knowledge available in this context, in which the magical/embodied modes of knowing have not been entirely repressed by instrumental rationality. The fact that much of the film is set in a prison, however, suggests that this repression is an inevitable condition of existence, wherever there is human culture.

There is a final surprise at the end of the title sequence: the fact that the film does not simply have the title "Carmen" but rather "Karmen Geï," and the question arises as to what this change might mean. The "C" is changed to "K" in keeping with Wolof, the local Senegalese language, and "Geï" is in fact a version of a surname common to many Senegalese, including Ramaka and his lead actress and wife, Djeïnaba Diop Gaï. However, the director had a specific purpose in mind when he named Karmen. He links Karmen to the *sabar* drumming that runs throughout the film when he says: "I thought of the rhythm of the *sabar* called 'Ndèye Guèye.' The person who gave her name to this particular rhythm was a beautiful and exceptional dancer. She was a Carmen. So the title of my film is *Karmen Geï*" (quoted in Powrie 2004:286). Karmen's name summons her role, in the film, as the representative of embodiment (since her name refers to a dancer and to a rhythm). It also, however, suggests that embodiment is always specific to context, since the addition of a surname to Karmen's name implies the intermeshing of personal and cultural identities in Karmen, and her relation to a specific place—as well as to a Senegalese woman who actually existed. The nationalization of Carmen's name is complemented, further, by Ramaka's situating her in a lineage of famous Senegalese heroines, of whom the chorus at Chez Ma Penda sings. Among the heroines named are the women of Nder, who chose to burn themselves to death rather than be taken by the Islamic invaders of their town on March 5, 1820, and Aline Sitoé Diatta, queen of the Casamance region in southern Senegal from 1940 to 1942, who tried to resist children from Casamance being taken by the French to fight in World War II, but who was arrested and deported by French officials, never to be heard of again. Thus, while Karmen does seem to represent embodiment in the film, her position in a tradition of strong Senegalese women would imply that she is similarly a symbol of positive resistance to external (Islamic, colonial, and masculine) control.

Karmen's powerful vitality does, however, seem to be an instance of the kind of pure being that "blinds" those who encounter it. Her fellow prison inmates recognize this when, in the rowdy scene in which they sing of Karmen's abandonment of them, they protest that all female bodies are the same, and have the same ability to seduce: Karmen, they suggest, must possess some force that is greater than the female. Similarly, some critics acknowledge that Karmen is "more polysexual than 'lesbian'" (London Lesbian and Gay Film Festival 2003), thereby recognizing that—through Karmen—Ramaka seems to represent more than a woman with a particular sexual identity. Ramaka speaks of Karmen's embodiment of both "mind" and "body," but also of her lack of understanding, in certain cases, of her body's own power and meaning:

> She struggles to grasp the message that her body gives her. She does not exist in the opposition between mind and body; her body is living, her mind confuses itself with the movements of her body. While the signs announcing her imminent death come to her, she does not understand them very well. She has not lost the meaning of her quest, but she does not grasp the meaning of her body. (Quoted in Barlet 2001)

Ramaka does not wish to endorse the Cartesian dualism of mind and body, but suggests here that the body in itself, without any element of rationality, is located outside of cognition, is not able to offer any kind of knowledge. The dialectic between embodiment and rationality played out between Karmen and Angelique is particularly pronounced through the juxtaposition of their respective deaths and burials. Whereas Angelique's death is represented as tragic and paralyzing, Karmen's death is represented through movement. Unlike typical representations of death—as terrifying, dark, oppressive—Karmen's visions of her own death are surprisingly colorful and calm, and represent a kind of revision of the Fanonian black skins/white masks dualism. Death, to Karmen, is shown by two sequences that are almost, but not quite, replicas of one another. In both cases death is represented by a handheld shot of rows of black people with their faces painted in various colors (*not* white). In the first instance, when this image is still only a premonition to Karmen, the sequence is edited together in a montage of shots that are almost continuous, but which—through their cuts—offer a sense of stultified movement. In the second instance, which is Karmen's vision after she is murdered by Lamine (the Don José equivalent) and is actually slipping into death, the sequence is continuous, without cuts, suggesting that death and movement are not mutually exclusive, but that death is the ultimate form of embodied knowledge.[8] Whereas Angelique receives a formal institutional burial—her body is invisible, encased in a coffin—Karmen's burial is simple, with her body wrapped in a cloth and carried to an open grave by her friend Samba.

The story of Carmen has achieved mythical status because of its power to motivate multiple performances in different media, and to produce strongly partisan interpretations by the public and by academic critics alike. This process of "mythification" is staged in *Karmen Geï*, in the scene in which Karmen is killed by Lamine above the stage on which her story is being performed. This scene would seem to enact the film's resistance to the reifying rational discourse of criticism, and this, in turn, raises the question as to how criticism, or critique, may be achieved at all. Susan Sontag, in her well-known essay "Against Interpretation," argues that interpretation in certain cultural contexts manages to be a "liberating act" that escapes "the dead past." She says:

> Interpretation must itself be evaluated, within a historical view of human consciousness. In some cultural contexts, interpretation is a liberating act. . . . In a culture, whose already classical dilemma is the hypertrophy of the intellect at the expense of energy and sensual capability, interpretation is the revenge of the intellect upon art. (1967:7)

The killing of Carmen/Karmen can, in some sense, be read as this kind of revenge of the intellect against art, the silencing of embodied modes of being by an extreme form of rationality. The murder above the stage could be seen as Ramaka's visualization of the process that is achieved discursively by the final chapter of Mérimée's novella, but it goes further, however, to implicate not only the rationalist discourse of interpretation but also the artistic media—also inevitably a mode of rationality—in the process of reification and mythification. Ramaka's hybrid aesthetic mode, exceeding that of Mérimée and Bizet, expresses an energetic rejection of the conventions of film-making, in the attempt to bring into play—through the forms of mimesis offered by the cinematic experience—the sensual as well as intellectual faculties of the viewer. While the figure of Karmen enacts a critique of rationality, the film does not produce a facile rejection of rational modes of knowing, and it is perhaps significant in this respect that Ramaka refers to his own filmmaking practice as that of "going out to meet my mental structure" (quoted in Barlet 2000:194).

It is possible to argue that *Karmen Geï*, as a radical African interpretation of *Carmen*, is a liberating act, a "means of revising, of transvaluing, of escaping the dead past" (Sontag 1967:7). In this sense, Ramaka's film works similarly to those West African films that deal irreverently with living West African myths, adapting them and demythologizing them in the service of performing a critique of contemporary violence, by both individuals and institutions, in Africa and elsewhere.[9] Given this reading of the film, Ramaka's attitude toward *Karmen Geï*'s position in the continuum of this myth—his simply asking why there should *not* be an African Carmen—is rather too modest. *Karmen Geï* not only provides a strikingly distinct representation of the story but also succeeds in strategically revitalizing the myth at its source, by adapting to the anxieties of Mérimée's and Bizet's versions while simultaneously radically revising them from a self-confident and critical African point of view. In the final analysis, the film is far more than an "indigenization" of *Carmen*, as Linda Hutcheon argues (2006:158-63); in its reclamation of *Carmen* as a human text belonging to all, *Karmen Geï* renders the very idea of *indigenization* irrelevant.

9 Humanizing the Old Testament's Origins, Historicizing Genocide's Origins

Cheick Oumar Sissoko's *La Genèse* (1999)

My aim has been to return Africa to the center of consciousness and events, to build bridges between the concerns of Africans and of other people. Because *La Gènese* associates universal themes with a profound anchorage in African reality, I believe it constitutes a new stage in our cinema.   CHEICK OUMAR SISSOKO (1999)

La Genèse (1999) is the first African film adaptation of the Old Testament.[1] It was made by a Malian filmmaker who is a Muslim, for viewers in a country that is 90 percent Muslim and 1 percent Christian, although laic by policy (Imperato 1989:87). However, it was also intended to reach an international audience. Sissoko thus speaks of his choice of the Book of Genesis as representing the shared story of origins of all three monotheistic religions, which share the same prophets. He says, "The Bible—it is also the Qur'an and the Torah [the first five books of the Tanakh]" (2003b). His intended audience, then, is a large and universal one: not only are Malian audiences very familiar with the narratives of the Old Testament as part of their own history and religion, but Jewish, Islamic, and Christian spectators throughout the world know the tales intimately. What Sissoko does, then, is to challenge directly those claims that his work is an adaptation of a canonical *Western* text—rather, his film adapts a canonical *human* narrative. The bias of certain Western critics is evident in their firm belief that this film is an adaptation of the Christian Bible. A *Variety* critic writes, "Casting Africans in all the roles certainly puts a new spin on an old story" (California Newsreel 1999), as though it were surprising that Africans are impersonating the Old Testament characters. Such perspectives ignore the fact that Africa has a long history of engagement with the Qur'an, the Bible, and also the Torah.

Western critics are compelled to rethink their assumptions about religious heritage when the opening scene shows Malian actors playing the roles of the characters and speaking in Bambara, with the popular Malian musician Salif Keïta as Esau, leading his clan through an easily recognizable part of northeastern Mali, beneath Mount Hombori Tondo—a landscape, it has been conceded, that is "perhaps not too different from the biblical Canaan" (California Newsreel 1999). Sissoko speaks in an interview about the symbolism he intended to invest in the film through Hombori: "The peace of the world finds itself again in the places that redeem this mystery, which men cannot master but that they can use to create their happiness. This mountain [Hombori] is ceaselessly present, like the symbol of a place of regrouping where men—no matter what their differences, their origins, their religion, their color—might understand one another" (1997). In this way, Sissoko registers his universal and inclusive message. He wants to challenge non-African audiences to reconsider their perspective on spirituality, and at the same time he invites such audiences to participate in the dialogue initiated by the film.

Sissoko has said: "I don't choose the films I make—if I made *La Genèse* and *Guimba* [*the Tyrant*], it was because through them there were situations of urgency that interpellated me" (2003b). This is the expression of a sense of responsiveness—and responsibility—from a filmmaker who has had a varied and remarkable career. He has been Mali's Minister of Culture since 2002 and describes here his evolution toward filmmaking:

> I was a student of mathematics—it was the militant who chose to express
> himself and to study history and sociology, and then the cinema, in order
> to pursue his ideal of liberty, in an Africa that would not have allowed
> a mathematics teacher to be affiliated, to take sides, to hold political
> meetings, to express himself in the press. At that time, in the seventies,
> it was impossible. Therefore I chose the cinema. (2003b)

Choosing to become a filmmaker, then, was a step for Sissoko toward allowing the "militant" and "idealist" within himself to emerge. Yet he speaks of the necessity of setting *aside* his filmmaking activities in 1991 while he was actively fighting the Malian dictator Moussa Traoré's autocratic regime and attempting to establish political democracy in Mali. And he saw as necessary to his development as a filmmaker the pursuit of higher education—he holds diplomas in Cinema and History, and in History and African Sociology from the École des Hautes Études en Sciences Sociales in Paris. In this

way, he suggests that, while the filmmaker does possess the ability to play a certain kind of "interventionist" role, he cannot *make* the revolution in and of itself. African filmmakers, he argues, are able to play the role of critics, but not simultaneously of militants.

In Sissoko's film *Guimba the Tyrant* (1995), the "situation of urgency" that "interpellated" him was Traoré's repressive regime, which lasted from 1968 until 1991. In his earlier film *Finzan* (1989), on the other hand, it was domestic patriarchal violence against women (through the practice of female excision) that concerned him. When asked about those "situations of urgency" that might have called on him to make *La Genèse*, Sissoko answers:

> The project of adapting a part of the Bible is linked to urgent situations in Africa and in the world. The situation of conflict—the situation of conflict in Africa, Rwanda, but also the conflicts in Europe, Bosnia, the Balkans, the situation of marginalization in America, the Chiapas Indians, but at the same time the development and the understanding in the world with the increase of xenophobia and racism. (2003b)

By dedicating *La Genèse* to "all those in the world who are the victims of fratricidal conflict," Sissoko offers a reminder of the age-old and ubiquitous nature of violent conflict, a reminder that violence and injustice are no more inherent in Africa than they are in other parts of the world. While his primary audience must be seen as Malian, his sense of responsibility extends beyond the local, and it is clearly his hope to address audiences around the world. In this sense, *La Genèse* is completely aligned with Burkinabé director Fanta Régina Nacro's *La Nuit de la Vérité* (2005), which was made as a response not only to the Rwandan genocide of 1994, but to ethnic cleansing in the former Yugoslavia. These two African films are remarkably similar in the way that they have chosen to represent the Rwandan genocide not directly, but through fictionalized, somewhat delocalized tales that take on universal weight: the use of an imaginary setting and fictional names for the two warring tribes (the Nayaks and Bonandés) in *La Nuit de la Vérité* achieves the same effect as the use of the Old Testament in *La Genèse*. In both cases, the focus is shifted away from blame—from what Feldman calls the "historiography of excuse"—through either "confirming" or "denying" acts of violence and genocide, and onto the need for the cycles of violence to be halted by strong leadership (2000). The prioritization of peace over even family ties becomes apparent in both films: in *La Nuit de la Vérité*, the Nayak president kills his wife Edna for setting the cycle of violence aflame once again; and in *La Genèse*, Jacob renounces his sons for their violence against Hamor's clan and sees their reconciliation with their brother Joseph as a prerequisite for being welcomed into his home once more. Notably, it is only filmmakers from outside Africa who have made fiction films that directly address the Rwandan genocide, and many of them glamorize that genocide in the process.[2]

Sissoko says that he deliberately chose to adapt chapters 24 to 38 of the Book of Genesis since this allowed him to focus on those parts of Genesis that stage violent, fraternal conflicts representative of much contemporary violence: the conflict between the twin brothers Jacob and Esau, and the conflict between different human communities (lorded over by Jacob, Esau, and Hamor, respectively) that live alongside one another and that have "every reason to love each other, certain reasons to hate each other, and yet they choose to hate each other" (2003b). The chapters adapted include the following narratives: Abraham sending his servant to Mesopotamia to find a wife for Isaac, and Isaac's marriage to Rebekah (ch. 24); Esau's selling his birthright to Jacob for a bowl of lentil soup (ch. 25); Isaac's blessing of Jacob (ch. 27); the Angel of God's "wrestling" with Jacob and giving him the name of "Israel" (ch. 32); Shechem's rape of Dinah, and the circumcision and genocide of Hamor's Canaanites (ch. 34); Jacob's mourning of Joseph's "death" from wild beasts (ch. 36); and Judah's marriage to Ada and his unexpected sexual relations with his daughter-in-law, Tamar (ch. 38). In spite of Sissoko's aiming to adapt simultaneously the Qur'an, the Torah, and the Bible, Sissoko's screenwriter Jean-Louis Sagot Duvauroux[3] worked from the Judeo-Christian text, which is why I will refer to this particular text rather than to the Qur'an.

While the narratives and dialogue within individual chapters are generally retained, the chronology of the chapters is radically revised. The film opens with a scrolling epigraph telling the viewer that two hundred years have passed since the flood. Jacob's "éleveurs" (monotheistic nomadic stockbreeders, dressed in blue to reference the nomadic Tuareg peoples of Mali, popularly known as the "Blue Men of the Desert") now find themselves in conflict with Hamor's "cultivateurs" (settled farmers, dressed in gold) and with Esau's "chasseurs" (hide-wearing hunter-gatherers), who are plotting revenge. For those familiar with Old Testament genealogy, the mention of the flood will be a reminder of the curse that Noah placed on Canaan, the son of Ham, ancestor of the Canaanites. The film's first image is that of Dinah attempting to scrub the blood from Joseph's coat while Jacob sits in his tent, mourning Joseph's apparent death (ch. 36); the second scene cuts to Esau's plotting vengeance against Jacob (such scenes punctuate the relatively slow movement of the film until Esau finally confronts Jacob toward the film's conclusion) (ch. 25); Shechem's rape of Dinah follows, and leads to the circumcision and genocide of the Canaanites (ch. 34); a scene is then added in which Jacob and Dinah meet with Hamor, who, in the film, is not killed, as he is in the original narrative. The two leaders decide to arrange an Assembly of Nations between Jacob's people and Hamor's Canaanites; during the Assembly of Nations, at which Jacob's sons are put on trial for Joseph's death, the civilians gaily perform other stories told in Genesis chapters 24 to 38—such as Judah's marriage to the Canaanite Ada, and Judah's deception by Tamar, which is visualized in flashback (ch. 38).

When it seems that the Assembly is on the verge of deteriorating into war, Benjamin hastens to fetch Jacob, who leaves his mourning tent and comes to tell the crowd the story of his father Isaac's marriage to Rebekah, also visualized in flashback (ch. 24). Esau then interrupts the Assembly of Nations, forcing Jacob to recount to Benjamin the story of how Jacob bought Esau's birthright, again visualized through flashback (ch. 25). Esau raises his spear to kill Jacob, but a small boy halts Esau, warning him that it is only for God to mete out punishment. Jacob "wrestles" with the Angel of God and survives, earning himself the name of Israel (ch. 32). The film ends with the reconciliation of Esau, Israel, and Hamor, and with Israel sending his sons to Egypt (Misraim) on Esau's advice (ch. 38).

The changes in chronology mean that the filmic narrative as a whole is framed by the story of Joseph, which is present as a kind of subtext, or linking device, holding the episodic structure together. This episodic structure, determined to a large extent by the nature of the Old Testament narratives, is also typical of a certain trend in African films, fashioned in the manner of oral tales, with an emphasis on digression in the eventual construction of a strong ethical message. Within the film's diegesis, a number of different storytellers are featured: the last third of the film is dominated by Jacob's stories, visualized in flashback, while the Assembly of Nations, as I will argue, balances rational discussion with theatrical, embodied storytelling, led by an African griot.

In the film, the story of Joseph's betrayal by his brothers seems to function as an extra-diegetic initiating event, followed by the second initiating event, which is the rape of Dinah by Shechem, the son of Hamor. These two events—fraternal envy and betrayal, and the violation of a woman—seem to trigger further, more widespread, violence. They are visually linked in the film through the similar framing and composition of two shots—one shot in which Jacob holds the bloodied cloth that is all that supposedly remains of Joseph; and one in which a woman from Hamor's clan holds up a bloodied cloth to prove that Shechem has raped Dinah. These two acts of violence set off a chain of violent acts of retribution, a series of metonymic displacements, which are brought to an end (in the film) only by the mission to recover Joseph. In the Book of Genesis, Jacob, out of purely economic incentive, sends his sons to buy corn in Egypt to bring back to famine-ridden Canaan; in *La Genèse*, Jacob knows (thanks to information provided by Esau) that he is sending his sons to recover their brother and to seek reconciliation with him, and this is the point at which the film concludes.

Within the diegesis of the film, the rape of Dinah initiates the violence. This would seem to be a reference to the universal tendency, on the part of warring parties, to use rape as a physical and psychological strategy to destroy the Other. In keeping with the typical modesty of African representations of violence, however, Sissoko refrains from depicting the actual rape. All that is shown is a long, wide-angle shot of Shechem carrying Dinah away across a field while three small boys with a goat pass across the foreground; this is followed by a medium close-up shot panning across the faces of Hamor's clan as they await the outcome of the rape; after the crowd banters about Jacob's clan and how nomads "cannot be trusted," the woman holding the bloodstained sheet emerges out of the stone hut in which the rape has occurred and triumphantly holds it up for the people to inspect. The woman initiates a song, proclaiming that the "bull's desire cannot be denied," and the people join in, clapping and singing, until Shechem emerges from the hut, after which they fall silent. Hamor storms onto the scene and stares angrily at his son Shechem, but says nothing. Instead, he goes inside the hut to berate Dinah, who notably replies through a convoluted string of Bambara proverbs, such as "Princes carry gold to their in-laws, they speak softly at their weddings, but if the ass requests a wife, his father-in-law covers his ears and his brothers-in-law flog him." The sequence as a whole works at both a sensory and symbolic level, and evokes a sense of ritual violence, sanctioned by the community (the rape is altogether shown to be a public event, "owned"

Figure 9.2
Two acts of violence
from *La Genèse*.
(Images courtesy
of California
Newsreel)

by the community, members of which are filmed en masse rather than in individual close-up shots), with the blood of the violated woman suggesting the blood of the sacrificial scapegoat.

Dinah's use of proverbs in the face of Hamor's "rational" authority sets in motion her descent into a state of enlightened insanity during the course of the film: in the Assembly of Nations sequence, instead of sitting among the women of her clan, she wanders from group to group, dressed in her white bridal clothes, laughing hysterically, dancing with the performers, and interjecting with wise but enigmatic statements. At one point, for example, she attempts to observe her footprints, and exclaims (in Bambara): "My steps leave no traces! How is that possible? Like the passing night! Does the passing night leave traces on the earth? No, that is impossible. [She looks up to the sky.] And what about the day? That too passes, but it cannot wear night's mourning." There appears to be a subtle kind of symbolism at work here, a reminder of the marginal status of those women who become mere items of

Figure 9.3
Circumcision
sequence from *La
Genèse*. (Images
courtesy of
California
Newsreel)

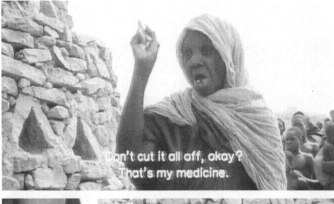

exchange in patriarchal cultures, but also a suggestion that Dinah is capable of representing, through her insanity and outcast status, an alternate mode of knowing. Notably, the actress who plays Dinah, Fatoumata Diawara, plays a very similar role in Dani Kouyaté's *Sia, le rêve du python* (2001), as Sia, a beautiful young virgin raped by male elders in her village who pretend to be executing traditional sacrifices in the name of the "python god." Sia escapes murder, but becomes mad after the rape; however, it is her madness that ironically brings the villagers to an understanding of the crime of the male elders. The film offers by way of conclusion one of the most powerful images of any African film: Sia, transported from the past into the present, takes on the role of a griot, striding along in her rags on one of the main streets of Ouagadougou, shouting her wise words at the deaf ears of people driving past in cars.

Following Shechem's rape of Dinah, the Canaanites come with gifts to ask for Dinah to be Shechem's wife, and Jacob deceives them into thinking that he will give his consent if they agree to be circumcised. The mass circumcision is shown with some humor (and it has certainly made audiences everywhere laugh), but, at the same time, the scene of the men going one by one to face the hatchet is capable of producing a strong sense of anticipated pain in the viewer. This act of symbolic violence against the culture of the Canaanites is thus rendered in strongly physical terms.

The genocide that follows represents the perpetrators of the violence (Jacob's sons) as victims of their own violence as much as those on whom they enact this violence (the Canaanites) since the filmmakers offer no cinematic "clues" as to whom the audience should align itself with morally. The sequence is played out in the dark of night, through a montage of fast shots (some handheld) in which it is difficult to discern which man belongs to which clan. The violence is heard rather than seen, with women wailing, children crying, the sound of a spear being driven through the body of a baby, and—finally—deathly silence. In this way the gratuitousness of the killing, its terrifying proximity, and—as with the rape scene—its mundane, unglamorous banality is conveyed. The scene closes with the following sequence: a slow pan across the bodies of the victims, overlaid by the lone weeping of a woman, no longer a mother; a close-up on the agonized face of this woman; a slow tilt up to reveal Hamor in close-up—the whites of his eyes glowing in the dark, conveying the utter desolation of his position as leader of a murdered clan; and a long, still, low-angle shot of the moon above, from Hamor's point of view. The universal symbol of the moon seems to unite all of humankind who have suffered the violence to which Hamor's clan has been subjected.

Following the massacre, Jacob's sons are immediately called to account for their violence against the Canaanites, and the next scenes show the Assembly of Nations, which takes on the form of a West African palaver and involves extensive dialogue among the people who have just been engaged in acts of extreme violence. Montage in which verbal analysis of violence is placed directly after the violence itself would be highly unusual in a Hollywood film, in which such structuring would mute the impact and entertainment value of the violence. In La Genèse, however, the utter gratuitousness of the killing is conveyed as the question arises as to why—if the leaders are now open to discussion—the massacre could not have been prevented by dialogue in the first place. The Assembly creates a forum for intense debate around issues of xenophobia, racism, and violence, and Barlet points out

Figure 9.4
Genocide sequence
from *La Genèse*.
(Images courtesy
of California
Newsreel)

263

that "the narratives respect the gestures and the form of the oral traditions, which the subtitles cannot unfortunately render in their entirety" (1999). He goes on to describe the criticism that has been leveled against this scene for its wordiness—which could be seen as an infidelity to the medium of film itself—and says that "a scriptwriter more used to film might have conveyed the message better." However, he defends what appears to be the excessive verbosity of these scenes, asking:

> Can't the spectator be asked to make an effort? Is it impossible to count on his/her intelligence today? Is a film hermetic because it is badly made, or because I am unable to listen to its density? Complex does not mean confused. If *La Genèse* accords such importance to the word, it is because words are of capital importance in African narrative. The strength of arguments and the impact of words make dialogue the prime route for resolving conflicts. . . . This film is worth the effort it asks of us. (Barlet 1999)

It is not surprising that the film is focused on words when one considers that the Qur'an is, in essence, an oral narrative. The very word *Qur'an* in Arabic means "he read" or "he recited," and Qur'anic schools (*msids*) concentrate on memorization of the text. While the Christian Bible and the Tanakh are of course also frequently recited, the emphasis is as much on silent reading as on recitation. A Christian or Jewish perspective may thus encourage interpretations of the film as excessively verbal.

Furthermore, the discussion among the various clans is important since it allows for the presentation of the different, sometimes conflicting, memories of characters, each of whom is shown to have his or her own experience of the episode. In this way, the individual experiences of the violence are emphasized, and Sissoko suggests that the film is inevitably able to present only one version of events. It is perhaps significant in this respect that the film was made at a time when the National Seminars on the History of Rwanda were being held (in December 1998 and October 1999), resulting in discussion around all aspects of Rwanda's colonial and postcolonial history. The need to accurately historicize the genocide that, in 1994, resulted in the death of more than 800,000 people (mostly people classified as Tutsis by people classified as Hutus) is recognized by Deo Byanafache, the dean of the School of Arts and Letters at the National University of Rwanda, who

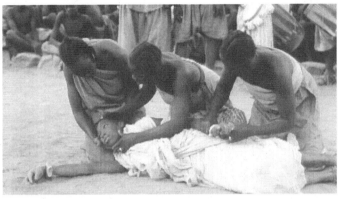

Figure 9.5
Assembly of
Nations sequence
from *La Genèse*.
(Images courtesy
of California
Newsreel)

says: "The historians who lived through these events [of 1994] are now more conscious that there is a big gap between what is written and the reality" (*Hopes on the Horizon* [film, 2000]). Problems of terminology arise—such as how to define the 1959 Hutu overthrow of the Tutsi minority. Hutus wish to call these events a "revolution"; Tutsis argue that it was simply a "political change." However, Ancilla Mukarubuga, the founder of the Genocide Victims Support Organization, argues that, "Reconciliation is not a cure. It is a process. So it is not the rewriting of history alone that will bring about reconciliation. There will be other phases, especially justice and rehabilitation: moral, physical, economic, etc." (*Hopes on the Horizon*). Laurent Nkusi, professor of journalism at the National University, says: "The history of Rwanda is irreplaceable. If it can at least be a lesson for the other people of Africa, then the genocide will have served a purpose" (*Hopes on the Horizon*). The way in which Sissoko represents the genocide of the Canaanites and its aftermath appears to be his way of participating in the process of reconciliation, of making the genocide serve the only kind of (positive) purpose that is now possible. While there is a need for writing the correct history of the Rwandan genocide, Sissoko refrains from participating in such a process and chooses rather to tell a story that is related metaphorically to genocides that have occurred throughout the world. The racial and ethnic insults that are bandied about by all of the different tribes in *La Genèse* (Hamor's people condemn Jacob's people for being nomadic; and Judah is berated for having slept with a "peasant") are a reminder of the racism that continues to exist everywhere.

At the same time, in the tragicomic generic vein of much West African myth and literature, Sissoko's impulse seems to be toward balancing pain and tragedy with laughter and comedy. While violence, and the rational discussion of violence, is treated very seriously in the film, the focus is not on violence alone. Something that Barlet overlooks in his description of the verbose scene of the Assembly of Nations or palaver, for example, is the mise-en-scène of Koteba theatrical performances that replay the rational discussions around violence from a performative angle. In West Africa, the practice of the Koteba popular theater has traditionally played the role of satirical critique, as Thackway points out:

In addition to playing an educational role, oral tales and other live performances, such as song and theatre, have always provided a forum for protest and criticism. The focus is often the abuse of power, and is usually articulated through satire. The traditional outdoor theatrical performances of the Koteba in Mali continue to serve as a vehicle for social commentary as the younger generations satirise and mock the behaviour of their elders. (2003:54)

Throughout the Assembly of Nations, such Koteba performances interrupt and dramatize the intense dialogue: for instance, Judah's bigotry toward the Canaanites is addressed both through abstract discussion among the chiefs (the legal authorities), and through a raucous performance by the people themselves which reveals that Judah not only married a Canaanite, but slept with his own daughter-in-law. When Judah grows wrathful toward the performers, one of the Canaanite chiefs advises him: "Truth speaks with two tongues. One is insolent. The other is modest. Judah! Listen well to our slave! His immodest eyes can see into places where your modesty is blind." In this way, the importance of both intellectual discussion and storytelling/performance/mythology is endorsed, and both are shown to be fully "African." Rational discourse may represent one truth, but the words of griots and performers represent another way of knowing, and the performances provide a sanctioned space for the kind of criticism of authority that is not normally permitted. The tolerance, or even celebration, of the griot in African culture, we might note, is a remarkable way of creating a sanctioned space for the entry of what Scott (1990) calls "hidden transcripts" (speaking the truth to power) into the public sphere. Beyond this, however, Sissoko's use of the griot and of forms such as Koteba theater reveal how the cinema, being a heterogeneous art, is able to incorporate elements of other African arts, such as the fine arts, photography, epic tales, music, masking, masquerade, theater, and dance. The question, then, of whether African cinema is as "indigenous" as other popular art forms (Givanni 2000:183–94) rests solely with the questions, Sissoko says, of "artistic and financial freedom" and "audience" (2000:193). Sissoko expresses fear at the effects of the "invasion of violent films and porn" on African television channels, and argues that "an African film only really exists as such when it has conquered an African public" (2000:193).

Sissoko has therefore taken it upon himself to exhibit his film throughout Mali and conduct postscreening discussions with Malian audiences. He describes the first screening of *La Genèse* in Mali, in Salif Keïta's home village (Djoliba), as one entailing identification and self-criticism on the part of Malians, and thus as leading to a good deal of animated postfilm discussion. Another of his reasons for adapting the Book of Genesis was "its parallel with the Malian agricultural and pastoral context, and the recent conflict with the Tuareg" (Barlet 1999). Sissoko says that the violence between farmers and stockbreeders in Salif Keïta's region, and the state violence against nomadic Tuaregs in northern Mali in 1993 (following the "Second Tuareg Rebellion" against the government of Mali on June 27, 1990), were conflicts he wished to address. He describes the screening experience in Djoliba:

> The first time the film was shown, it was in the village of Salif Keïta, Djoliba. We debated for two hours. I was enthusiastic because they showed that they recognized the conflict between the stockbreeders and farmers. It was the same type of conflict. And nevertheless outside of these conflicts they live together, in Mali, among us. (2003b)

The villagers—comprised of stockbreeders (*éleveurs*) and farmers (*paysannes*)—were able to identify with the characters, saw their own problems and fraternal conflicts in those of the Book of Genesis, and were able to engage in self-criticism. They could relate, too, to Sissoko's "augmentation" of the biblical narrative in which he places emphasis on the droughts from which the three clans are suffering in the film—this was intended, Sissoko says, to refer to the great droughts in Mali of 1972–1974 and 1983–1985, during which almost half of Mali's herds were decimated (2003b). The casting of world-famous Salif Keïta of Djoliba in the film, furthermore, does not appear to be accidental. Keïta's own ostracization from his community due to his albinism (seen as bad luck in Mandinka culture), and his transgression of the rules of his lineage (he is a direct descendant of Soundjata Keïta, founder of the Mali empire), which forbade him to become a singer, find resonance with the themes of *La Genèse*, making the film all the more moving in its tackling of racism and the rigidity of social classes.

Turning from the most local of audiences, in Djoliba, to consider Western responses to the film, it is important to remember that Sissoko has said that it was his wish to speak, through the Book of Genesis, to people of all faiths, and to encourage interreligious dialogue. As he says, "The Bible is a historic document shared by humanity, and cannot be reserved for the West" (quoted in Barlet 1999). *La Genèse* is clearly not intended as an act of appropriation in an adversarial sense—that is to say, it is not intended as a struggle for representation by one group via the canonical text of another group. There are, nevertheless, ways in which aspects of the film do have the potential to cause Western viewers to reflect on certain Eurocentric assumptions relating to the Old Testament. For example, the casting of the familiar Old Testament figures as black West Africans, rather than as whites (as in most biblical film adaptations) might serve as a reminder that the Old Testament has its provenance in the Middle East and that Africans have been excluded from Judeo-Christian histories.[4]

Sissoko's film adaptation, alongside the adaptations of Bekolo and Ramaka, reinserts Africans not simply into prehistory, but into a universal human history from which they have often been excluded or, as Sylvia Wynter says, "dysselected" (2000:36). In this sense, all three of these West African films participate in a (future) cinematic movement that Wynter believes will "redefine what it is to *be* human" where the historical concept of the human has been associated with the (securalized) Judeo-Christian West (2000:25). *La Genèse* does this by offering a critique of violence, using to great effect the embodied potential of the cinematic experience as well as the rational analysis that is promoted by the re-historicizing and contextualizing effect of adaptation. Viewers of *La Genèse* cannot turn away from the violence, nor take pleasure from it, but are required to respond both critically and compassionately to it. At a recent screening of *La Genèse*,[5] viewers—none of them African, but all theologians—expressed surprise at the "violence" of the film. Having expected Sissoko to adapt the less violent parts of the Book of Genesis (the Creation, the Garden of Eden, Noah embarking the Ark), they were shocked to find themselves confronted instead with scenes of rape, circumcision, pillage, and genocide. This response is perhaps a measure of the extent to which the extreme violence of the Old Testament is elided from contemporary thought. The film is a vivid reminder of the sacrificial and vengeful culture in which *all* the monotheistic religions originated, and of the perpetuation of the same kind of metonymic displacement of violence in the present by people of all religions. This is a particularly important project at a time when the Qur'an has been subject to interpretation which claims that it sanctions violent action against non-Muslims or "infidels" (Spencer 2003). Certain Islamic scholars have been quick to point out the Qur'an's position on violence, as with the Christian Bible or Tanakh, is a matter of interpretation (Miller and Hashmi 2001).

Although violent passages from the Book of Genesis were chosen for adaptation, there is a complete absence of sensationalism in the way in which the events are shown. The film's social realist aesthetic privileges modest long shots with more than one character in the frame. The slow tempo is further protracted by the magisterial compositions of Michael Risse and Pierre Sauvageot. As Barlet says:

> Right from its prologue, *La Genèse*, the tale of the dawn of humanity, is poignantly and painfully relevant today. But it is not *Saving Private Ryan*, nor the sordid imagery of the television: it is not just about juxtaposing testimony and using emotion to write History in a Spielbergesque style. This tale does not content itself with exploring humanity at its origins, it ausculates the innermost depths of man. (1999)

What sets Sissoko's audio-visualization of violence apart from, for instance, Mel Gibson's graphic depiction of violence in *The Passion of the Christ* (2004) is that Sissoko eschews using special effects and emotionally charged extra-diegetic music as a way of evoking a facile mimetic response from the viewer in the acceptance of the filmmaker's own construction of "victim" and "villain." Films like *The Passion of the Christ* or Visual Bible International's recent "word-for-word" adaptation of *The Gospel of St. John*, are, of course, made specifically for a worldwide Christian community, and, unlike *La Genèse,* with the primary aim of proselytizing.

Made with the intention of promoting interreligious and intercultural dialogue, *La Genèse* offers a specific challenge to the kind of criticism traditionally practiced in the field of historical and theological scholarship, which tends to examine the ways in which Africans have been "Christianized" or "Islamized" and not the ways, as Richard Rathbone argues, that these movements and events have themselves been "Africanized" (2002:20). Sissoko, as a Muslim who Africanizes the Book of Genesis, would seem to be participating actively in that task of exploring the relationship between the Bible and other sacred texts "in those parts of Africa where Christianity and Islam substantially encounter each other" and where this "analysis and reflection" is needed (West 2001:339). Lamin Sanneh's exploration of the ways in which Africans have refashioned the Bible for their own purposes can be applied to Sissoko's radical re-historicization of the Book of Genesis. In his foundational work on missionary culture, *Translating the Message: The Missionary Impact on Culture* (1989), Sanneh argues that the translation of the Bible into African vernaculars resulted not only in hegemonic "external transmission" of the Scriptures but also in the constructive outcome of African agency through the "internal appropriation" and "charismatic renewal" of the Bible (3).

I would argue that Sissoko's *La Genèse* plays a vital role in drawing attention not only to situations of violence across the contemporary world but also to the impact that Africa has had, or can have, on of all of the sacred texts—the Christian Bible, the Qur'an, and the Tanakh—and their interpretation. Moreover, in its "unfaithful" interpretation of the Book of Genesis, *La Genèse* would seem to perform what Morgan and Barton acknowledge in *Biblical Interpretation* (1988) when they talk about the necessity for liberated interpretation of the sacred texts at this time of violent conflict between Muslims, Christians, and Jews. At the same time, in its infidelity to multiple sacred texts, Sissoko might be seen to critique *any* kind of belief system that attempts to secure a monopoly on the "truth" or that exercises violence and dominance over another group. In this sense, his film—while "adapting to" the Book of Genesis—also reminds viewers of the violence with which Christianity and Islam were sometimes enforced upon Africans throughout the continent, thereby suppressing longstanding polytheistic, animist traditions. *La Genèse* might be watched in conjunction with Sembene's *Ceddo* (1976), which explores the struggle of West African peoples against the imposition of Christianity and Islam, and *Guelwaar* (1992), in which a Christian leader is accidentally buried in a Muslim cemetery. It might also be used, however, to consider current religious conflicts in West Africa—particularly in Nigeria's Plateau State, where two thousand people have died since 2001—and the attempts to end cycles of violence initiated or fueled by religion. That Christianity was first promoted in West Africa by means of film slide shows, that cinemas are now being bought up and converted into mosques and Pentecostal churches throughout West Africa, and that many southern Nigerian and Ghanaian video films use extensive Christian iconography to justify their narratives of retributive violence, means that the critique of religion and the promotion of restorative justice through film has additional relevance.

The choreography of the film's final shot clearly symbolizes Sissoko's message of reconciliation and restorative justice: a wide long shot, it shows Hamor (in gold), Jacob (in blue), Dinah (in white), and Esau (in brown hide) standing together in the Sahelian semiarid landscape facing Mount Hombori, watching Jacob's sons in the distance, thus pointing forward, also, to their reconciliation with their brother, Joseph. Showing that reconciliation is possible, Sissoko says, was his reason for deciding to keep Hamor (who is killed in the Book of Genesis by Jacob's sons) alive (2003a). Read from a Christian perspective, the recovery of Joseph, who was believed to be dead, prefigures the resurrection of Christ, thereby pointing forward to a time when the violent, sacrificial culture of the pre-Christian era is (apparently) brought to an end by Christ's teachings on nonviolence. Even without this perspective, however, what is anticipated in the meeting in Egypt is a scene in which Joseph shows no desire for retributive justice, but weeps and embraces his brothers, and in which Judah offers to give himself into slavery in the place of Benjamin, the youngest brother. As Barlet says:

> [Sissoko] adds a dimension [to the Book of Genesis] that is essential at present, namely the surpassing of the conflict. Jacob seeks to be reconciled with Esau, but it is with God that he has to fight, and thus with himself. Without spirituality, without a questioning of the self, there is no reconciliation. Especially as racism is first and foremost a projection on the Other of what frightens me in my self: that stranger who disturbs me in my divided self. For, as the Rwandan proverb puts it: *Nta wiyanga nk'uwanga undi* (No one hates himself more than he who hates others). (1999)

By drawing on the shared Book of Genesis as a means for interrogating past and present violence—the conflicts between rural communities in Mali, and ethnic and religious conflicts worldwide—Sissoko would seem to align himself with those Africans who, according to professor of religion Vincent Wimbush, are "creatively pragmatic and selective in their use of the Bible so that the Bible may enhance rather than frustrate their life struggles" (quoted in West, 341). The radical infidelities of the film result in a narrative that offers a critique of violence, and thus the Africanization of the Book of Gen-

Figure 9.6
Reconciliation
sequence from *La
Genèse*. (Images
courtesy of
California
Newsreel)

esis is achieved precisely through the renouncing of violence. While the film
suggests that violence is "inherent to human fraternity," according to Barlet,
"it is not just the stating of this that makes the film so pertinent today," but
rather that Sissoko attempts, through *La Genèse*, "to work toward a solution"
(1999).

Sissoko offers a challenge to anyone who assumes that his film is a transformation of a text external to Mali. While reclaiming the Book of Genesis as a human source, Sissoko simultaneously adapts local Malian traditions—the griotic, and the Koteba theatrical traditions—which he uses to rewrite an old, familiar narrative for the sake of contemporary audiences in Africa and abroad. His film thus participates in that movement by African film adapters to erode the boundaries between African and non-African epistemologies, allowing them to inflect and influence each other. In this way Sissoko himself can be seen as a griot, intervening in world culture to speak the truth to global violence. That this griot offers his critique of violence from the continent that is most often associated with violence is extremely moving and powerful.

Conclusion

"Fear Stalks Darfur Camps as Violence Begins to Take Hold." "Tribal Violence Spirals in Kenya." "Thousands Flee Fighting in Chad." "DR Congo: Voices of Violence." "Mogadishu Emptied by Fighting." "Children Terrified by South African Xenophobia." These were the news headlines circulating in Europe in early 2008. One cannot deny the existence of violence in Africa, but the crystallization of violence into neatly packaged, easily digested newsbites engages in precisely the kind of repetition and reproduction for which Adorno condemns the mass-culture industry. These kinds of headlines have become so predictable in relation to African countries that they could even be characterized as a form of Baudrillardian simulation: readers have been inundated by such statements to the extent that they are likely to be completely desensitized to them, and utterly distanced from any empathy for the actual suffering and pain to which millions of Africans are being subjected on a daily basis. It is for this reason that I want to preserve the genre of "African film" within the broader genre of "African screen media," and the practice of "African film adaptation" within the broader category of "film adaptation." For African film, embodying all the imaginative possibilities of fiction, and African film adaptation, with its tendency to historicize, deepen, and make sense of the realities of the present, clearly have a role to play in counteracting the excessively negative and depressing image created of Africa through the news media.

In Abderrahmane Sissako's film *Bamako* (2006), one of the few African films to succeed in gaining mainstream distribution in Europe, a legal trial is staged in a courtyard in which the plaintiff is the Malian people and the defendant global institutions such as the International Monetary Fund (IMF) and the World Bank. Sissako's film perhaps offers the most plangent and urgent testimony and critique of violence of any African film. The critique of violence here is leveled not at Africa, but squarely at the West, and the tools Sissako uses are mimetic: a combination of rational logic and embodied evidence. One of the witnesses for the prosecution, Aminata Traoré, speaks eloquently about the way that Africa has been underdeveloped by the West, while another, the old farmer and master of the balafon Zegué Bamba, simply sings out his suffering. One witness stands before the court silently, saying nothing. And yet, the defense continually asks for written documents as proof of the claims being made by the Malians. Sissako attempts to show us that the evidence is before our very eyes: in the thoughts and embodied experiences of these Africans. These people are not hidden behind depersonalized, shocking headlines. They express themselves through their unique facial expressions, bodily gestures, and voices due to the film medium's indexical recording abilities and Sissako's commendable patience. If their evidence did not exist before because it was not written down, it exists now forever—in Sissako's audiovisual document of their experiences. Negotiating between the immediacy of documentary, by inviting his actors to improvise their arguments, and the clarity of fiction, by complementing the plaintives' words with the heartrending narrative of a couple's breakup, Sissako stretches the possibilities of the film medium to show how the global economic system manifests itself, causing pain, in the most personal and intimate of ways. The film medium—and fiction film in particular—allows us to focus on stories of individual suffering while also collectively imagining a more positive future.

Similarly, Suleman, Hood, Dube, Roodt, Bekolo, Ramaka, and Sissoko stretch the possibilities of film adaptation, molding it into a form of mimesis that pays respect to age-old oral and performative African practices while also allowing it to intervene in contemporary African and international debates. Ignoring expectations that film adaptations should be "faithful" to their source texts, these directors collectively make a powerful statement through radical infidelity to texts that nevertheless provide an important backdrop for the scenes of contemporary violence visualized in the films. Turning to adaptation has allowed the filmmakers to rewrite history and remake literary texts for contemporary audiences, both "subaltern" and "elite," and to invest their films with textured layers of meaning that open up rather than foreclose discussion and debate. At a time when certain world leaders are all too ready to uncritically condemn violence as the work of "evil," thereby de-historicizing the use of force, African film adapters have summoned the adaptation process precisely to reveal the historical and rational roots to all acts of violence. According to the perspective put forward by these film-makers, violence is not the consequence of bodily impulses, brute force, or pure unfathomable evil, but of rational(izable) events and actions—if only people take the trouble to trace, study, and attempt to explain these events and actions. To understand violence is not to excuse it, as is implied in the French proverb: *Tout comprendre, c'est tout pardonner.* To see violence as reasonable is both terrifying and empowering: for it means that the solution to violence is a complex, arduous process of restoring trust and good faith between individuals and communities.

From the critique of sexual, class, and racial violence and the expression of a certain degree of hope for the future in South African film adaptations, to the reinstatement of the shared human foundations to critical, artistic, and religious texts in the West African film adaptations, these films—in spite of their violent content—are among the most optimistic and inspir-ing of African feature films. Although as diverse in their strategies and styles as Africa is in its cultures, these films can be collectively character-ized through the common solution to violence that they pose: the rejection of retributive strategies, which will inevitably lead to ongoing cycles of vio-lence, and the embracing of restorative justice, whether it be through truth commissions in South Africa, through Rwanda's gacaca courts, or through Sissako's makeshift fictional "court"-yard in which structural economic vio-lence against Africa is taken to task on film. As I have argued, these adap-tations are themselves complementing processes of restorative justice, both literally—through the way that Sissoko used *La Genèse* to mediate the con-flict between the Tuaregs and the Malian government—and symbolically, through the filmmakers' implicit message that making films about violence can help to exorcise and explain violence in a way that either the taking up of arms or solely rational, disembodied discussion cannot.

NOTES

Preface

1. See Vieyra 1969, 1972, 1975, and 1983; Bachy 1982 and 1983; Pfaff 1984 and 2004; Boughedir 1987; Gardies and Haffner 1987; Tomaselli 1988 and 2006; Diawara 1992; Ukadike 1994 and 2002; Barlet 2000; Thackway 2003; Gugler 2003.

Introduction: "African Cinema": Problems and Possibilities

1. Momar Thiam's short film *Sarzan* (1963) is an adaptation of a story by Birago Diop.

2. For example, *Niaye* (1964), *La Noire de . . .* (1965), *Mandabi* (1968), *Xala* (1974), and *Guelwaar* (1992) are all adaptations.

3. Dani Kouyaté's *Keïta! L'héritage du griot* (1994) and *Sia, le rêve du python* (2001), and Zimbabwean director Tsitsi Dangarembga's *Kare Kare Zvako* (2004), are examples.

4. See Stam and Raengo 2005; Hutcheon 2006; Leitch 2007; Cartmell and Whelehan 2007; Sanders 2007.

5. There has been significant confusion in African film criticism around the precise meaning of the word *griot*. Too often this word is simply conjured in nonspecific terms as a means of labeling African filmmakers as "storytellers" without adequate historical contextualization. What is most important to recognize is that griots are not found in every African country or context: they are concentrated in West Africa, where they again have different sociocultural roles depending on which community one is addressing. In broad terms in West Africa, the word *griot* refers to a group of professional musicians and historians. For a comprehensive study on griots throughout West Africa, see Hale (1998). For more specific studies of the role of the griot in Mandinka (Malian and Gambian) society, see Darbo (1976), Hoffman (2000), and Ebron (2002), and in Wolof (Senegalese) culture, see Panzacchi (1994) and Castaldi (2006).

6. The filmmakers, writers, and actors interviewed include Moussa Sene Absa (Senegal), Breyten Breytenbach (South Africa), Tsitsi Dangarembga (Zimbabwe), Mark Dornford-May and Pauline Malefane (South Africa), Tayeb Louhichi (Tunisia), Sarah Maldoror (France/Angola), Zola Maseko (South Africa), Sechaba Morojele (South Africa), Njabulo Ndebele (South Africa), Oliver Schmitz (South Africa), Ousmane Sembene (Senegal), Patrick Shai (South Africa), Cheick Oumar Sissoko (Mali), Shawn Slovo (South Africa), and Mansour Sora Wade (Senegal).

7. See Marks 2000 and 2002; Jayamanne 2001; Bruno 2002; Sobchack 2004; Attridge 2004; Scarry 2007; and Beugnet 2007.

8. Whereas Sada Niang has claimed that Sembene's fourth film, *Mandabi* (1968), is "a serious plea for . . . *social* rationality" (1996:56; my emphasis), Birgit Meyer has examined the way that Ghanaian video films often exhibit a form of *spiritual* rationality, representing Christianity as the solution to problems raised in the film (whether related to love, family, or government corruption). She contrasts these video films, which tend to see the origin of problems as located within occult forces, with celluloid films made by the Ghana Film Industry Corporation (GFIC) that "tried to describe problems arising in the city as *social*" (2003:201). She does point out, however, that the representation of occult and spiritual forces in Ghanaian video films "do not primarily and necessarily reflect the convictions of the filmmakers but spectators' expectations" (ibid.). Similarly, one could argue that many African celluloid filmmakers have figured solutions to social problems through animist practices in which they do not necessarily believe: the spitting scene that concludes Sembene's *Xala* is one example. Although Sembene himself is a professed atheist, his films confirm his respect for the fact that he lives in a country that is 95% Muslim, with many who visit marabouts, and who would believe in the possibility that the *xala* (impotence) was indeed the result of an actual curse placed on El Hadji. As David Murphy points out, "In a society where people routinely believe in fetishes and the supernatural, one is obliged to consider such beliefs as a social reality, irrespective of one's own personal opinions on such matters" (2000a:100). Beyond recognizing "such beliefs" as a *social reality*, it is necessary to recognize them—as Meyer would argue—as a form of spiritual rationality. A similar philosophy is offered by Senegalese filmmaker Joseph Gaï Ramaka (see chapter 7).

9. I am indebted to my colleague, Dr. Alena Rettová, for drawing my attention to these works.

10. See Bhabha 1984, 1994; Comaroff and Comaroff 2000; Cooper 2002, 2005; and Povinelli 2002.

11. Some of the earliest film adaptations set in Africa fall into this category—such as H. Rider Haggard's *King Solomon's Mines* (1885), adapted to film by H. Lisle Lucogue (1919), Geoffrey Barkas (1937), and Compton Bennett (1950); and C. S. Forester's *The African Queen* (1935), adapted to film in 1951 by John Huston.

12. In other parts of the continent, film production began much earlier, under the auspices of commercial film industries (as in Egypt and "white" South Africa).

13. Second Cinema is typified by those counter-cinemas developed in Europe after World War II, such as the French Nouvelle Vague.

14. I do not mean to claim that such a mode is the only one that has existed in African cinematic production. African cinema in the Portuguese ex-colonies, for example, represents an alternate case, having been founded on revolutionary principles.

15. Here, as throughout the book, translation from French to English is my own.

I. Cinema and Violence in South Africa

1. See Gutsche 1972; Tomaselli 1988, 2006; Blignaut and Botha 1992a; Botha and Van Aswegen 1992; Davis 1996; Balseiro and Masilela 2003; and Maingard 2007.

2. This anniversary, originally called Dingaan's Day, later came to be called the Day of the Vow or the Day of the Covenant by radical, right-wing Afrikaners, since they saw their victory as a message from God that they were the rightful owners of South Africa. Now, post-1994, the name has been changed to the Day of Reconciliation.

3. Tomaselli and Hees point out that Grierson identified with the Afrikaners as a Scotsman who felt the humiliation his people had suffered under the English. They suggest, however, that this partiality to the Afrikaners blinded Grierson to the link between state and ideology—he accepted the Afrikaner discourse around "cultural emancipation" at face value, ignoring apartheid's concomitant fascism.

4. See Dovey and Impey (forthcoming).

5. See Gairoonisa Paleker's forthcoming Ph.D. dissertation from the University of Cape Town for a fascinating and in-depth discussion of general and "black" subsidy schemes and the films they funded.

6. I am indebted to Paula Callus for making me aware of these films and the possibilities inherent in the animation process.

7. The state sector in South Africa, including the government-run NFVF and the state-owned Industrial Development Corporation (IDC), provides only about 2.6% of financing for films, the remainder coming from private financiers or from overseas (mainly from the United States). In order to increase its investment, the state sector has to encourage the production of films that are guaranteed to win box-office success (Sukazi 2003). This in itself hinders the possibility of the development of a truly independent national film industry, free from compromises imposed by external players.

8. *Cry Freedom* (1987), an adaptation of Donald Woods's factual books *Biko* (1978) and *Asking for Trouble* (1980), *A World Apart* (1988), based on Ruth First's prison diary *117 Days* (1965), and *A Dry White Season* (1989), adapted from André Brink's 1979 novel of the same name, all make use of a white intermediary. Euzhan Palcy, the Martinican director of *A Dry White Season*, explains that she wanted to make "a film about South Africa entirely from the point of view of black characters" but "clearly nobody wanted to put money into a black filmmaker making a movie about

blacks in South Africa. So I decided I had to find a book that would help me tell the story another way" (quoted in Nixon 1991:513). Shawn Slovo explains that in order to escape potential censorship, she had to convert the name of her Communist mother Ruth First into "Diana Roth," thereby invoking sympathy through the obvious connection to the Princess of Wales (Slovo 2003).

9. FEPACI, an organization of 33 member countries, was set up in 1969, mainly under the auspices of Francophone Africa.

10. Lucia Saks points out that not only are South Africa's home-grown television dramas and soap operas, such as *Generations* and *Yizo Yizo*, outperforming imported U.S. television shows, but also that it is the most gritty and realistic of these South African television products—such as *Isidingo* and *Yizo Yizo*—that are most watched by South African audiences (2003:145). This would imply that there is a large South African audience that would welcome critical feature films on violent South African realities were they more widely available.

11. At the time of this book's publication, the Cape Town World Cinema Festival and Sithengi Film Market were suspended due to financial problems (see ScreenAfrica 2008). It is uncertain whether they will continue.

12. It should be noted that African filmmakers' response to the AFL initiative has not been entirely positive, due to the very low, once-off acquisition fee that M-Net offers filmmakers in exchange for the rights to their films.

2. *Fools* and Victims: Adapting Rationalized Rape into Feminist Film

1. French, South African, Zimbabwean, and Mozambican film production companies collaborated in the making of the film, which also received financial support from the European Union, the Hubert Bals Fund, the SABC, and the French Ministry of Foreign Affairs.

2. The film's French audience total for 1997 was 4,369 (Barlet 2000:251).

3. Government statistics show that violent crime increased by 33% between 1994 and 2001 (Harris 2003), and according to statistics provided by the nongovernmental organization Rape Crisis South Africa, there were 52,160 reported rapes alone in South Africa in 1997 (Rape Crisis South Africa 2004).

4. A *stokvel* is a mutual benefits society in black South African society, where money is made available for such occasions as weddings and funerals.

5. This scene is presented with some ambiguity—it could be seen as a miscarriage—possibly because abortion is a very contentious issue in certain black South African communities.

6. In *Disgrace* (1999), J. M. Coetzee's protagonist David Lurie is notably a lecturer in Romantic poetry who also uses the discourse of Romanticism to "cloud" the reality of his rape of Melanie Isaacs in the telling of it. In many ways *Disgrace* can itself be seen as a rewriting or adaptation of Ndebele's "Fools."

3. Redeeming Features: Screening HIV/AIDS, Screening Out Rape in Gavin Hood's *Tsotsi*

1. In Lovinsa Kavuma's powerful documentary film, *Rape for Who I Am* (2005), not only does the director show that South African lesbians are "put in their place" by men through rape, but also that certain men believe that it is their "right" to have sex with their daughters. One father in the film proclaims: "If I have planted a peach tree, why should I not pluck the peaches from it?"

2. The animated film, *And There in the Dust* (2004), is—to my knowledge—the only fictional film that deals with baby rape in South Africa. It is based on the true story of 9-month-old Baby Tshepang, who was raped on October 27, 2001, in the settlement of Louisvale Road near Upington. The horrific event was first translated into a play, *Tshepang*, written and directed by Laura Foot Newton, one of the producers and directors of *And There in the Dust*. The film, only 8 minutes long, reveals that the particularly subtle techniques of animation allow Tshepang's story to be told in a way that is true to her pain while steering away from sensationalizing the rape. I wish, once again, to express my gratitude to Paula Callus for bringing this film, and the techniques of animation, to my attention.

3. The dilemma is perhaps most strikingly summed up (although not wittingly) in a recent Louis Vuitton adveriesement, photographed by Annie Leibovitz, in which Mikhail Gorbachev sits in the back of a car, a Louis Vuitton bag at his side, the Berlin Wall visible in the rear window of the car. Gorbachev apparently agreed to become the new face of Louis Vuitton after the company decided to donate money to the organization he founded, Green Cross International.

4. From Black and White to "Coloured": Racial Identity in 1950s and 1990s South Africa in Two Versions of *A Walk in the Night*

1. At its release the film was given the title 'Nagstappie, an Afrikaans translation of the phrase "a short night walk." Subsequently, it was altered to *A Walk in the Night*, possibly since this title is more accessible to non–South African audiences.

2. The term *Coloured* was applied by the apartheid government to people of mixed race, who are the descendants of whites, blacks, Khoisan, and indentured slaves from Ceylon (Sri Lanka), the Dutch East Indies (Malaysia and Indonesia), Mozambique, and Madagascar who were shipped to South Africa in the 1600s. Dube, and La Guma, like the protagoninst of *A Walk in the Night*, Mikey, have been classified as Coloured.

3. This is contrary to the way that La Guma's work has subsequently been read, for example by Balasubramanyam Chandramohan, who sees Coloured identity as central to La Guma's literary project (1992).

4. Mikey's reclaiming of his Coloured identity, and of the Afrikaans language used by Coloured people, perhaps emphasizes the fact that 72 percent of Afrikaans

speakers in South Africa are not in fact white, but Coloured, and that the Afrikaans language thus cannot be seen only as the language of apartheid oppression.

5. Coetzee argues that although La Guma's "A Walk in the Night" has no hero, "it is indicated clearly who the potential hero is: Franky Lorenzo" (1971:10). To Coetzee, Franky Lorenzo—through his embodiment of class solidarity—is the novella's representative for the possibility of a Marxist reading of the South African situation. It is thus of import that in the film Mikey is granted some of Franky's attributes.

6. See www.youtube.com/watch?v=E36-9_0_ENE for a short television report about the Johan Nel case, which was filmed, edited, and narrated by Paula Chowles for the *Times* multimedia in January 2008. For the ANC's Statement on the racial abuse at Free State University, issued February 28, 2008, see www.anc.org.za/ancdocs/pr/2008/pr0228.html.

7. See Du Pré 1994; James et al. 1996; Erasmus 2001; Hendriks 2004; and Adhikari 2005.

5. Audio-visualizing "Invisible" Violence:
Remaking and Reinventing *Cry, the Beloved Country*

1. Roodt and Singh previously made the B-grade thriller, *City of Blood* (1983), set in Johannesburg; *Place of Weeping* (1986), a film which they publicized as the "first anti-apartheid feature film made in South Africa"; and the hugely popular musical *Sarafina!* (1992), adapted from Mbongeni Ngema's stage musical. Their most recent film, *Yesterday* (2004), was nominated for an Academy Award for Best Foreign-Language Film.

2. It is worth noting that the 1951 film makes use of a heterodiegetic narrator, with a strong British accent, and in this way appears to rerender faithfully the novel's location of autonomy and Ultimate Authority in this narrator.

6. Cinema and Violence in Francophone West Africa

1. In order to ground Genova's claims, it is necessary to contextualize Senegal's early colonial relationship to France and to cinema. The centrality of cinema to Senegal is no doubt partly due to the manner in which the French colonized sub-Saharan Africa. The first French presence was established on the island of Ndar off Senegal in 1659, and colonizing activity started in the early 1800s from the port town of St. Louis in Senegal and moved inland while retaining Senegal as its base. The French general Louis Faidherbe, who was put in charge of the eastward expansion, was made governor of Senegal in 1854, and Senegal became the first French African colony in 1864. Faidherbe encountered a great deal of opposition from inland African leaders, which meant that very little civilian French presence was established in countries other than Senegal, although children were forced to learn French at school and there was a strong French military presence. West Africa—and particularly Senegal—was

clearly the focus of the French colonizing authorities, and French Equatorial Africa was allocated to the French later, at the Berlin Conference. Senegal was a "privileged" country, too, in terms of its access to cinema, with COMACICO and SECMA opening more than 70 theaters with 35mm and 16mm projectors in the country (Vieyra 1983:18). As Vieyra points out, "The cinema . . . installed itself in Dakar for its essential activities, whether distribution-exhibition or production" (ibid.).

2. Rouch also played a key role in the development of Mozambican national cinema (see Diawara 1992).

3. Instead of providing African filmmakers with the necessary skills to work independently of French control, the Bureau was structured so that funding was given to half-completed projects, or toward financing postproduction costs in France rather than paying the Africans themselves. The words of French editors during this period reveal the minimal creative power African filmmakers had over their work. Frequently not provided with adequate training or production materials, African filmmakers relied on French editors to "save" their films (Andrade-Watkins 1996:119–26). A clause in contracts also meant that African filmmakers had to sign away their noncommercial rights to their films in exchange for the Bureau's assistance (115).

4. See Vieyra 1969, 1972, 1975, 1983; Martin 1982; Pfaff 1984; Boughedir 1987; Gardies and Haffner 1987; Diawara 1992; Ukadike 1994.

5. Although after independence West African governments professed an interest in developing cinematic infrastructures, Diawara argues that they "failed to ground their politics of national production in an economically viable plan" (1992:77). Notably, those West African countries with socialist postindependence governments, such as Mali, Burkina Faso, and Guinea, were much more successful at nationalizing film production than were the more economically liberal countries such as Senegal, Niger, and Cameroon, which relied too greatly on French support (see Diawara 1992).

6. In Senegal, Mansour Sora Wade has adapted Mbissane Ngom's novel *Le Prix du Pardon* (1983) into a film of the same name (2001).

7. Ousmane Sembene and Bassek Ba Kobhio have engaged in what Tcheuyap calls "auto-adaptation" (2001, 2005), bringing their own novels to the screen.

8. Guinean filmmaker David Achkar has adapted his father's prison letters to the screen in *Allah Tantou* (1992), which criticizes Sekou Touré's regime for its betrayal and torture of his father. This practice of "familial adaptation" finds a parallel in South African filmmaker Shawn Slovo's adaptation, *A World Apart* (1988), of her mother's prison diary, *117 Days* (1965), and in the work of Burkinabé director Dani Kouyaté, the son of the griot Sotigui Kouyaté, who has adapted West African myths to film.

9. Many of the video films that have been made in Nigeria are adaptations of Yoruba traveling plays.

10. These films include Malian filmmaker Cheick Oumar Sissoko's *Battu* (2000),

adapted from Senegalese writer Aminata Sow Fall's novel *La Grève des Battu* (Beggars' Strike) (1986), Mauritanian filmmaker Med Hondo's film *Sarraounia* (1986), adapted from the Nigerian writer Abdoulaye Mamani's eponymous novella (1980), and Joseph Gaï Ramaka's film *So Be It/Ainsi soit-il* (1997), from Nigerian writer Wole Soyinka's English play *The Strong Breed* (1964).

11. Cameroonian and Gabonese filmmakers Bassek Ba Kobhio and Didier Ouénangaré's film *Le Silence de la Forêt/The Silence of the Forest* (2003) is adapted from a novel by Etienne Goyémidé (1985), set in the Central African Republic.

12. Nigerian filmmaker Tunde Kelani's *Thunderbolt* (2000) is a "half-adaptation" of *Othello*, while Mambety's *Hyenas* draws on Dürrenmatt's play only in part.

7. Losing the Plot, Restoring the Lost Chapter: Aristotle in Cameroon

1. See Butcher 1951; Eden 1986; Halliwell 1987; Belfiore 1992; Barnes 1995; Nuttall 1996; and Halliwell 2002.

2. See Kierkegaard 1942; Gombrich 1965; Lowell 1971; Greene 1982; Hillis Miller 1982; Johnson 1985; and Melberg 1995.

3. The symbol of the grandfather is of great importance in African films, as attested to by the opening words of Safi Faye's film *Fad' jal/Grand-père raconte/ Come and Work* (1979), which state that losing an old man is akin to the destruction of a library.

8. African Incar(me)nation: Joseph Gaï Remaka's *Karmen Geï* (2001)

1. Forty of these are silent films, made before the first sound film version of *Carmen* appeared in 1931. Some of the film versions of *Carmen* include Charlie Chaplin's *Burlesque on Carmen* (1916); *The Campus Carmen* (1928), which features a female Don José; a fascist reinterpretation commissioned by Hitler called *Andalusische Nachte/Carmen, la de Triana* (Germany/Spain 1938); *Carmen Jones* (1954), which was set on a military base in the U.S. South and starred an all-black cast; and even a pornographic version, *Carmen Baby* (1967).

2. For an analysis of *U-Carmen eKhayelitsha* (2005), see Dovey, "Return to (Questions of) Source: A Case Study of *U-Carmen eKhayelitsha*" (2007).

3. These include films by Peter Brook, Jean-Luc Godard, Francesco Rosi, and Carlos Saura.

4. Notably, although such an interpretation could be related to the subtextual concerns of *Karmen Geï*, it would be difficult to apply the same reading to some of the other recent film adaptations of *Carmen*, such as Vicente Aranda's 2003 Spanish version, *Carmen*, which depoliticizes the novella.

5. See Nietzsche 1967; Clément 1979; Furman 1988; McClary 1991; and Collier 1993.

6. For a more profound analysis of the ways in which Africans were constructed

as irrational, embodied Others through the framework of "fetishism," see Dovey (2005).

7. Alexie Tcheuyap gives an illuminating account of representations of and reactions to sexuality and homosexuality in African films in Africa (2005a). He does not analyze *Karmen Geï* but does notably suggest in a footnote that lesbianism in the film is best interpreted in relation to context rather than identity politics (2005a:152–53).

8. This view, notably, conforms to the philosophy of death in many African religions (Mbiti 1969; Idowu 1973; Bosch 1975; Blakely et al. 1994; Magesa 1997).

9. Examples include Dani Kouyaté's *Keïta! L'héritage du Griot* (1995) and *Sia, le rêve du python* (2001), adaptations of the West African myths of Soundjata and Wagadu, respectively.

9. Humanizing the Old Testament's Origins, Historicizing Genocide's Origins: Cheick Ouman Sissoko's *La Genèse* (1999)

1. Mark Dornford-May and Pauline Malefane's *Son of Man* (2006) is the first African adaptation of the New Testament, again inspiring suggestion that South African filmmakers are following in the footsteps of West African directors' interest in adapting canonical texts. Ivorian director Roger Gnoan M'bala's film *Au Nom du Christ* (1993), winner of FESPACO's Etalon de Yennenga, is the most well-known African feature film on the topic of religion. In this case, unlike in *La Genèse* and *Son of Man*, the filmmaker is caustically critical of religion (especially Christianity) and the way in which it might be harnessed for abuse through power.

2. The fiction films that have been made about the Rwandan genocide are: Nick Hughes's *100 Days* (2001), Terry George's *Hotel Rwanda* (2004), Michael Caton-Jones's *Shooting Dogs* (2005), Raoul Peck's *Sometimes in April* (2005), and Lee Isaac Chung's *Munyurangabo* (2007). One might speculate that films representing the Rwandan genocide have been made only by foreigners since there are very few film facilities in Rwanda, but there also seems to be a non-African preoccupation and fascination with the so-called "ethnic" violence as something "Other" to the West, which denies the Rwandan genocide's origins in Belgian colonial violence and the division of the Hutus and Tutsis through identity cards.

3. Duvauroux, a Biblical specialist, is the author of *Héritiers de Caïn—Identités, fraternité, pouvoir* (1997).

4. The only well-known film adaptation of the Bible with an all-black cast, *The Green Pastures* (1936), adapted from Marc Connelly's Pulitzer Prize–winning play of the same name, falls into the same trap of representing Africans as children and their religious practice as naïve. Ssali points out, however, that *Green Pastures*, after being sent to South Africa for distribution, was banned simply because it suggested that all of the Old Testament characters were black (1996:94).

5. Given at the Cambridge University Divinity Faculty, Feb. 12, 2004.

FILMOGRAPHY

100 Days (2001). Dir. Nick Hughes. UK/Rwanda. 100 min. English and French. Prod. Eric Kabera. Not in distribution.

L'Afrance (2001). Dir. Alain Gomis. Senegal/France. 91 min. French. Prod. Edouard Mauriat and Anne-Cécile Berthomeau. Mercure Distribution.

Africa Dreaming (1997). Directors: Richard Pakleppa, Abderrahmane Sissako, Joseph Gaï Ramaka, João Ribeiro. South Africa/Mozambique/Namibia/Senegal/Tunisia. 4 x 26 min. Ex. Prod. Jeremy Nathan. Distr. California Newsreel.

The African Queen (1951). Dir. John Huston. UK/USA. 105 min. Prod. Horizon Films. Adapted from C. S. Forester, *The African Queen* (1935).

Afrique 50 (1950). Dir. René Vautier. France/Congo. 20 min. French. Distr. Cinémathèque de Bretagne (claude.arnal@cinematheque-bretagne.fr).

Afrique, Je Te Plumerai (Africa, I will fleece you) (1992). Dir. Jean-Marie Teno. Cameroon. 88 min. French. Distr. California Newsreel.

Afrique sur Seine (1955). Dir. Paulin Soumanou Vieyra and Mamadou Sarr. France. 21 min. French. Prod. Le Groupe Africain du Cinéma. Available for viewing at the African Film Library, French Ministry of Foreign Affairs, Paris.

Allah Tantou (God's will) (1991). Dir. David Achkar. Guinea/France. 62 min. French. Distr. California Newsreel.

Andalusische Nachte/Carmen, la de Triana (1938). Dir. Herbert Maisch. Germany/Spain. 94 min. German. Prod. Carl Froelich-Film. Distr. Ufa Film Company. Adapted from Prosper Mérimée, *Carmen* (1845–1847).

And There in the Dust (2004). Dir. Lara Foot Newton, Gerhard Marx, and Wesley France. Animation. South Africa/Zimbabwe. 8 min. Prod. Lara Foot Newton. Not in distribution.

Aristotle's Plot (1997). Dir. and Screenplay: Jean-Pierre Bekolo. Cameroon/Zimbabwe. 70 min. English. Prod. JBA Production (France), British Film Institute (GB), and Framework International (Zimbabwe). Distr. JBA Production.

L'arrivée d'un train en gare de Ciotat (1896). Dir. Auguste and Louis Lumière. France. 1 min. Silent. Prod. Lumière Brothers. Distr. Kino Video.

L'arroseur arosé (1895). Dir. Louis Lumière. France. 1 min. Silent. Prod. Lumière Brothers. (Viewable at www.youtube.com/watch?v = Ei6nJfXAuHQ.)

Au Pays Dogon (1938). Dir. Marcel Griaule. Mali. 15 min. Not in distribution.

Bab el Hadid (1958). Dir. Youssef Chahine. Egypt. 95 min. Arabic. Prod. Gabriel Talhami Productions. Distr. Misr Films, Egypt.

Bal poussière (1988). Dir. Henri Duparc. Ivory Coast. 91 min. French. Prod. Focale 13. Available for viewing at the African Film Library, French Ministry of Foreign Affairs, Paris.

Bamako (2006). Dir. Abderrahmane Sissako. Mali/USA/France. 115 min. French and Bambara. Prod. Archipel 33. Distr. Artificial Eye.

Battu (2000). Dir. Cheick Oumar Sissoko. Senegal/Mali. 105 min. Wolof and French. Prod. David Christophe Barrot and Sheryl Crown. Distr. UGC International. Adapted from Aminata Sow Fall, *La Grève des Battu* (1986).

Beyond Freedom: The South African Journey (2006). Dir. Jacquie Trowell. Animation. Germany/South Africa. 13 min. English. Prod. Atom Films. (Partially viewable at www.youtube.com/watch?v = _3v1JqlnvIw&feature = related.)

Bicycle Thieves (1948). Dir. Vittorio de Sica. Italy. 93 min. Italian. Prod. Produzioni De Sica. Distr. Arrow Film Distributors. Adapted from Luigi Bartolini, *Ladri di bicicleta* (1946).

The Birth of a Nation (1915). Dir. D. W. Griffith. USA. 187 min. Silent. Prod. David W. Griffith Corporation. Distr. Kino Video. Adapted from Thomas F. Dixon, Jr., *The Clansman: An Historical Romance of the Ku Klux Klan* (1905).

Blood Diamond (2006). Dir. Edward Zwick. USA/Germany. 143 min. Mende, English, and Afrikaans. Prod. Warner Brothers. Distr. Warner Home Video.

Boesman and Lena (1974). Dir. Ross Devenish. South Africa. 102 min. English. Prod. Bluewater Productions. Not in distribution. Adapted from Athol Fugard, *Boesman and Lena* (stage play) (1969).

Borom Sarret (1963). Dir. Ousmane Sembene. Senegal/France. 22 min. French. Prod. Filmi Doomirew and Actualités Françaises. Distr. New Yorker Films (USA).

Boy Called Twist (2004). Dir. Tim Greene. South Africa. 115 min. English. Prod. Twisted Pictures. Distr. TripFlix. Adapted from Charles Dickens, *Oliver Twist* (1838).

Burlesque on Carmen (1916). Dir. Charlie Chaplin. USA. 67 min. Silent. Prod. Essanay Film Manufacturing Company. Distr. Reel Media International. Adapted from Prosper Mérimée, *Carmen* (1845–1847) and Georges Bizet, *Carmen* (opera) (1875).

Le cake-walk des négres du nouveau Cirque (1902). Dir. Georges Méliès. Senegal. Not in distribution. No further information available.

The Campus Carmen (1928). Dir. Alfred J. Goulding. USA. 20 min. Silent. Prod.

Mack Sennett Comedies. Distr. Video Classic. Adapted from Prosper Mérimée, *Carmen* (1845–1847).

Cape of Good Hope (2004). Dir. Mark Bamford. South Africa/USA. 107 min. Afrikaans, English, and Xhosa. Prod. Wonder View Films. Distr. New Yorker Films.

Carmen (1983). Dir. Carlos Saura. Spain. 102 min. Spanish. Prod. Emiliano Piedra. Distr. The Criterion Collection. Adapted from Prosper Mérimée, *Carmen* (1845–1847) and Georges Bizet, *Carmen* (1875).

Carmen (2003). Dir. Vicente Aranda. Spain/Italy/UK. 119 min. Spanish. Prod. Parallel Pictures. Distr. Parasol Pictures Releasing. Adapted from Prosper Mérimée, *Carmen* (1845–1847) and Georges Bizet, *Carmen* (1875).

Carmen Baby (1967). Dir. Radley Metzger. USA/West Germany/Yugoslavia. 97 min. English. Prod. Amsterdam Films. Distr. Sma Distribution. Adapted from Prosper Mérimée, *Carmen* (1845–1847) and Georges Bizet, *Carmen* (1875).

Carmen Jones (1954). Dir. Oscar Hammerstein. USA. 105 min. English. Prod. Carlyle Productions. Distr. Twentieth Century Fox. Adapted from Prosper Mérimée, *Carmen* (1845–1847) and Georges Bizet, *Carmen* (1875).

Ceddo (1976). Dir. Ousmane Sembene. Senegal. 120 min. Wolof and French. Prod. Filmi Doomirew. Distr. (16mm) BFI (UK).

Chikin Biznis—The Whole Story (1999). Dir. Ntshaveni Wa Luruli. South Africa. 103 min. English, Afrikaans, and Zulu. Distr. Film Resource Unit.

City Lovers (1982). Dir. Barney Simon. South Africa. 60 min. English. Prod. Profile Productions. Distr. MGM video. Adapted from the story by Nadine Gordimer (1972).

City of Blood (1983). Dir. Darrell James Roodt. South Africa. 95 min. English. Prod. Anant Singh Productions. Distr. New World Pictures.

Come Back, Africa (1959). Dir. Lionel Rogosin. USA/South Africa. 90 min. English and Zulu. Distr. (35mm) Cineteca di Bologna.

The Constant Gardener (2005). Dir. Fernando Meirelles. Germany/UK. 129 min. Italian, English, Swahili, and German. Prod. Potboiler Productions. Distr. Universal. Adapted from John Le Carré, *The Constant Gardener* (2001).

Conversations on a Sunday Afternoon (2005). Dir. Khalo Matabane. South Africa. 80 min. French, English, Swahili, and Zulu. Prod. Matabane Filmworks.

Country Lovers (1972). Dir. Manie van Rensburg. South Africa. 60 min. English. Prod. Profile Productions. Distr. MGM video. Adapted from the story by Nadine Gordimer (1972).

Cri du Coeur (1994). Dir. Idrissa Ouedraogo. France/Burkina Faso. 85 min. French. Prod. Les Films de la Plaine and La Centre Européen Cinématographique Rhône-Alpes. Not in distribution.

Cry Freedom (1987). Dir. Richard Attenborough. USA/UK/Zimbabwe. 157 min. English. Prod. Warner Brothers and Marble Arch Productions. Distr. Swank Motion Pictures (USA). Adapted from Donald Woods, *Biko* (1978) and *Asking for Trouble* (1980).

Cry, the Beloved Country (1951). Dir. Zoltan Korda. Screenplay: Alan Paton. South Africa/UK. 111 min. English. Prod. Lion Film Corporation. Distr. British Lion Film Corporation. Adapted from Alan Paton, *Cry, the Beloved Country* (1948).

Cry, the Beloved Country (1995). Dir. Darrell James Roodt. Screenplay: Ronald Harwood. South Africa. 109 min. English. Prod. Anant Singh. Distr. (35mm) Swank Motion Pictures (USA) and (VHS) Film Resource Unit (South Africa). Adapted from Alan Paton, *Cry, the Beloved Country* (1948).

Daratt (2006). Dir. Mahamat-Saleh Haroun. Chad/France/Belgium/Austria. 96 min. Arabic/French. Prod. Chinguitty Films. Distr. Soda Pictures (UK).

The Dark Heart (2004). Dir. Cliff Bestall and Pearlie Joubert. South Africa. 44 min. English. Prod. BBC. Not in distribution.

Den Muso (1975). Dir. Souleymane Cissé. Mali. 88 min. Bambara. Prod. Cissé Films. Not in distribution.

Drum (2004). Dir. Zola Maseko. South Africa/USA. 94 min. English, Afrikaans, and German. Prod. Armada Pictures. Distr. Armada Pictures International.

A Dry White Season (1989). Dir. Euzhan Palcy. USA/UK. 106 min. English. Prod. MGM with Star Partners II. Distr. Swank Motion Pictures (USA). Adapted from André Brink, *A Dry White Season* (1979).

Dust (1985). Dir. Marion Hänsel. Belgium/South Africa. 87 min. English. Prod. Man's Films and Daska Film International. Distr. Kino International (USA). Adapted from J. M. Coetzee, *In the Heart of the Country* (1978).

Un enfant d'Ireli (1958). Dir. Mario Marret. Mali. 13 min. Not in distribution. No further information available.

Et la neige n'était plus (1966). Dir. Ababacar Samb-Makharam. Senegal. 22 min. French. Available for viewing at the African Film Library, French Ministry of Foreign Affairs, Paris.

Et si Latif avait raison (2006). Dir. Joseph Gaï Ramaka. Senegal. 22 min. French. Prod. Les Atéliers de l'Arche. Not in distribution.

Ezra (2007). Dir. Newton I. Aduaka. Nigeria/France. 103 min. English. Prod. Arte France Cinéma. Distr. California Newsreel.

Fad'jal/Grand-père raconte/Come and Work (1979). Dir. Safi Faye. Senegal. 108 min. Serere. Not in distribution. No further information available.

Finzan (1989). Dir. Cheick Oumar Sissoko. Mali/Germany. 107 min. Bambara. Prod. Kora Films, Zweites Deutsches Fernsehen, and CNPC. Distr. (VHS) California Newsreel.

Finye (1982). Dir. Souleymane Cissé. Mali. 100 min. Bambara. Prod. Cissé Films. Not in distribution.

Flame (1996). Dir. Ingrid Sinclair. Zimbabwe/France/Namibia. 85 min. English and Shona. Prod. Black and White Film, JBA Production, and Onland Productions. Distr. (35mm and VHS) California Newsreel. Adapted from Shimmer Chinodya, *Harvest of Thorns* (1989).

Fools (1997). Dir. Ramadan Suleman. Screenplay: Bhekizizwe Peterson and Ramadan Suleman. France/South Africa/Mozambique/Zimbabwe. 90 min. Zulu and English. Prod. JBA Production, Natives at Large, Ebano Multi-Media, Framework International, M-Net Africa, and Périphérie Production. Distr. Film Resource Unit (South Africa). Adapted from the novella "Fools" by Njabulo Ndebele (1983).

Forgiveness (2004). Dir. Ian Gabriel. South Africa. 112 min. English and Afrikaans. Prod. Giant Films. Distr. California Newsreel.

La Genèse [Genesis] (1999). Dir. Cheick Oumar Sissoko. Screenplay: Jean-Louis Sagot Duvauroux. Mali/France. 102 min. Bambara. Prod. Kora Films, Centre National de Production Cinématographique du Mali, and Cinéma Public Films. Distr. (35mm and VHS) California Newsreel. Adapted from the Old Testament.

God Is African (2001). Dir. Akin Omotoso. South Africa. 93 min. English, Afrikaans, and Sotho. Prod. TranxAfrica Films. Distr. Bony Entertainment (South Africa).

The Gospel of St. John (2003). Dir. Philip Saville. Canada. 180 min. English. Prod. Toronto Film Studios and Visual Bible International. Not in distribution.

The Green Pastures (1936). Dir. Marc Connelly. USA. 93 min. English. Prod. Warner Brother Pictures. Distr. Warner Home Video. Adapted from the Old Testament.

Guelwaar (1992). Dir. Ousmane Sembene. Senegal/France. 105 min. Wolof and French. Prod. Filmi Doomirew, Galatée Films, and FR3 Film Production. Distr. New Yorker Films (USA) and BFI (UK). Adapted into Ousmane Sembene, *Guelwaar* (1996).

Guimba the Tyrant (1995). Dir. Cheick Oumar Sissoko. Mali. 93 min. Bambara. Prod. Kora Films. Distr. (35mm and VHS) California Newsreel and Kino International (USA).

Hijack Stories (2000). Dir. Oliver Schmitz. Germany/France/UK. 91 min. English and Zulu. Prod. Schlemmer Film, Septième Production, and Xenos Pictures. Distr. (35mm) Momentum (UK) and Ster-Kinekor (South Africa).

Hopes on the Horizon (2000). Dir. Onyekachi Wanbu. USA. 120 min. Prod. and Distr. (VHS) PBS.

Hotel Rwanda (2004). Dir. Terry George. USA/UK/Italy/South Africa. 121 min. English. Prod. Kigali Releasing Ltd. Distr. (DVD) Entertainment in Video.

How Long? (1976). Dir. Gibson Kente. South Africa. Held by the National Film, Video, and Sound Archives, South Africa.

Hyenas/Hyènes (1992). Dir. Djibril Diop Mambety. Senegal. 113 min. Wolof. Prod. ADR Productions. Distr. (35mm, VHS) BFI (UK) and California Newsreel. Adapted from Friedrich Dürrenmatt, *Der Besuch der Alten Dame* (1956).

Imbazo, the Axe (1993). Dir. Mickey Madoda Dube. South Africa/USA. 24 min. Prod. Mickey Madoda Dube. Held by the University of Southern California, School of Cinema-Television.

In Darkest Hollywood: Cinema and Apartheid (1993). Dir. Peter Davis and Daniel Riesenfeld. USA/Canada. 112 min. English. Prod. Nightingale and Villon. Distr. Villon Films (Canada).

In Desert and Wilderness (2001). Dir. Gavin Hood. Poland. 111 min. Polish. Distr. Vision Film Distribution. Adapted from Henryk Sienkiewicz, *W pustyni i w puszczy* (1912).

In My Country (2004). Dir. John Boorman. UK/Ireland/South Africa. 105 min. English and Afrikaans. Prod. Chartoff Productions, IDC, UKFC. Distr. Sony Pictures. Adapted from Antjie Krog, *Country of My Skull* (1998).

Jaguar (1954). Dir. Jean Rouch. France/Niger/Ghana. 110 min. French. Prod. Les Films de la Pléiade. Distr. Documentary Educational Resources.

Jim Comes to Jo'burg/African Jim (1949). Dir. Donald Swanson. South Africa. 58 min. English and Zulu. Prod. Warrior Films. Distr. Villon Films (Canada).

Jozi Zoo (2006). Dir. Mike Scott. Animation. South Africa. English. 5 min. 35 sec. Not in distribution.

Jump the Gun (1997). Dir. Les Blair. South Africa/UK. 124 min. English. Prod. Channel Four Films. Distr. Film Resource Unit.

Kare Kare Zvako (2002). Dir. Tsitsi Dangarembga. Zimbabwe. 30 min. Prod. Nyerai Films. Distr. Nyerai Films. Adapted from an oral tale, one version of which is Charles Mungoshi, "The Spirit of the Ashpit" (1989).

Karmen Geï (2001). Dir. and Screenplay: Joseph Gaï Ramaka. Senegal/France. 82 min. French and Wolof. Prod. Euripide, Mataranka, Les Atéliers de l'Arche, and Zagarianka. Distr. (35mm and VHS) California Newsreel. Adapted from Prosper Mérimée, *Carmen* (1845–1847) and Georges Bizet, *Carmen* (1875).

Keïta! L'héritage du griot (Keïta! The Heritage of the Griot) (1995). Dir. Dani Kouyaté. Burkina Faso/France. 94 min. French and Jula. Prod. AFIX Productions, Les Productions de la Lanterne, Sahélis Productions, and the Government of Burkina Faso. Distr. (35mm and VHS) California Newsreel and (35mm) La Lanterne (France). Adapted from the myth of Soundjata Keïta, one version of which is D. T. Niane, *Sundiata, an Epic of Old Mali* (1976).

Last Grave at Dimbaza (1974). Documentary by Nana Mahomo. South Africa/UK. 55 min. English. Prod. Morena Films. Distr. Villon Films (Canada).

The Last King of Scotland (2006). Dir. Kevin Macdonald. UK. 121 min. English, French, and German. Prod. DNA Films. Distr. Momentum.

Long Night's Journey into Day (2000). Dir. Deborah Hoffmann and Frances Reid. USA/South Africa. 94 min. English and Afrikaans. Prod. Reid-Hoffmann Productions. Distr. California Newsreel.

Madame Brouette (2002). Dir. Moussa Sene Absa. Canada/Senegal/France. 104 min. French. Prod. Productions de la Lanterne. Not in distribution.

Les Maîtres Fous (1954). Dir. Jean Rouch. Ghana. 30 min. French. Distr. Documentary Educational Resources.

Mandabi (1968). Dir. Ousmane Sembene. Senegal. French version 90 min. Wolof version 105 min. Prod. Comptoir Français du Film/Filmi Doomirew. Distr. New Yorker Films. Adapted from Ousmane Sembene, *Le Mandat* (1966).

Mapantsula (1988). Dir. Oliver Schmitz. South Africa/Australia/UK. 104 min. Zulu,

English, and Afrikaans. Prod. One Look Productions, David Hannay Productions, and Haverbeam. Distr. California Newsreel.

La Marche de Dakar (no date). Dir. Georges Méliès. No further information available.

Marigolds in August (1978). Dir. Ross Devenish. South Africa. 87 min. English. Prod. R. M. Productions. Not in distribution.

Max and Mona (2004). Dir. Teddy Mattera. South Africa/Sweden. 98 min. English, Afrikaans, and Zulu. Prod. Ice Media, Dv8. Distr. Ster Kinekor.

Moi et Mon Blanc (Me and my white guy) (2003). Dir. S. Pierre Yameogo. France/Burkina Faso. 90 min. French and Moré. Prod. Dunia Productions. Distr. Médiathèque des Trois Mondes.

Moi, un noir (1958). Dir. Jean Rouch. Niger. 70 min. French. Available for viewing at the African Film Library, French Ministry of Foreign Affairs, Paris.

Moolaadé (2004). Dir. Ousmane Sembene. Senegal/Burkina Faso/France/Cameroon/Morocco/Tunisia. 124 min. Bambara and French. Prod. Filmi Doomirew and Ciné-Sud Promotion. Distr. Artificial Eye.

Munyurangabo (2007). Dir. Lee Isaac Chung. USA/Rwanda. 98 min. Kinyarwanda. Prod. Almond Tree Productions. Distr. UMédia.

The Native Who Caused All the Trouble (1989). Dir. and produced by Manie van Rensburg. South Africa. 90 min. English. Distr. (VHS) Film Resource Unit.

Niaye (1964). Dir. Ousmane Sembene. Senegal/France. 35 min. French. Prod. Les Actualités Françaises and Filmi Doomirew. Available for viewing at the African Film Library, French Ministry of Foreign Affairs, Paris. Adapted from Ousmane Sembene, "Véhi Ciosane" (1962).

Noces d'eau (1953). Dir. Jean Capron and Serge Ricci. Burkina Faso. French. 26 min. No further information available.

La Noire de . . . (1965). Dir. Ousmane Sembene. Senegal/France. 65 min. Les Actualités Françaises and Filmi Doomirew. Distr. New Yorker Films/Médiathèque des Trois Mondes. Adapted from Ousmane Sembene, "La Noire de . . ." (1962).

No Past to Speak Of (2006). Dir. Jeremy Gans. South Africa/Canada. 55 min. English.

La Nuit de la Vérité (2005). Dir. Fanta Régina Nacro. Burkina Faso/France. 100 min. Dioula, French. Prod. Acrobates Film. Distr. First Run Features.

Paradise Now (2005). Dir. Hany Abu-Assad. Palestine/France/Germany/Netherlands/Israel. 90 min. Arabix. Prod. Augustus Film. Distr. A-Film Distribution.

The Passion of the Christ (2004). Dir. Mel Gibson. USA. 127 min. Aramaic/Latin/Hebrew. Prod. Icon Productions. Distr. Icon Entertainment. Adapted from the New Testament.

Paysans du Niger (1959). Dir. Eric Duvivier and A. Luzuy. Niger. 20 min. No further information available.

Paysans Noirs/Famoro le Tyran (1947). Dir. Georges Régnier. France/Burkina Faso. 99 min. French. No further information available.

Petit à Petit (1968). Dir. Jean Rouch. France. 96 min. French. Prod. Les Films de la Pléiade. Distr. Pantheon Films.

Place of Weeping (1986). Dir. Darrell James Roodt. South Africa. 88 min. English and Afrikaans. Prod. Place of Weeping Productions. Distr. New World Pictures.

Le Prix du Pardon/The Price of Forgiveness/Ndeysaan (2001). Dir. Mansour Sora Wade. Senegal. 90 min. Lébou. Distr. (VHS) California Newsreel. Adapted from Mbissane Ngom, *Le Prix du Pardon* (1983).

The Promised Land (2002). Dir. Jason Xenopolous. South Africa. Afrikaans and English. 100 min. Prod. Film Afrika. Distr. (35mm and VHS) Film Afrika. Adapted from Karel Schoeman, *Na die Geliefde Land* (1972).

Proteus (2003). Dir. John Greyson. South Africa/Canada. 100 min. English, Afrikaans, and Dutch. Prod. Pluck Productions. Distr. Parasol Peccadillo.

The Quarry (1998). Dir. Marion Hänsel. Belgium/South Africa. 112 min. English and Afrikaans. Prod. Man's Films. Adapted from Damon Galgut, *The Quarry* (1995).

Quartier Mozart (1992). Dir. Jean-Pierre Bekolo. Cameroon. 79 min. French. Prod. Kola Case. Distr. Médiathèque des Trois Mondes.

Rape for Who I Am (2005). Dir. Lovinsa Kavuma. South Africa. 27 min. English. (Viewable at www.youtube.com/watch?v = YWTqutKtZ5A.)

A Reasonable Man (1999). Dir. Gavin Hood. South Africa/France. 103 min. English. Prod. African Media Entertainment and M-Net. Distr. Pandora Cinema.

Red Dust (2004). Dir. Tom Hooper. South Africa/UK. 110 min. English and Afrikaans. Prod. BBC. Distr. Videovision Entertainment. Adapted from Gillian Slovo, *Red Dust* (2000).

Un Retour d'un Aventurier (1966). Dir. Moustapha Alassane. Niger/France. 30 min. Hausa and French. Prod. Argos Films. Available for viewing at the African Film Library, French Ministry of Foreign Affairs, Paris.

Les Saignantes (The Bloodletters) (2006). Dir. Jean-Pierre Bekolo. Cameroon. 92 min. French. Prod. Quartier Mozart Films. Not in distribution.

Sambizanga (1972). Dir. Sarah Maldoror. Angola. 102 min. Portuguese. Distr. Annouchka de Andrade (France).

Sarafina! (1992). Dir. Darrell James Roodt. France/South Africa/UK/USA. 117 min. English. Prod. BBC. Distr. Buena Vista. Adapted from Mbongeni Ngema, *Sarafina* (stage play) (1988).

Sarraounia (1986). Dir. Med Hondo. Burkina Faso/Mauritania/France. 120 min. Dioula, Peul, and French. Prod. Les Films Soleil O. Adapted from Abdoulaye Mamani, *Sarraounia* (1980).

She's Gotta Have It (1986). Dir. Spike Lee. USA. 88 min. English. Prod. 40 Acres and a Mule Filmworks. Distr. MGM Home Entertainment.

Shooting Dogs (2005). Michael Caton-Jones. UK/Germany/Rwanda. 115 min. English and French. Prod. CrossDay Productions. Distr. A-Film Home Entertainment.

Sia, le rêve du python (Sia, the dream of the python) (2001). Dir. Dani Kouyaté. France/Burkina Faso. 96 min. Jula. Prod. Les Productions de la Lanterne, Sahélis Productions, and the Government of Burkina Faso. Distr. La Lanterne (France).

Adapted from Moussa Diagana, *La Légende du Wagadu vu par Sia Yatabéré* (stage play) (no date).

Le Silence de la Forêt/The Silence of the Forest (2003). Dir. Bassek Ba Kobhio and Didier Ouénangaré. Central African Republic/Cameroon/Gabon/France. 93 min. French. Prod. Centre National du Cinéma. Distr. California Newsreel. Adapted from Etienne Goyémidé, *Le Silence de la Forêt* (1985).

So Be It/Ainsi soit-il (1997). Dir. Joseph Gaï Ramaka. Senegal. 26 min. French and Wolof. Prod. Jeremy Nathan (Africa Dreaming Series). Distr. (VHS) California Newsreel. Adapted from Wole Soyinka, *The Strong Breed* (stage play) (1964).

Soleil O (1969). Dir. Med Hondo. France/Mauritania. 98 min. French and Arabic. Prod. Grey Films and Shango Films. Available for viewing at the African Film Library, French Ministry of Foreign Affairs, Paris.

Sometimes in April (2005). Dir. Raoul Peck. France/USA/Rwanda. 140 min. English and Kinyarwanda. Prod. and Distr. HBO Films.

Song of Africa (1951). Dir. Emil Nofal. South Africa. 59 min. English and Zulu. Prod. African Film Productions. Distr. Villon Films (Canada).

Son of Man (2006). Dir. Mark Dornford-May. South Africa. 86 min. Xhosa and English. Prod. Spier Films. Distr. Spier Films. Adapted from the New Testament.

Sous les masques noirs (1938). Dir. Marcel Griaule. Mali. 15 min. No further information available.

Les Statues Meurent Aussi (1953). Dir. Alain Resnais and Chris Marker. France. 30 min. French. Prod. Présence Africaine and Tadié Cinéma. Not in distribution.

The Storekeeper (1998). Dir. Gavin Hood. South Africa. 22 min. Prod. Hood Productions. Distr. with *Tsotsi* by Miramax.

Tengers (2007). Dir. Michael Rix. Claymation. South Africa. 60 min. Prod. and Distr. Mirror Mountain Pictures.

Teranga Blues (2007). Dir. Moussa Sene Absa. Senegal. 95 min. Wolof and French. Prod. MSA Productions. Not in distribution.

This is Nollywood (2007). Dir. Franco Sacchi. Nigeria/USA. 56min. English. Prod. Centre for Digital Imaging Arts, Boston. Distr. California Newsreel.

Thunderbolt (2000). Dir. Tunde Kelani. Nigeria. 110 min. Distr. (VHS) California Newsreel. Adapted in part from Shakespeare's *Othello*.

Touki Bouki (The journey of the hyena) (1973). Dir. Djibril Diop Mambety. Senegal. 85 min. French. Prod. Cinegrit. Distr. Kino Video.

Tsotsi (2006). Dir. and Screenplay: Gavin Hood. South Africa/UK. 94 min. Zulu, Xhosa, Afrikaans, English. Prod. The UK Film & TV Production Company PLC. Distr. Miramax. Adapted from Athol Fugard, *Tsotsi* (1980).

Ubuntu's Wounds (2001). Dir. Sechaba Morojele. USA/South Africa. 32 min. Prod. HBO. Distr. Sechaba Morojele (South Africa).

U-Carmen eKhayelitsha (2005). Dir. Mark Dornford-May. South Africa. 120 min. Xhosa. Prod. Spier Films. Distr. Tartan. Adapted from Georges Bizet, *Carmen* (1875).

U-Deliwe (1975). Dir. Simon Sabela. South Africa. 60 min. Prod. Haynes Films. No further information available.

The Unfolding of Sky (1998). Dir. Antjie Krog and Ronelle Loots. South Africa. 27 min. English. Prod. Don Edkins. Distr. Film Resource Unit.

La Vie est Belle (1987). Dir. Mweze Ngangura and Benoît Lamy. DRC/Belgium/France. 80 min. French. Distr. California Newsreel.

Visages des Femmes (1985). Dir. Désiré Ecaré. Ivory Coast/France. 105 min. Aidoukrou and French. Prod. Films de la Lagune. Distr. Kino Film.

De Voortrekkers (1916). Dir. Harold M. Shaw. South Africa. 60 min. Silent. Prod. African Film Production. Distr. Villon Films (Canada).

Voyage au Congo (1927). Dir. Marc Allégret. France. Silent. Adapted from André Gide, *Voyage au Congo* (1927). No further information available.

Waati (1995). Dir. Souleymane Cissé. France/Mali/Burkina Faso. 140 min. Bambara, French, and English. Prod. Cissé Films, La Sept Cinéma. Not in distribution.

A Walk in the Night (1998). Dir. Mickey Madoda Dube. Screenplay: Mickey Madoda Dube, Mandla Langa, and Molefi Moleli. South Africa. 78 min. Afrikaans and English. Prod. Interface Productions. Distr. (VHS) California Newsreel. Adapted from the novella "A Walk in the Night" by Alex La Guma (1962).

Wa 'n Wina (2001). Dir. Dumisani Phakathi. South Africa. 52 min. Sotho, Zulu, and English. Prod. Steps for the Future. Distr. Film Resource Unit.

The Wilby Conspiracy (1974). Dir. Ralph Nelson. South Africa/UK. 105 min. English. Prod. Baum/Dantine. Distr. (DVD) MGM Home Entertainment.

A World Apart (1988). Dir. Chris Menges. Screenplay: Shawn Slovo. UK/Zimbabwe. 114 min. English. Prod. Working Title. Distr. (35mm) Working Title (UK). Adapted from Ruth First, *117 Days* (1965).

Xala (1974). Dir. Ousmane Sembene. Senegal. 123 min. Wolof and French. Prod. Société Nationale de Cinématographie and Filmi Doomirew. Distr. (35mm) New Yorker Films (USA) and BFI (UK). Adapted from Ousmane Sembene, *Xala* (1973).

Yeelen (Brightness) (1987). Dir. Souleymane Cissé. Mali. 105 min. Bambara. Prod. Cissé Films. Distr. (35mm) Kino International (USA).

Yesterday (2004). Dir. Darrell James Roodt. South Africa. 96 min. Zulu. Prod. Distant Horizon and HBO Films. Distr. HBO Video.

Yizo Yizo (television series) (2004). Dir. Barry Berk, Andrew Dosunmu, Angus Gibson, Teboho Mahlatsi. South Africa. 1,664 min. English and Zulu. Prod. SABC. Distr. SABC.

Zonk! (1950). Dir. Hyman Kirsten. South Africa. 58 min. English and Zulu. Prod. Ike Brooks Baruch. Distr. Villon Films (Canada).

Zulu (1964). Dir. Cy Endfield. South Africa/UK. 133 min. Prod. Diamond Films. Distr. Paramount Home Video.

Zulu Love Letter (2004). Dir. Ramadan Suleman. South Africa/Germany/France. 100 min. English, Zulu, and French Sign Language. Prod. JBA Production. Distr. JBA Production.

BIBLIOGRAPHY

Absa, Moussa Sene. 2003. Filmed interview with author (Mar. 2).

Adamu, Y. M. 2002. "Between the Word and the Screen: A Historical Perspective on the Hausa Literary Movement and the Home Video Invasion." *Journal of African Cultural Studies* 15.2 (Dec.): 201–213.

Adesanya, Afolabi. 1997. "From Film to Video." In Haynes 1997: 13–20.

Adhikari, Mohamed. 2005. *Not White Enough, Not Black Enough: Racial Identity in the South African Coloured Community.* Athens: Ohio UP.

Adorno, Theodor W. 1978. *Minima Moralia: Reflections from Damaged Life* (1951). Trans. E. F. N. Jephcott. London: Verso.

——. 1981–82. "Transparencies on Film." Trans. Thomas Y. Levin. *New German Critique* 24–25: 199–205.

——. 1984. *Aesthetic Theory* (1970). Ed. Gretel Adorno and Rolf Tiedermann. Trans. C. Lenhardt. London: Routledge and Kegan Paul.

——. 1991. "The Schema of Mass Culture." In J. M. Bernstein, ed., *The Culture Industry: Selected Essays on Mass Culture*, 53–84. London: Routledge.

——. 2000. "Culture Industry Reconsidered" (1963). In Brian O'Connor, ed., *The Adorno Reader*, 231–38. Oxford and Malden, Mass.: Blackwell.

AfriCiné. 2007. "Violence et cinema africain." Le bulletin de la Fédération Africaine de la Critique Cinématographique. No. 6 (Mar. 1).

Akomfrah, John. 2000. "Response to Diawara." In Givanni: 90–91.

Aldama, Arturo J., ed. 2003. *Violence and the Body: Race, Gender, and the State.* Bloomington: Indiana UP.

Algiers Charter on African Cinema. 1975. Rpt. in Bakari and Cham: 25–26.

Allen, Richard. 1987. "The Aesthetic Experience of Modernity: Benjamin, Adorno, and Contemporary Film Theory." *New German Critique* 40: 225–40.

Amarger, Michel. 2001. "Les cinémas d'Afrique au-delà des comédies musicales." *Africultures* 37 (Apr.). Accessed July 20, 2004 (*see* www.africultures.com/index. asp?menu = revue_affiche_article&no = 1985).

Anderson, Benedict. 1983. *Imagined Communities: Reflections on the Origin and Spread of Nationalism*. London: Verso.

Andrade-Watkins, Claire. 1996. "France's Bureau of Cinema—Financial and Technical Assistance, 1961–1977: Operations and Implications for African Cinema" (1990). Rpt. in Bakari and Cham: 112–27.

——. 1996a. "Portuguese African Cinema: Historical and Contemporary Perspectives, 1969–1993" (1995). Rpt. in Bakari and Cham: 132–47.

Appiah, Kwame Anthony. 1992. *In My Father's House: Africa in the Philosophy of Culture*. London: Methuen.

Aragay, Mireia, ed. 2005. *Books in Motion: Adaptation, Intertextuality, Authorship*. Amsterdam: Rodopi.

Aristotle. 1996. *The Poetics*. Trans. Malcolm Heath. London and New York: Penguin.

Armes, Roy. 1987. *Third World Film Making and the West*. Berkeley and London: U of California P.

Armes, Roy and Liz Malkmus. 1991. *Arab and African Film Making*. London: Zed Books.

Ashcroft, Bill, Gareth Griffiths, and Helen Tiffin. 2000. *Post-Colonial Studies: The Key Concepts*. London and New York: Routledge.

Ashcroft, Bill, Gareth Griffiths, and Helen Tiffin, eds. 1995. *The Post-Colonial Studies Reader*. London and New York: Routledge.

Askew, Kelly and Richard Wilk, eds. 2002. *The Anthropology of Media: A Reader*. Oxford and Malden, Mass.: Blackwell.

Asmal, Kader, Louise Asmal, and Ronald Suresh Roberts. 1997. *Reconciliation Through Truth: A Reckoning of Apartheid's Criminal Governance*. 2d ed. Cape Town: David Philip; Oxford: James Currey; New York: St. Martin's.

Attridge, Derek. 2004. *J. M. Coetzee and the Ethics of Reading: Literature in the Event*. Chicago and London: U of Chicago P.

Attwell, David, ed. 1992. *Doubling the Point: Essays and Interviews*. Cambridge: Harvard UP.

Auerbach, Erich. 2003. *Mimesis: The Representation of Reality in Western Literature*. Trans. Willard R. Trask. Princeton and Oxford: Princeton UP.

Auret, Michael. 2008. Interview with author (Jan. 17).

Axmaker, Sean. 2006. "Gavin Hood: 'These Issues are Timeless'" (Mar. 1). Accessed Aug. 27, 2007 (*see* www.greencine.com/article?action = view&articleID = 277& pageID = 510).

Bâ, Mariama. 2002. *Une si longue lettre* (1981). Dakar: Les Nouvelles Éditions Africaines du Sénégal.

Bachy, Victor. 1982. *Le Haute-Volta et le Cinéma*. Brussels: OCIC (Organisation Catholique Internationale du Cinéma).

——. 1983. *Le Cinéma au Mali*. Brussels: OCIC.

Bakari, Imruh. 2000. "Introduction: African Cinema and the Emergent Africa." In Givanni: 3–24.

Bakari, Imruh and Mbye Cham, eds. 1996. *African Experiences of Cinema*. London: British Film Institute.

Ba Kobhio, Bassek. 2000. "Response to Taylor." In Givanni: 147–50.

Balseiro, Isabel and Ntongela Masilela, eds. 2003. *To Change Reels: Film and Film Culture in South Africa*. Detroit: Wayne State UP.

Bangré, Sambolgo. 1996. "African Cinema in the Tempest of Minor Festivals" (1994). Rpt. in Bakari and Cham: 157–61.

Banham, Martin, ed. 2004. *A History of Theatre in Africa*. Cambridge: Cambridge UP.

Barber, Karin. 1987. "Popular Arts in Africa." *African Studies Review* 30.3 (Sept.): 1–78.

——. 2000. *The Generation of Plays: Yoruba Popular Life in Theater*. Bloomington: Indiana UP.

——. 2006. *Africa's Hidden Histories: Everyday Literacy and Making the Self*. Bloomington: Indiana UP.

Barlet, Olivier. 1999. Review of *La Genèse* by Cheikh [*sic*] Oumar Sissoko. *Africultures* 18 (May). Nouvelles créations africaines. Accessed July 20, 2004 (*see* www.africultures.com/index.asp?menu = revue_affiche_article&no = 835).

——. 2000. *African Cinemas: Decolonizing the Gaze*. Trans. Chris Turner. London and New York: Zed Books. (Trans. and updated version of *Cinémas d'Afrique Noire: Le regard en question*. Paris: L'Harmattan, 1996.)

——. 2001. "Entretien avec Joseph Gaye [*sic*] Ramaka" (Cannes, May). *Africultures*. Accessed July 20, 2004 (*see* www.africultures.com/popup_article.asp?no = 2371 &popup = 1).

——. 2002a. "Karmen censuré: Entretien avec Jo Gaye [*sic*] Ramaka." *Africultures* 47 (Apr.). Accessed July 20, 2004 (*see* www.africultures.com/index.asp?menu = revue_affiche_article&no = 2171&dispo = &retour = 1).

——. 2002b. "Universal as a Tale." Interview with Dani Kouyaté (Cannes, May). *Africultures* 49 (June 2002). Accessed July 20, 2004 (*see* www.africultures.com/index. asp?menu = revue_affiche_article&no = 2293).

——. 2003. "'Sia, le rêve du python': L'adaptation littéraire au cinéma." *Africultures* (Feb. 13). Accessed July 20, 2004 (*see* www.africultures.com/index.asp?menu = revue_affiche_article&no = 2775).

——. 2004. "Le renouvellement de l'Afrique se fera par la culture." Conférence de presse d'Ousmane Sembène au festival Ecrans noirs (Yaoundé, June 6, 2004). *Africultures* 59. Accessed July 20, 2004 (*see* www.africultures.com/index.asp?menu = revue_affiche_article&no = 3440&section = cahier).

——. 2007. "*Les Saignantes* by Jean-Pierre Bekolo" (Aug. 15). Accessed Aug. 27, 2007 (*see* www.africultures.com/index.asp?menu = affiche_article&no = 6642&lang = _en).

Barnes, John. 1992. *Filming the Boer War*. London: Bishopgate.

Barnes, Jonathan, ed. 1995. *The Cambridge Companion to Aristotle*. Cambridge: Cambridge UP.

Barnett, Ursula A. 1983. *A Vision of Order: A Study of Black South African Literature in English (1914–1980)*. London: Sinclair Brown.

Baudrillard, Jean. 1988. "Simulacra and Simulations." In Mark Poster, ed., *Jean Baudrillard: Selected Writings*, 166–84. Stanford: Stanford UP.

BBC News. 2001a. "Senegal's Carmen Controversy" (Sept. 10). Accessed July 20, 2004 (*see* http://news.bbc.co.uk/1/hi/world/africa/1535781.stm).

——. 2001b. "Senegal Director Wants Karmen Released" (Dec. 18). Accessed July 20, 2004 (*see* http://news.bbc.co.uk/1/hi/world/africa/1718284.stm).

——. 2006a. "SA Pirates 'Hijack' Tsotsi Movie" (Mar. 20). Accessed Aug. 27, 2007 (*see* http://news.bbc.co.uk/1/hi/world/africa/4825220.stm).

——. 2006b. "SA 'Tsotsi' Returns Baby" (Apr. 25). Accessed Aug. 27, 2007 (*see* http://news.bbc.co.uk/1/hi/world/africa/4942016.stm).

Behind the Mask: A Web Site on Gay and Lesbian Affairs in Africa. "About Senegal." Accessed July 20, 2004 (*see* www.mask.org.za/SECTIONS/AfricaPerCountry/ABC/senegal/senegal_index.html).

Beittel, Mark. 2003. "'What Sort of Memorial?' *Cry, the Beloved Country* on Film." In Balseiro and Masilela: 70–87.

Bekolo, Jean-Pierre. 2000. "Aristotle's Plot." In Maureen Eke, Kenneth Harrow, and Emmanuel Yewah, eds., *African Images: Recent Studies and Text in Cinema*, 19–29. Trenton, N.J., and Asmara (Eritrea): Africa World Press.

——. 2002. Interview. In Ukadike 2002: 217–38.

Belfiore, Elizabeth S. 1992. *Tragic Pleasures: Aristotle on Plot and Emotion*. Princeton: Princeton UP.

Benjamin, Walter. 1999. "On the Mimetic Faculty" (1933). Rpt. in Michael W. Jennings and Howard Eiland, eds., *Walter Benjamin: Selected Writings*. Vol. 2, *1927–1934*. Cambridge: Belknap Press of Harvard UP.

——. 1935. "The Work of Art in the Age of Mechanical Reproduction." Rpt. in Leo Braudy and Marshall Cohen, eds., *Film Theory and Criticism: Introductory Readings*, 731–51. 5th ed. 1999. New York and Oxford: Oxford UP.

Berardinelli, James. 1995. Review of *Cry, the Beloved Country* (the film). Accessed Nov. 20, 2004 (*see* http://movie-reviews.colossus.net/movies/c/cry_beloved.html).

Bernstein, J. M. 1991. "Introduction." In J. M. Bernstein, ed., *The Culture Industry: Selected Essays on Mass Culture*, 1–25. London: Routledge.

Bester, Rory. 1998. "*Fools*." Review for New York African Film Festival 2000–2001. Accessed July 20, 2004 (*see* www.africanfilmny.org/network/news/Rbester.html).

Beugnet, Martine. 2007. *Cinema and Sensation: French Film and the Art of Transgression*. Edinburgh: Edinburgh UP.

Bhabha, Homi. 1984. "Of Mimicry and Man: The Ambivalence of Colonial Discourse." *October* 28 (Spring): 125–33.

——. 1994. "The Other Question: Stereotype, Discrimination, and the Discourse of Colonialism." In *The Location of Culture*, 94–120. London and New York: Routledge.

Bickford-Smith, Vivian and Richard Mendelsohn, eds. 2007. *Black and White in Colour: African History on Screen*. Oxford: James Currey; Athens: Ohio UP; Cape Town: Double Storey.

Biko, Steve. 1979. *Steve Biko, 1946–1977—I Write What I Like*. Ed. C. R. Aelred Stubbs. Oxford and Johannesburg: Heinemann.

Blakely, Thomas D., Walter E. A. van Beek, Dennis L. Thomson et al., eds. 1994. *Religion in Africa: Experience and Expression*. London: James Currey.

Blaise-Fonkoua, Romuald. 2002. "Trente ans d'écriture filmique en Afrique: d'Ousmane Sembène à Jean-Pierre Bekolo." *Notre Librairie* "Cinémas d'Afrique" 149 (Oct.–Dec.): 2–7.

Blignaut, Johan and Martin Botha, eds. 1992a. *Movies, Moguls, Mavericks: South African Cinema, 1979–1991*. Cape Town: Showdata.

——. 1992b. "Statements on 'Ethnic' Cinema." In Blignaut and Botha: 255–76.

Bloom, Harold. 1973. *Anxiety of Influence*. Oxford and New York: Oxford UP.

Bøås, Morten. 2003. "Weak States, Strong Regimes: Towards a 'Real' Political Economy of African Regionalization." In J. Andrew Grant and Fredrik Söderbaum, eds., *The New Regionalism in Africa*, 31–46. Hants, Eng., and Burlington, Vt.: Ashgate.

Bolly, Moussa. 2007. "Un fléau, trois therapies." *AfriCiné* 6 (Mar. 1): 1.

Bordwell, David and Kristin Thompson. 1997. *Film Art: An Introduction*. 5th ed. New York: McGraw-Hill.

Born, Georgina. 2004. "Against Negation, For a Politics of Cultural Production: Adorno, Aesthetics, the Social" (1993). In Gerard Delanty, ed., *Theodor W. Adorno*, vol. 4:95–117. London and Thousand Oaks (Calif.) and New Dehli: Sage.

Bosch, David J. 1975. *The Traditional Religions of Africa*. Tshwane: U of South Africa P.

Botha, Martin, ed. 2008. *Marginal Lives and Painful Pasts: South African Cinema After Apartheid*. Johannesburg: Genugtig!

Botha, Martin and Adri Van Aswegen. 1992. *Images of South Africa: The Rise of Alternative Film*. Pretoria: Human Sciences Research Council.

Boughedir, Férid. 1987. *Le cinéma africain de A à Z*. Brussels: OCIC.

——. 1995. "Cinéma et Libertés en Afrique." In Fepaci: 34–46.

Bouzid, Nouri. 1996. "On Inspiration." In Bakari and Cham: 48–59.

Bowen, Barbara E. 1993. "Writing Caliban: Anticolonial Appropriations of *The Tempest*." *Current Writing* 5.2 (Oct.): 80–99.

Bradshaw, Peter. 2004. "Baby, I Don't Love You." *The Guardian* (Feb. 11). Accessed July 20, 2004 (*see* http://film.guardian.co.uk/festivals/news/0,11667,1145667,00.html).

Braude, Claudia. 1996. "The Archbishop, the Private Detective, and the Angel of History: The Production of South African Public Memory and the Truth and Reconciliation Commission." *Current Writing* 8.2: 39–65.

Braudy, Leo. 1998. "Afterword: Rethinking Remakes." In Andrew Horton and Stuart

Y. McDougal, eds., *Play it Again, Sam: Retakes on Remakes*, 327–34. Berkeley and London: U of California P.

Breytenbach, Breyten. 2003. Filmed interview with author (Mar. 9).

Breytenbach, Cloete. 1997. *The Spirit of District Six*. Cape Town: Human & Rousseau.

Brink, André. 1979. *A Dry White Season*. London: Vintage.

Brunkhorst, Hauke. 1999. *Adorno and Critical Theory*. Political Philosophy Now. Cardiff: U of Wales P.

Bruno, Giuliana. 2002. *Atlas of Emotion: Journeys in Art, Architecture, and Film*. New York and London: Verso.

Buck-Morss, Susan. 1991. *Dialectics of Seeing: Walter Benjamin and the Arcades Project*. Cambridge and London: MIT Press.

Butcher, S. H. 1951. *Aristotle's Theory of Poetry and Fine Art*. 4th ed. London: Dover.

Cabral, Amilcar. 1973. *Return to the Source: Selected Speeches by Amilcar Cabral*. Ed. Africa Information Service. New York and London: Monthly Review Press (with Africa Information Service).

Cahn, Michael. 1984. "Subversive Mimesis: T. W. Adorno and the Modern Impasse of Critique." In Spariosu 1984a: 27–64.

California Newsreel. 1995a. "About the Film" (*Keïta* by Dani Kouyaté). Accessed July 20, 2004 (*see* www.newsreel.org/films/keita.htm).

——. 1995b. "About the Film" (*Rouch in Reverse* by Manthia Diawara). Accessed July 20, 2004 (*see* www.newsreel.org/nav/title.asp?tc = CN0078).

——. 1999. "About the Film" (*La Genèse* by Cheick Oumar Sissoko). Accessed July 20, 2004 (*see* www.newsreel.org/nav/title.asp?tc = CN0040).

——. 2000. "About the Film" (*Thunderbolt* by Tunde Kelani). Accessed Aug. 23, 2007 (www.newsreel.org/nav/title.asp?tc = CN0129).

——. 2001. "About the Film" (*Karmen Geï* by Joseph Gaï Ramaka). Accessed July 20, 2004 (*see* www.newsreel.org/films/karmen.htm).

Calhoun, Dave. 2007. "White Guides, Black Pain." *Sight & Sound* (Feb.): 32–35.

Callan, Edward. 1982. *Alan Paton*. Boston: Twayne.

Cardwell, Sarah. 2002. *Adaptation Revisited: Television and the Classic Novel*. Manchester: Manchester UP.

Castaldi, Francesca. 2006. *Choreographies of African Identities: Négritude, Dance, and the National Ballet of Senegal*. Urbana: U of Illinois P.

Cattrysse, Patrick. 1997. "The Unbearable Lightness of Being: Film Adaptation Seen from a Different Perspective." *Literature/Film Quarterly* 25.3: 222–30.

Chabi, Godefroy Macaire. 2007. "Acrimonie du regard." *AfriCiné* 6 (Mar. 1): 3.

Cham, Mbye. 1996. "Introduction." In Bakari and Cham: 1–16.

——. 2004. "Film and History in Africa: A Critical Survey of Current Trends and Tendencies." In Pfaff 2004: 48–68.

——. 2005. "Oral Traditions, Literature, and Cinema in Africa." In Robert Stam and

Alessandra Raengo, eds., *Literature and Film: A Guide to the Theory and Practice of Film Adaptation*, 295–312. Malden, Mass., and Oxford: Blackwell.

Chandramohan, Balasubramanyam. 1992. *A Study in Trans-Ethnicity in Modern South Africa: The Writings of Alex La Guma, 1925–1985*. Lewiston (New York) and Lampeter (Wales): Edwin Mellen Press.

Childs, Peter and Patrick Williams. 1997. *An Introductory Guide to Postcolonial Theory*. New York: Prentice-Hall.

Chinodya, Shimmer. 1989. *Harvest of Thorns*. Zimbabwe: Baobab.

Chrisman, Laura and Benita Parry, eds. 2000. *Postcolonial Theory and Criticism*. Cambridge, Eng.: D. S. Brewer.

Clément, Catherine. 1979. *L'Opéra ou la défaite des femmes*. Paris: Grasset & Fasquelle.

Coetzee, Carli. 2004. "Truth and Power: The Truth and Reconciliation Commission of South Africa." *Journal of Southern African Studies* 30.1 (Mar.): 192–93.

Coetzee, J. M. 1971. "Alex La Guma and the Responsibilities of the South African Writer." *Journal of the New African Literature and the Arts* 9–10: 5–11.

——. 1974. "Man's Fate in the Novels of Alex la Guma." In Attwell 1992: 344–60.

——. 1978. *In the Heart of the Country*. Johannesburg: Ravan Press.

——. 1986. "Into the Dark Chamber: The Writer and the South African State." In Attwell 1992: 361–68.

——. 1988. *White Writing: On the Culture of Letters in South Africa*. New Haven and London: Yale UP.

Cohen, Derek. 1984. "Beneath the Underworld: Athol Fugard's *Tsotsi*." *World Literature Written in English* 23.2: 273–84.

——. 1991. "Fugard and the Liberal Dilemma." *Brick: A Literary Journal* 40: 11–18.

Collier, Mary Blackwood. 1993. "Carmen: Femme Fatale or Modern Myth?" Paper presented at the Eighteenth Annual Colloquium on Literature and Film. West Virginia University (Morgantown), Sept. 1993.

Collins, Harold Reeves. 1953. "*Cry, the Beloved Country* and the Broken Tribe." *College English* 14.7 (Apr.). Rpt. in Gerstung: 39–46.

Comaroff, Jean and John Comaroff, eds. 2000. "Millennial Capitalism and the Culture of Neoliberalism." Special Issue of *Public Culture* 12.2 (Spring).

Conklin, Alice. 1997. *A Mission to Civilize: The Republican Idea of Empire in France and West Africa, 1895–1930*. Stanford: Stanford UP.

Cookson, Rich. 2003. "Who Calls the Shots?" *The Guardian* (June 27). Accessed July 20, 2004 (*see* http://film.guardian.co.uk/features/featurepages/0,4120,985465,00.html).

Cooper, Frederick. 2002. *Africa Since 1940: The Past of the Present*. Cambridge: Cambridge UP.

——. 2005. *Colonialism in Question: Theory, Knowledge, History*. Berkeley: U of California P.

Cottenet-Hage, Madeleine. 1996. "Decolonizing Images: *Soleil O* and the Cinema of

Med Hondo." In Dina Sherzer, ed., *Cinema, Colonialism, Postcolonialism: Perspectives from the French and Francophone World*, 173–87. Austin: U of Texas P.

Dangarembga, Tsitsi. 2006. Panel discussion at 2006 Stockholm African Film Festival. Stockholm, Sweden, October 18–25.

Darbo, Seni. 1976. *A Griot's Self-portrait: The Origins and Role of the Griot in Mandinka Society as Seen from Stories Told by Gambian Griots*. Banjul: Gambia Cultural Archives.

Das, Veena, Arthur Kleinman, Mamphela Ramphele, and Pamela Reynolds, eds. 2000. *Violence and Subjectivity*. Berkeley: U of California P.

Davis, Peter. 1996. *In Darkest Hollywood: Exploring the Jungles of Cinema's South Africa*. Johannesburg: Ravan Press.

——. 2004. "Introduction." In *Come Back, Africa—Lionel Rogosin: A Man Possessed*, 6–15. Johannesburg: STE Publishers.

Daymond, M. J. 1981. "Fugard's Baby." *The Bloody Horse* (Johannesburg) 1.3: 85–88.

De Bruyn, Pippa. 2006. "Soft Target." *ZA@Play* (Mar. 3). Accessed Aug. 27, 2007 (*see* www.chico.mweb.co.za/art/2006/2006mar/060303-tsotsi.html).

Denman, Kamilla Lee. 1996. "Haunted Scenes and Shadowed Texts: Film Adaptations of British Victorian Prose Fiction." Ph.D. diss., Harvard University.

De Turegano, T. H. 2003. "Featuring African Cinemas." *World Literature Today* 77.3–4: 14–18.

Deutsch, Jan-Georg, Peter Probst, and Heike Schmidt, eds. 2002. *African Modernities*. Oxford: James Currey.

Diagana, Moussa. 1994. *La légende du Wagadu vue par Sia Yatabéré*. Wallonie (Belgium) and Montréal: Editions Lansman.

Diawara, Manthia. 1988. "Black Spectatorship: Problems of Identification and Resistance." Rpt. in Leo Braudy and Marshall Cohen, eds., *Film Theory and Criticism*, 845–53 (5th ed., 1999). New York and Oxford: Oxford UP.

——. 1992. *African Cinema*. Indianapolis: Indiana UP.

——. 1996. "Popular Culture and Oral Traditions in African Film." In Bakari and Cham: 209–218.

——. 2000. "The Iconography of West African Cinema." In Givanni: 81–89.

Diouf, Mamadou. 1996. "History and Actuality in Ousmane Sembène's *Ceddo* and Djibril Diop Mambety's *Hyenas*." Trans. Robert Julian. In Bakari and Cham: 239–51.

Donaldson, Andrew. 2000. "Starched Dashiki Brigade Wide of Mark on Picasso." *Sunday Times* (Mar. 19): 21.

Dornford-May, Mark and Pauline Malefane. 2006. Filmed interview with author (May 16).

Dovey, Lindiwe. 2002. "Towards an Art of Adaptation: Film and the New Criticism-as-Creation." *Iowa Journal of Cultural Studies* 2 (Fall): 51–61.

——. 2005. "Fetishizing Feminism: Representing/Reading Women in African Cinema." Paper presented at conference, "The Politics of Visual Pleasure 30 Years

On: The Work of Laura Mulvey." University of Cambridge, Cambridge (June 18).

——. 2007. "Return to (Questions of) Source: A Case Study of *U-Carmen eKhayelit-sha*." Paper presented at conference, "Cinematographic Aesthetics and Cultures of Africa," organized by CODESRIA at FESPACO (Burkina Faso, Mar. 1).

——. 2007a. "The 'Nation' and Inter-Nationalism in West African Cinemas: The Dilemma of West African 'Art' Cinema vs. 'Commercial' Cinema." Paper presented at African Film Conference, University of Illinois, Urbana-Champaign, Nov. 8–10.

——. Forthcoming. "Postcolonial Writing and Film." In Ato Quayson, ed., *Cambridge History of Postcolonial Literature*. Vol. 2. Cambridge: Cambridge UP.

Dovey, Lindiwe and Angela Impey. Forthcoming. *"Music in Early 'Black' South African Cinema: Discerning Black South African Performers and Audiences of the 1940s and 1950s."*

Downing, John D. H. 1996. "Post-Tricolor African Cinema: Toward a Richer Vision." In Dina Sherzer, ed., *Cinema, Colonialism, Postcolonialism: Perspectives from the French and Francophone World*, 188–228. Austin: U of Texas P.

Dube, Mickey Madoda. 1999. "Criticising the Critic." *ZA@Play* (Oct. 14). Accessed Aug. 27, 2007 (*see* www.chico.mweb.co.za/art/film/9910/991014-drama.html).

Dubowski, Sandi. 2005. "The People's Opera: Township Cinema in the New South Africa." *Filmmaker Magazine* (Spring). Accessed May 8, 2006 (*see* www.filmmakermagazine.com/spring2005/reports/peoples_opera.php).

Du Pré, Roy H. 1994. *Separate but Unequal: The "Coloured" People of South Africa—A Political History*. Johannesburg: Jonathan Ball.

Durix, Jean-Pierre. 1998. *Mimesis, Genres, and Postcolonial Discourse: Deconstructing Magic Realism*. New York: St. Martin's.

Dürrenmatt, Friedrich. 1962. *The Visit*. Trans. Patrick Bowles. New York: Grove Press. Trans. of *Der Besuch der alten Dame* (1956).

Dzobo, N. K. 1992. "Knowledge and Truth: Ewe and Akan Conceptions." In K. Wiredu and K. Gyekye, eds., *Person and Community: Ghanaian Philosophical Studies* I. Washington, D.C.: Council for Research in Values and Philosophy. See also www.crvp.org/book/Series02/II-1/chapter_iii.htm.

Ebron, Paulla. 2002. *Performing Africa*. Princeton: Princeton UP.

Eden, Kathy. 1986. *Poetic and Legal Fiction in the Aristotelian Tradition*. Princeton: Princeton UP.

Ellis, Stephen. 2003. "Violence and History: A Response to Thandika Mkandawire." *Journal of Modern African Studies* 41.3 (Sept.): 457–75.

Else, Gerald F. 1958. "'Imitation' in the Fifth Century." *Classical Philology* 53.2: 73–90.

Englehart, Lucinda. 2003. "Media Activism in the Screening Room: The Significance of Viewing Locations, Facilitation, and Audience Dynamics in the Reception of HIV/AIDS Films in South Africa." *Visual Anthropology Review* 19:1–2 (Spring-Summer): 73–85.

Erasmus, Zimitri, ed. 2001. *Coloured by History, Shaped by Place: New Perspectives on Coloured Identities in Cape Town*. Colorado Springs: International Academic Publishers.

Eze, Emmanuel Chukwudi. 1997. "Toward a Critical Theory of Postcolonial Identities." In E. C. Eze, ed., *Postcolonial African Philosophy: A Critical Reader*, 339–44. Oxford and Cambridge (Mass.): Blackwell.

Fanon, Frantz. 1967. *Black Skin, White Masks*. Trans. Charles Lam Markmann. London and Sydney: Pluto Press.

——. 1983. *The Wretched of the Earth* (1961). Trans. Constance Farrington. Harmondsworth: Penguin-Pelican.

Farid, Samir. 2000. "Response." In Givanni: 191–93.

Feld, Stephen, ed. 2003. *Cine-Ethnography Jean Rouch*, Minneapolis and London: U of Minnesota P.

Feldman, Allen. 2000. "Violence and Vision: The Prosthetics and Aesthetics of Terror." In Das et al.: 46–78.

Fepaci, ed. 1995. *L'Afrique et le Centenaire du Cinéma/Africa and the Centenary of Cinema*. Paris: Présence Africaine; Dakar: Fepaci.

Films for the Humanities and Sciences. 2004. "Ray Phiri." Accessed July 20, 2004 (*see* www.films.com/Films_Home/Item.cfm/1/7648).

First, Ruth. 1965. *117 Days: An Account of Confinement and Interrogation under the South African Ninety-Day Detention Law*. London: Bloomsbury.

Fischer, Lucy. 1980. "*Xala*: A Study in Black Humor." *Millenium Film Journal* 7–9: 165–72.

Foley, Andrew. 1996. "Liberalism in South African English Literature, 1948–1990." Ph.D. diss., University of Natal.

——. 1998. "'Considered as a Social Record': A Reassessment of *Cry, the Beloved Country*." *English in Africa* 25.2 (Oct.): 63–92.

Foucault, Michel. 1977. *Discipline and Punish: The Birth of the Prison*. Trans. Alan Sheridan. London: Allen Lane. Translation of *Surveiller et punir: Naissance de la prison* (1975).

Frassinetti, Paola. 1990–91. "Introduction." In "Athol Fugard's *Tsotsi*: When Loveless Meets Loveless," 9–20. Ph.D. diss., University of Venice.

Fugard, Athol. 1980. *Tsotsi: A Novel*. New York: Grove Press.

Furman, Nelly. 1988. "The Languages of Love in *Carmen*." In Arthur Groos and Roger Parker, eds., *Reading Opera*, 168–83. Princeton: Princeton UP.

Gabriel, Teshome. 1982. *Third Cinema in the Third World: The Aesthetics of Liberation*. Ann Arbor: UMI Research Press.

——. 1995. "Other Place, Other Approaches." In Fepaci: 236–44.

——. 2002. "Foreword: A Cinema in Transition, a Cinema of Change." In Ukadike 2002: ix–xii.

Galgut, Damon. 1995. *The Quarry*. London: Penguin-Viking.

Gardies, André and Pierre Haffner. 1987. *Regards sur le cinéma negro-africain*. Brussels: OCIC.

Garritano, Carmela. 2003. "Troubled Men and the Women Who Create Havoc: Four Recent Films by West African Filmmakers." *Research in African Literatures* 34.3 (Fall): 159–65.

Gates, Henry Louis, Jr. 1999. *Wonders of the African World*. New York: Knopf.

Genette, Gérard. 1980. *Narrative Discourse*. Trans. Jane E. Lewin. Oxford: Basil Blackwell.

——. 1997. *Palimpsests: Literature in the Second Degree*. Trans. Channa Newman and Claude Doubinsky. Lincoln: U of Nebraska P. (Translated version of *Palimpsestes: La Littérature au Second Degré*. Paris: Editions du Seuil, 1982.)

Genova, James. 2004. *Colonial Ambivalence, Cultural Authenticity, and the Limitations of Mimicry in French-Ruled West Africa*. New York: Peter Lang.

Gerima, Haile. 2003. "Afterword: Future Directions of African Cinema." In Balseiro and Masilela: 201–229.

Gerstung, Estella Baker, ed. 2001. *Readings on "Cry, the Beloved Country."* San Diego: Greenhaven Press.

Ginsburg, Faye. 1995. "Mediating Culture: Indigenous Media, Ethnographic Film, and the Production of Identity." In Leslie Devereaux and Roger Hillman, eds., *Fields of Vision: Essays in Film Studies, Visual Anthropology, and Photography*. Berkeley: U of California P.

Ginsburg, Faye, Lila Abu-Lughod, and Brian Larkin, eds. 2002. *Media Worlds: Anthropology on New Terrain*. Berkeley: U of California P.

Girard, René. 1986. *The Scapegoat*. Trans. Yvonne Freccero. London: Athlone Press.

Givanni, June, ed. 2000. *Symbolic Narratives/African Cinema: Audiences, Theory, and the Moving Image*. London: British Film Institute.

Glaser, Clive. 2000. *Bo-tsotsi: The Youth Gangs of Soweto, 1935–1976*. Portsmouth: Heinemann; Oxford: James Currey.

Gombrich, E. H. 1965. *Meditations on a Hobby Horse and Other Essays on the Theory of Art*. London: no publisher given.

Gould, Evlyn. 1996. *The Fate of Carmen*. Baltimore and London: John Hopkins UP.

Graham, Lucy. 2005. "Reading the Unspeakable: Rape in J. M. Coetzee's *Disgrace*." In Flora Veit-Wild and Dirk Naguschewski, eds., *Body, Sexuality, and Gender: Versions and Subversions in African Literatures* 1:255–67. Amsterdam and New York: Rodopi.

Gray, Stephen. 1981. "The Coming into Print of Athol Fugard's *Tsotsi*." *Journal of Commonwealth Literature* 16.1: 56–63.

——. 1982. "Fugard on Film: Interview with Ross Devenish (Johannesburg, 13 June 1980)." In Stephen Gray, ed., *Athol Fugard*, 136–38. Johannesburg: McGraw Hill.

——. 1985. "Third World Meets First World: The Theme of 'Jim Comes to Joburg' in South African English Fiction." *Kunapipi* 7.1: 61–80.

Green, Michael. 1999. "Social History, Literary History, and Historical Fiction in South Africa." *Journal of African Cultural Studies* 12.2 (Dec.): 121–36.

Greene, Thomas. 1982. *The Light in Troy: Imitation and Discovery in Renaissance Poetry*. New Haven: Yale UP.

Gugler, Josef. 2003. *African Cinema: Re-imagining a Continent*. Oxford: James Currey.

——. 2004. "Fiction, Fact, and the Critic's Responsibility: *Camp de Thiaroye, Yaaba*, and *The Gods Must be Crazy*." In Pfaff 2004: 69–85.

Gugler, Josef and Oumar Cherif Diop. 1998. "Ousmane Sembène's *Xala*: The Novel, the Film, and Their Audiences." *Research in African Literatures* 29.2: 147–58.

Gutsche, Thelma. 1972. *The History and Social Significance of Motion Pictures in South Africa, 1895–1940*. Cape Town: Howard Timmins.

Hall, Stuart. 1973. "Encoding and Decoding in the Television Discourse: Paper for the Council of Europe Colloquy on 'Training in the Critical Reading of Television Language.'" Birmingham: Birmingham University.

Hale, Thomas. 1998. *Griots and Griottes: Masters of Words and Music*. Bloomington: Indiana UP.

Hallen, B. and J. Olubi Sodipo. 1997. *Knowledge, Belief, and Witchcraft: Analytic Experiments in African Philosophy*. Stanford: Stanford UP.

Halliwell, Stephen. 1987. *The "Poetics" of Aristotle: Translation and Commentary*. London: Duckworth.

——. 2002. *The Aesthetics of Mimesis: Ancient Texts and Modern Problems*. Princeton: Princeton UP.

Hamilton, Carolyn and Litheko Modisane. 2007. "The Public Lives of Historical Films: The Case of *Zulu* and *Zulu Dawn*." In Bickford-Smith and Mendelsohn: 97–119.

Hänsel, Marion. 2002. Filmed interview with author (Nov. 12).

Hansen, Miriam. 1981–82. "Introduction to Adorno, 'Transparencies on Film' (1966)." *New German Critique* 24–25: 186–98.

——. 1992. "Mass Culture as Hieroglyphic Writing: Adorno, Derrida, Kracauer." *New German Critique* 56: 43–73.

Harding, Frances, ed. 2003a. "Special Issue Focusing on the Media in and about Africa." *Journal of African Cultural Studies* 16.1 (June).

——. 2003b. "Editor's Preface: The Media and Africa." In Harding 2003a: 5–6.

——. 2003c. "Africa and the Moving Image: Television, Film, and Video." In Harding 2003a: 69–84.

Harris, Bronwyn. 2001a. "'Violent Crime That's Our Daily Bread'": Vigilante Violence During South Africa's Period of Transition." Violence and Transition Series. Vol. 1 (May). Accessed July 20, 2004 (*see* www.csvr.org.za/papers/papvtp1.htm).

——. 2001b. "A Foreign Experience: Violence, Crime, and Xenophobia During South Africa's Transition." Violence and Transition Series. Vol. 5 (Aug.). Accessed July 20, 2004 (*see* www.csvr.org.za/papers/papvtp5.htm).

——. 2003. "Spaces of Violence, Places of Fear: Urban Conflict in Post-apartheid South Africa." Paper presented on the Conflicts and Urban Violence panel, Foro Social Mundial Tematico, Cartagena (Colombia), June 16–20. Accessed July 20, 2004 (*see* www.csvr.org.za/papers/paphar2.htm).

Harris, Iain. 2004. *"God Is African*—The Guerilla Tactics of Akin Omotoso." *South African Film* Accessed July 20, 2004 (*see* www.safilm.org.za/news/article.php?uid = 231).

Harrow, Kenneth W., ed. 1999a. *African Cinema: Post-Colonial and Feminist Readings*. Trenton and Asmara: Africa World Press.

——. 1999b. "Introduction." In Harrow 1999a: ix–xxiv.

Haynes, Jonathan. 1999a. "African Filmmaking and the Postcolonial Predicament: *Quartier Mozart* and *Aristotle's Plot*." In Harrow 1999a: 21–43.

——. 1999b. "Nigerian Cinema: Structural Adjustments." In Harrow 1999a: 143–76.

——. 2006. "Political Critique in Nigerian Video Films." *African Affairs* 105.421 (2006): 511–33.

Haynes, Jonathan, ed. 1997. *Nigerian Video Films*. JOS: Nigerian Film Corporation.

——. 1997a. "Preface." In Haynes 1997: 9–10.

Heath, Stephen. 1981. *Questions of Cinema*. Bloomington: Indiana UP.

Hees, Edwin. 1993. "Film in Africa and South Africa." *Critical Arts* 7.1–2. Accessed Sept. 23, 2003 (*see* www.und.ac.za/und/ccms/articles/hees.htm).

——. 2003. "The Birth of a Nation: Contextualizing *De Voortrekkers* (1916)." In Balseiro and Masilela: 49–69.

Hendriks, Cheryl. 2004. "Burdens of the Past and Challenges of the Present: Coloured Identity and the Rainbow Nation." In Bruce Berman, Dickson Eyoh, and Will Kymlicka, eds., *Ethnicity and Democracy in Africa*. Oxford: James Currey.

Higgins, Lynn and Brenda Silver, eds. 1991. *Rape and Representation*. New York: Columbia UP.

Hillis Miller, J. 1982. "Two Forms of Repetition." In *Fiction and Repetition: Seven English Novels*, 1–21. Oxford: Basil Blackwell.

Hiltunen, Ari. 2002. *Aristotle in Hollywood: The Anatomy of Successful Storytelling*. Bristol (Eng.): Intellect Books.

Hoffman, Barbara. 2000. *Griots at War: Conflict, Conciliation, and Caste in Mande*. Trans. with Kassim Koné. Bloomington: Indiana UP.

Hogg, David. 1978. "Unpublished Fugard Novel." *Contrast* 12.1: 60–78.

Hondo, Med. 1996. "What Is Cinema for Us?" In Bakari and Cham: 39–41.

Horkheimer, Max and Theodor W. Adorno. 1973. *The Dialectic of Enlightenment* (1947). Trans. John Cumming. London: Allen Lane.

Horton, Andrew and Joan Magretta. 1981. *Modern European Filmmakers and the Art of Adaptation*. New York: Ungar.

Hough, Barrie. 1980. "Interview with Athol Fugard (Port Elizabeth, Nov. 30, 1977)." In Stephen Gray, ed., *Athol Fugard*, 121–29. Johannesburg: McGraw Hill.

Howlett, Jana and Rod Mengham, eds. 1994. *The Violent Muse: Violence and the Artistic Imagination in Europe, 1910–1939*. Manchester and New York: Manchester UP.

Hughes, Scott. 2003. "God—The Hollywood Years." *The Guardian* (June 20). Accessed July 20, 2004 (*see* http://film.guardian.co.uk/features/featurepages/0,4120,981027,00.html).

Hutcheon, Linda. 2006. *A Theory of Adaptation*. London and New York: Routledge.

Iannone, Carol. 1997. "Alan Paton's Tragic Liberalism." *American Scholar* 66.3 (Summer). Edited version rpt. in Gerstung: 93–102.

IDC (Industrial Development Corporation). 2006. "'Tsotsi' Smashes Local Box Office Records" (Apr. 10). Accessed Aug. 27, 2007 (*see* www.idc.co.za/IDC%20News%20and%20Media%20releases.asp?GroupCode = 0&ArticleId = 166).

Idowu, E. Bolaji. 1973. *African Traditional Religions*. London: SCM Press.

Imperato, Pascal James. 1989. *Mali: A Search for Direction*. Boulder: Westview Press.

Jacoby, Tamar. 1983. "Tsotsi" (1981). In Jean Stine, ed., *Contemporary Literary Criticism*, 174–75. Gale.

Jakobson, Roman. 1987. *Language in Literature*. Cambridge (Mass.): Belknap Press.

James, Wilmot, Daria Caliguire, and Kerry Cullinan, eds. 1996. *Now That We Are Free: Coloured Communities in a Democratic South Africa*. Boulder: Lynne Rienner.

James, Wilmot and Linda Van de Vijver. 2000. *After the TRC: Reflections on Truth and Reconciliation in South Africa*. Athens: Ohio UP; Cape Town: David Philip.

Jameson, Fredric. 1992. *The Geopolitical Aesthetic: Cinema and Space in the World System*. Bloomington: Indiana UP; London: British Film Institute.

Jarvis, Simon. 1998. *Adorno: A Critical Introduction*. Key Contemporary Thinkers. Oxford: Blackwell-Polity.

Jayamanne, Laleen. 2001. *Toward Cinema and Its Double: Cross-Cultural Mimesis*. Bloomington: Indiana UP.

Jeyifo, Biodun. 1984. *The Yoruba Popular Travelling Theatre of Nigeria*. Lagos: Nigeria Magazine Publications.

Johnson, Barbara. 1985. "Taking Fidelity Philosophically." In Joseph F. Graham, ed., *Difference in Translation*. Ithaca: Cornell UP.

Jolly, Rosemary Jane. 1996. *Colonization, Violence, and Narration in White South African Writing: André Brink, Breyten Breytenbach, and J. M. Coetzee*. Athens: Ohio UP; Johannesburg: Witwatersrand UP.

Kennedy, Lisa. 2006. "'Tsotsi' Prompts a Viva!" *Denver Post*, Mar. 24, F8.

Kierkegaard, Søren. 1942. *Repetition: An Essay in Experimental Psychology*. Trans. Walter Lowrie. Oxford: Oxford UP; London: Humphrey Milford.

King James Bible. 1991. New York: Ivy Books.

Kleinman, Arthur. 2000. "The Violences of Everyday Life: The Multiple Forms and Dynamics of Social Violence." In Das et al.: 226–41.

Kline, T. Jefferson. 1992. *Screening the Text: Intertextuality in New Wave French Cinema*. Baltimore and London: Johns Hopkins UP.

Kriedemann, Kevin. 2005. "Proudly South African Filmmaking: Are SA Films Making Any Money?" *The Callsheet* (July 4). Accessed May 8, 2006 (*see* www.writingstudio.co.za/page860.html).

Kriger, Robert and Abebe Zegeye. 2001. *Culture in the New South Africa: After Apartheid*. Vol. 2. Cape Town: Kwela Books; Maroelana: South African History Online.

Krog, Antjie. 1998. *Country of My Skull: Guilt, Sorrow, and the Limits of Forgiveness in the New South Africa*. New York: Three Rivers Press.

Labour Relations Act. 1995. South African Office of the President. Accessed July 20, 2004 (*see* www.labour.gov.za/docs/legislation/lra/act95-066.html#ch8).

La Guma, Alex. 1967. "A Walk in the Night" (1962). In *A Walk in the Night and Other Stories*, 1–96. African Writers Series. London, Ibadan (Nigeria), Nairobi (Kenya), and Lusaka (Zambia): Heinemann.

Lalu, Premesh and Brent Harris. 1996. "Journeys from the Horizons of History: Text, Trial, and Tales in the Construction of Narratives of Pain." *Current Writing* 8.2: 24–38.

Landy, Marcia. 1984. "Political Allegory and 'Engaged Cinema': Sembene's *Xala*." *Cinema Journal* 23.3: 31–46.

Laremont, Ricardo René. 2002. "The Causes of War and the Implications of Peacekeeping in Africa." In Laremont, ed., *The Causes of War and the Consequences of Peacekeeping in Africa*, 3–18. Portsmouth, Eng.: Heinemann.

Larkin, Brian. 2002. "The Materiality of Cinema Theatres in Northern Nigeria." In Ginsburg et al.: 319–36.

Lazarus, Neil. 2004. "Introducing Postcolonial Studies." In Neil Lazarus, ed., *The Cambridge Companion to Postcolonial Literary Studies*, 1–16. Cambridge: Cambridge UP.

Leahy, James. 1988. "Sarraounia." *Monthly Film Bulletin* 55.648 (Jan.): 8–10.

Leclerq, Emmanuel. 2002. "Afrique 1990–2002: État Des Lieux Du Cinéma Militant." *Les Temps Modernes* "Afriques du Monde" 620–21 (Aug.–Nov.): 526–44.

Lefevere, André (1984). "On the Refraction of Texts." In Spariosu 1984a: 217–37.

Lindlow, Megan. 2005. "Carmen's New Conquest: How a Film Version of Bizet's Famous Opera, Relocated to a South African Township, Is Seducing the Locals." *Time Europe Magazine* (Apr. 17). Accessed May 8, 2006 (*see* www.time.com/time/europe/html/050425/carmen.html).

Lledo, Jean-Pierre. 2004. Filmed presentation at the 24th Cambridge Film Festival (July 14).

London Lesbian and Gay Film Festival. 2003. "Karmen Geï" (Apr. 7). Accessed July 20, 2004 (*see* www.outuk.com/cgi-bin/llgff/filmdetail.pl?link_ref = 1035).

Louhichi, Tayeb. 2003. Filmed interview with author (Mar. 4).

Lowell, Robert. 1971. *Imitations*. London: Faber & Faber.

Lyons, John D. 1982a. "Introduction." In Lyons and Nichols: 1–19.

Lyons, John D. and Stephen G. Nichols, Jr., eds. 1982b. *Mimesis: From Mirror to Method, Augustine to Descartes*. Hanover and London: UP of New England.

MacCabe, Colin. 1992. "Preface." In Jameson: ix–xvi.

Magesa, Laurenti. 1997. *African Religion: The Moral Traditions of Abundant Life*. New York: Orbis.

Magogodi, Kgafela oa. 2003. "Sexuality, Power, and the Black Body in *Mapantsula* and *Fools*." In Balseiro and Masilela: 187–200.

Mahoso, Tafataona. 2000. "Unwinding the African Dream on African Ground." In Givanni: 197–226.

Maingard, Jacqueline. 2003. "Framing South African National Cinema and Television." In Balseiro and Masilela: 115–31.

——. 2007. *South African National Cinema*. London: Routledge.

Maldoror, Sarah. 2003. Filmed interview after screening at 2003 Cambridge African Film Festival (May 10).

Malkmus, Lizbeth and Roy Armes. 1991. *Arab and African Film Making*. London: Zed Books.

Mambety, Djibril Diop. 2002. Interview in Ukadike 2002: 121–31.

Marks, Laura. 2000. *The Skin of the Film: Intercultural Cinema, Embodiment, and the Senses*. Durham and London: Duke UP.

——. 2002. *Touch: Sensuous Theory and Multisensory Theory*. Minneapolis and London: U of Minnesota P.

Martin, Angela, ed. 1982. *African Films: The Context of Production*. London: BFI.

Marx, John. 2004. "Postcolonial Literature and the Western Literary Canon." In Neil Lazarus, ed., *Cambridge Companion to Postcolonial Literary Studies*, 83–96. Cambridge: Cambridge UP.

Maseko, Zola. 2008. Telephone interview with author (Jan.).

Masilela, Ntongela. 2001. "Thelma Gutsche: A Great South African Film Scholar." In Kriger and Zegeye: 207–28.

——. 2003. "The New African Movement and the Beginnings of Film Culture in South Africa." In Balseiro and Masilela: 15–30.

Mast, Gerald. 1983. *Film/Cinema/Movie: A Theory of Experience*. Chicago and London: U of Chicago P.

Mazrui, Ali. 1969. *Violence and Thought: Essays on Social Tensions in Africa*. London: Longmans.

——. 1986. *The Africans: A Triple Heritage*. Boston: Little Brown.

Mbalo, Eddie. 2007. "La couleur du futur." Entretein avec Vincent Malausa. *Cahiers du Cinéma*. "Le Cinéma Africain au Présent." Supplement to No. 620: 11.

Mbembe, Achille. 2001. *On the Postcolony*. Berkeley: U of California P.

——. 2002. Interview with Christian Hoeller. *Springerin* 3. Accessed Apr. 20 2003 (*see* www.springerin.at).

Mbiti, John S. 1969. *African Religions and Philosophy*. London: Heinemann.

McClary, Susan. 1991. *Feminine Endings: Music, Gender, and Sexuality.* Minneapolis: U of Minnesota P.

McClary, Susan (with chapter by Peter Robinson). 1992. *Georges Bizet: Carmen.* Cambridge Opera Handbooks. Cambridge: Cambridge UP.

McClintock, Anne. 1992. "The Angel of Progress: Pitfalls of the Term Post-Colonialism.'" *Social Text* 31-32: 84-98.

McFarlane, Brian. 1996. *Novel To Film: An Introduction to the Theory of Adaptation.* Oxford: Clarendon Press.

McKinney, Devin. 2000. "Violence: The Strong and the Weak." In Prince 2000a: 99-109.

Medalie, David. 1998. "'A Corridor Shut at Both Ends': Admonition and Impasse in Van der Post's *In a Province* and Paton's *Cry, the Beloved Country.*" *English in Africa* 25.2 (Oct.): 93-110.

Meiring, Piet. 1999. *Chronicle of the Truth Commission: A Journey Through the Past and Present into the Future of South Africa.* Vanderbijlpark (South Africa): Carpe Diem.

Melberg, Arne. 1995. *Theories of Mimesis.* Cambridge: Cambridge UP.

Mensah, Alexandre. 2004. Review of *Karmen Geï. Africultures.* Accessed July 20, 2004 (*see* www.africultures.com/index.asp?menu = revue_affiche_article&no = 2342& lang = _en).

Mercer, Kobena. 2000. "Response to Taylor." In Givanni: 145-47.

Mérimée, Prosper. 2001. "Carmen." *Carmen suivi de Les âmes du purgatoire (1845-1847).* Pössneck (Allemagne): Librio.

Metz, Christian. 1974. *Film Language: A Semiotics of the Cinema.* New York: Oxford UP.

Meyer, Birgit. 2003. "Ghanaian Popular Cinema and the Magic in and of Film." In Birgit Meyer and Peter Pels, eds., *Magic and Modernity: Interfaces of Revelation and Concealment,* 200-222. Stanford: Stanford UP.

Miller, Daniel, ed. 2005. *Materiality.* Durham and London: Duke UP.

Miller, David and Sohail Hashmi. 2001. *Boundaries and Justice: Diverse Ethical Perspectives.* Princeton and Oxford: Princeton UP.

Mkandawire, Thandika. 2003. "Rejoinder to Stephen Ellis." *Journal of Modern African Studies* 41.3 (Sept.): 477-83.

Mondolini, Dominique, ed. 2002. *Notre Librairie* 148 (July-Sept.), "Penser La Violence." Accessed July 20, 2004 (*see* www.adpf.asso.fr/librairie/derniers/148/texte148.htm).

Moore, Gerald. 1980. *Twelve African Writers.* London: Hutchinson Group.

Morgan, Robert with John Barton. 1988. *Biblical Interpretation.* Oxford: Oxford UP.

Morojele, Sechaba. 2003. Filmed interview with author (Mar. 1).

Morphet, Tony. 1983. "Alan Paton: The Honour of Meditation." *English in Africa* 10.2 (Oct.): 1-10.

Mudimbe, V. Y. 1988. *The Invention of Africa: Gnosis, Philosophy, and the Order of Knowledge.* Bloomington: Indiana UP.

——. 1994. *The Idea of Africa*. Bloomington: Indiana UP; London: James Currey.

Mulvey, Laura. 1988a. "Visual Pleasure and Narrative Cinema" (1975). In Penley: 57–68.

——. 1988b. "Afterthoughts on 'Visual Pleasure and Narrative Cinema' Inspired by *Duel in the Sun*" (1981). In Penley: 69–79.

——. 1994. "*Xala*. Ousmane Sembene 1976: The Carapace That Failed." In Laura Chrisman and Patrick Williams, eds., *Colonial Discourse and Post-Colonial Theory: A Reader*, 517–34. London: Harvester Wheatsheaf.

Murphy, David. 2000a. *Sembene: Imagining Alternatives in Film and Fiction*. Oxford: James Currey; Trenton: Africa World Press.

——. 2000b. "Africans Filming Africa: Questioning Theories of an Authentic African Cinema." *Journal of African Cultural Studies* 13.2 (Dec.): 239–49.

Naficy, Hamid. 2001. *An Accented Cinema: Exilic and Diasporic Filmmaking*. Princeton: Princeton UP.

Naremore, James, ed. 2000. *Film Adaptation*. London: Athlone Press.

Nathan, Jeremy. 2007. Presentation at "Power to the Pixel: The Digital Distribution Forum for Independents" at the *Times* BFI London Film Festival 2007 (Oct. 26).

Ndebele, Njabulo. 1983. "Fools." In *Fools and Other Stories*, 152–280. Johannesburg: Ravan Press.

——. 1994a. *South African Literature and Culture: Rediscovery of the Ordinary*. Manchester and New York: Manchester UP.

——. 1994b. "The Rediscovery of the Ordinary: Some New Writings in South Africa." In Ndebele 1994a: 41–59.

——. 1994c. "Turkish Tales and Some Thoughts on South African Fiction." In Ndebele 1994a: 17–40.

——. 2003. *The Cry of Winnie Mandela*. Claremont (Cape Town): David Philip.

——. 2003a. Filmed interview with author (May 20).

Newbury, Catharine. 2002. "States at War: Confronting Conflict in Africa." *African Studies Review* 45.1 (Apr.): 1–20.

Ngakane, Lionel. 2002. Interview. In Ukadike 2002: 73–83.

Ngangura, Mweze. 1996. "African Cinema—Militancy or Entertainment?" Trans. Paul Willemen. In Bakari and Cham: 60–64.

Ngom, Mbissane. 1983. *Le prix du pardon*. Dakar: Les Nouvelles Éditions Africaines du Sénégal; Vanves (France): EDICEF (Editions Classiques d'Expression Française).

Niane, D. T. 1960. *Soundjata: Ou l'épopée mandingue*. Dakar: Présence Africaine.

Niang, Sada. 1996. "*Mandabi*: Character, Context, and Wolof language." *Jump Cut* 40 (Mar.): 55–61.

Nichols, B., ed. 1976. *Movies and Methods: An Anthology*. Berkeley: U of California P.

Nietzsche, Friedrich. 1967. *The Birth of Tragedy and the Case of Wagner*. Trans. Walter Kaufmann. New York: Random House.

Niven, Alistair. 1980. " . . . and Sophiatown." *Times Literary Supplement* (May 2), 500.

Nixon, Rob. 1987. "Caribbean and African Appropriations of *The Tempest*." *Critical Inquiry* 13: 557–78.

——. 1991. "Cry White Season: Apartheid, Liberalism, and the American Screen." *South Atlantic Quarterly* 90.3 (Summer): 499–529.

Norton, David. 1993a. *The History of the Bible as Literature*. Vol. 1. Cambridge: Cambridge UP.

——. 1993b. *The History of the Bible as Literature*. Vol. 2. Cambridge: Cambridge UP.

Notcutt, L. A. and G. C. Latham. 1937. *The African and the Cinema: An Account of the Work of the Bantu Educational Cinema Experiment During the Period March 1935 to May 1937*. London: Edinburgh House Press (for The International Missionary Council).

Nuttall, A. D. 1996. *Why Does Tragedy Give Pleasure?* Oxford: Clarendon Press.

Ogunleye, Foluke, ed. 2003. "Preface." *African Video Film Today*, ix–xi. Swaziland: Academic Publishers.

Okpewho, Isidore. 1979. *The Epic in Africa: Towards a Poetics of the Oral Performance*. New York: Columbia UP.

Open Democracy. 2003. "Africa in the Mirror of Cinema" (Nov. 13). Accessed July 20, 2004 (*see* www.opendemocracy.net/debates/article-1-67-1575.jsp).

Orr, Wendy. 2000. *From Biko to Basson: Wendy Orr's Search for the Soul of South Africa as a Commissioner of the TRC*. Saxonwold (South Africa): Contra.

Osborne, Sara. 2000. "The Role of an Ultimate Authority in Restorative Justice: A Girardian Analysis." *Contagion: Journal of Violence, Mimesis, and Culture* 7 (Spring): 79–107.

Owens, Craig. 1983. "The Discourse of Others: Feminists and Postmodernism." In Hal Foster, ed., *Postmodern Culture*, 57–82. London and Sydney: Pluto Press.

Owolabi, Kolawole. 1996. "Regional Integration and the Imperative of Cultural Rehabilitation: A Philosopher's Response to the Issues of Dependency and Integration in West Africa." *UFAHAMU* 24.2–3: 82–96.

Owoo, Kwate Nii. 2000. "Response to Mahoso." In Givanni: 228–31.

Panzacchi, Cornelia. 1994. "The Livelihood of Traditional Griots in Modern Senegal." *Africa: Journal of the International African Institute* 64.2: 190–210.

Parry, Benita. 2005. "The New South Africa: The Revolution Postponed, Internationalism Deferred." *Journal of Postcolonial Writing* 41.2 (Nov.): 179–88.

Paton, Alan. 2002. *Cry, the Beloved Country* (1948). London, Sydney, Auckland, and Endulini (South Africa): Random House–Vintage.

Pechey, Graham. 1994. "Introduction." In Ndebele 1994a: 1–16.

Pellow, C. Kenneth. 1994. *Films as Critiques of Novels: Transformational Criticism*. Lewiston (New York) and Lampeter (Wales): Edwin Mellen Press.

Penley, Constance, ed. 1988. *Feminism and Film Theory*. New York: Routledge; London: BFI.

Perry, G. M. and Patrick McGilligan. 1973. "Ousmane Sembene: An Interview." *Film Quarterly* 26.3 (Spring): 36–42.

Peterson, Bhekizizwe. 2003. "The Politics of Leisure During the Early Days of South African Cinema." In Balseiro and Masilela: 31–46.

Pfaff, Françoise. 1984. *The Cinema of Ousmane Sembene: A Pioneer of African Film.* Westwood, Conn.: Greenwood Press.

——. 1996. "Africa from Within: The Films of Gaston Kaboré and Idrissa Ouédraogo as Anthropological Sources." In Bakari and Cham: 223–28.

Pfaff, Françoise, ed. 2004. *Focus on African Films.* Bloomington: Indiana UP.

——. ed. 2004a. "Introduction." In Pfaff 2004, 1–11.

Philips, David. 2007. "Looking the Beast in the (fictional) Eye: The Truth and Reconciliation on Film." In Bickford-Smith and Mendelsohn: 300–322.

Phillips, Barnaby. 2001. "Baby Rape Shocks South Africa." BBC News (Dec. 11). Accessed Feb. 7, 2008 (*see* http://news.bbc.co.uk/1/hi/world/africa/1703595.stm).

Piot, Charles. 1999. *Remotely Global: Village Modernity in West Africa.* Chicago and London: U of Chicago P.

Porton, Richard. 1997. Review of "Hyenas." *Cineaste* 23.2 (Dec.): 51. Accessed July 20, 2004 (*see* www.ebertfest.com/four/hyenas_rev.htm).

Posel, Deborah and Graeme Simpson, eds. 2002. *Commissioning the Past: Understanding South Africa's Truth and Reconciliation Commission.* Johannesburg: Witwatersrand UP.

Povinelli, Elizabeth. 2002. *The Cunning of Recognition: Indigenous Alterities and the Making of Australian Multiculturalism.* Durham and London: Duke UP.

Powdermaker, Hortense. 1950. *Hollywood the Dream Factory: An Anthropologist Looks at the Movie-makers.* Boston: Little, Brown.

Powrie, Phil. 2004. "Politics and Embodiment in *Karmen Geï*." *Quarterly Review of Film and Video* 21.4: 283–91.

Pretorius, William. 1994. "New Life for an Old Classic." *Weekly Mail and Guardian* (Johannesburg), Dec. 9–14.

Prince, Stephen, ed. 2000a. *Screening Violence.* London: Athlone Press.

——. 2000b. "Introduction." In Prince 2000a: 1–44.

Prins, Harald. 2002. "Visual Media and the Primitivist Perplex: Colonial Fantasies, Indigenous Imagination, and Advocacy in North America." In Ginsburg et al.: 58–74.

Quayson, Ato. 2000. *Postcolonialism: Theory, Practice, or Process?* Cambridge (Eng.): Polity Press.

Rape Crisis South Africa. 2004. "Statistics." Accessed July 20, 2004 (*see* www.rape-crisis.org.za/statistics.html).

Rathbone, Richard. 2002. "West Africa: Modernity and Modernization." In Deutsch et al.: 18–30.

Rebelo, Nicky. 1981. "Socio-Cultural Determinants in Athol Fugard's Early Works." Fourth Year Long Essay. University of Witwatersrand.

Renders, Luc. 2007. "Redemption Movies." In Botha: 221–53.

Rich, Paul. 1984. *White Power and the Liberal Conscience: Racial Segregation and South African Liberalism, 1921–60.* Manchester: Manchester UP.

Rive, Richard. 1987. *District Six.* Cape Town: David Philip.

Robertson, Janet. 1971. *Liberalism in South Africa, 1948–1963.* Oxford: Clarendon Press.

Robinson, Peter. 1992. "Mérimée's *Carmen.*" In McClary 1992: 1–14.

Rose, Jacqueline. 1996. *States of Fantasy.* Oxford: Clarendon Press.

Rosenstone, Robert. 1995. *Visions of the Past: The Challenge of Film to Our Idea of History*, 45–79. Cambridge: Harvard UP.

Rotten Tomatoes. 2006. "Tsotsi." Accessed Aug. 27, 2007 (*see* www.rottentomatoes. com/m/tsotsi/about.php).

Russell, Sharon A. 1998. *A Guide to African Cinema.* Westport (Conn.) and London: Greenwood Press.

Sagnane, Fatoumata. 2007. "Vision-violence dans les films africains." *AfriCiné* 6 (Mar. 1): 2.

Said, Edward W. 1993. *Culture and Imperialism.* London: Chatto & Windus.

Saks, Lucia. 2003. "The Race for Representation: New Viewsites for Change in South African Cinema." In Balseiro and Masilela: 132–59.

Sanneh, Lamin. 1989. *Translating the Message: The Missionary Impact on Culture.* New York: Orbis.

Sartre, Jean-Paul. 1983. "Preface." In Fanon 1983: 7–26.

Scarry, Elaine. 2007. Clark Lectures, delivered at the University of Cambridge (Jan.).

Schmidt, Nancy J. 1982. "African Literature on Film." *Research in African Literatures* 13.4 (Winter): 518–31.

——. 1994. *Sub-Saharan African Films and Filmmakers, 1987–1992: An Annotated Bibliography.* London: Hans Zell.

Schmitz, Oliver. 2003. Filmed interview after screening at 2003 Cambridge African Film Festival (May 10).

Schoeman, Karel. 1972. *Na Die Geliefde Land.* Kaapstad (Cape Town) and Pretoria: Human & Rousseau.

Schultz, Karla L. 1990. *Mimesis on the Move: Theodor W. Adorno's Concept of Imitation.* New York U Ottendorfer Series. Berne and New York: Peter Lang.

Schwab, Peter. 2001. *Africa: A Continent Self-Destructs.* New York: Palgrave.

Scott, James C. 1990. *Domination and the Arts of Resistance: Hidden Transcripts.* New Haven and London: Yale UP.

Screen Africa. 2008. "Sithengi Saved" (Jan. 4). Accessed Feb. 9, 2008 (*see* www. screenafrica.com/latest_edition/763601.htm).

Sé, Anne K. 2002. "Afrique du Sud: Années zero pour le cinéma noir." Accessed July 17, 2007 (*see* www.africultures.com/index.asp?menu=revue_affiche_article&no= 612).

Segal, Naomi. 1994. "Who Whom? Violence, Politics, and the Aesthetic." In Howlett and Mengham: 141–49.

Sembene, Ousmane. 1974. "The Promised Land." *Tribal Scars*. Trans. Len Ortzen. London, Ibadan, and Nairobi: Heinemann.

——. 1976. *Xala*. Trans. Clive Wake. London, Nairobi, and Ibadan: Heinemann.

——. 1989. "A Glint in His Eyes: An Interview with Ousmane Sembene." *African Concord* 4.24 (Oct. 9): 49.

——. 1995. Interview with Sada Niang and Samba Gadjigo. "African Cinema." Special issue of *Research in African Literatures* 26.3 (Fall): 174–78.

——. 1996. *Guelwaar*. Paris and Dakar: Présence Africaine.

——. 2000. "Commentary." In Givanni: 185–86.

——. 2003. Filmed interview with author (Mar. 4).

Shai, Patrick. 2003. Filmed interview with author (Mar. 1).

Shea, Martin. 1998. Review of "*Aristotle's Plot*: Lampooning Cinema & Identity" by Michael Dye. *African Media Project*. Michigan State University. Accessed July 20, 2004 (*see* www.und.ac.za/und/ccms/amp/reviews/aristot2.htm).

Sheen, Erica. 2000. "Introduction." In Sheen and Giddings: 1–13.

Sheen, Erica and Robert Giddings, eds. 2000. *The Classic Novel: From Page to Screen*. Manchester: Manchester UP.

Shehu, Brendan. 1995. "Cinema and Culture in Africa." In Fepaci: 97–104.

Shepperson, Arnold and Keyan Tomaselli. 2001. "Culture, Media, and the Intellectual Climate: Apartheid and Beyond." In Kriger and Zegeye: 41–63.

Shohat, Ella Habiba. 2000. "Post-Third-Worldist Culture: Gender, Nation, and the Cinema." In Diana Brydon, ed., *Postcolonialism: Critical Concepts*. Vol. 5. London and New York: Routledge.

Shohat, Ella Habiba and Robert Stam. 1994. *Unthinking Eurocentrism: Multiculturalism and the Media*. London: Routledge.

Simkins, Charles. 1986. *Reconstructing South African Liberalism*. Johannesburg: South African Institute of Race Relations.

Simpson, G. 2001. "Shock Troops and Bandits: Youth, Crime, and Politics." In J. Steinberg, ed., *Crime Wave: The South African Underworld and Its Foes*, 115–28. Johannesburg: Witwatersrand UP.

Sissako, Abderrahmane. 2007. "Finding Our Own Voices." Interview with Ali Jaafar in *Sight & Sound* (Feb.): 30–31.

Sissoko, Cheick Oumar. 1997. Interview with Olivier Barlet (Feb.). Accessed July 20, 2004 (*see* www.africultures.com/index.asp?menu = affiche_artiste&no = 461).

——. 1999. "*La Genèse*" (California Newsreel). Accessed Aug. 27, 2007 (*see* www. newsreel.org/nav/title.asp?tc = CN0040).

——. 2000. "Response." In Givanni: 193–94.

——. 2003a. Cambridge Arts Picturehouse Presentation (Dec. 8).

——. 2003b. Filmed interview with author (Dec. 8).

——. 2003c. Interview. In Thackway: 201–203.

Sklar, Robert. 1995. *Film: An International History of the Medium*. New York: Harry N. Abrams.

Slavin, David. 2001. *Colonial Cinema and Imperial France, 1919–1939: White Blind Spots, Male Fantasies, Settler Myths*. Baltimore and London: Johns Hopkins UP.

Slovo, Shawn. 2003. Filmed interview with author (Mar. 8).

Smith, Charlene. 2003. "The Virgin Rape Myth—A Media Creation or a Clash Between Myth and a Lack of HIV Treatment?" Accessed Aug. 27, 2007 (*see* www. speakout.org.za/about/child/child_virgin_rape_myth.html).

Smith, Robert. 1976. *Warfare and Diplomacy in Pre-Colonial West Africa*. London: Methuen.

Snipe, Tracy D. 1998. *Arts and Politics in Senegal, 1960–1996*. Trenton (N.J.): African World Press.

Sobchack, Vivian. 2004. *Carnal Thoughts: Embodiment and Moving-Image Culture*. Berkeley: U of California P.

Solanas, Fernando and Octavio Getino. 1969. "Towards a Third Cinema." Rpt. in Nichols 1976: 44-64.

Sontag, Susan. 1967. "Against Interpretation" (1964). *Against Interpretation and Other Essays*, 3–14. London: Eyre & Spottiswoode.

Sorel, Georges. 1999. *Reflections on Violence* (1907). Ed. Jeremy Jennings. Cambridge Texts in the History of Political Thought. Cambridge: Cambridge UP.

Sosibo, Kwanele. 2006. "True to Tsotsis?" *ZA@Play* (Feb. 3). Accessed Aug. 27, 2007 (*see* www.chico.mweb.co.za/art/2006/2006feb/060203-tsotsi.html).

South Africa. 2006/2007. Arts and Culture. In *South Africa Yearbook 2006/7*, ch. 5. Accessed Aug. 27, 2007 (*see* http://66.102.9.104/search?q = cache:TqRbhsu-DmUJ:www.gcis.gov.za/docs/publications/yearbook/chapter5.pdf+Tsotsi+%22So uth+African+viewers%22&hl = en&ct = clnk&cd = 6&client = safari).

SouthAfrica.info reporter. 2005. "Young Women Rise from Poverty" (May 23). Accessed Aug. 27, 2007 (*see* www.southafrica.info/women/bappies-160505.htm).

Soyinka, Wole. 1973. "The Strong Breed." *Collected Plays I*, 113–46. Oxford and New York: Oxford UP.

——. 1988. "From a Common Backcloth: A Reassessment of the African Literary Image" (1963). In *Art, Dialogue, and Outrage: Essays on Literature and Culture*. London: Methuen.

Spaanderman, Barbara. 1982. "Development of Characterization in the Plays *No-Good Friday* and *Nongogo* and in the Novel *Tsotsi* by Athol Fugard." Honors Essay, Rand Afrikaans University.

Spariosu, Mihai, ed. 1984a. *Mimesis in Contemporary Theory: An Interdisciplinary Approach*, vol. 1: *The Literary and Philosophical Debate*. Cultura Ludens: Imitation and Play in Western Culture. Philadelphia and Amsterdam: John Benjamins.

——. 1984b. "Introduction." In Spariosu 1984a: i–xxix.

Spencer, Robert. 2003. *Onward Muslim Soldiers: How Jihad Still Threatens America and the West*. Washington, D.C.: Regnery.

Ssali, Ndugu Mike. 1996. "Apartheid and Cinema." In Bakari and Cham: 83–101.

Stam, Robert. 2000. *Film Theory: An Introduction*. Oxford and Malden, Mass.: Blackwell.

Stam, Robert and Ella Habiba Shohat. 2000. "Film Theory and Spectatorship in the Age of the 'Posts.'" In Christine Gledhill and Linda Williams, eds., *Reinventing Film Studies*, 381–401. London: Arnold; New York: Oxford UP.

Sukazi, John. 2003. "Cape Town Hits the Big Time in Global Film Industry." *Sunday Times* (Jan. 12): Business 2.

Suleman, Ramadan. 1997. Program Notes. 50th Locarno International Film Festival, Aug. 6–16, 1997. Accessed Aug. 27, 2007 (*see* www.pardo.ch/1997/filmprg/r008.html).

——. 2002. Interview. In Ukadike 2002: 281–99.

——. [N.d.] Interview with Olivier Barlet. *Africultures*. Accessed July 20, 2004 (*see* www.africultures.com/index.asp?menu=revue_affiche_article&no=159&lang=_en).

Tapsoba, Clément. 1995. "De L'Orientation de la Critique du Cinéma Africain." In Fepaci: 157–65.

Taussig, Michael. 1993. *Mimesis and Alterity: A Particular History of the Senses*. New York and London: Routledge.

Taylor, Clyde. 2000. "Searching for the Postmodern in African Cinema." In Givanni: 136–44.

Tcheuyap, Alexie. 2001. "Entre films romans: Des réécritures textuelles en Afrique Francophone." Ph.D. diss., Queen's University (Canada).

——. 2001–2002. "La Littérature à l'Écran: Approches et Limites Théoriques." *Protée* (Hiver): 87–96.

——. 2005. *De l'écrit à l'écran: Les Réécritures Filmiques Du Cinéma Africain Francophone*. Ottawa: U of Ottawa P.

——. 2005a. "African Cinema and Representations of (Homo)Sexuality." In Flora Veit-Wild and Dirk Naguschewski, eds., *Body, Sexuality, and Gender: Versions and Subversions in African Literatures* 1:143–54. Amsterdam and New York: Rodopi.

Teer-Tomaselli, Ruth. 2001. "Nation-Building, Social Identity, and Television in a Changing Media Landscape." In Kriger and Zegeye: 117–37.

Thackway, Melissa. 2003. *Africa Shoots Back: Alternative Perspectives in Sub-Saharan Francophone African Film*. Oxford: James Currey.

——. 2007. "Future Past: Integrating Orality into Francophone West African Film." In Julie Codell, ed., *Genre, Gender, Race, and World Cinema: An Anthology*, 458–70. Oxford: Blackwell.

Tomaselli, Keyan. 1988. *The Cinema of Apartheid: Race and Class in South African Film*. London and New York: Routledge.

——. 1995. "Some Theoretical Perspectives on African Cinema: Culture, Identity, and Diaspora." In Fepaci: 105–134.

——. 1996. "'African' Cinema: Theoretical Perspectives on Some Unresolved Questions." In Bakari and Cham: 165–74.

——. 2006. *Encountering Modernity: Twentieth-Century South African Cinemas*. Rozenberg: UNISA Press.

Tomaselli, Keyan and Maureen Eke. 1995. "Secondary Orality in South African Film." *Iris* 18 (Spring): 61–71.

Tomaselli, Keyan and Edwin Hees. 1999. "John Grierson in South Africa: Afrikaaner [*sic*] Nationalism and the National Film Board." July 1. Latrobe University. Accessed Mar. 10, 2004 (*see* www.latrobe.edu.au/screeningthepast/firstrelease/fro799/ktfr7e.htm).

Tomaselli, Keyan and Jeanne Prinsloo. 1992. "Third Cinema in South Africa: The Anti-Apartheid Struggle." In Blignaut and Botha 1992a: 329–73.

Trotter, David. 2000. *Cooking with Mud: The Idea of Mess in Nineteenth-Century Art and Fiction*. Oxford and New York: Oxford UP.

Turegano, T. H. 2004. "On Questions and Critical Methodology of African Cinemas." *Film Philosophy* 8.13 (Apr.).

Turner, Terence. 2002. "Representation, Politics, and Cultural Imagination in Indigenous Video: General Points and Kayapo Examples." In Ginsburg et al.: 75–89.

Ukadike, Nwachukwu Frank. 1994. *Black African Cinema*. Berkeley: U of California P.

——. 1995. "African Films: A Retrospective and a Vision for the Future." In Fepaci: 47–68.

——. 1996. "Reclaiming Images of Women in Films from Africa and the Black Diaspora." In Bakari and Cham: 194–208.

——. 2002. *Questioning African Cinema: Conversations with Filmmakers*. Minneapolis and London: U of Minnesota P.

University of Newcastle Upon Tyne. 2002. "Exposed: The Film Industry's 100-Year Love Affair with Carmen" (June). *The Carmen Project*. Accessed July 20, 2004 (*see* www.scienceblog.com/community/older/2002/B/20026439.html).

van Eeden, Janet. 2003. "Devenish Back in SA to Make Films." *ScreenAfrica* 15 (Feb.): 44.

Vieira, José Luandino. 1978. *The Real Life of Domingos Xavier* (1971). Trans. Michael Wolfers. London, Nairobi, Lusaka: Heinemann.

Vieyra, Paulin Soumanou. 1969. *Le Cinéma et l'Afrique*. Paris: Présence Africaine.

——. 1972. *Ousmane Sembene: Cinéaste. Première Période, 1962–1971*. Paris: Présence Africaine.

——. 1975. *Le Cinéma Africaine: Des Origines à 1973*. Paris: Présence Africaine.

——. 1983. *Le Cinéma au Senegal*. Paris: Présence Africaine.

Villa-Vicencio, Charles and Wilhelm Verwoerd. 2000. *Looking Back, Reaching Forward: Reflections on the Truth and Reconciliation Commission of South Africa*. Cape Town: U of Cape Town P; London: Zed Books.

Wade, Mansour Sora. 2003. Filmed interview after screening at 2003 Cambridge African Film Festival (May 10).

Wagner, George. 1975. *The Novel and the Cinema*. Rutherford (N.J.): Fairleigh Dickinson UP.

Walden, Diane. 2004. "Critical Theory and Film: Adorno and "The Culture Industry" Revisited." In Gerard Delanty, ed., *Theodor W. Adorno*, vol. 4: 55–77. London, Thousand Oaks (Calif.), and New Dehli. Sage.

Walder, Dennis. 1984. *Athol Fugard*. Basingstoke: Macmillan.

West, Gerald. 2001. "Liberation Theology: Africa and the Bible." In John Rogerson, ed., *The Oxford Illustrated History of the Bible*, 330–42. Oxford: Oxford UP.

White, Hayden. 1973. *Metahistory: The Historical Imagination in Nineteenth-Century Europe*. Baltimore: Johns Hopkins UP.

Wilk, Richard. 2002. "Television, Time, and the National Imaginary in Belize." In Ginsburg et al.: 171–86.

Williams, Amie. 1989. "Dancing with Absences: The Impossible Presence of Third World Women in Film." *UFAHAMU* 17.3 (Fall): 44–56.

Wilson, David. 2003. "Local Isn't Lekker Enough." *Varsity* (University of Cape Town) 62.3 (May 15): Arts 14.

Wilson, Richard. 2001. *The Politics of Truth and Reconciliation in South Africa: Legitimizing the Post-Apartheid State*. Cambridge: Cambridge UP.

Woods, Donald. 1978. *Biko*. London: Paddington Press.

——. 1980. *Asking for Trouble: Autobiography of a Banned Journalist*. London: Gollancz.

Woolfalk, Saya. 2003. "*Karmen Geï*: Political Sex Icon." New York African Film Festival. Accessed July 20, 2004 (*see* www.africanfilmny.org/network/news/Rwoolfalk.html).

Wynter, Sylvia. 2000. "Africa, the West, and the Analogy of Culture: The Cinematic Text after Man." In Givanni: 25–78.

Young, Robert J. C. 2001. *Postcolonialism: An Historical Introduction*. Oxford: Blackwell.

Zacks, Stephen. 1999a. "The Theoretical Construction of African Cinema." In Harrow: 3-20.

——. 1999b. "A Problematic Sign of African Difference in Trinh T. Minh-ha's *Reassemblage*." In Harrow: 75–88.

Zomorodi, Manoush. 2006. "'Tsotsi' Takes Foreign Film Oscar." BBC (Mar. 6). Accessed Aug. 27, 2007 (*see* newsvote.bbc.co.uk/mpapps/pagetools/print/news.bbc.co.uk/2/hi/entertainment/4754790.stm).

INDEX

100 Days, 287n2

117 Days, 281n8

Achebe, Chinua, 199

Adesanya, Afolabi, 22

Adorno, Theodor, 247, 275; ideas on adaptation, 208; ideas on film, 208–210; logic of sacrifice, 227–28; theory of enlightenment, 216; theory of mass culture, 209–210; theory of mimesis, 16–21, 154, 228–29

L'Afrance, 17

Africa: origin of name, 2; as represented in films by European and North American filmmakers, 28–29, 45; as represented in the Western news media, 25–26, 45

Africa Dreaming, 57

African Cinema: birth of, 29–31; debate around term "African Cinema," 1–2, 8; theories of, 8, 23–24, 30, 194–96, 206

Africa Film Group, 189

Africa Film Summit, 58

African Film Library (AFL), 61

African Jim. See Jim Comes to Jo'burg

African languages. *See* language use in African films

The African Queen, 280n11

Afrikaner: identity, 34–39; national cinema, 46–47; representation of in cinema, 65

Afrique 50, 189

Afrique Occidentale Française, 180–81

Afrique sur Seine, 189, 192

agency, 11, 12, 215

AIDS. *See* HIV/AIDS

Alassane, Moustapha, 211

Allah Tantou, 285n8

Allégret, Marc, 189

Almoravid invasions, 198

ANC (African National Congress), 49, 56, 69, 109, 122, 174

And a Threefold Cord, 120

Anderson, Benedict, 4

Andrade-Watkins, Claire, 9, 189–90

And There in the Dust, 51, 283n2

Anglo Boer War, 36, 40, 42

Anglophone: critique of term, 196; West African industry, 202

animation, 51

anthropology: as a discipline, xiv; and fantasy, 4; shared anthropology, 187. *See also* ethnography

anti-apartheid: cinema, 44, 48; discourse, 65

anticolonial: cinema, 189; uprisings, 189

apartheid: Biko's analysis of, 25; British reaction to through film, 37–39; control of film industry, 45–47; critique of in cinema, 48; origins of, 34–37

Appiah, Kwame Anthony, 5

appropriation, 5, 193, 199

Aristotle, 205

Aristotle's Plot, 57, 205–217

Asking for Trouble, 281n8

Atlantic slave trade. *See* slave trade

Phiri, Chikapa Ray, 71
piracy, 91
Plaatje, Solomon T., 43
Place of Weeping, 284*n*1
Plan Images Afrique, 191
Plato, 16, 207
Plomer, William, 150
The Poetics, 205–217
Poitier, Sidney, 146
popular art, 202–204, 214
Portuguese. *See* Lusophone
post-apartheid discourse, 65
postcolonial theory: appropriation and, 5, 12; in relation to Africa, 2, 7; in relation to African cinema, 213–16; in relation to the nation, 4; in relation to South Africa, 39
postmodernism, 212–15
poststructuralism, 11–12, 15
Powdermaker, Hortense, 209
Preller, Gustav, 34
Prénom Carmen, 219
Prince, Stephen, 40–41
Le Prix du Pardon, 285*n*6
production. *See* film production
protest writing, 65, 122
Proteus, 52
psychoanalysis, 4

Quartier Mozart, 213–15
Qur'an, 252–74

Raberono, 6
racism, 25, 43, 220, 255; representation in film, 86–87
Ramaka, Joseph Gaï, 218–51, 280*n*8
rape, 258–60; baby rape, 92, 106; representation in *Fools*, 73–84 ; representation in literature, 107; South African statistics of, 89, 106, 282*n*3; representation in *Tsotsi*, 103–107
Rape for Who I Am, 52, 283*n*1
Rathbone, Richard, 270
realism: in African arts, 8; in African film, 8–9
A Reasonable Man, 93
reconciliation, 272–73; in South African cinema, 55–57. *See also* TRC
Red Dust, 54–55
regionalism: Francophone, 178–81; in response to the failure of national cinemas, 198; in South Africa, 57; in West Africa, 5–6, 180–81, 195–98; through war, 180
Regnault, Felix-Louis, 185
Régnier, Georges, 182
Reid, Frances, 54
remakes (cinematic), 145–76, 147–48
repetition, 11
representation: crisis of, 23, 193
Resnais, Alain, 177, 189
restorative justice, 23, 53, 154–57, 272
Un Retour d'un Aventurier, 211
retributive justice, 23, 56, 93, 154–57, 167–76, 202, 271
La Revue des Deux Mondes, 220, 224
Riverwood, 22
Robinson, Peter, 220
Rogosin, Lionel, 48
Romanticism, 74–75, 85, 283*n*7
Roodt, Darrell James, 145–76, 283*n*1
Rose, Jacqueline, 4
Rosenstone, Robert, 38
Rouch, Jean, 186–89, 285*n*2
Rwanda: gacaca courts, 277; genocide in, 255, 264–66, 287*n*2; genocide on film, 256, 287*n*2; "Hillywood" in, 204

SABC (South African Broadcasting Corporation), 49, 60–61, 66, 121
sabar, 248; dancing, 244–46; drumming, 221, 245–46
Sabela, Simon, 47
sacrifice, 229, 242, 259–60
Les Saignantes, 215
Saks, Lucia, 282*n*10
Sanneh, Lamin, 271
Sarafina! 284*n*1
Sarraounia, 286*n*10
Sarzan, 279*n*1
Saura, Carlos, 223
scapegoating, 154–55, 167–76, 194, 259
Schmitz, Oliver, 49
Schreiner, Olive, xi
Scott, James C., 38–39, 46, 267
screen griots, 13. *See also* griots
screen media, 2
SECMA (Société d'Exploitation Cinématographique Africaine), 183
Second Cinema, 29, 281*n*13
Segal, Naomi, 136

Seiphemo, Rapulana, 117
Selassie, Haile, 3
Sembene, Ousmane, 6, 8, 14, 30–31, 61, 186, 190, 191, 192, 201, 285n7
Senegal, 5–7, 196; censorship of films in, 190; history, 284–85n1; relationship to France, 184–85
Senghor, Léopold Sédar, 185
sex: representation in African film, 33
sexuality: representation in African film, 52
Shai, Patrick, 70–71
Sharpeville massacre, 49, 95, 99, 124
Shaw, Harold, 34–35
Sheen, Erica, 12
She's Gotta Have It, 213
Shohat, Ella, 28
Shooting Dogs, 287n2
Shout Cinemas, 60, 61
Sia, le rêve du python, 260, 279n3, 287n9
Le Silence de la Forêt, 286n11
Sinclair, Upton, 124
Singh, Anant, 145, 284n1
Sissako, Abderrahmane, 50, 191, 203, 275–77
Sissoko, Cheick Oumar, 9, 14, 252–74
Sithengi Film Market, 60, 61, 282n11
slave trade, 7, 198, 246–47
Slavin, David, 182–83
Slovo, Gillian, 54
Slovo, Shawn, 282n8
Smith, Charlene, 106
Smith, Robert, 179
Smuts, Jan, 151
So Be It, 229, 286n10
social realism, 8, 140, 194
Solanas, Fernando, 29, 195
Sometimes in April, 287n2
SONAVOCI (Société Nationale Voltaïque du Cinéma), 183
Song of Africa, 46
Son of Man, 57, 287n1
Sontag, Susan, 250
Sophiatown, 51; demolition of, 95–96, 99; Renaissance, 43–44
Soundjata Keïta, 181
South African Coloured People's Congress, 123
South African Liberal Party, 109, 149
South African National Party. See National Party
Soweto, 58, 64

Soyinka, Wole, 123, 150, 229
spectatorship: in Africa, 20; colonial spectatorship, 28; early film spectatorship, 41–42; parodied in *Aristotle's Plot*, 209–211; participatory, 13–14; problems of in Africa, 21–22, 24, 203–204; resistant spectatorship, 28; in South Africa, 57–62, 66
Spier Films, 59
spirituality, 252–74, 280n8
Ssali, Ndugu Mike, 35
Stam, Robert, 28
Les Statues Meurent Aussi, 177, 189
stereotypes, 27, 239; in films, 182
Ster-Kinekor, 59–60, 91
Stimela, 71
The Stone Country, 120
The Storekeeper, 92–93
The Story of an African Farm, xi
The Strong Breed, 229, 286n10
subsidy schemes for film production, 46–47, 281n5
Suleiman, Elia, 211
Suleman, Ramadan, 14, 54, 63–89, 70

Tanakh, 252–74
Taussig, Michael, 26–27, 42, 48
Taylor, Clyde, 24, 193, 214
Tcheuyap, Alexie, 11
television: African collaboration in, 61; as medium, 2; ownership in South Africa, 59–60, 282n10; Senegalese, 246; showing African films on, 24, 58, 66. *See also* M-Net and SABC
The Tempest, 199
Tengers, 51
Teno, Jean-Marie, 22
Teranga Blues, 198
terrorism, 48, 136
Thackway, Melissa, 9, 183
theater: Malian, 266–67; South African, 70, 150; Yoruba (*See* Nigeria)
Themba, Can, 43–44, 48, 150
theology, 269–74
Third Cinema, 29–31
Thunderbolt, 286n12
Tomaselli, Keyan, 9, 57
Torah, 252–74
Touki Bouki, 8, 193
Touré, Mamadou, 6, 189

Touré, Sekou, 285n8
tragedy, 212, 222
transcultural, 213
Traoré, Mahama, 32
Traoré, Moussa, 190, 253, 255
TRC (Truth and Reconciliation Commission), 53–57, 139, 146, 154, 157; documentaries about, 54, 121; fiction films about, 54
Trotter, David, 124–26
Tsotsi (film), 59, 90–118, 119, 121, 176
Tsotsi (novella), 90–118
tsotsis: definition of, 94–95; as film spectators, 93–94; representation of in film, 95. *See also* gangsters
Tuareg, 256, 268, 277
Tutu, Archbishop Desmond, 53, 109–110

ubuntu, 16, 157
Ubuntu's Wounds, 54, 56
U-Carmen eKhayelitsha, 57, 59–60, 199, 218, 286n2
U-Deliwe, 47
Uganda, 204
ujamaa, 16
Ukadike, Frank, 7, 181, 185, 187
The Unfolding of Sky, 54
unhu, 16
United States: cinema trade policy, 209; relationship to South Africa, 44

Van der Post, Laurens, 150
Vautier, René, 189
video films: in Cameroon, 21; critique in, 23; critiques of, 22–24; in Ghana, 21, 280n8; in Kenya, 21; in Sierra Leone, 21; in Tanzania, 21; in Uganda, 21. *See also* Kanywood, Riverwood, Bongowood
video halls, 204
video jockeys, 204
Vieyra, Paulin Soumanou, 182
violence: in Africa, 25–33, 50; in African cinema, xiv, 6–7, 9–10, 23, 25–33, 51, 193–194; in African video films, 23; censorship of film violence, 41–42; different kinds of, 26; good and bad violence, 154–55; in Hollywood film, 32; and the introduction of cinema in Africa, 27–29; in Mali,

14; mimicry of, 210; in post-apartheid South Africa, 50; representation of in literature, 32; representation of in *Tsotsi*, 105–106; retributive violence, 23, 193–94; revolutionary violence, 29–30; and surveillance, 47; and the TRC in South Africa, 53–57; and visuality, 47–48; monitoring of in West Africa, 197; against women, 255. *See also* genocide
Visages des Femmes, 214
Voyage au Congo, 189

Waati, 57
Wade, Abdoulaye, 229
A Walk in the Night (film), 52, 92, 119–44, 145, 148, 176
A Walk in the Night (novella), 119–44
Wa 'n Wina, 49
war, 26; in pre-colonial West Africa, 179–80; in South African films, 34–39 ; "War Against Terror," 48; World War I, 183–84; World War II, 184, 248. *See also* civil war
White, Hayden, 224
The Wilby Conspiracy, 44
A World Apart, 44, 281n8, 286n8
World Bank, 276
Wright, Richard, 124
Wynter, Sylvia, 206

Xala, 190, 279n2, 280n8
xenophobia, 255; representation of in film, 133, 135, 143; and riots in South Africa, 140

Yeelen, 193
Yesterday, 51, 58, 284n1
Yizo Yizo, 49–50, 282n10
Yoruba plays. *See* Nigeria
Young Communist League, 123

ZIFF (Zanzibar International Film Festival), 3, 202, 204
Zimbabwe, 208
Zola, 101
Zonk!, 46
Zulu, 37–39
Zulu Love Letter, 54

Film and Culture

A series of Columbia University Press

Edited by John Belton